D0897858

# THE POLITICAL ECONOMY
# OF INTEGRATION
# IN THE EUROPEAN UNION

To Nancy and Graeme, the new Europeans

# The Political Economy of Integration in the European Union

Jeffrey Harrop

*Lecturer in Economics, Department of European Studies, University of Bradford, UK*

*Third Edition*

**Edward Elgar**
Cheltenham, UK • Northampton, MA, USA

337.142
H32þ3

Published by
Edward Elgar Publishing Limited
Glensanda House
Montpellier Parade
Cheltenham
Glos GL50 1UA
UK

Edward Elgar Publishing, Inc.
136 West Street
Suite 202
Northampton
Massachusetts 01060
USA

A catalogue record for this book is available from the British Library.

**Library of Congress Cataloguing-in-Publication Data**
Harrop, Jeffrey.
    The political economy of integration in the European Union / Jeffrey
    Harrop.—3rd ed.
    Rev. ed. of: International library of critical writings in economics. 2nd
    ed. 1999.
    Includes bibliographical references and index.
    1. European Union. 2. Europe—Economic integration. I. Harrop,
Jeffrey. Political economy of integration in the European Community.
II. Title.

    HC240.H3516 2000
    337.1'42—dc21                            99–049222

ISBN 1 84064 099 5 (cased)
ISBN 1 84064 114 2 (pb)

Typeset by Manton Typesetters, Louth, Lincolnshire, UK.
Printed and bound in Great Britain by MPG Books Ltd, Bodmin, Cornwall

cau

# Contents

*v*

# Figures

# Tables

# Preface to the third edition

Momentous changes occurred between the first and second editions of this book. The reunification of Germany and the end of the cold war led to a gravitation of East European countries towards the EU and NATO. Likewise, the period that has elapsed since the second edition has seen even more significant changes. These include the continued painful transition process in Eastern Europe, and the Maastricht and Amsterdam Treaties which provide for a further deepening and widening of integration within the European Union. The new name 'European Union' is now used in the title of this book to reflect the significant Maastricht Treaty on European Union. While the first and main pillar economically of the EU is the European Community, I felt that the term 'European Union' was more appropriate to reflect the whole edifice and political aspirations of economic integration.

I have been encouraged to produce this new edition in response to the many readers who deserve a revised and more up-to-date review of the EU's activities. It is never easy to decide how much to modify an existing structure or to delete some older descriptive material. Essentially, the basic structure and three-fold division in each chapter has been retained, but some deletions have been made in order to make way for new material. This can be seen especially in terms of updating Chapter 2 with the new Treaties, and altered numerical composition of the EU institutions as a consequence of the membership enlargement. There is a new Chapter 6 which combines energy, transport and environmental policy, and enhanced coverage is given to regional and social policy in Chapter 7. The significant introduction of the euro is covered in Chapter 8. Chapter 9 includes the Budget in the early years of the new millennium. Chapter 10 on world-wide trading links has been condensed, since the growing attractiveness of the EU has brought some countries into full membership of the EU. A lengthier Chapter 11 reflects this enlargement process of the EU and is forward-looking in anticipation of embracing certain countries of Eastern and Central Europe. The conclusions in Chapter 12 reflect the dynamic integration that has taken place in recent years.

I have benefited from TEMPUS visits to the following universities in Eastern Europe: Szeged in Hungary, Poznan and Warsaw in Poland,

Prague in the Czech Republic, Bratislava in Slovakia, Cluj-Napoca and Bucharest in Romania. The British Council financed a visit to the University of Riga, Latvia, at the end of 1997 and a visit to the university of Wroclaw in Poland in 1998. Visits to these countries provide added richness to standard economic and statistical analysis of these countries and their degree of readiness for EU entry. I am indebted to many people for their time, their views and discussion about the EU, but the interpretation of events is ultimately mine.

JEFFREY HARROP

# Abbreviations

| | |
|---|---|
| AASM | Associated African States and Malagasy (countries which participated under the Yaoundé Convention) |
| ACP | African, Caribbean and Pacific (countries which participate in the Lomé Convention) |
| BRIDGE | Biotechnology Research for Innovation, Development and Growth in Europe |
| BRITE | Basic Research in Industrial Technologies for Europe |
| CADDIA | Co-operation in Automation of Data and Documentation for Imports, Exports and Agriculture |
| CAP | Common Agricultural Policy |
| CEDEFOP | European Centre for the Development of Vocational Training |
| CEECs | Central and East European Countries |
| CET | Common External Tariff |
| CFE | Conventional Forces in Europe |
| CFP | Common Fisheries Policy |
| CFSP | Common Foreign and Security Policy |
| CHIEF | Customs Handling of Import and Export Freight |
| COCOM | Co-ordinating Committee on Multilateral Export Controls |
| Comecon or CMEA | Council for Mutual Economic Assistance (grouping of East European countries) |
| COMETT | Community Programme for Education and Training in Technologies |
| COPA | Committee of Agricultural Organizations (Comité des Organisations Professionelles Agricoles des Pays de la Communauté Economique Européenne) |
| COR | Committee of the Regions |
| COREPER | Committee of Permanent Representatives (Comité des Répresentants Permanents de la CEE) |
| CSCE | Conference on Security and Co-operation in Europe (now OSCE) |
| DG | Directorate-General of the European Commission |
| EAGGF | European Agricultural Guidance and Guarantee Fund (FEOGA, Fonds Européen d'Orientation et Garantie Agricole) |

| | |
|---|---|
| EBRD | European Bank for Reconstruction and Development |
| EC | European Community |
| ECs | European Communities (EEC, Euratom and ECSC) |
| EC(6) | European Community: Belgium, France, Germany, Italy, Luxembourg and the Netherlands |
| EC(9) | The EC(6) plus Denmark, Ireland and the UK |
| EC(10) | The EC(9) plus Greece |
| EC(12) | The EC(10) plus Spain and Portugal |
| EC(15) | The EC(12) plus Austria, Finland and Sweden |
| ECB | European Central Bank |
| ECE | (United Nations) Economic Commission for Europe |
| ECJ | European Court of Justice |
| ECOFIN | Council of Economics and Finance Ministers |
| ECOWAS | Economic Community of West African States |
| ECSC | European Coal and Steel Community |
| ECU | European Currency Unit (a basket of European currencies) |
| EDC | European Defence Community |
| EDF | European Development Fund |
| EEA | European Economic Area |
| EEC | European Economic Community |
| EFA | European Fighter Aircraft |
| EFTA | European Free Trade Association |
| EIB | European Investment Bank |
| EMCF | European Monetary Co-operation Fund |
| EMF | European Monetary Fund |
| EMS | European Monetary System |
| EMU | Economic and Monetary Union |
| EP | European Parliament |
| EPU | European Payments Union |
| ERASMUS | European Action Scheme for the Mobility of University Students |
| ERDF | European Regional Development Fund (FEDER, Fonds Européen de Développement Régional) |
| ERM | Exchange Rate Mechanism |
| ESC | Economic and Social Committee |
| ESF | European Social Fund |
| ESPRIT | European Strategic Programme for Research and Development in Information Technology |
| ETUC | European Trade Union Confederation |

| | |
|---|---|
| EU | European Union |
| EUA | European Unit of Account |
| Euratom | European Atomic Energy Community |
| EUREKA | European Research Co-ordination Agency |
| EUT | European Union Treaty |
| EWC | European Works Council |
| FDI | Foreign Direct Investment |
| FIFG | Financial Instrument for Fisheries Guidance |
| FTA | Free Trade Area |
| GATT | General Agreement on Tariffs and Trade |
| GDP | Gross Domestic Product |
| GEMSU | German Economic, Monetary and Social Union |
| GNP | Gross National Product |
| GSP | Generalized System of Preferences |
| IEA | International Energy Agency |
| IEPG | Independent European Programme Group (defence industry) |
| IGC | Inter-Governmental Conference |
| ILO | International Labour Organization |
| IMF | International Monetary Fund |
| IMPs | Integrated Mediterranean Programmes |
| IT | Information Technology |
| JET | Joint European Torus |
| JHA | Justice and Home Affairs |
| LDC | Less-Developed Country |
| LEADER | Liaison Entre Actions de Développement de l'Économie Rurale |
| LEDA | Local Employment Development Action |
| LINGUA | Programme for the improvement of foreign language teaching |
| MCA | Monetary Compensatory Amount |
| MEP | Member of European Parliament |
| MFN | Most Favoured Nation |
| MNC | Multinational Corporation |
| NATO | North Atlantic Treaty Organization |
| NCB | National Central Bank |
| NCE | Non-Compulsory Expenditure |
| NIC | Newly Industrializing Country |
| NICE | Nomenclature des Industries Établies dans les Communautés Européennes |

| | |
|---|---|
| NTB | Non-Tariff Barrier |
| NOW | New Opportunities for Women |
| NUTS | Nomenclature of Territorial Units for Statistics |
| OCA | Optimum Currency Area |
| OECD | Organization for Economic Co-operation and Development |
| OEEC | Organization for European Economic Co-operation (forerunner of the OECD) |
| OPEC | Organization of Petroleum Exporting Countries |
| PHARE | Poland and Hungary Aid for Reconstruction of the Economy (later extended to other East European countries) |
| QMV | Qualified Majority Voting |
| R&D | Research and Development |
| RACE | Research and Development in Advanced Communications Technologies for Europe |
| RETI | Régions Européennes de Tradition Industrielle |
| SAD | Single Administrative Document |
| SEA | Single European Act |
| SEDOC | European system for the international clearance of vacancies and applications for employment |
| SEM | Single European Market |
| SMEs | Small and Medium-sized Enterprises |
| STABEX | Export Revenue Stabilization Scheme |
| SYSMIN | Scheme for Mineral Products (Système Minérais) |
| TARIC | Community Integrated Tariff |
| TEMPUS | Trans-European Mobility Programme for University Students |
| TENs | Trans-European Networks |
| UA | Unit of Account |
| UNCTAD | United Nations Conference on Trade and Development |
| UNICE | Industrial Confederation of the European Community (Union des Industries de la Communauté Européenne) |
| UNRRA | United Nations Relief and Rehabilitation Administration |
| VAT | Value Added Tax (TVA, Taxe sur valeur ajoutée) |
| VER | Voluntary Export Restraint |
| WEU | Western European Union |
| WTO | World Trade Organization |

# Introduction

This book on the European Union (EU), formerly with the title European Community (EC), was written mainly for undergraduate students, in particular those studying within the context of an interdisciplinary European Studies degree and whose chief interest is in Economics. The increased provision of such courses at both undergraduate and postgraduate level partly reflects the greater European orientation in the United Kingdom, signalled by UK entry to the EC in 1973. At that time there was also an awakening of general public consciousness about the EC and since then there has been a growing demand for information about it. Some universities responded by providing adult education courses, and some of the material and ideas for this book were first collected for a diploma course in European Studies at the University of Hull and later for a similar course run jointly by the Universities of Bradford and Leeds. The book has a common format for each chapter. Initially there is an outline of some of the basic issues; this is followed by the heart of each chapter which examines the progress of economic integration in the EU. Finally, the consequences of integration are examined from the perspective of the UK. The view from this angle is not intended to reflect any undue national preoccupation, but to meet the needs of most readers for an understanding of the extent to which the UK has become integrated in the EU and some of the difficulties that it has experienced.

Each chapter is self-contained and readers interested in a particular aspect of the Community need only turn to that chapter. However, I hope they will go on to read the rest of the book since one of the purposes in writing it has been to show the links between the different economic sectors which have provided the momentum for the process of integration.

The EU provides a natural interdisciplinary area for analysis, crossing the boundaries of many individual subjects. The two main disciplines considered here are Economics and to a lesser extent Politics. The book adopts a political-economy approach covering both economic policies and institutions. Whilst economic integration may not be an end in itself but more a means to political union, most emphasis is placed upon the economic aspects of integration. However, it was felt that a wholly theoretical economics book would fail to encapsulate fully the multidimensional elements of events in the EU over the past 40 years or more. Interpretation of these developments is naturally influenced by value judgements, and from the UK economic perspective the writer's views of its relationship with the EU show the critical problems that have existed in many areas of integration.

Detailed knowledge and information about the EU have generally been low, despite the establishment of several European Information Centres. To aid understanding, this book contains as much up-to-date material as possible, whilst avoiding the mass of detailed, jargonized Euro-legislative material which students do not need to memorize. Whilst Euro-jargon has been kept to a minimum, some key terminology is used where necessary to explain the EU's operation in an accessible way. Hence key terms such as the following will be found: *'acquis communautaire'* (the Community's system of legislation and commitments); 'subsidiarity' (the EU conducts activities in accordance with this principle and acts only when decisions cannot be taken or acted upon more effectively at a lower member-state level); 'additionality' (EU funds to be additional to and not to replace national spending on Structural Funds); 'cohesion' (transfer to less-developed member states and regions); and 'flexibility' (allowing the more progressive member states to push integration ahead of others in different policy areas). However, the main aim is to go beyond the descriptive level to a real understanding of issues and principles that underlie the various sectors of integration in the EU.

I became conscious when gathering material over the years that it was accumulating faster than it could be digested and it became urgent to produce something concise and concrete. The beginning of the next millennium marks a very appropriate time to analyse past and prospective developments. With the Mediterranean enlargement (entry of Greece, Portugal and Spain) and rejection of full Turkish membership, membership of the EU rose to 12. The enlargement of the EU in 1995 to incorporate the former EFTA members of Austria, Sweden and Finland means that the term EU(15) is referred to mainly in the book. There was concern that further enlargement of the EU might constrain a deepening of its policies in some areas such as political developments in foreign policy, security and defence. The EU re-examined its long-term destination after the Single European Act negotiated in December 1985 and in force in 1987, and in the Maastricht Treaty on European

Union negotiated in 1991 and in force in 1993. It was decided that deepening should initially take precedence over enlargement until the single market was firmly in place. The Amsterdam Treaty, signed in October 1997, consolidated integration further. Later in 1997 the European Commission presented its 'Agenda 2000', taking account of the prospects of an enlarged EU and the Commission published its opinion on each prospective new applicant. In the first wave, applications from the better-placed countries in Eastern Europe would be considered, such as those from Hungary, the Czech Republic, Poland and Estonia, together with parts of the former Yugoslavia such as Slovenia, and micro-states such as Cyprus. Further enlargement including most of the remaining countries of Eastern Europe could in the long term lead to a union of 25–30 states.

Evidently the book could not be exhaustive in coverage and it focuses on the main developed sectors of economic integration. Some sectors are still given limited treatment, such as energy, transport and environmental policy, though the progress in these areas has led me to group them together in a separate new Chapter 6 (instead of subsuming them in other parts of the book). Most attention and the sharpest focus are given in depth to sectors such as the customs union and internal market, agriculture, industry, regional and social policy, monetary and fiscal integration, external trade and enlargement. Agriculture remains a stubborn problem because of its centrality, high budgetary costs and the need to reform it substantially before enlargement. Although direct income payments to farmers represent an improvement over high price-support policies, the former are still extremely costly because an agricultural EU is loath to face up to more radical change. It is industrial policy that needs to be placed higher on the agenda so that the EU can raise its international market share in high-technology products. The internal market programme constituted an attempt to remedy this deficiency to allow the EU to compete more effectively with the USA and Japan.

For readers who wish to pursue areas excluded here, or to work even more deeply through the areas covered in the book, there are many sources available. The EU itself produces many publications – indeed, the mountain of printed papers might be likened to the agricultural surpluses! Nevertheless, some of these publications are valuable and readers are encouraged to sift through some of the material, which is located in European Documentation Centres in many libraries. Information is also available on the Internet from EU websites. There is material emanating from the Commission, with reports from the various Directorates-General, from the European Parliament (EP), the Council and the European Court of Justice (ECJ). Material from bodies such as the Economic and Social Committee (ESC), the European Investment Bank (EIB) and the Committee of the Regions (COR) is somewhat less profuse.

There is plentiful documentation covering both primary legislation from the foundation of the ECSC in 1951 and the EEC and Euratom in 1957, and secondary legislation which is promulgated daily and published in the Official Journal. Community legislation is of four types:

1. *Regulations* which must be imposed and are directly applicable in the law of all member states in order to ensure uniform application.
2. *Directives* which are binding as to ends to be achieved, but leave discretion to the national authorities over the means of introducing them.
3. *Decisions* which are addressed to specific groups, which are binding in their entirety.
4. *Recommendations* and *opinions* which have no binding legal force.

The starting point was the European Coal and Steel Community, followed by two further communities: Euratom and the very important European Economic Community (EEC). A decision was taken to merge their separate institutions and they are referred to either as Communities or (in the singular) the European Community. There has been further progress post-Maastricht to create a European Union which refers to the three pillars: pillar 1 (the central pillar) – the European Community; pillar 2 – Foreign and Security Policy; pillar 3 – Judicial and Home Affairs.

The process of international integration is one of combining countries, leading towards a union between them in a regional bloc. The term integration conveys more precisely the development of the EU than other words that are sometimes used: consultation, collaboration, concertation, co-operation and co-ordination. Progress towards integration has developed considerably in the postwar years between countries which consider that the elements they share are more important than those that divide them. Economic integration has removed major national barriers and increased competition. However, integration is not an end in itself but an instrument to achieve certain goals more effectively than nation states can deliver themselves, such as economic prosperity. The book is concerned with a very limited model of integration in Europe, specifically that of the EU. While focus on its key features exemplifies many aspects of integration, readers should recognize the distinctiveness of the EU experience, which has spawned many other examples of integration in the rest of the world that have gained new encouragement from the EU's continued success. Its predominantly market-based approach proved it superior to the centrally planned type of economic integration of Eastern Europe in Comecon, which took a different and less durable form. The disintegration in Eastern Europe which began in 1989 reminds us that an imposed integration by a dominant power is always likely to be impermanent. Disintegration has also spread beyond Comecon to countries such as Yugoslavia.

Most economies are moving towards market systems, encouraged by the EU's experience, though we are unlikely to see a complete convergence of economic systems. Integration in the EU has been rooted firmly in market principles whereby market signals determine the allocation of resources. The Treaty of Rome (1957) reflected a liberal approach, particularly influenced by West German trade and competition policy. Fundamental global changes, especially trade and capital flows, plus new electronic technology, have reinforced the dominance of markets. However, over the years the EU has also developed some more interventionist policies, alongside those of individual member states with their more mixed economies. The EU has moved beyond its dominant focus on allocation through the liberal market to add more moderate policies of redistribution (through the Structural and Cohesion Funds) and into a stabilization role via EMU. These are desirable to the extent that they underpin solidarity and citizenship and help to create a greater degree of economic stability in the EU.

# 1 Organizational stepping stones

## Disintegration and integration in Europe

*Pre-1945*

During the nineteenth century the European economy became much more highly integrated, based initially on overlapping regional industrial developments and freer trade. The formation of the Zollverein in 1833 created a large free-trade area and enabled tariff concessions to be extracted from other countries. Italy was unified in 1860, creating a free-trade area. Other countries signed treaties to reduce tariffs, such as France with the UK. Numerous international organizations were established, relating to spheres such as communications (Pollard 1974). However, a setback was provided by depression in the late nineteenth century which encouraged greater protectionism; also, national power caused international rivalry which was to result in the two catastrophic world wars in the first half of the twentieth century.

The First World War resulted in devastating losses of labour and capital, and for the first time even the victors had to conclude that war did not pay. It has been estimated that the war resulted in a slowdown of industrial production by approximately eight years; that is, the 1929 level of production, assuming pre-1914 trends, would have been achieved in 1921 (Svennilson 1954). The European economy disintegrated and the reshaping of national boundaries at the end of the war increased the number of separate customs unions in Europe from 20 to 27. Territorial realignments caused massive problems, creating dislocation in industrial links; for example, coal in the Ruhr and iron in Lorraine. Both Germany and the Austro-Hungarian Empire suffered substantial territorial losses. Massive reparation payments were imposed on Germany and these exceeded its capacity to repay them, contributing to instability in the 1920s (Aldcroft 1978, pp. 60–64). Inflationary finance and massive borrowings were undertaken. Unfortunately much of the borrowing was not used for productive investment; nearly half of it was short term and eventually countries were borrowing just to pay back interest on the earlier borrowings. A collapse of the financial system resulted, and in the late 1920s capital inflows into

Germany were withdrawn, especially by the USA, resulting in enforced deflation. Economic activity turned down after 1929 and the depression was aggravated by speculative activity. The Great Depression was international in scope and marked a deep collapse in industry, trade and finance. While there was some recovery after 1932, this was very weak in North America and also weak in some European countries such as France and Austria. The most successful economic recoveries took place in Sweden, the UK and Germany. In Sweden recovery was based on enlightened budgetary policies, unlike the UK, where there was greater concern with balanced budgets. In the UK cheap finance for investment stimulated key sectors such as housing. Recovery was also helped by the growth of new industries, and sales to an expanding domestic market were assisted by protection. In Germany a great economic recovery occurred on a different basis with a massive growth in public spending, particularly on armaments. Germany's export trade was also well adjusted to the new trends in world demand, with a larger share being held by metal manufacture, machinery and chemicals. In its trade policy Germany sought to raise its level of self-sufficiency and the weaker European countries fell under its economic hegemony. German expansionist military ambitions plunged Europe and the rest of the world into yet another devastating war.

The adverse effects of the Second World War were similar to those of the First World War: there were massive losses of labour and capital, and millions of people were killed and wounded, while others found themselves refugees. Homes were in ruins and the transport system disrupted supplies, with shortages of essentials such as food and fuel. There was massive financial indebtedness to the USA which finally established itself as the major power in the world.

### Post-1945

Peace did not automatically result in an improved situation, and in the late 1940s there was continuing political and economic chaos. The division of Europe into two parts resulted in the Soviet Union consolidating its hold over Eastern European states. The Soviet Union was seen as posing a threat to the West, turning the screw at sensitive points such as Berlin. In some West European countries, for instance France and Italy, the Communist parties scored major electoral gains.

Attempts to achieve integration by military aggression had recently failed disastrously under Hitler, just as they had under Napoleon. Given the impermanence of European history, there was a need to create an irreversible process of integration on a new basis. Most European countries were in such a dreadful condition that there was a greater receptiveness to integration.

It was not so much the ideas for integration that were new, but the conditions that were conducive for this to occur after 1945. Unlike the failure of Count Coudenhove-Kalergi's ideas to be applied after the First World War, the collapse of continental nations at the end of the Second World War left them with little choice but to integrate. The impetus for integration stemmed from a revulsion against nationalism; concern over the future of Germany; and a reaction against the adverse effects of protectionism. A peaceful process of integration on a voluntary basis was the only way to full recovery and to provide Europeans with a better future. Wartime resistance movements had gradually recognized this fact. The immediate practical problem was how to turn the dreams and aspirations of integration into reality. The driving force in this was provided by leading national figures who, through force of personality and persuasion, were able to enlist the support of the political élite. Jean Monnet's role was crucial and his ideas were favourably received by politicians such as Robert Schuman in France, Konrad Adenauer in Germany and Alcide de Gasperi in Italy. These politicians came from the frontier areas which had been ravaged by war.

Other support was forthcoming from political parties, with Catholic political parties, for instance, more prepared to consider supranational instead of national solutions (Spinelli in Hodges 1972). Spinelli himself perceived scope for tapping popular support of the general public for the process of integration (Pryce 1987, p. 24). There was a high level of public support for European unification in the 1950s, even including the UK at the time.

The external influences on integration, in particular from the two superpowers – the USA and the USSR – created a constellation of new international circumstances. The USA was generally a benevolent and supportive influence on European integration, providing its own federal model as one that Europe could imitate. It recognized the need for European integration based upon the recovery and involvement of Germany, which was central to the elimination of the German threat to European security. In contrast, the USSR constituted a very great threat, with fear of further extension of Soviet imperialism pushing European countries closer together for their own protection and security. Cold war pressures were especially acute in the early postwar years, but even in the mid-1950s there were constant reminders of vulnerability to Soviet power; for example, intervention in Hungary in 1956. That, along with other international events such as the Suez crisis, provided the background for renewed economic integration in the EEC.

## European organizations
Although there were different views about the process of integration and the best ways of achieving it, there was much goodwill and idealism; these ideals were well reflected in the Council of Europe.

### The Council of Europe
The Council of Europe was established in 1949 and its founding members comprised the United Kingdom, France, Belgium, the Netherlands, Luxembourg, Denmark, Norway, Sweden, Ireland and Italy, with other countries joining later. Its aim is expressed in Article 1 of the Statute: 'To achieve a greater unity between its members for the purpose of safeguarding and realizing the ideals and principles which are their common heritage and facilitating their economic and social progress …'. It was decided to locate the Council in Strasbourg on the ravaged Franco-German border. The phrase 'Council of Europe' was used by Winston Churchill during the Second World War and the title reflected Britain's influence on the structure of the organization.

It is an intergovernmental organization whose institutions comprise a Committee of Ministers, with most decisions needing a two-thirds majority and those important decisions addressed to governments requiring unanimity; a consultative Parliamentary Assembly whose debates lead to recommendations to the Committee of Ministers; and a Congress of Local and Regional Authorities of Europe, with one chamber for local authorities and another for regions, which aim to strengthen local democracy and have become useful for the new democracies of Eastern Europe.

The Council has been concerned with all matters excluding defence, and its prime concern is to organize co-operation in social and human rights, public health, education, culture and sport, youth activities, the environment and planning, local and regional authorities, and law. It has a large membership, though it is limited to European parliamentary democracies that provide basic human rights. Its most tangible achievements are enshrined in the Council's Conventions and Agreements. A most important Convention is that for the Protection of Human Rights and Fundamental Freedoms to create a civilized society. After this came into force, the European Commission of Human Rights was set up, and later the European Court of Human Rights. Although the Council failed to achieve political unity in Western Europe, its initiatives in the field of human rights and meetings of its parliamentarians have represented useful achievements. The neutral countries have been keen on the Council of Europe, with countries such as Austria, Sweden and Switzerland playing a prominent role. After the momentous changes in Eastern Europe and the concern to improve human rights there, in the 1990s several countries applied for full membership.

*Defence organizations*
Other organizations have been established mainly to help states to tackle their many national problems more effectively in a co-operative framework; this is exemplified by the defence and security problems of Western Europe. The division of Europe into two halves resulted in Western European defence initiatives, notably in co-operation with the USA.

Various organizations were created, starting with the Dunkirk Treaty between Britain and France in 1947, followed by the Brussels Treaty in 1948. This agreement between Belgium, France, Luxembourg, the Netherlands and the UK provided for automatic mutual defence assistance in Western Europe. It was concerned with the possibility of a revived German aggression, but the main preoccupation was with the Soviet Union. It established a military agency, the Western European Defence Organization. The French refused to agree to the rearmament of an independent Germany. France, along with other members of the European Coal and Steel Community (ECSC), agreed to set up a European Defence Community (EDC). Although a treaty to establish this was proposed in 1952, it was not ratified by the French. France would not participate in a European army which included Germany unless Britain also took part, and the latter's support was lacking. The failure of the EDC and of the Belgian Paul-Henri Spaak's proposals to combine the institutions of the ECSC and the EDC into a European political community marked a failure for the federal approach to integration.

In 1954 the rejection of the EDC gave way to the extension of the Brussels Treaty Organization to include West Germany and Italy in the Western European Union (WEU). It enabled the rearmament of West Germany to occur in an acceptable form. The WEU also facilitated political consultations between the EC and the UK (until the latter joined the Community). The WEU was not a very effective organization, but difficulties in developing a security and defence profile for the EC, such as Ireland's neutrality, led in 1984 to attempts to reactivate it. France decided that it wanted to contribute more fully to discussions on European security; hence 1984 marked the first ministerial meeting for eleven years. Both Spain and Portugal decided to apply to join the other seven members of the WEU in 1984.

The WEU is an intergovernmental body and though militarily it is part of the North Atlantic Treaty Organization (NATO) defence system, it had the advantage of including France, which lay outside the integrated military structure of NATO. When the WEU Treaty expired in 1998 there were proposals that its activities should be taken over eventually by the EU and together they drew up an arrangement for enhanced co-operation (though kept minimal by the UK). This may pose difficulties for non-members of the WEU – especially Denmark and Ireland – worried about increased militarization of the EU. A strengthening of the European pillar of NATO is thought by some to be desirable and the WEU came to the fore even more after the Gulf crisis (1991) because, unlike NATO, its actions under Article 6 of the Treaty were not confined geographically. The Gulf crisis showed the need for a common European position to match that of the USA, and to be capable of operating beyond the NATO area, such as in the Middle East, where continuing military threats seem likely to occur.

It is NATO, founded in 1949, that has constituted the main basis of Western defence. It linked ten European countries with the USA and Canada (Germany, Greece, Turkey and Spain joining later). Its Treaty is brief and not set out in arcane language, the core of it being Article 5 which begins: 'The Parties agree that an armed attack against one or more of them in Europe or North America shall be considered an attack against all of them ...'. NATO has been confronted by the Warsaw Pact, but despite the latter's Polish base, whereby any countries leaving have to give notice to Poland, it has been under effective control by the Soviet Union – far more so than NATO has been controlled by the USA.

NATO is an intergovernmental organization and within its framework the Eurogroup, an informal association of European defence ministers, promoted closer European co-operation in the alliance after 1968. In 1984 they created the Independent European Programme Group, which includes France. The IEPG is the principal forum for promoting equipment co-ordination and has been given the stimulus to create a European defence industry. This is the defence equivalent of 1992: the aim is to go beyond collaboration, creating a common market in military products in the same way as the EC has done in civil products. As an alliance NATO was a widely stretched defensive grouping whose strategy was based upon détente and deterrence, and if the latter failed then its flexible response was to defend itself. Nations have faced many competing demands on their limited resources and during the cold war NATO was worried about its quantitative inferiority in conventional forces to the Warsaw Pact. However, an aggressor would have required a large enough quantitative superiority to be certain of success. The qualitative technical superiority of NATO also lessened with improvements to equipment in Eastern Europe. NATO has a triad of forces: conventional, non-strategic nuclear forces and strategic nuclear forces. NATO strategy was to hold any attack by the Warsaw Pact as far forward as possible with its conventional defence. The concern was that if this failed, NATO would be forced to resort to the use of nuclear weapons at a very early stage. But the short-range nuclear flexible response was eliminated by the Intermediate Nuclear Forces Treaty signed at the end of 1987 which destroyed launchers and marked the first time the Soviets conceded on-site inspection. Agreements to eliminate intermediate nuclear forces were criticized strongly by certain NATO commanders on the grounds that to do so would significantly diminish the doctrine of flexible response.

NATO stayed strong but was prepared to negotiate after the Harmel Report of 1967. Mutually balanced force-reduction talks began in 1973 in Vienna. In 1990 the Conventional Forces in Europe (CFE) agreement finally put an end to the cold war, mandating the physical destruction of arms and establishing rough equality between East and West. It equalized numbers across a range of five weapon systems: tanks, armoured personnel carriers, artillery, fixed-wing combat aircraft and military attack helicopters. In addition, zones were established in which to spread out the equipment, and no one country was to possess more than one-third of these armaments. The effect was to reduce the level of confrontation, removing the likelihood of a surprise attack. CFE provides added confidence since it is verifiable with various forms of inspection. In reducing the massive Soviet superiority in conventional weapons, the Treaty ran into problems. For example, the Soviet military moved equipment east of the Urals and also switched some of their tanks to the navy, since the maritime area was excluded by the Treaty. Furthermore, the Treaty said nothing about troop numbers, nor the quality of equipment, and obviously the oldest equipment was destroyed first on both sides.

The ending of the cold war, with the decline of the USSR and dissolution of its empire, has ushered in a more optimistic phase of co-operation. For example, Poland, the Czech Republic and Hungary are moving closer to the EU and to NATO. The EU has not rushed into economic integration with these countries because of difficult adjustment problems, but moved more quickly on NATO expansion, with the three countries joining NATO in 1999, the costs of up to $2 billion being far less than those for EU enlargement. The EU has tried not to present a military challenge to the Russians, which might be more likely with Baltic enlargement. NATO still has to plan for a worst-case scenario of a threatening Russian military dictatorship, plus new contingencies of ethnic unrest in Europe, as in the Balkans, plus problems in the rest of the world, such as the Middle East. Thus NATO is revising its strategy since its forward-defence strategy has changed with the reunification of Germany and the abolition of the military component of the Warsaw Pact. New NATO strategy will rely on smaller, more mobile forces.

The Conference on Security and Co-operation in Europe (CSCE), which started at Helsinki in 1973, brought together 34 NATO, Warsaw Pact and neutral nations. It has provided greater confidence-building measures, such as notification of military-force levels and manoeuvres, leading on to mandatory confidence- and security-building measures. Since the London declaration in mid-1990 on a transformed NATO alliance, the aim is to develop a strengthened institutionalized role for the CSCE, now called the Organization for Security and Co-operation in Europe (OSCE). The OSCE is providing the outline of a new East–West order, with regular meetings; it has a small semi-permanent secretariat in Prague and a conference centre in Vienna exchanging information. It has increased to over 50 members and in the late 1990s was active in maintaining peace through verification in areas such as Kosovo. Ultimately, however, NATO action became necessary on humanitarian grounds to deal with the return of ethnic conflict in 1999.

*Economic organizations*

The United Nations Relief and Rehabilitation Administration (UNRRA) provided some relief and rehabilitation during the war and early post-war years. European governments created a few emergency organizations to complement UNRRA's activities and these were subsequently absorbed into an Economic Commission for Europe (ECE) to facilitate reconstruction throughout the whole of Europe. It was successful in bringing about all-European co-operation in research; in the exchange of technological and statistical information; and in the removal of many obstacles to East–West trade.

*The Organization for European Economic Co-operation (OEEC)*   The USA agreed to donate aid under the Marshall Plan if European countries would come together to frame their own recovery programme. It has been regretted by federalists that the aid was not made conditional on the creation of supranational political unity. Although assistance was offered throughout Europe, it was refused by the Soviets, who distrusted American intentions. Hence, rather than channel US aid through the ECE, a new body, the OEEC, was created in 1948. Sixteen West European countries, plus the commanders-in-chief of the western zones of Germany, signed the Convention establishing the organization. Canada and the USA became associate members of the OEEC in 1950; Spain and Yugoslavia also participated in the 1950s.

A major problem in all organizations has been whether to operate on an intergovernmental basis like the OEEC, or whether to operate at a more supranational level, as favoured by France at that time, though France has had to square this with its concerns relating to its own national independence. The decision-taking in the OEEC was on the basis of unanimity to protect the interests of the smaller countries.

The basic international problem in the early postwar years was recognized as one of restoring freer trade and payments, since if industry were to recover and expand it would need access to a large international market. Freer international payments were helped by the European Payments Union (EPU), set up in 1950 to assist countries that faced balance-of-payments deficits.

By the beginning of the 1960s over 90 per cent of trade was free from quotas. After this, attention focused mainly on the other impediments to both visible and invisible trade. Unfortunately, a lack of consensus on the approach to reducing tariffs was to lead to the fragmentation of the OEEC. This led it to concentrate more on other international issues, symbolized by its change of name to the Organization for Economic Co-operation and Development (OECD). The Convention establishing the OECD was signed by 20 countries in 1961 and it subsequently increased its membership with more European countries, plus the USA, Canada, Australia, New Zealand and Japan.

*The European Coal and Steel Community (ECSC), the European Atomic Energy Community (Euratom) and the European Economic Community (EEC)* There is a very significant difference between the three Communities compared with the organizations discussed previously which have been intergovernmental ones, in which unanimity is the normal voting procedure and in which the Secretariat usually has little scope for initiative. In contrast, in the European Communities the Commission has far more weight than a Secretariat. Both the ECSC and the EEC were designed to be more supranational in character, in particular the former.

The Schuman Declaration in 1950 had proposed the pooling of French and German coal and steel in an organization open to all European countries. In 1951 Belgium, France, Germany, Italy, the Netherlands and Luxembourg (the Six) accepted the Schuman Plan and signed the ECSC Treaty. It allotted strong supranational powers to its High Authority and the Council did not appear in the original plans of Schuman and Monnet. In the EEC greater weight was given to the Council since countries were reluctant to relinquish sovereignty over many other sectors of their economy. The ECSC offered France some control of these key strategic and heavy industrial resources to prevent any potential renewed German aggression. For West Germany it offered better prospects than the system of Allied control. Tariffs and quotas were removed to create a single market for coal, coke, iron ore, scrap iron, pig iron and steel among the Six, with some initial exemptions for Italian coke and steel products and Belgian coal. Generally the creation of the ECSC worked out more easily than expected, resulting in increased trade. The ECSC was also quite an interventionist body, though it had no common trade policy.

A limitation of the ECSC was its confinement to two main sectors and the recognition that to enjoy greater success, integration had to be widened to include other sectors. For example, although trade restrictions in the ECSC were removed by 1953, it was not until 1957, with the introduction of the international through-rates for transport, that competition took place on a fairer basis. In transport, countries tended to have lower freight charges for domestic products and subsidies for exports. Imports often had to face terminal charges for reloading at frontiers. Hence there was a need to develop a common transport policy, and also to go further with energy policy beyond coal and cover other sources.

The creation of the EEC in 1957 with the signing of the Treaty of Rome included oil, natural gas and electricity. Meanwhile, research on atomic energy came under Euratom, which seemed to offer considerable potential for co-operation. Indeed, in some quarters there was greater optimism about Euratom than the EEC. For instance, France was very keen to form Euratom, whereas West Germany and the Benelux countries showed greater interest in achieving an EEC customs union. Unfortunately, the desire by national governments to control their own nuclear programmes has hampered the progress of Euratom. In addition, expectations of the role of nuclear power were too high, and only after 1973 did the need for such a supplementary energy source become vital.

The Benelux countries had already experimented with their own customs union. They agreed to form one during the later stages of the war and from the beginning of 1948 they removed all intra-tariffs, establishing a common external tariff (CET) to outsiders, and making some attempt to harmonize economic policies. Benelux sought to go further, and it was Paul-Henri Spaak, a Belgian closely involved with the process of postwar integration, who was chosen to chair an intergovernmental committee which produced the important report bearing his name in 1955–56; this laid the foundation for the Treaty of Rome.

The smaller European countries, not being major powers, have had less to lose through integration, though they recognized that there would have to be a satisfactory voting system to ensure that their views would not be overridden by larger European partners. The smaller members have been able to exercise international influence via the EEC, in particular when occupying the Presidency of the Council of Ministers. Both Belgium and Luxembourg house European institutions, with Brussels being acknowledged as the capital of the Community: these institutions are an important source of revenue, and Luxembourg has fought hard to try to retain its position. These smaller countries are all highly dependent on trade, and access to an open trading system is crucial to them.

The EEC was the most important of the three Communities, and economic spillover has occurred with the interdependence of different sectors. The starting-point was the customs union in which a precise and detailed timetable was laid down for removing intra-bloc trading barriers. Individual national tariffs were replaced by a common external tariff which was applied on imports from outside countries – this, the CET, was the visible symbol of the EC's presence to the rest of the world. The EC has become most integrated in the free flow of goods, but a free flow of factors of production has also taken place. These intra-EC factor flows are less than those for goods, and the EC has not reached the same common external policy on factor flows (Molle 1990). Nevertheless, this first phase of integration created a Common Market in which the internal barriers which had been erected were steadily removed.

Another phase of integration has consisted of positive policies in new fields leading towards economic union, and this has proved difficult and contentious, since whereas negative integration was underpinned by Treaty provisions, positive integration has depended more upon new agreements. Its economic justification has been to create conditions of fair competition and to avoid a situation of 'second best'. The latter arises if countries are importing from their partners not because of natural comparative advantage, but because of different national policies subsidizing particular sectors of the economy. For example, those countries with cheaper food, lower taxes, lower charges for transport and energy, and so on, would have an unfair trading advantage; hence the rationale for a high degree of economic integration. This has been carried out more extensively in some sectors, such as agriculture, than in others.

Apart from natural economic spillover, political pressures have also underscored the process of integration. The EC has shown a bureaucratic appetite for expansion into new areas, sometimes impinging upon the work of more specific organizations. Nevertheless, progress has not been as automatic as expected, since countries have fought obdurately to defend particular national interests. The process of bargaining has often produced 'package deals', whereby countries have only been willing to make concessions in return for some *quid pro quo* in an ancillary area. Indeed, the actual formation of the EEC along with Euratom exemplified the linking of interests in its inception, but over the years the process has become more pronounced, such as with the linking of the internal market to institutional changes of greater majority voting by the Council, and additional powers for the European Parliament; likewise the two intergovernmental conferences on political union and on EMU in 1991. In some respects it is paradoxical that inability to reach agreement on one issue has at times resulted in more widespread integration in other fields in which some countries perceive prospective gains. This process of integration may be a source of potential problems, and has on occasions invoked national interests which resulted in complete deadlock; for example, the Community seized up in the mid-1960s after the French boycott and its opposition to moves towards majority voting.

New goals were established for integration during the 1970s to move it towards a real Community. On the eve of EC enlargement in 1973, the widening of EC membership from six to nine was also to be accompanied by deeper integration in an attempt to create the ambitious goal of European union by 1980. In some respects Community enlargement actually seems to be incompatible with a deeper and faster process of integration. Nevertheless the EC has sought to progress from microeconomic policies of integration in particular sectors towards macroeconomic integration. The progression towards monetary union became necessary because free trade and common pricing in a sector such as agriculture is undermined when national exchange rates are highly unstable. Monetary union in turn has reinforced the case for strengthening the Community's regional policy. Monetary integration itself can only be sustained by the adoption of convergent economic policies, in particular to avoid disparities in national rates of inflation. In the long run, if macroeconomic policy-making becomes more centrally controlled, with a larger budget, then political institutions at a supranational level may develop more fully towards a political union – provided they are not frustrated by continuing national interests.

Unfortunately, a setback to macroeconomic integration was provided by the steep rise in oil prices after 1973. Since then the Community has resembled more closely a zero-sum game in which gains are made in one country increasingly at the expense of another country. Progress is much easier where a variable-sum game exists, since all countries expect to gain real benefits from EC membership. The minimum condition that needs to be fulfilled is laid down by Paretian social welfare in stating that 'changes are desirable if it is possible to compensate losers so that no one is worse off and at least some people are better off' (Dosser et al. 1982, p. 5); hence some countries need to be better off and to compensate losers so that the latter are no worse off.

During the 1980s EC integration recovered its dynamism as the Community decided to reinforce its original basic theme of completing the Common Market via its internal market initiatives. It has had to couple this with enhanced structural funding to help weaker member states, particularly those in Southern Europe; otherwise the latter would lose out if the focus were solely on the internal market, the central feature of the Single European Act which came into force on 1 July 1987. The single market is also to be accompanied by a single currency in the new millennium. The EU is an organization growing in importance, moving towards an integrated foreign policy, towards a common security policy and towards a common defence policy.

*European Free Trade Association (EFTA)*  The OEEC split created a Europe of 'Sixes and Sevens' in which seven countries opted for a looser free-trade area instead of joining the six in a customs union. Seven countries signed the Stockholm Convention in 1960: Austria, Denmark, Norway, Portugal, Sweden, Switzerland and the UK; they were joined later by Finland and Iceland.

The departure of the UK and Denmark from EFTA in 1973 – along with the later withdrawal of Portugal – and their entry into the EC led to the conclusion in some quarters that EFTA was a failure and that it would disintegrate totally. This was a premature but mistaken conclusion since EFTA continued to exist, providing an interesting comparison, particularly for the members which have belonged to both organizations. In 1973 the bridge-building between the enlarged EC and EFTA led to the establishment of much closer economic relations between the two organizations; this was decisively reinforced after the Ministerial Declaration of Luxembourg in 1984.

A primary and distinctive difference between EFTA and the EC is that the former has been concerned solely with economic integration. It never sought political integration as its goal, unlike the EC, and this originally deterred most EFTA countries from joining the EC. For example, Austria and Finland were constrained initially by Soviet pressure, while Switzerland has been concerned with preserving its long-standing neutrality. Finland was only an associate member of EFTA, but decided to become a full EFTA member after the departure of Portugal into the EC.

EFTA is an intergovernmental organization; its key institution is the Council, which consists of occasional meetings attended by representatives of its member governments, while the Heads of the Permanent Delegations meet more frequently. EFTA has made little use of voting and has generally proceeded on the basis of unanimity. It lacks a body such as the Commission of the EC to provide initiatives for federal integration and has only a very small secretariat of under one hundred employees. The official language continues to be English, even though after the UK's departure in 1973 German might have seemed more appropriate, given the membership of countries such as Austria and Switzerland. EFTA reflects pragmatic traditions, with its absence of supranational institutions. Unlike the situation in the EC, as evidenced by the growing workload of the Court of Justice, relationships in EFTA have been relatively harmonious, with only a few disputes arising, and those were referred to the Council. The operating costs of EFTA have been low, not only because of its limited scope and falling membership but also because of its low institutional overheads. For example, EFTA budgetary expenditure was only 7.0 million Swiss francs in 1967–8 and 9.4 million Swiss francs in 1978–9.

EFTA has been concerned with industrial free trade and each country retains its own tariff to outsiders. This necessitated rules of origin to prevent imports creeping in through the country with the lowest tariff. EFTA also failed to develop the range of common policies that characterizes the EC. Nevertheless, EFTA has shown a high degree of success for its members in terms of macroeconomic performance. The growth of trade led to low rates of unemployment in all EFTA countries and the problem countries – the UK and Portugal – transferred their problems to the EC.

EFTA constituted, after the withdrawal of Portugal and the UK, a more homogeneous group and some of its members were better candidates for progress towards full economic integration than some of the Southern European members that have enlarged the European Community. Many EFTA countries gained economic benefits from free-trade access into the Community market, via the Common Economic Space, without paying the full price of membership. The EC's developments of the internal market by 1992 tested EFTA's ultimate intentions since if it wished to maintain its preferential position with the EC then it would have to fall into line, perhaps ultimately applying the EC's CET and approximating taxes.

EFTA steadily declined in economic significance and its members had a limited range of options. The least attractive was to cling to the existing arrangements, since the internal market made EC businesses more efficient with lower costs, and multinational investment more attractive in the EC than in EFTA. Hence EFTA countries began to apply the internal market measures and held joint discussions with the EC to create a European Economic Area (EEA). Difficult stumbling-blocks to be resolved included agriculture, and in particular fisheries; the role of the Court of Justice; and EFTA's participation in decision-making. The EEA created a close legal and economic relationship which increased the participation of the EFTA pillar and also led to financial obligations in contributing to EU Structural Funds. However, Swiss participation was rejected in a referendum in 1992, with Switzerland negotiating a bilateral agreement with the EU, leaving the others in the EEA. In 1995 Austria became a full member of the EU, along with Finland and Sweden, whose relative economic position has declined and its role as a 'model' for others has diminished. The benefits from neutrality appear increasingly less convincing in the 1990s, with the ending of the cold war divisions in Europe. However, for Switzerland and Liechtenstein, Iceland and Norway, EFTA was to remain as a preferable option.

**The United Kingdom**
The UK's ambivalent postwar relationship with the EC has something of a tragic farce about it. Various phases can be distinguished and in the 1950s, when the ECSC and the EEC were being formed and UK participation would have been welcomed, the UK remained aloofly outside. In the 1960s, when the UK sought to join, the boot was on the other foot, and British overtures were rejected. Finally, after eventually joining the EC in 1973, the UK agonized over whether it had taken the right decision, with the trauma of the referendum in 1975 followed by perpetual disputes over agricultural and budgetary issues.

*The mistake of standing aside in the 1950s*
The pressures underlying European integration were much greater on the Continent than in the UK, which had held firm during the war. Although at that time Churchill had proposed a union between France and Britain, in the early postwar years the UK was reluctant to participate in any continental integration that went beyond intergovernmental organizations. The UK was unwilling to join the ECSC at its inception since the British coal and steel industries had been nationalized by the Labour government and there was opposition to placing these key industries under a higher supranational authority. At that time the UK produced about half the coal and about a third of the steel output of Europe, so that its absence from the ECSC was significant, as was its later failure to join Euratom – in a field where the UK again held a strong position. The UK stood apart since it had very real doubts as to whether European integration could be successfully achieved in a durable way. With its glorious history, why should it choose to take the risky jump into the unknown when it could continue with its more certain, reliable and traditional partners such as the USA and the Commonwealth? The UK had sufficient political power in the 1950s and hoped that EFTA would provide a sufficient additional economic stop-

gap. The UK was able to mould EFTA so that it could play a similar pivotal role to that which it exercised in the Commonwealth. EFTA was a complementary organization enabling the continuance of traditional Commonwealth trading links such as those for the import of cheap food. Unfortunately the UK failed to maximize its opportunities in EFTA, partly because it was always seen as a temporary creation, and British business had to make special marketing arrangements for the different Scandinavian and Alpine markets.

The case for joining the Six was so much less compelling for the UK at the time than it was for its continental neighbours, who appreciated the political and economic benefits from reconciliation. Whereas they opted for change, the UK chose continuity. It saw its past and its future as an outward-looking maritime power that did not wish to be drawn into an inward-looking continental bloc. In retrospect the UK made a crucial and major miscalculation in the 1950s. It took the safe decision, and the one that most people would probably have taken in the circumstances at that time. But with the benefit of hindsight it was a fundamental error, given that later the UK was to withdraw from EFTA and join the EC, which had been moulded and developed to suit different continental interests. The UK joined in an even weaker position, with poorer terms.

*Courtship of the Community from the 1960s*
In the early 1960s the UK decided that it wanted to join the EC and its change in position can be attributed to both political and economic factors. The political arguments for joining increased because of the weakening links with the Commonwealth, while those with the USA also deteriorated, notably after the Suez crisis. Unfortunately, in 1963 entry negotiations were called off after President de Gaulle stated that the time was not ripe for British membership of the Community. De Gaulle still harboured some resentment towards the UK; whereas Britain felt that it had treated France well during the war, de Gaulle was less than flattered by his wartime relationship with Churchill. In the 1960s de Gaulle was also very concerned about the dangers of increased American influence creeping into the Community via UK entry. In the suggestion that Britain was not ready for membership one can detect a recognition of the competitive threat posed by British industry that was greater at that time than later. France would hardly welcome such competition unless the UK accepted the key aspects of integration, particularly the Common Agricultural Policy. Negotiations became

bogged down not only over agriculture and the Commonwealth, but over a multiplicity of other items. The EC doubted whether the UK was prepared to play a constructive role in the Community. The USA, which had pursued an equal Atlantic partnership with Europe based upon the UK in the EC, found its strategy rebuffed. Instead of enlarging the Community, France and Germany reinforced their partnership, signing a Treaty of Co-operation which was ratified in 1963. West Germany added a preamble to the Treaty to reduce criticism from outside, such as that from the USA, though de Gaulle considered that it diminished the value of the Treaty (Groeben 1985).

The Labour government in 1966 decided to pursue British membership of the Community. This arose partly from some disillusionment with the Commonwealth and problems in particular countries, such as the illegal Unilateral Declaration of Independence (UDI) in Rhodesia. The Prime Minister and Foreign Secretary (Harold Wilson and George Brown) made a tour of capital cities in the Community, pointing out, amongst other things, the technological advantages that Britain could bring to the Community. In 1967 de Gaulle said '*non*' yet again.

De Gaulle may have been right in thinking that the British would not turn out to be '*communautaire*', though France itself had often been unco-operative when it suited national interests. For example, while de Gaulle was prepared to use the EC to pursue French economic interests, politically he believed that only national governments could deal with the high policy areas. France withdrew from EC institutions in the latter half of 1965 since it was concerned to perpetuate a national veto on decisions of major importance. Similarly, in 1966 France decided to withdraw from the integrated command structure of NATO. The French preferred their own '*force de frappe*', objecting to an American dominance of NATO and being less certain of the US nuclear guarantee to Europe.

After the resignation of de Gaulle in 1969 the UK made better progress since France was prepared to recognize that the UK could provide some counterweight to the growing power of West Germany. France also saw that enlargement could be linked to the completion of the Community's budgetary system of own resources. The Hague Summit in 1969 cleared the way for a round of new and successful negotiations. The UK was worried about particular issues such as agriculture, fisheries, the Budget, and so on. In 1971 Heath (UK) and Pompidou (France) compromised, with the UK accepting the own-resources budgetary system, and France giving ground over its concern about the overhanging sterling balances.

*The first enlargement, 1973*
The UK agreed to accept the existing treaties, but negotiated a period of transitional adjustment for five years in which it aligned itself to the EC system. The UK would have preferred a shorter transitional period for its industry and a longer one for agriculture. The interests of the Commonwealth were accommodated for imports of dairy produce from New Zealand and sugar cane from important Commonwealth producers. The attempt to meet specific Commonwealth interests has aggravated subsequent agricultural problems in the Community, adding to its embarrassing surplus of farm products. The entry terms for the UK were approved by the House of Commons with a vote of 356 to 244 in favour of joining the Community. Ireland and Denmark also entered the EC.

It was inevitable that Ireland would be drawn towards the EC because of the UK's application. In some ways Irish membership was less contested than that of the UK since Ireland had not incurred the strength of French opposition. Ireland also stood to benefit strongly from the Community's agricultural policy: indeed, the absence of agricultural concern in EFTA was one reason why Ireland was a non-member of that organization. A referendum produced overwhelming support in Ireland with an 83 per cent 'yes' vote for EC membership. Ireland has generally fared quite well, though the restraints on agricultural spending have proved unpopular. In addition, closer co-operation on issues such as European security, as part of the Single European Act (SEA), led to Irish delay in ratifying this. In May 1987 the Irish government arranged a referendum on the SEA, with a majority of 70 per cent in favour.

Denmark saw the UK as one of its major export markets agriculturally which had to be retained. In the EC efficient Danish farmers have been able to improve further on their already adequate incomes. The economic benefits have cemented Denmark in the Community, despite considerable opposition, and in 1986 a further referendum was necessary so that Denmark could sign the Single European Act.

A Nordic Council had been created in 1954 and Denmark co-operated closely with other Scandinavian countries. In joining the Community Denmark also expected Norwegian entry but unfortunately, whereas Denmark voted 63.5 per cent in favour of entry, the Norwegian referendum rejected membership, with 53.5 per cent voting 'no'. The major sources of opposition in Norway were the primary and peripheral sectors comprising agriculture and fisheries, but also other fringe protest groups. These were confronted by industry, commerce, shipping and consumers, but in the end the more urban groups were defeated (Allen 1979). Norway negotiated a trade agreement with the Community, after hard bargaining over several sensitive industrial products and the level of fishing tariffs.

*A referendum to resolve the issue of UK membership*
The UK was finally relieved to achieve its objective of membership of the Community, but it soon seemed to forget why it had joined, and pressure resurfaced for a withdrawal. Although the UK had committed itself firmly to the EC for an unlimited time period, this was not necessarily considered to be binding since Westminster was in a position to revoke membership. The Labour government that was returned to office in 1974 was highly dissatisfied by the terms of entry achieved under the Conservative Prime Minister Edward Heath. There is little doubt that the gradual weakening in the UK's bargaining position and its determination to join the EC almost at any cost had not resulted in the negotiation of the best terms. Community policies had moved on in areas such as agriculture, fishing and budgetary matters, and these were to prove contentious for the UK. The Labour government sought a review of particular items and was determined to secure better terms. In June 1975 the UK underwent the innovation of a referendum – whereas greater use is made of referenda in other European countries.

The old issues were reopened and the major political parties were divided. Consequently, the campaign was between two groups: Britain in Europe, which was pro-market, and the National Referendum Campaign, which was anti-market. The major political figures supporting Britain in Europe made important pleas. Edward Heath asked: 'Are we going to stay on the centre of the stage where we belong, or are we going to shuffle off into the dusty wings of history?' Roy Jenkins, who was President of the Britain in Europe Organizing Committee, argued that 'not to have gone into Europe would have been a misfortune, but to come out would be an altogether greater scale of self-inflicted injury'. In the pamphlet urging a 'yes' vote for Britain in Europe, some of the following points were made: traditions would be safe; jobs would be retained; food secured at fair prices; and ultimately no better alternatives were foreseen. The financial weight of this group was stronger than that of the National Referendum Campaign, which urged a 'no' vote. The latter was concerned with the UK's right to rule itself, and with the adverse effects on food prices, jobs and the trade deficit. It also recognized the favourable alternatives available to EFTA countries. The decisive factor was the government's own position and its pamphlet entitled 'Britain's New Deal in Europe'. The Prime Minister, Harold Wilson, claimed that the renegotiation objectives had been substantially achieved; therefore the government 'decided to recommend to the British people to vote for staying in the Community'. The voters were naturally inclined to trust the government's advice and the referendum outcome reconfirmed UK membership, though holding a referendum on whether to withdraw from the EC was a different matter from the decision not to hold a referendum on whether to join in the first place.

The referendum was a way of helping to heal the intra-party divisions which were most intense in the Labour Party. The turnout in the UK was 64.5 per cent: some 17 million people voted 'yes' to stay in the EC and about 8 million people voted 'no', although the result concealed wide regional and local variations. In the north less support was recorded, but only Shetland and the Western Isles voted against remaining in the Community.

The electorate has had considerable difficulty in understanding the complex subject of the EC, and public opinion on the issue has been extremely volatile. Unfortunately, in the EC there tended to be an over-optimistic interpretation of the referendum result in deducing an apparently new-found enthusiasm by the UK for the Community. This was largely mistaken, but at least the main virtue of the referendum was that it settled the issue, confirming that the UK's future role and destiny lay in the EC. Withdrawal would have been a setback, although Greenland withdrew from the Community in February 1985. Obviously a UK decision to withdraw would have had far more devastating consequences.

# 2 The structure and operation of EU institutions

**The decision-making process**

It is important to understand the institutions that engage in decision-making and exercise power in the EU, and to consider the changes that have taken place in the interplay between them. It has been suggested that the EU's achievements have been constrained by failings in its decision-making and also that decision-making procedures need to become more democratic. The institutions examined in this chapter are the Commission, the Council of Ministers, the European Parliament (EP), the Economic and Social Committee (ESC), the European Court of Justice (ECJ) and lastly the Committee of the Regions (COR). No coverage is given here of the Court of Auditors, nor of the European Central Bank, since these are touched upon in later macroeconomic chapters. It should be borne in mind when discussing the European Communities that there were differences between the ECSC, the EEC and Euratom, since each had separate Commissions and Councils, but with a common Parliament and Court. A Treaty to merge the three was signed in April 1965 and came into force in July 1967. Since that time there has been a single Commission and Council.

While the main concern of economists is with policy outputs, as shown in subsequent chapters, it is important to understand the inputs into the decision-making process. This is crucial not only for political scientists but for all those seeking to influence and participate in decision-making. It is true that there has still not been the decisive transfer of identity and power towards the EU that was hoped for, and the key actors are still the nation states. Also, the political spillover brought about by European interest groups has so far not kept pace with the economic spillover of integration. Nevertheless, over time more and more crucial decisions are being taken at the EU level, with far-reaching implications both for business and for citizens in the EU.

The decisions that are taken are not imposed secretively by the bureaucracy in Brussels, as perhaps the media might imply, but represent the articulation of many different views in a very open, participative and consensual system. This framework results in a very slow process of decision-making – on average a period of three years before proposals are turned into law, with difficult issues often taking very much longer. Thus there are considerable opportunities to influence policy-making, but to do this effectively it is necessary to identify the role of the institutions and to exercise timely and appropriate lobbying. It is preferable to do so at an early a stage as possible, starting when the Commission is formulating new legislative proposals and these are being considered by experts and working parties.

Further channels to reshape policies occur when the proposals are being considered by the Economic and Social Committee and by the European Parliament, and since the latter now has enhanced powers to amend legislation, it is being lobbied far more. A mass of lobbying organizations has gravitated towards the power centre of the EU. Another opportunity to influence policy arises when the revised draft is being reworked by the Commission and discussed by the Committee of Permanent Representatives (COREPER), before being submitted to the Council of Ministers. Since policies evolve and are moulded to suit the different national interests of the 15 member states, there is considerable scope to modify legislation. While influence is best brought to bear at the European level, it should not be neglected at national level where Community legislation is also examined.

It will be shown that power has shifted over time from the Commission – which is now just one among several other bodies – to the Council, and in particular the European Council. Furthermore, since direct elections in 1979 to the EP, the latter has increased in influence following Treaty revisions, tending to diminish the role of the ESC. With the growing demands by the EP to enhance its powers to reduce the democratic deficit, important concessions were made to it in the Single European Act, increasing the EP's role in important areas such as the internal market. Whereas the Community was originally on a 'journey to an unknown destination', this has given way to a clearer political destination.

## EU institutions

### The Commission

*Structure*   The Commission is a small and open bureaucracy. Nearly two-thirds of the staff are based in Brussels, with other significant numbers based mainly in Luxembourg. Around a quarter of the graduate staff are engaged in linguistic work, made necessary by the number of working languages. The Commission is the EU's Civil Service and has been able to operate with modest staffing levels since it depends heavily upon national civil servants for implementing its policies, such as the Common Agricultural Policy (CAP). The Commission has also sought to improve its internal management and working practices, along with the devolution of some of its tasks to specific agencies.

A distinction has to be drawn between the Commissioners and their staff. The Commissioners were appointed for a period of four years, with the President appointed for two years, on the assumption that this would be renewable. However, under the Maastricht Treaty the term of office was increased to five years. The first President, Walter Hallstein of Germany, served for an even longer stint; subsequently it proved difficult at times to match the excellent spirit of co-operation in the first Commission (Groeben 1985, p. 47). The President has to mould the team together and has usually been an important national figure. The Frenchman Jacques Delors's long occupation of office enabled him to make a very significant contribution in moving the EU forward from the Single European Market (SEM) to Maastricht.

The President is assisted in his tasks by a number of Vice-Presidents. The Commission consists of two Commissioners from the larger countries and one Commissioner from the smaller countries. There has been some concern about the body becoming unwieldy as a consequence of enlargement, but proposals to appoint only one Commissioner from each country have been opposed by the large countries. In the allocation of portfolios between the Commissioners, some are thought to be more significant and rewarding than others; hence some haggling occurs over the initial distribution of posts. The 20 Commissioners exercise influence according to their portfolios and their personal characteristics of charisma and drive. Some strong personalities, including those from smaller countries, have often wielded considerable power (Butler 1986, p. 18). Many Commissioners have had some ministerial experience in their own countries before coming to the Commission.

The Commission is an appointed body which many would prefer to be democratically elected, though this would elevate it further at the expense of the Council of Ministers. The Commissioners, despite differing political views, have to work together effectively, transferring their allegiance to the EU. While naturally they retain close links back home, they are definitely not delegates following national instructions. They have to act impartially in the interests of the EU and occasionally in doing this they have incurred national criticism. However, Commissioners cannot be dismissed during their term of appointment either by their national governments or by the President of the Commission. Although the Commission as a whole is directly responsible to the Parliament – which can dismiss it by a two-thirds majority – the Parliament cannot take formal action against individual Commissioners. This point was well illustrated in January 1999 when the Commission was censured by the EP for its corruption, incompetence and fraud, but the EP declined to dismiss the whole Commission, partly for fear of setting back the progress of the EU. However, after a critical report the Commission itself resigned in March 1999. The discredited Jacques Santer had proved too weak to control the Commission and was replaced as President by the Italian Romano Prodi, the former Italian Prime Minister.

The Commission is organized into 24 Directorates-General (DGs) and they are usually identified by number, ranging from DGI on External Relations to DGXXIV on Consumer Policy. Some DGs are of greater importance than others: for example, DGVI on Agriculture and DGXV on the Internal Market and Financial Services. The main organizational links are vertical, with fairly weak horizontal links between the DGs.

The Commission takes several decisions routinely and other straightforward matters follow a written procedure: if no reservations are entered, then the proposals are adopted. For more important issues, majority voting is used. Where a vote is taken, the Commission operates like a college and the minority abide by the collective decision.

Each Commissioner is supported by the French form of private office or Cabinet, which helps to keep the Commissioner well informed and is usually filled with his or her personal choice of staff. The Chef de Cabinet will deputize for an absent Commissioner. The power of the Chefs de Cabinet may have reduced some of the authority of the Directors-General. Each of the Directorates-General covers broad policy areas and is divided into sections dealing with various aspects, presided over by Directors, beneath whom are the Heads of Division.

The allocation of posts in the DGs is distributed to secure a balance between the 15 members of the EU. To enable this balance to be maintained after previous enlargements, some existing staff took early retirement on generous terms. A blending together of different nationalities has generally worked well, avoiding a splintering into rival national factions. The main dissatisfaction arises from career-minded staff who, although well paid, may feel that their promotion is restricted because of national quotas on staff in different grades and areas. However, in the lower-grade posts the quota is disregarded and a disproportionate number of staff are nationals of the countries in which the institutions are located.

*Functions of the Commission*  The Commission embodies the ideals of the EU and carries out a range of political and administrative functions which can be classified in five main ways. In the first instance, the Commission proposes new policies since the Treaty establishing the EC was more of an outline sketch than that of the ECSC or Euratom. Hence the Commission has filled in the details of existing policies and initiated new policies. It is the master of both the form and the timing of new proposals, without which the Council cannot act. The Commission often has to modify these proposals, but tries to act as the powerhouse of closer integration. Commission power is strongest where it has clear Treaty provisions supporting its actions.

Secondly, the Commission carries out executive powers to implement the policies in the Treaties. It prepares decisions and regulations to implement the provisions of the Treaty, such as on trade, and enactments of the Council; for example, a mass of regulations is passed each year relating to the CAP. The Commission also administers EU Funds and research programmes. The Commission works closely with member countries to operate policies effectively, often by means of management committees, such as those for agriculture. While national administrators may lack the Commission's commitment to integration, they have been helpful in monitoring proposals and in reducing the administrative burden. The Commission needs to proceed further with more devolved administration of more of its programmes to ensure that they are managed more effectively.

Thirdly, the Commission acts as guardian of the Treaties: it fulfils a watchdog role and investigates any action which it considers infringes the Treaties. It demands explanations for actions which may arise from a misinterpretation of the Treaties. If the Commission is still dissatisfied with the explanations given, it issues a reasoned opinion with which the state must comply. If the state does not do this, the matter is referred to the Court of Justice, although in the case of competition and cartels the Commission itself has direct powers to fine offending companies.

Fourthly, the Commission has the formal right to attend Council meetings where it presents its views vigorously in order to pilot through its legislation. Likewise, the President of the Commission attends meetings of the European Council ('summit meetings'). The Commission seeks to steer through its own proposals, being the centre of bargaining and an additional member of the Council, and even though the Commission has no vote, it possesses the expertise. It mediates and strives to secure agreement between the differences of the member states, as does the President of the Council. The Commission is also the hinge between the Parliament and the Council at the second stage. Often the overall policy outcome is simply one of establishing the lowest common denominator, far removed from the initial Commission proposal based on a strong, adventurous initiative for integration.

In addition to the functions outlined, a final responsibility of the Commission is to represent the EU in various international organizations and also in the EU's external relations with non-member countries. The Commission DGs, in conducting their activities, have developed over time a very bureaucratic organization, though the Commissioners can provide political leadership.

## The Council of Ministers

*Structure*   The Council of Ministers was given only a minor role in the ECSC, but had a very important position to play in the EC, and its power has grown in significance. Ministerial representatives from the member states, along with their officials, make up the Council. Its meetings are usually held in Brussels but also in Luxembourg, and the latter, having suffered from the decision of Parliament not to hold its meetings there, was keen to retain some Council meetings.

Unlike the case in other EU institutions, the Ministers' mandate is to represent their own country. The most frequent visitors to Council meetings are the Ministers of Foreign Affairs and of Agriculture. Ministers of Finance also meet on a regular basis in ECOFIN, whereas other Ministers meet less frequently. Sometimes Ministers, even from the same country, may adopt contradictory positions; for example, Ministers of Agriculture have supported farming interests, whereas Ministers of Finance have been concerned to limit financial expenditure on agriculture. The Foreign Ministers have the most important responsibility since they are also expected to provide the general roles of supervision and co-ordination. An improvement would be greater openness of the Council, publishing the voting record and moving to the holding of some of its sessions in public.

The Presidency of the Council is held by each member state on a rotating basis for a period of six months. The President has an important job in exercising political weight of mediation to try to secure agreement, with the Commission's role being to produce the technical solutions to the problems. The establishment of the Council's own Secretariat has altered the Commission's role in servicing the Council. The Council's Secretariat has over two thousand employees and is organized, like the Commission, into a small number of Directorates-General. The major administrative task of the Secretariat is to organize and administer the Council's decision-making: it makes EU legislation available in different languages and many of its staff are translators and legal linguists.

The Council of Ministers has extended vertically over the years, spreading downwards to include the Committee of Permanent Representatives (COREPER). This comprises both the Permanent Representatives and their Deputies, with the former (COREPER 2) dealing with external questions, significant political questions and highly contentious issues. Meanwhile the Deputies (COREPER 1) focus more on internal issues such as the internal market, transport, social affairs and the environment. Note that agriculture has its own Special Committee, staffed by senior officials either from the Permanent Representatives or from national Ministries of Agriculture. COREPER resolves many issues, providing the groundwork for the Ministers themselves to approve agreements (as 'A points') on their agenda, and to enable them to make greater progress on more important and difficult matters ('B points').

*Functions of the Council* Power resides in the Council of Ministers since it takes the decisions, but being the least supranational of bodies in the EU it has provided a brake on developments. Its role has been enhanced further as a consequence of the two intergovernmental pillars of the EU. There has been concern about the way in which some decisions are taken: voting can be by unanimous vote or by absolute or qualified majority vote. Unanimity is generally needed for the initiation of new policies (or if an existing policy framework is to be modified or developed further), and when the Council is seeking to amend a Commission proposal against the Commission's wishes. Majority voting usually applies where proposals are concerned with the operation of existing policies (Nugent 1994).

The Treaty of Rome laid down a voting procedure which in the earlier years required a unanimous vote for most of the decisions. But in other areas, such as agriculture, a qualified majority vote was sufficient. France raised objections to Commission proposals in 1965 for a package deal to develop agricultural policies more completely and to move towards decision-making by majority voting. France not only opposed the substance of the latter but objected to the way in which the Commission's proposals were first delivered to the EP before being forwarded officially to the Council of Ministers. The paralysis of the Community was resolved by an extraordinary meeting of the Council of Ministers, which was held in Luxembourg rather than Brussels, and the outcome was the so-called Luxembourg Compromise. De Gaulle was not prepared to see France outvoted where very important national issues were at stake. It was agreed, therefore, that countries would continue to negotiate with each other until unanimous agreement was reached. After the enlargement of the EU, most new members supported this new national right of veto which can still be invoked where important national interests are involved.

A general reluctance to make wide use of majority voting slowed down the decision-making in a search for compromise and consensus. It became obvious after the southern enlargement of the EU in the 1980s that changes were needed to bring about greater use of majority voting; otherwise the EU was likely to grind to a halt in many fields. The Single European Act (SEA) made an important breakthrough by introducing majority voting for most aspects of the creation of the internal market. It thus embodied a significant step forward in improving the decision-making process. The Council's Rules of Procedure were formally amended in July 1987 in order to allow not just the President but any national representative and the Commission to have the right to call for a vote, and a vote must be held if the majority agree. However, it is important for the EU to progress as far as possible in a united and consensual way to ensure that legislation is implemented. For example, at the end of 1990, whilst technically the qualified majority voting system could have been applied in GATT, Italy did not wish to expose Franco-German opposition to this.

Under the qualified majority voting system the votes are distributed so that the 'big four' – Germany, France, Italy and the UK – have 10 votes each; Spain has 8 votes; Belgium, Greece, the Netherlands and Portugal have 5 votes each; Austria and Sweden have 4 votes each; Denmark, Ireland and Finland have 3 votes each; and Luxembourg has 2 votes. It can be seen that in relation to population size the larger countries such as Germany are under-represented in the Council voting system, while smaller countries such as Luxembourg are over-represented. From this total of 87 votes the threshold for a qualified majority vote is 70 per cent, and after the 1995 enlargement of the EU a qualified majority requires 62 votes and a blocking minority of 26. The whole issue of the blocking minority was considered, due to concerns in the UK, and the Council made a further compromise to ensure that when 23–26 votes are cast against a proposal, every effort will be made to ensure a satisfactory solution that could be adopted by 68 votes within a reasonable time.

*The European Council*   The vertical links of the Council have also extended upwards, reflected in the activities of the European Council: this consists of regular meetings of Heads of Governments. These Summit Meetings were not provided for in the Treaty of Rome, but it was agreed to establish them in 1974 and they were written into the SEA under Article 2. Although they have limited the supranational characteristics of the EU in favour of intergovernmentalism, they have been vital in breaking the log-jam of business and in propelling the EU forward. The European Council has met three times a year and now meets twice a year; the meetings are held in the capital cities of the countries which hold the Presidency during the year.

Membership of the European Council is restricted to Heads of Government (or Heads of State), Ministers for Foreign Affairs, and two representatives from the Commission. While the European Council symbolizes intergovernmentalism, the Commission has been able to inject important ideas which promote further integration. The relatively small group, operating in a fairly informal way with a flexible agenda, is able to focus on current EU and international issues and can resolve immediate problems. Often a package deal emerges as the easiest resolution, sewing up several problems together; for example, the Fontainebleau Summit in 1984, tackling Britain's agricultural and budgetary problems. At other Summits new direction has been provided, such as in 1985 on the internal market programme, or in 1990 at the Rome Summit, with the Italians making further progress on dates for EMU.

Heads of Government interact less frequently than Foreign Ministers, but when they have enjoyed amicable personal relationships, these have been most helpful to progress in the EU. For example, Franco-German links are crucial and the meeting of minds between Schmidt and Giscard d'Estaing and later between Kohl and Mitterrand provided the Community with leadership in fields such as economic and monetary union. Sometimes relations have been strained and meetings unsuccessful as Heads of Government have become bogged down with too many details which they have been incapable of comprehending, and an over-lengthy agenda. Problems have been compounded by some indecisive national Ministers who might have settled some of the issues themselves in the Council instead of leaving these to be shifted upwards to the European Council. With greater use of majority voting in the Council of Ministers the European Council will be able to focus on fewer problems; it is the one body that can set a clear agenda of objectives (Tugendhat 1986). The European Council's role in the more intergovernmental Common Foreign and Security Policy (CFSP) has also increased.

*The European Parliament*

*Structure*   The European Parliament used to be called the Assembly. Its structure can be examined in two ways: the Members of the European Parliament (MEPs) can be divided either by their national membership or by their party-political distribution. There were 410 MEPs after the first direct elections in 1979, since when the total number of MEPs for the EU (15) has risen to 626. Of the 'big four', a united Germany has 99 seats, while France, Italy and the UK each have 87 seats. Spain has 64 MEPs, the Netherlands 31, and there are 25 MEPs each from Belgium, Greece and Portugal; 22 from Sweden, 21 from Austria, plus 16 from Denmark and 16 from Finland, 15 from Ireland, and 6 from Luxembourg.

The MEPs, drawn from very many national political parties, come together into a small number of political groups. These transnational groups seek a common approach to issues, aiming to grow into real political parties. The strength of the party groups and their national membership in the EP has varied over the years in each election and provisional estimated group sizes immediately after the June 1999 elections indicated further re-alignments as shown in Table 2.1.

There are nine party groups, including the independent non-attached MEPs. The largest transnational group before the 1999 elections was the Socialists, with MEPs belonging to it from every country. In the 1999 elections the Socialists lost seats, despite the dominance of centre–left governments in many member states. Seats were lost especially in Germany and the UK, and the Group of the Party of European

Table 2.1   New 1999 political groups in the European Parliament

| | B | DK | D | GR | E | F | IRL | I | L | NL | A | P | FIN | S | UK | Total |
|---|---|---|---|---|---|---|---|---|---|---|---|---|---|---|---|---|
| EPP/ED | 6 | 1 | 53 | 9 | 28 | 21 | 5 | 34 | 2 | 9 | 7 | 9 | 5 | 7 | 37 | 233 |
| PES | 5 | 3 | 33 | 9 | 24 | 22 | 1 | 17 | 2 | 6 | 7 | 12 | 3 | 6 | 30 | 180 |
| ELDR | 5 | 6 | | | 3 | | 1 | 7 | 1 | 8 | | | 5 | 4 | 10 | 50 |
| GREENS/EFA | 7 | | 7 | | 4 | 9 | 2 | 2 | 1 | 4 | 2 | | 2 | 2 | 6 | 48 |
| EUL/NGL | | 1 | 6 | 7 | 4 | 11 | | 6 | | 1 | | 2 | 1 | 3 | | 42 |
| UEN | | 1 | | | | 13 | 6 | 9 | | | | 2 | | | | 31 |
| TGI | 2 | | | | | 5 | | 11 | | | | | | | | 18 |
| EDD | | 4 | | | | 6 | | | | 3 | | | | | 3 | 16 |
| IND | | | | | 1 | | | 1 | | | 5 | | | | 1 | 8 |
| TOTAL | 25 | 16 | 99 | 25 | 64 | 87 | 15 | 87 | 6 | 31 | 21 | 25 | 16 | 22 | 87 | 626 |

Abbreviations

| | |
|---|---|
| EPP/ED | European People's Party/European Democrats |
| PES | Party of European Socialists |
| ELDR | Group of the European Liberal, Democratic and Reformist Party |
| Greens/EFA | Green Group in the European Parliament/European Free Alliance |
| EUL/NGL | Confederal Group of the European United Left–Nordic Green Left |
| UEN | Union for a Europe of Nations |
| TGI | Technical Group of Independents |
| EDD | The Europe of Democracies and Diversities Group |
| IND | Non-attached |

*Source*:   EU Directorate-General for Information and Public Relations, EP Elections, Results and Elected Members – June 1999 (revised edition – 28 July 1999).

Socialists (PES) fell to 180 MEPs. The Socialist MEPs manifest some differences in their approach, with one cleavage (among others) being whether they represent urban or rural areas. There are also often differences in their links with the national party; for example, the Spanish Socialists have greater links with their party at home than do others, such as their Danish colleagues.

The second largest group has traditionally been the European People's Party, but after the 1999 elections the EPP and the European Democrats (ED) became the largest party with 233 seats (since the largely Euro-sceptical 36 British Conservatives rejoined the EPP). The Christian Democrats in this group have most representation from Germany, from the CDU and Christian Social Union and from Italy, plus comprehensive representation across the EU. MEPs reflect business interests including agriculture, and they have strongly supported the progress of European integration. While the EPP has become the biggest party, it still lacks a majority, needing to work with other centre–right parties to obtain the required 314 votes to overturn the Council.

In comparison, the other party groups have had a much smaller representation. The Liberal, Democratic and Reformist (ELDR) group maintained its membership with 50 MEPs and has members from most countries. This group is perhaps the least coherent ideologically since there are wide interpretations of the word 'liberal', but it has shown concern for a liberal economy based on private enterprise to guarantee human civil rights.

The Green membership of the EP, which had been strengthened by Scandinavian enlargement in the previous Parliament, has increased its membership to 38 MEPs. Its members reflect concern for environmental interests with a reduced number of Greens in Germany, being strengthened by increased representation from other countries, especially France and Belgium. The Greens have formed an alliance with 10 MEPs from Scottish, Welsh and Spanish home rule parties in the European Free Alliance (EFA). Membership of the Group of the European Left/Nordic Green Left rose to 42 MEPs and comprises Left/Green parties plus members of Communist parties. The European electorate has continued to record a vote for anti-integration parties in the Union for Europe of Nations group and this has increased to 31 MEPs (including, among others, traditionally mainly French MEPs, plus Italian 'Allianza Nazionale', Irish 'Fianna Fail', two Portuguese and one Danish MEP). The creation of the Technical Group of Independents with 18 MEPs from various parties of differing political complexions in Italy, France and Belgium has been contested and referred to the Legal Affairs Committee. The Europe of Democracies and Diversities Group with 16 MEPs includes the French pro-hunting/defence of rural traditions group, anti-EU Danes, Dutch Calvins and members of the UK Independence Party. Finally, there are a number of non-aligned members: after the June elections of 1999 there were eight unattached MEPs comprising mainly the Freedom Party in Austria and mavericks such as Ian Paisley.

The Parliamentary groups receive financial assistance and Parliament has laid down that for this the minimum number of Parliamentarians needed to form a political group is 14 if they have representatives from four countries or more, 18 from three member states, 23 MEPs if they come from only two states, and if they all come from only one member state, 29 MEPs (CEPR 1995, p. 33). The speaking-time in the Parliament is in relation to the strength of the groups. There have been only a few MEPs who are independent of party groups – such are the perceived advantages of group assistance.

The political groups do much work, not just in Parliament, but in over 20 Permanent Committees: these comprise the engine-room of the Parliament. Each group's membership of the Committees is proportional to its size, while the independent members have the right to membership of one Committee only. Some Committees have much more importance that others: for example, Agriculture, Budgets, Economic and Monetary Affairs, and the Political Committee. By increasing the number of its Committees, Parliament showed that it was concerned to be a working Parliament. The political groups have the right to fill the chairmanships of the various Committees. The Committees appoint a rapporteur, following French tradition, who draws up a draft Report for discussion, modification, and redrafting and revision into a final draft Resolution for adoption. The Committees' Reports then go to a plenary session.

Parliament has been peripatetic: its Committee meetings and party group meetings are held regularly in Brussels and there is little doubt that it would have been more efficient and economic originally to site the Parliament itself in Brussels, beside the Commission and the Council. For example, mediation and co-decision could be carried out much more smoothly. Unfortunately the location of the Parliament's activities has been very much a tug-of-war between Brussels, Strasbourg and Luxembourg, with the Parliament's Secretariat based in Luxembourg beside EU institutions such as the European Court of Justice and the

European Investment Bank. The wish of France to consolidate Strasbourg as the seat of Parliament has been achieved by considerable expenditure to facilitate EP operations there.

*Functions of the EP*   The EP's role was originally strongly consultative and advisory in non-budgetary matters, but since direct elections in 1979 it has sought to increase its powers significantly, based upon democratic electoral support. However, with regard to the latter, in the EU as a whole voting turnout in EP elections has fallen slightly: 62.5 per cent in 1979; 59.0 in 1984; 57.2 per cent in 1989; 56.5 per cent in 1994; and around 50 per cent in 1999. The range of turnout has varied widely between the member states, with a particularly high turnout in Belgium and Luxembourg, 95 and 90 per cent respectively in 1999, where voting is compulsory.

The normal functions of any parliament, apart from expressing views, are to legislate, to exercise financial responsibility and to control government. It was argued that the EP did not properly fulfil the traditional powers of a national parliament (Lodge 1989). This is partly because some of the traditional Parliamentary powers lie with the Commission and the Council. Parliament has sought to influence both these bodies, especially the Commission (whose appointment it approves), giving its opinions, with the latter often making changes to incorporate its suggestions. The EP can also take the initiative, trying to encourage the Community to legislate in particular fields. Parliament has had considerable scope for questions that have been directed especially to the Commission and to a lesser extent to the Council. The EP also approves agreements with outside countries. In addition, it has the power to set up a committee to investigate maladministration and also can appoint an ombudsman to receive citizens' complaints about maladministration. The EP's role in the budgetary process is covered in Chapter 9. Any substantial accretion of the EP's power has been seen as a direct challenge by the Council. While the Council is appointed from elected national MPs, who are largely held to account, the operation of national officials in COREPER has been criticized, especially for not being accountable to the EP.

The EP has been locked into a vicious circle in which it failed to command popular support because it lacked powers to match those of national parliaments. This has resulted in citizens focusing their main allegiance and expectations on the latter. One attempt to tackle the EP's remoteness from Community citizens has been to encourage those with grievances to appeal to its Committee on Petitions. Further institutional changes were made to raise the EP's profile, under the SEA and the Maastricht and Amsterdam Treaties. The EP's role has been increased incrementally, fundamentally reformed and greatly enhanced so that it is part of a legislature alongside the Council, with joint decision-making powers of co-operation and co-determination with the Council in various areas (some are discussed more fully later).

*The Economic and Social Committee*
The Economic and Social Committee (ESC) is marginal to the main decision-making process, though it has an influence on some policy details. The ESC meets once a month in Brussels and consists of 222 representatives of interest groups in the 15 member states. It parallels the national systems for institutionalizing interest-group participation which have a long history, going back to the 1920s in Germany and France. The ESC under the Treaties has been consulted compulsorily on many issues, and where appropriate in other areas. Since 1974 it has had the rights of initiative on questions affecting the EU, with the high level of unemployment, for example, one of the issues raised frequently since that time.

The ESC consists of three groups: employers (group 1); workers (group 2); and various other interest groups (group 3), including representatives of agriculture, transport, trade, small enterprises, the professions and consumers. The trade unions in group 2 feel that in some issues the group 3 members tend to vote with the group 1 employers. The ESC's functions are consultative and its influence has tended to be eroded by the elected EP and later by the creation of the Committee of the Regions. The ESC has been criticized further for being a 'quango' in its appointments and in its procedures, since it has been consulted only at a late stage. Its influence has also been diluted by the growth of the independent interest groups themselves, with farmers represented by the Comité des Organisations Professionelles Agricoles (COPA); for employers, the Confederation of Industries of the European Community (UNICE); and for trade unions the European Trade Union Confederation (ETUC).

If the ESC is to be of influence it must have well-produced recommendations, but on some economic and social affairs each group has used the Committee as a platform for its own views, though on other issues such as safety standards (for example, cars) the three sides have been much more in agreement. The Committee is a non-elected body like the Commission and has seen the latter as its ally, needing to prevent the overlap and duplication of the ESC with a stronger elected EP. The EP often waits for ESC deliberation, but also deals more directly with other pressure groups. The ESC sends its opinions to the Commission and Council before the latter takes its decisions.

A consensus among the 222 members is difficult, so the ESC is divided into a small number of sections covering key areas. If the Commission asks for an opinion, it is sent to one of these sections. Each member of the ESC sits on two or three sections. A small study group is then set up, representative as far as possible of the three interest groups and member states. The study group elects a rapporteur and listens to the members, and where a very technical issue is concerned, such as that of nuclear power stations, there is also a resort to outside expertise. Over the years the ESC has issued hundreds of opinions, including many on its own initiative, and a few information reports.

*The Court of Justice*

The Court of Justice has no connection with the Council of Europe Court on Human Rights in Strasbourg. The Court of Justice sits in Luxembourg and comprises 15 judges from each member state who are appointed for a period of six years, with provision for re-appointment. Although the judges come from member states, they are expected to be independent of the pressure of national governments. This is facilitated by judgement emanating from the Court instead of from individual judges.

The judges are assisted by advocates-general, appointed from the member states. The office of advocate-general is based on the French system; those appointed prepare the ground for the Court by giving a reasoned opinion. There is an advocate-general for each case.

The Court is supranational and its main function has been to ensure that in the member states EU law is applied, with the Treaties being understood and implemented correctly. Where a citizen goes to the national court and the latter is in doubt, it can refer to the European Court for clarification. Given that the EU's prime concern is with economic integration, the Court has been occupied very much in ensuring that key economic objectives are met: for example, free trade, where the Court has ruled against different types of protectionist measures; the CAP has also resulted in numerous Court cases. In addition, the Court has been active in tackling business practices that are contrary to its competition policy.

The Court has resolved cases of infringement of the Treaty which have been referred to it. Member states have preferred not to bring proceedings against other members states, leaving it to the Commission to do so. The Court has also ruled on Community institutions' actions and failures to act properly. Even the EP has gone to the Court, for example, claiming that the Council breached its obligations under the Treaty in relation to the pace of introduction of a common transport policy.

The Court is sovereign, overruling national courts, but the latter apply the law. The European Court itself has no EU army or police force for this purpose! The Court of Justice is very active and has dealt with thousands of cases since first taking up its duties in 1953. It has a growing workload, and to relieve this the SEA provided for the establishment of an additional European Court of First Instance in which each state has a member (and has no advocates-general). It has limited jurisdiction which has been expanded, and its competencies can be extended further by unanimity.

*Committee of the Regions*

The Committee of the Regions (COR), the latest of the EU's institutions, reflects a federalist EU vision to elevate the regional level of representation (as in Germany with the Länder, and in Belgium). It gives the regions recognition, enabling the Commission to obtain additional views to those of national governments, providing a more bottom-up approach. The COR, which had its first meeting in Brussels in March 1994, has 222 full members (and 222 alternates). Its numerical composition is the same as that for the ESC. There are 24 members each from Germany, France, Italy, and the UK; 21 from Spain, 12 each from Austria, Belgium, Greece, the Netherlands, Portugal, and Sweden; 9 each from Denmark, Finland and Ireland; finally, 6 from Luxembourg. The COR has a bureau elected every two years with a president, vice-president and 34 members who organize the plenary assembly and opinions. There are 8 Commissions (and 4 sub-Commissions). Commission 1 is for regional development and finance, with a sub-Commission on local regional finance. Commission 2 relates to spatial planning and agriculture, while sub-Commission 2 covers tourism and rural areas. Commission 3 covers communications and transport networks, and sub-Commission 3 is for telecommunications. Commission 4 is for urban policies. Commission 5 is for land use planning, the environment and agriculture. Commission 6 is for education and training. Commission 7 is for citizens' Europe, research, culture, youth and consumers, with a sub-Commission 7 for youth and sport. Finally, Commission 8 covers economic and social cohesion, social policy and public health.

The COR issues opinions on the basis of three types of referrals. The first are mandatory referrals which are required by the Treaty on European Union. Second, there are optional referrals by the Commission or Council. Third, there are self-referrals which are opinions by the Committee on its own initiative on matters involving specific regional interest or on any area that the COR wishes to address. The COR held a Summit on the European Regions and Cities in 1997 in Amsterdam to provide an input into the Inter-Governmental Conference (IGC). The COR saw its own Summit being complementary to the Summit of Heads of State and Government. The two representative associations of local and regional authorities in Europe, the Assembly of European Regions (AER) and the Council of European Municipalities and Regions (CEMR), contributed to the organization of the Summit. The COR presented the Stoiber-Gomes Report as a working document for the Amsterdam Summit. It called for consultation over more areas, and for all its members to be elected, and it wanted to be fully autonomous from the ESC. It was supportive of adding a new title of employment to the Amsterdam Treaty and supported territorial employment pacts to bring together public and private sectors locally at grass-roots level. It also emphasized the need for the subsidiarity principle to be paramount, seeking a demarcation of its own rights under subsidiarity. Notwithstanding the COR's limitation mainly as a consultative body, it does represent a useful democratic addition of sub-national interests to the institutional framework.

*The changing relationship between the institutions and the impact of reform*
What was the initial relationship established between institutions and how has this changed over the years? In the first instance, the Commission wielded great power, its strength providing the driving force for integration. However, after the Luxembourg Compromise of 1966 to maintain a national veto, the Commission became somewhat subdued, lacking the leadership necessary to ensure the progress that neo-functionalists sought. The Commission has tried to create greater backing for its proposals, but it has had to be flexible and compromise, for example, with the EP and particularly with the Council. Its main limita-

tion, which has to be emphasized, is that it consists of a non-elected bureaucracy, with many unaccountable committees of national experts or civil servants. It is no longer the dominant institution and is just one among several. Nevertheless, it remains the most central and permanent of the EU's institutions. Furthermore, its powers in some fields, such as competition policy, are highly developed.

There have been many proposals for institutional change; for example, in 1979 the Spierenburg Report focused on the Commission's decline and made various proposals. These included recommendations to strengthen the role of the Commission President and to reduce both the number of Directorates and the number of Commissioners. While the latter move has been resisted for many years, further enlargement of the EU makes it even more imperative.

Over the years the power of the Council has increased, especially after the Luxembourg Compromise in 1966. Countries have been able to block developments. To alleviate this problem, 'package deals' have been resorted to increasingly to offer compensatory gains to countries in some areas in an attempt to offset losses elsewhere and to secure agreement. But the pursuit by countries of their own national interests and their attempts to claim domestic victories has created slow, inefficient decision-making. With enlargement of the EU, complete paralysis would probably have occurred without the introduction of more qualified majority voting. Greater use of this was recommended by the Committee of Three (Biesheuvel, Dell and Marjolin) in its Report in 1979. Certainly, the wider application of qualified majority voting after the SEA, and the Maastricht and Amsterdam Treaties, represented a valuable step forward in cutting through the vast growth of EU business to ensure that it was executed more effectively.

The elected EP has been concerned to increase its power in relation to the Commission and especially *vis-à-vis* the Council. Under the influence of Altiero Spinelli it took the lead in bringing about institutional reform by drafting a Treaty to establish European Union (EUT). There was strong support for this, particularly from Italian and German MEPs, in keeping with the earlier Genscher–Colombo Plan. There was a Solemn Declaration on European Union in 1983, with strong support from the EP for the EUT. It led the European Council at the Fontainebleau Summit in 1984 – having dealt with the UK budgetary issues – to establish two committees on European Union. These were the Dooge Committee on Institutional Affairs (along the lines of the earlier Spaak Committee which provided the basis for the Treaty of

Rome) and the Adonnino Committee which was concerned with improving the EU to create a so-called People's Europe. This included, among other things, aspects such as a Community flag, emblem and anthem; introduction of common postage stamps; and minting of the ECU as European coinage. The European Council Meeting in 1985 proposed an intergovernmental conference in Luxembourg in autumn 1985 which led to agreement to amend the Treaty of Rome and to sign the SEA in 1986. Although this was a far-reaching development, it fell short of the radical proposals by the EP for European Union.

Some of the speeches and statements at the signing of the SEA reflected these disappointments, in particular that the EP had not been given even greater democratic control. However, at least the EP was recognized in the SEA as a Parliament and not as an Assembly. Furthermore, since the SEA the power of the EP has been significantly enhanced. There is a complex system of decision-making which has fallen into different categories for the EP. The first, its traditional role, is that it is consulted and gives an opinion, after which the Council votes with qualified majority or with unanimity, depending on the policy area. The second, since the SEA, is under the co-operation procedure in which, if the EP accepts, the Council votes with qualified majority, and if it refuses, the Council votes with unanimity. The third procedure, particularly after the Maastricht Treaty on European Union, involves co-decision in which if the EP accepts, the Council votes with qualified majority and if the EP refuses, then the conciliation committee has to be formed between the EP and the Council. This applies very much to the fundamental market freedoms of the Single European Market, and to the newer areas of policy following the Maastricht Treaty, such as Trans-European Networks (TENs). An amended proposal requires both the vote of the EP and the Council with a qualified majority. Fourth, under the conformity vote, if the EP accepts, the Council must vote unanimously, and where the EP refuses, the proposal is rejected: this applies to accession of new members and to international association agreements (for details of which policy areas fall under each procedure, see CEPR 1995, pp. 35–6).

Both the Commission and the Council are having to pay greater attention to the EP, and after the Amsterdam Treaty co-decision-making was enhanced greatly and covers about half of all legislation. Also, some pillar 3 issues, such as free movement and migration, were brought under the influence of the EP for the first time and are no longer exclusively intergovernmental. The new Treaty also confirmed that the size of the EP after enlargement would be kept at 700 MEPs, meaning more competition for positions and better-quality candidates. The smaller EU countries are keen to go further in dealing with the democratic deficit to improve support for the EP and to make the Council more open. For example, members of the Council are not obliged even to consult their national parliaments before taking a decision (though the Danish representatives do). Some critics suggest further improvements might be attained by the Council being made more open through the publication of its minutes and also by enabling European political parties to put forward candidates for the Commission Presidency. Unfortunately the problem for the European electorate is that they know they cannot remove the executive, as they can in national parliamentary elections. This has led to very different electoral turnouts, with the low appeal of European elections perhaps underpinning the Maastricht subsidiarity principle which recognizes that the EU will only act when policies cannot be conducted more effectively at national level.

*Accelerated integration after the Maastricht and Amsterdam Treaties*
Negotiations were first launched in 1990 and concluded at Maastricht in December 1991. The Treaty brought together the conclusions of two intergovernmental conferences, one on political union and the other on monetary union. The Treaty was 'a new stage in the process of creating an ever closer union among the peoples of Europe'. Despite various protocols allowing exemptions, the Treaty was significant in creating Union citizenship and in introducing many new areas of EU competence. As mentioned above, it increased the powers of the EP significantly in terms of amendments, greater conciliation with the European Council, and ultimately the possibility of a final veto by the EP. The EP also has a greater role in appointing the Commission and, while governments nominate Commissioners (in consultation with the EU President), these nominations need the assent of the EP, which could reject the Commissioners. The EP's assent is also needed for major international agreements.

The Maastricht Treaty constructed a new European architecture of three pillars and in addition to pillar 1 of the EC, pillar 2, the Common Foreign and Security Policy (CFSP), was created. Consultation on foreign policy had taken place since the Davignon Report in 1969. This was kept at an informal intergovernmental level, with regular meetings of Foreign Ministers. Common views were reached on international issues, with a tendency to vote together at the United Nations. The SEA carried foreign policy a stage further by recognizing that it should endeavour to formulate and implement a European foreign policy. The new pillar in Maastricht provided the beginnings of a new common foreign and security policy through the WEU. This was to be pursued in two ways: systematic co-operation (which already occurred within the framework of European political co-operation); and common action within broad guidelines laid down by the European Council acting unanimously.

Divisions led to little progress on the CFSP, though following the Amsterdam Treaty the Council Secretary-General is to be the 'High Representative of the CFSP' (Devuyst 1997, p. 10). Javier Solana, the Secretary-General of NATO, was appointed to this position in 1999. Decision-making by unanimity remains necessary for common strategies, though a novelty in the second pillar is that some constructive abstention is possible. The member state abstaining will also, according to the Treaty, be bound not to undertake any action which conflicts with or impedes that taken by the EU. It was agreed that the WEU would carry out a supportive role with the minor Petersberg tasks such as humanitarian aid, rescue tasks, peacekeeping and crisis management. The EU CFSP still has 'bark without bite', exemplified by the USA chairing the London conference between Israel and the Palestinians.

Another new pillar 3 is co-operation on Justice and Home Affairs (JHA); for example, asylum and immigration policy affecting third-country nationals, and co-operation in police matters such as drugs and fraud. These two new policy areas have shifted from national control to EU control, with power concentrated especially in the Council of Ministers (rather than the Commission). The EU is now at the centre of more affairs and the two new pillars (CFSP and JHA) were previously ones in which co-ordination was being carried out outside the EU framework. The Treaty of Amsterdam has provided incremental consolidation, building upon the three pillars of the EU. The Amsterdam Treaty switched some matters relating to the free movement of people, asylum and immigration from the intergovernmental pillar 3 to pillar 1. However, in Germany, Kohl, conscious of the vast influx of asylum refugees there, still limited decision-making during the first five years mainly to intergovernmental procedures. The UK and Ireland also obtained protocols related to keeping separate border checks, and both countries also remained outside the Schengen Acquis, which has been largely transferred into pillar 1.

The results at Amsterdam reflected the lack of a grand project (such as EMU) in the Maastricht Treaty. The supranational element was checked and the results mainly consolidated intergovernmentalism. Amsterdam highlighted the problem of seeking to make progress through consensus, as each country sought a qualification for its own special interests. At Amsterdam the EU failed to resolve the institutional issue of voting reform in the Council before further enlargement takes place. It is necessary to ensure that the accession of many more small states does not lead to an overweighting in their favour in an enlarged EU. Another deficiency at Amsterdam is that all the exceptions sought by the existing member states for their own interests are likely to be noted by potential new entrants to the EU as a basis for pressing for special recognition of their own national interests.

### UK adjustment to the institutions

The EU has tended to affect and shape the UK rather more than the latter has shaped the EU. The UK had to adjust to a continental system after 1973, but had not participated in its construction. The UK national voting system based on 'first past the post' – rather than the system of proportional representation (PR) as in other EU states – distorted the representation from the UK political parties to the EP. For example, this was most marked in relation to Liberal Democrats, who might have strengthened Liberal forces in the EP. Only by the 1999 Euro-elections had the continental PR system spread to the UK, and this increased the representation of the Liberal Democrats and gave votes for the first time to minority parties with 2 seats to the Greens and 3 seats to the UK Independence Party.

Both Labour and particularly Conservative MEPs fitted uneasily into the EP's political parties. Although Labour MEPs are part of the Socialist group, the anti-market views of some Labour MEPs reduced the cohesiveness of the group. Furthermore, the Conservative Party was for many years unable to fit into existing party groups and hence formed the European Democrats, though it was eventually able to join the European People's Party.

The EP has not had the impact that was hoped for, failing to receive anything like the media coverage given to Westminster. Most of the major political personalities are still attracted to Westminster, with some MEPs from the UK using the EP either at the beginning or the end of their political careers. There has been a reluctance to see any overwhelming transfer of powers from Westminster to the EP, though national parliaments have lost some of their influence over the increasing areas covered by the EU. Meanwhile, scrutiny of EU affairs is often limited and retrospective, with the scrutiny committee of the House of Commons, and the more effective one in the House of Lords, sifting through material and trying to highlight important issues. Lack of enthusiasm for the EU has been shown by low electoral turnout in the UK, and the apathy in 1999 produced an all-time low turnout of around 23 per cent. Eurobarometer national opinion polls showed that most people considered that they had not benefited from EU membership. At times there appears to have been some weakening of the mass commitment to European integration which has been driven forward mainly by the élite. Various polls of public opinion have shown that the percentage of people who believe that the UK has benefited from being in the EU is much lower than in most other EU countries. The lack of popular support in the UK for EU policies has arisen because of conflictual problems relating especially to the costs of the CAP, the inequity of the Budget and reluctance in some quarters to abandon the pound in favour of the euro.

The UK has despatched some distinguished political figures to the Commission, whose own self-image is one of a political bureaucracy. One of the most significant was Roy Jenkins who, in his capacity as President of the Commission, was successful in launching the EMS, though unfortunately he failed to carry the UK forward enthusiastically towards EMU. Other senior figures appointed have included Christopher Soames, Arthur Cockfield, Leon Brittan, Neil Kinnock and Chris Patten. The second Commissioner appointed has reflected a bipartisan political approach, being a member of the opposition party.

In the Council, governments have defended their own national interests tenaciously and the British have proved no exception. They have been concerned to ensure that alterations in the voting system do not reduce the UK's influence in favour of smaller states; there has also been vigorous defence of crucial issues, based especially upon a dominant Treasury philosophy to restrict spending with regard to issues such as the budget and agriculture. The pattern has tended to be one in which Northern European countries have fought very strongly in the Council and created more difficulties than Southern European countries. Nevertheless, the former, including the UK, have a good record in implementing the law, with relatively few cases against them, whereas the latter have raised problems of implementation. For this reason the UK was instrumental in enabling the ECJ in the Maastricht Treaty to fine member states which had failed to comply with earlier judgements from the Court.

The UK has natural problems with the EU, having joined late, and with late entry into EU monetary integration and EU social policy. UK problems have been partly self-imposed by the two main political parties and their lack of visionary leadership, with the exception of Edward Heath. The problems were intense, particularly for the Conservative Party. For example, Mrs Thatcher's vision of Europe, and one supported by the Bruges group, was based upon a limited co-operation of independent states, being opposed to the creation of any federal and bureaucratic superstate. Divisions over Europe led to the departure of pro-European members of her Cabinet, such as Heseltine, Lawson and Howe, and finally the downfall of Mrs Thatcher herself. She will be remembered for her conflictual policy style, although it was under her government that the UK signed the SEA and entered the ERM of the EMS – albeit reluctantly. The SEA was a pale shadow of the draft European Treaty and was seen as an opportunity for the UK to benefit, particularly from the internal market. Under the UK Presidency in the second half of 1986, many measures were pushed through to create a successful internal market. However, there has been a natural tendency both by politicians and the media to use the EU as a scapegoat for the UK's own problems in many other fields. The support by John Major to appoint Jacques Santer as President, based on the mistaken assumption that he would not pursue a dynamic federal agenda, was a misconception, since the role of any President is to drive integration forward, and the only consequence was to provide ineffectual leadership.

Old Labour was also divided significantly over the EU, but new Labour after the election of the Blair government in 1997 has struck a much more positive note. This was reflected in its approach to the Amsterdam Treaty and in the UK Presidency of the EU in the first half of 1998. Nevertheless, aspirations to a leadership role and being at the heart of the EU based, for example, upon a successful flexible economy, were hampered by the UK retaining its discreet distance from EMU. Overall, the British achievements in the Presidency were disappointing when set against its lofty ambitions, and UK absence from the Euro-Committee of Finance Ministers on euro matters could diminish the UK input into monetary and economic policy-making.

# 3 Free trade, the customs union and internal market

## GATT's efforts to maintain a free trade system

The signing of the General Agreement on Tariffs and Trade (GATT) in 1947, originally by 23 countries, was a crucial step forward in ensuring that a freer system of trade would predominate in the postwar years. It has provided the best defence for the international economy, minimizing the re-emergence of a paralysing protectionism. It is founded on basic principles, such as that of non-discrimination. Advantages in trade conferred on one party have had to be extended to all, which then received Most Favoured Nation (MFN) treatment. Since exceptions already existed for preferential agreements, such as those in the British Commonwealth, further advantage was taken of the exceptions which were made for customs unions.

Both the ECSC and the EEC took advantage of the concessions that were permissible, though they failed in some respects to comply completely with the conditions for creating customs unions; for example, these specified that they were to cover virtually all the trade between member countries, whereas the ECSC was sectoral and covered only coal, iron and steel. Hence the ECSC necessitated a special waiver from GATT, and the only opposition to this came from Czechoslovakia. To be consistent with GATT, the Common External Tariff (CET) was not to be fixed at a higher or more restrictive level than that which the member countries themselves applied before the formation of the customs union. While the CET in the EEC was set below the tariff rates of many individual members, initially it involved higher tariff levels in countries such as West Germany. The development of the EC since the 1970s has also manifested several restrictive tendencies; for example, the free trade area between the EC and EFTA excluded agricultural products. In addition, there was concern over whether the extension of the customs union between the EC and certain Mediterranean countries could be completed within a reasonable time period (Hine 1985). Similarly, the association agreements between the EU and the CEECs did not establish free agricultural trade, and where an associated country applies restrictive safeguard measures the EU has a preference for its exports over others.

Fortunately any potential conflict between preferential trade in the EC and the multilateralism of GATT has been largely resolved by the EC taking over from the individual member states that were the contracting parties to GATT and participating in many rounds of global trade negotiations which have cut world-wide tariffs. These reduced the EC's CET from 12.5 per cent in 1958 to about 6 per cent after the Tokyo round of negotiations. The main achievement of the Tokyo round, which ended in 1979 after six years, was to reduce nominal industrial tariffs in the industrial world by nearly a third, on average. Unfortunately the impact of recession led some countries, including those in the EC, to infringe the general principles of GATT far more. Agriculture, textiles and clothing were to a large degree exempt from GATT rules and discipline, and trade in several other products became distorted by the use of quotas and by voluntary export restraints (VERs).

Countries in the EC for many years continued to retain national quotas on many imports, since these controls often pre-dated the Treaty of Rome. These national quantitative restrictions lost their effectiveness after the creation of a single European market in 1992 and the removal of internal border controls. Consequently most remaining national controls on imports from outside the EU have been replaced by controls on a Community-wide basis. This has on occasion added to conflict with outsiders, with Germany moving reluctantly in the case of its free imports of bananas to the contentious single EU market for banana imports.

There has been widespread resort to VERs, which despite the name are not really voluntary, as countries recognize that if they refuse to accept them they will be likely to experience a universal non-negotiable reduction in their exports. VERs have also been accepted since they enable sellers to obtain higher prices for their goods than if some other form of trade restriction were used. In the mid-1980s the EC had around 50 VERs, and over a third of Japanese exports to the EC were covered by these. It can be seen, therefore, that despite tariff liberalization, the EU was quite protectionist by use of other means. This issue of VERs and the growing use of non-tariff barriers (NTBs) needed to be tackled in a new tariff-cutting round.

In an attempt to salvage GATT, over one hundred countries participated in another long-drawn-out trade round: 1986–93, and this Uruguay Round covered a very large agenda. Somewhat unexpectedly, it led to the creation of a new, even more powerful World Trade Organization (WTO) to replace GATT and covering most countries. In the lead-up to

GATT suggestions had been made for a GATT-Plus (or Super-GATT), paralleling the kind of *à la carte* or variable geometry in EC integration in which the leaders move on more quickly (Tsoukalis 1986). Differences arose in the GATT negotiations between developed countries and less-developed countries (LDCs), but with the latter being less inward-looking though still sceptical about opening up trade in sectors such as services. In addition, the Code on Subsidies and Countervailing Duties, which had been negotiated during the Tokyo Round, had failed to tackle export subsidies effectively, particularly in agriculture, and even greater difficulties existed in tackling agricultural production subsidies, in which the EC was seen as the main obstacle to progress. This manifested itself clearly in the suspension of GATT talks in Brussels in December 1990, with acrimony between the USA and the EC over the issue of agricultural support systems. Subsequently negotiations resumed in 1991 and the EC showed itself willing to be more flexible on agriculture. Japan, which has come to the fore as a major beneficiary of GATT, also had to accept its new-found responsibilities by tackling its protectionist tendencies, especially on NTBs, and its rice protectionism. The Uruguay Round was a triumph for multilateralism and marked significant new progress in creating freer agricultural trade, cutting subsidies, particularly on exports, and moving towards tariffication on imports. It was also important in opening up trade in services. In addition, it banned VERs, though not anti-dumping and countervailing duties.

The WTO created a body to settle disputes to minimize unilateral actions. Its rulings cannot be blocked by guilty offenders. It is possible to appeal once against its rulings and if this is rejected again, there is a period of 15 months for compliance. The main flaw is that the losers have simply delayed and tinkered with changes. Although the plaintiffs can receive compensation or impose retaliatory action, a further improvement would be for independent arbitration to rule on whether a losing defendant has complied properly.

The main dangers to global multilateral trade still come from preferential regional trade agreements, and the whole issue of whether regional integration complements or conflicts with multilateralism has resulted in massive debate, with an enlarged EU becoming more protectionist to outsiders in several sectors from agriculture to footwear, and so on (Pomfret 1997). There is concern that the international economy has fragmented even more into blocs, with the USA following the EU pattern of more continental-based trade, and engaging in even closer trading relationships with North, Central and South America. The free trade area (FTA) with Canada later brought in Mexico in the creation of the North American Free Trade Agreement, which came into effect in 1994. In Europe, the move to market economies in Central and Eastern Europe has led to freer trade, but very much within the region. Apart from the trade agreements which they have entered with the EU, they have also established free trade agreements amongst themselves, reflected by the Central European Free Trade Area (CEFTA) and also the Baltic Free Trade Area (BFTA). However, trade between some of the CEFTA countries is only a low proportion of the total trade for most CEFTA members, apart from the high trade between the Czech Republic and Slovakia.

## The EU customs union and internal market

*Key concepts of a customs union: trade creation and trade diversion*
The most important characteristic of a customs union is a complete removal of tariffs between member countries. This constitutes a movement towards free trade, at least within the regional bloc. However, a customs union is also characterized by the imposition of a Common External Tariff (CET) on imports from the rest of the world, and the higher its level, the more adverse is its impact on outsiders.

Whether a customs union is beneficial depends, among other things, on the two concepts of trade creation and trade diversion. Trade creation occurs when a country in the customs union finds it cheaper to import from a partner country. Instead of producing a good domestically, it switches its supply to the partner, which has a lower price since the intra-tariff is removed. Let us examine three countries: 1, 2 and 3. Assume that initially the price of a good, $x$, is £4 in country 1, £3 in country 2 and £2.80 in country 3. If country 1 imposed a 50 per cent tariff against imports, then it would produce the good domestically, since it would cost £4.50 to import it from country 2 (£3 plus 50 per cent tariff) and £4.20 (£2.80 plus 50 per cent tariff) to import it from country 3.

If countries 1 and 2 form a customs union (and country 3 remains outside, facing a 50 per cent CET), then country 1 imports the product from country 2 at the price of £3. Figure 3.1 helps to clarify these production gains, assuming for simplicity elastic supply schedules (quantity supplied at constant costs); also, for the present, any demand effects are ignored, with a completely inelastic demand schedule being shown in country 1.

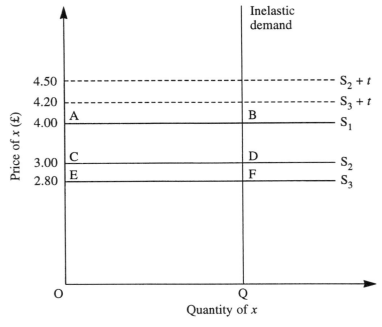

*Figure 3.1   Trade creation*

The total cost to country 1 of producing the good domestically is the area under its supply schedule OABQ. The total cost of importing the same quantity OQ from country 2 is OCDQ. The difference between the two rectangles constitutes a resource saving of ABDC. It is apparent that there would be greater consumer gains by enlarging the customs union to include country 3, since this would provide additional resource savings of rectangle CDFE.

A paradox exists as to why country 3 is excluded from the customs union. What are some of the implications for outside countries? The concept of trade diversion shows the consequences for outside country 3, which in the pre-customs union situation was the lowest-cost supplier to country 1, but was excluded by 1's tariff; that is, the tariff of 50 per cent resulted in country 3 being priced out of the market. Let us assume, therefore, that a pre-customs union tariff of only 10 per cent was originally in force. Then country 1 imported from country 3, since the cost of importing from country 3 was £3.08 (£2.80 plus 10 per cent tariff), while the cost of importing from country 2 was £3.30 (£3 plus

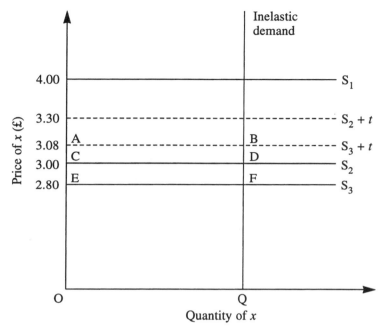

*Figure 3.2    Trade diversion*

10 per cent tariff). When a customs union is formed between countries 1 and 2, with country 3 excluded, trade is now diverted completely from a lower-cost supplier outside the union to a higher-cost member, since country 1 can save 8p by importing tariff-free from country 2 instead of from country 3 (which still faces the CET of 10 per cent) (see Figure 3.2).

Although in Figure 3.2 country 1 enjoys a consumer saving of rectangle ABDC by importing from country 2, it sacrifices welfare as shown by the rectangle CDFE, since country 3 has production costs of only OEFQ. The diversion of trade in this instance has clearly had adverse trading consequences for outside countries.

Jacob Viner was the pioneer of customs union theory, using partial equilibrium analysis to examine the effects on a single product. He was influenced by classical economists in thinking about production changes – even though consumption changes had already been introduced into the international trade literature. It is necessary therefore to modify the earlier analysis by adding changes in consumption. When prices are

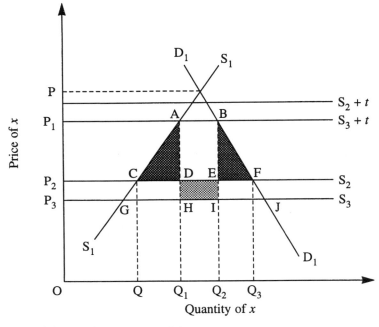

*Figure 3.3   Trade creation and diversion*

reduced (by removing tariffs), demand tends to increase and trade expansion takes place. Figure 3.3 shows the normal downward-sloping demand curve, plus a more normal upward-sloping supply curve for the home producer.

The demand and supply curves in country 1 intersect at price OP. By importing good $x$ consumers can enjoy a lower price than OP. With a tariff imposed by country 1 on imports from countries 2 and 3, country 1 produces domestically along its supply schedule up to OA and it imports quantity AB from country 3. What changes occur if a customs union is formed between countries 1 and 2 in which the lowest-cost producer, country 3, is excluded? This is not just a theoretical point but also reality, since the EU is open only to full membership by European countries, hence many low-cost world producers are excluded.

The welfare effects are that in a customs union, country 1 reduces its own domestic supply to OQ and switches all of its imports to country 2 and imports CF. In the trade-creating effects of the customs union there is the supply-side effect discussed earlier; this is now shown by a triangular area ACD. The costs of producing quantity $QQ_1$ in country 1 is the area under its supply curve; that is, $AQ_1QC$, whereas the cost of importing the same quantity from country 2 is $CQQ_1D$. The triangle ACD is the production gain between these two areas.

The new element shown in Figure 3.3 is the increase in demand of $Q_2 - Q_3$ resulting from the lower price. Consumers are potentially better off, and using the concept of consumer surplus as a representation of consumer utility – notwithstanding its limitations – a consumption gain can be shown by the triangle BEF. Consumers are prepared to pay the prices shown along the demand curve. The utility from consuming $Q_2 - Q_3$ is shown by the area $BFQ_2Q_3$, whereas the expenditure incurred for $Q_2 - Q_3$ was $EQ_2Q_3F$. The difference between these two areas is the triangle BEF.

The main customs-union problem is that since country 2 is not the lowest-cost producer, trade is diverted from country 3. The trade diversion is rectangle DEIH and in conventional analysis is clearly harmful. Furthermore, there is also a loss of tariff revenue, which may have to be raised by alternative domestic tax increases. However, it is possible that in the long run country 2 could reduce its cost significantly; also country 2 may on welfare grounds be a low-income country. Furthermore, even with trade diversion, prices for consumers fall with the removal of tariffs. It has been argued that trade diversion empirically is not widespread and a general presumption in favour of customs unions should be retained. In addition, where customs unions have contributed to rising internal incomes and outside countries have been supplying complementary products, the latter have been able to derive benefits – this has been true particularly where the CET has been set at a low level. Customs unions which are bigger in membership are likely to be better since they reduce the likelihood of the lowest-cost producer being excluded. Where the customs-union partners have a high proportion of intra-trade and only a low CET to outsiders, then the degree of trade diversion is likely to be small.

However, with completely free trade there would be no trade diversion at all and in Figure 3.3 there would only be gains: higher production gains AHG and higher consumption gains BIJ. Thus it has been argued that a non-preferential trade policy which reduces protection will always be superior to the formation of a customs union. Yet if the traditional consumer gains for importing countries can be obtained by unilateral tariff reductions, why do countries rarely reduce tariffs unilaterally but instead favour the formation of customs unions? They are prepared to accept a second-best solution partly because pursuit of consumer interests has to be modified and related in reality to the costs of industrial adjustment which are imposed. The reallocation of resources, even in a common market, is not painless but is accompanied by some unemployment.

*The rationale behind customs unions*
The initial reasons for forming customs unions were not wholly economic; they included both strategic and political considerations. However, it is helpful, where an economic explanation is given, to focus not only on consumer gains but also on the gains to producers in a customs union.

In Figure 3.4, a low-cost supplier in one EU country – where $D_i$ is domestic demand, $S_i$ is domestic supply and a low equilibrium price $OP_i$ prevails – is able to export quantity $QQ_1$ to the rest of the EU. Although its own consumers face higher prices (since supply is imperfectly elastic) its producers' export gain is the large shaded triangle in Figure 3.4(a). Thus industry is able to expand along its domestic supply curve ($S_i$) supplying the rest of the EU – with 'r' in Figure 3.4(b) referring to the rest of the Community. A common price $OP_c$ which equals the EU price, then exists throughout the Community, with its consumers benefiting from lower prices.

The concern with expanding production *per se* has led to perhaps the most cogent explanation for the formation of customs unions. It is argued that a country has some collective preference for domestic industrial and agricultural production which yields social benefits. In a predominantly trade-diverting customs union, a country that has a strong preference for such production, but with only a weak comparative advantage internationally, can achieve its preferences. But why do countries not achieve this by measures such as domestic subsidies and taxes? To achieve a sufficiently high level of production and exports countries would need to resort to export subsidies, and these have been used widely in agriculture. But industrially they infringe international trading agreements, whereas customs unions have been able to develop within the GATT framework. Therefore the constraints on the use of first-best domestic policies and constraints on trade policies help to explain the formation of customs unions (El-Agraa 1994).

Producer gains have been significant for another reason, which is that much of the trade expansion has been of an intra-industry type: that is, countries simultaneously export and import similar or even

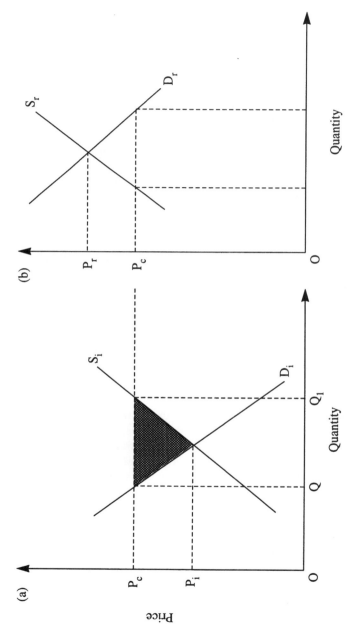

*Figure 3.4  (a) The market in an individual EU country  (b) The market in the rest of the EU*

homogeneous products in the same industry. Freer trade has enabled countries to concentrate production in fewer, larger plants. While intra-industry trade has always existed, it has increased significantly within the EU (Greenaway 1987; Millington 1988). In 1980 intra-industry trade ranged from 50 per cent for Italy to 65 per cent for both France and Belgium–Luxembourg. It exists particularly in differentiated products in which multinational companies are active, with a significant growth of intra-firm trade in, for example, passenger cars.

Countries in a customs union are able to derive other advantages. For example, by acting collectively rather than separately they can increase their bargaining power and their terms of trade may improve relative to outside countries. If the latter are producing competitive goods whose output is inelastic, then to avoid displacement of their exports, the price falls. EU countries have been able to get much better prices for their own exports relative to their import prices. Terms-of-trade gains of up to 1 per cent of GNP have been estimated (Petith 1977). However, later studies have been less optimistic about the size of these terms-of-trade gains, though they have confirmed that the larger the economic area, the more substantial is the improvement likely to be in the terms of trade (Marques Mendes 1987, p. 106).

Finally, the customs union is important as the basic starting-point along the road to more extensive integration in other sectors. A customs union, then, is part and parcel of the whole process of integration in a regional bloc.

*Dynamic gains in a customs union*
Modern industry is characterized by the growth of giant firms that are able to reap static and dynamic economies of scale within a large market such as that in the EU. These economies of scale enable firms to meet greater market demand by moving down their long-run average cost curves. Economies of scale are significant in the formation of all customs unions, not only the EU but also the customs unions that have been formed in other parts of the world between LDCs.

In the case of key industries, such as the motor industry, a customs union between LDCs helps to make the actual production of cars viable, whereas in developed countries it enables cars that are already being produced to be made at an even lower cost. Optimum economies of scale in the EU car industry would occur with a company output of up to 2 million cars annually, every doubling of output up to this level reducing unit costs by about 10 per cent – hence it became the long-term goal of a European manufacturer to reach this level of output. It indicates that the European market can accommodate only a few large companies. The more successful producers have been able to benefit from export opportunities, and French car producers have significantly increased their net sales to other markets in the Community. Germany has also been very successful in penetrating other EU markets, especially in the commercial vehicles sector. In this sector, economies of scale are lower, though the 100 000 unit producer had a cost advantage of about 16 per cent over the 20 000 unit producer (Owen 1983). In other sectors, for instance, white goods, it is Italy that has shown the way forward. Economies of scale in products such as refrigerators and washing machines have enabled Italy to sell with great success in other markets within the Community. Some economists have placed particular emphasis on the role of economies of scale in lowering unit costs in such industries (Owen 1983), and these have been given central prominence in delivering a significant proportion of the predicted gains from the internal market programme.

The scope for exploiting economies of scale naturally varies from one industry to another, and Owen may have exaggerated these by choosing atypical industries. In some industries the level of concentration which has been reached may well be above that which is justified by the need for economies of scale alone. Furthermore, large firms operating in oligopolistic markets and lacking sufficient competition are often prone to some X-inefficiency. Nevertheless, the aim of the EU has been to provide a sufficient market size to try to match the economies of scale, standardization and productivity levels of the USA. There the market has been large enough to support a sufficient number of optimally sized plants without resulting in the danger of monopoly exploitation, which was a problem in national European markets.

While multinational companies can only develop on the basis of a large market, historically some of the world's major multinationals have actually grown up in small national markets such as Switzerland and Sweden. But they have been able to grow mainly by selling to the international market rather than to the domestic one alone. Membership of EFTA and its free industrial trade agreement with the EC further facilitated the growth of such multinationals, even if they did not cause it initially. The smaller EFTA countries have also been able to co-operate with the EC in some industrial sectors in which scale is crucial to success. Not being full members of the EC did not preclude co-operation by outside countries in sectors such as aerospace. Even before

1973 the UK, for example, was an active participant in European aerospace projects. However, the appeal of belonging fully to a large EU market has attracted more and more of the businesses of the smaller European countries to press their governments for full membership of the EU.

Apart from economies of scale, another mechanism of dynamic gain is provided by increased competition, which can stimulate a higher level of efficiency. In a more competitive environment less efficient producers are undercut, being forced either to improve their production methods or be driven out of business. Monopolies in domestic markets find their position undermined by exposure to highly competitive imports. But for gains to be realized, these firms have to compete effectively by altering their existing pricing policies (Hine 1985, p. 28).

A further benefit is that a large expanding market is conducive to a greater level of both indigenous and inward investment – a key factor in raising the rate of economic growth. Foreign direct investment (FDI) has been significant in the EU, though some of this is diversion from the rest of the world. In the heyday of EC expansion, businesses feared the consequences of not investing aggressively in new plant and equipment, but in the recession after 1974 investment slackened. Although the EC has contributed to an increase in the aggregate rate of economic growth, some individual countries such as West Germany actually achieved a higher growth rate before joining the Community; also, the UK economic growth rate since joining the EC has not accelerated. While dynamic factors as a whole are important, they need to be sufficient to outweigh any losses which show up in a static analysis of customs unions.

*Empirical measurement*

There have been many studies which have tried to measure the growth in trade that can be attributed to the formation of a customs union *per se*. The two basic approaches are either *ex ante* or *ex post*. The former is a system of simulating the effects of tariff changes on the pattern of trade, with results depending on demand and supply elasticities. The *ex post* method, which has proved most popular, involves looking at the changes in trade patterns which have taken place as a result of a customs union. Balassa (1975), for example, used *ex post* income elasticities of demand (assuming that they would have been unchanged in the absence of the EC). He confirmed the predominance of trade-creating effects and that these were strongest in the early stages of the

EC. However, to avoid overstating trade creation it is generally useful to try to normalize the expected trade shares more realistically by examining how income elasticities have changed in other countries outside the EC, such as the USA. Even with such downward adjustments they showed trade creation exceeding trade diversion by at least four times.

There are great variations in both the empirical results and also in the welfare analysis of the implications of trade creation and trade diversion (El-Agraa 1994). Nevertheless, some sensible orders of magnitude of static effects are possible and in several studies trade creation has been around $10 billion and trade diversion $1 billion (Swann 1995, p. 131).

There are, though, a few early studies which showed significantly more trade diversion, such as those by Truman and Kreinin (Kreinin 1974). Overall, static customs-union gains are limited to 1 or 2 per cent of GNP, since not all goods and services are traded. Also, the gains are concentrated mainly in manufactured products with strong trade diversion in agriculture for the EU(15).

A particular dissatisfaction with traditional customs-union analysis has been expressed by some economists; for example, Millington (1988) found little support for the explanatory power of traditional customs-union theory. Meanwhile, Marques Mendes (1987) went further than the basic problems of trade creation and trade diversion and the unreliability of their results, pointing out the neglect in measuring the important dynamic effects, let alone all the other features of the Community. He questioned the underlying assumptions such as the automatic adjustment in the balance of payments. He adopted a different approach, using the foreign-trade multiplier to capture trade effects, relating those to output growth. His results showed a higher result than earlier estimates by other economists, with strong trade effects, leading him to conclude that integration resulted in a significantly higher GDP than in a non-integration situation (Marques Mendes 1987, p. 104). Despite all the empirical analysis, the conclusions on effects are highly contested and, though generally positive, they are still considered by some economists to be very small (Pomfret 1997, pp. 265–75).

*Intra-EU trade and the internal market*
The removal of tariffs between countries in the EC was much easier than anticipated since the countries were in a fairly similar competitive position (apart from the south of Italy). Also, at a time of general

economic growth in the 1960s, firms were able to expand, and any factors of production which became redundant could be absorbed with relative ease into other sectors. Over half of the EU's trade now consists of intra-trade; this growth has been assisted not only by the removal of tariff barriers but also by other developments such as the emergence of greater similarity in the pattern of consumer preferences. Once manufacturers have developed a competitive product, they look for exports in other markets which have similarity in both income per head and in the pattern of demand for those products. Thus more horizontal trade, at least in modern consumer durables, has developed between countries with similar factor proportions and not, as the Heckscher–Ohlin theory predicted, between countries with different factor proportions. Many products are the result of innovation, and the most developed EU countries with high R&D expenditure tend to dominate trade in new technological sectors. Export of such products enables both dynamic and static economies of scale to be reaped.

With the onset of economic recession after the early 1970s, member states in the Community sought to exploit Article 36 of the Treaty of Rome far more – this allowed justified exemptions to free trade. EU countries started to make greater use of NTBs to defend their products. NTBs can, for example, take the form of different technical standards to protect national health, safety and the welfare of citizens. These NTBs were even more welfare-reducing than tariffs, which at least generate revenue benefits. It was argued that the NTBs led to the lack of a complete common market, which constituted a significant obstacle to increasing the competitiveness of European industry. In exporting products, firms complained that the Community was an 'uncommon market' and that they had to make modifications to meet the separate national requirements of each European market.

It was to rectify these problems of continuing market obstacles that the Community began to pursue vigorously the completion of the internal market for which plans were first published in a White Paper in June 1985. It provided a catalyst for the Community's regeneration, and agreement on this proved possible since the lack of a single internal market was even more costly than the CAP, and tackling the former seemed less intractable than the latter. The distinctive features were that it was a complete programme and set within the time period for completion by 1992, though there was some slippage in application and enforcement. The internal market, according to Article 13 of the SEA and the new Article 8a of the EEC Treaty, 'shall comprise an area without internal frontiers in which the free movement of goods, persons, services and capital is ensured'. Article 14 of the SEA and the new Article 8b of the EEC Treaty were concerned with a balanced implementation of measures, with the Commission to report to the Council on the progress made, decisions being taken on the basis of qualified majority voting. Article 15 of the SEA and Article 8c in the EEC Treaty recognized the heterogeneous nature of the Community since its enlargement, with provisions for temporary derogations.

The single internal market became one which began to dominate all others during the late 1980s and 1990s. The focus in this section is on border controls, technical barriers and preferential public purchasing impeding the flow of goods and services in the customs union. Different aspects of the internal market are included in other chapters, such as taxation in Chapter 9, but it should be recognized that this is mainly the consequence of removing frontier controls, rather than any new macroeconomic preoccupation with fiscal integration *per se*. Indeed, the single European market indicates a recommitment to microeconomics to reap the benefits accruing from the free play of market forces, running in parallel with more liberal policies in many member states.

The stimulus towards the internal market programme came from a combination of external and internal pressures. The external threat provided urgency to greater EC integration in the 1980s in the form of the economic challenge from American and Japanese industrial power. This highlighted the EC's acute deficiency in the new rapidly growing high-tech sectors. Internally the EC found it easier to agree on the single market programme than on other more contentious avenues which might have been chosen for integration. Also, the links between the SEM and the SEA were important in the overall package. A variety of different political perspectives have been used to explain the dynamics of the process (Armstrong and Bulmer 1998). The single internal market was in many respects completing the negative phase of economic integration, rather than tackling additional new and more controversial elements of positive integration. However, regulation became increasingly necessary to deal with market failures of externalities and internalities; for example, cases of the latter which are important to the single market included harm to consumers resulting from product failure or breach of contract (for a further account of problems of moral hazard and adverse selection, see Pelkmans 1997, pp. 52–3).

The single market, in addition to completing fully the creation of the Common Market, largely refocused its profile away from the agricultural concerns of the 1950s towards policies for new growth sectors of the 1980s and 1990s. These embraced the high-tech sectors, and the rapidly growing service sector, which has been more pronounced domestically and in terms of employment than its growth in intra-EU trade. Although the emphasis on transport is not new, the attempt to liberalize financial services is a major new development, as is the attempt to open up trade and competition in the purchasing policy of the large public sector in member economies. Above all, what was crucial was the psychological recognition that there could be no turning back in the process of economic integration, thus providing a valuable stimulus to business confidence and new business strategies for the larger market which in future will be seen increasingly as a large home market.

*The barriers to be removed*   Barriers, according to European business groups, were crippling economic activity, and the Kangaroo Group, a European Parliamentary pressure group, drew attention to the multiplicity of barriers that still existed and campaigned for their abolition; these were expounded in issues of *Kangaroo News*. A major source of market fragmentation was the continuation of physical border controls. Despite the absence of intra-EU tariffs, controls provided a national safeguard by controlling the flow of particular imported goods to maintain health and safety; also, there has been the need to prevent drug smuggling. Border controls also fulfilled the necessary functions to collect trade statistics; to deal with VAT on imports; and the administration of the complex system of monetary compensatory amounts for agricultural products. Frontier controls have also been used to limit the undesirable movement of certain individuals, with some countries such as Spain and the UK having particular concerns to prevent the movement of terrorists across uncontrolled borders.

Some steps had already been taken to reduce a variety of irksome form-filling for traders. Although the customs union was completed in July 1968, checks at frontiers had continued. To simplify these, procedures were agreed on a package of customs' changes from January 1988. The Single Administrative Document (SAD) replaced about one hundred export and import forms and Community transit documents (T-forms) used in the EC and for trade with EFTA. Nevertheless, most firms considered that this had not helped them significantly, and only its abolition within the single market would make trade much easier after 1992. Some forms had to be retained, though revised and aligned to the SAD, in order to provide proof that certain goods, such as those covered by the CAP, were used or disposed of in a particular way.

After 'Customs 88' there was also a reclassification of tariff codes to a new Harmonized Commodity Description and Coding System. This consisted of six digits recognized world-wide; seven and eight digits for EU sub-divisions and nine for the UK; for imports from outside the EU and especially for agricultural products, an additional digit tariff was used. While the change in code changed some duties, the overall effect was neutral. A new computer system for Customs Handling of Import and Export Freight (CHIEF) was introduced to accommodate changes brought about by the SAD and the Community Integrated Tariff (TARIC). Automation of customs data speeded up administration and cut costs for industry and commerce: the programme for Co-operation in Automation of Data and Documentation for Imports, Exports and Agriculture (CADDIA) also proved very successful.

The EU Commission sponsored various studies to estimate the cost of different impediments to trade, including border-related controls. Ernst and Whinney for the Commission (1988) divided the costs on a six-country basis into three components which included: the costs to firms of meeting customs' formalities (ECU 7.5 billion); the costs to governments of administering the controls (ECU 500–1000 million) and some 15 000–30 000 staff; and the opportunity cost or potential business forgone by firms (ECU 4.5–5.0 billion). The study was based on six countries and the costs were highest for Italy and lowest for Benelux. The greatest burden was also imposed on smaller firms.

A further calculation was made for the Commission of the costs imposed by transport delays. This was based upon road transport and, like other studies, was dependent upon the response by firms, some of which were reluctant to disclose confidential information. The maximum cost of transport delays was estimated at ECU 830 million, and in order to avoid overstating cost savings, it may be better to take the range upwards from half of this figure; that is, ECU 415 million. This is because otherwise one would be assuming that replacement work would always be available for the driver and vehicle to fill the time saved. Another aim in transport policy was to remove the quantitative quota controls which require hauliers to apply for permits to transport goods across borders. In addition, the objective was to change 'cabotage'; that is, the restrictions on non-resident hauliers carrying and delivering goods within a member state. These have contributed to extra costs in the form of lorries having to make return journeys empty.

However, the costs of delays at frontiers are less than those that have arisen from the operation of different national technical standards. Firms engaged in exporting products have faced the extra burden of having to modify their exports to meet the national standards imposed. While the intentions in setting high standards are often very laudable, such as those to ensure health and safety, in some instances they have provided hidden forms of national industrial protection. Those industries most adversely affected have included engineering, chemicals, foodstuffs, and precision and medical equipment, though many other industries have been affected to a lesser degree (*European Economy* 1988, p. 51). For example, in foodstuffs intra-EU trade has tended to stagnate and major companies, apart from Unilever and Nestlé, tend to be American. Trade has been restricted and national prices kept higher than necessary for products such as pasta in some European countries and especially in Italy.

The European Court has decided that restrictions can only be justified if they conform to three criteria. These are, first, that of causality and a direct cause-and-effect relation between the measure and the objective or essential requirement being pursued. Second, the criterion of proportionality, whereby the measure should not be disproportionate to the objective. Finally, the criterion of substitution: if an alternative way that does not impede trade is available to reach the objective, then it should be used. In the case of the 1967 Italian pasta law, which laid down that pasta should consist exclusively of durum wheat and not less expensive soft wheat, the law failed on all three criteria. It fell at the first hurdle since mixed pasta is just as healthy; there was a disproportionate impact with negligible imports; and finally there are alternative ways of dealing with this, such as labelling, without adverse effects on trade. With the removal of the pasta law, imports should rise and prices be reduced.

A test case of considerable significance was that of Cassis de Dijon 1979 in which a French liqueur made from blackcurrants was deemed to have too low an alcoholic content for the West German market. The European Court of Justice decided otherwise and laid down that if a product had satisfied the standard requirements in one country then its import should in principle be allowed into another member country. The ruling has since provided precedent for other cases, such as that concerning beer imports into West Germany and Greece. In Germany the *Reinheitsgebot* insisted that beer could contain nothing more than malted barley, yeast, hops and water. Germany claimed that their law was not discriminatory since if national manufacturers made beer in this way they could sell to the German market. This claim was successfully contested by the European Court of Justice. However, Denmark, which has generally been progressive in opening up markets, also banned imports of beer from other members states, unless it was in reusable beer bottles. While this was a useful conservation measure, it again reduced imports of foreign beer because of the distances involved in comparison with the more convenient locations of Denmark's own breweries.

Standards have varied and in Germany the Standards Institute has imposed very high standards, whereas most French and British standards have not been compulsory. When every product has to be submitted for approval by each country, this has led to delays and often to imported products being subjected to a more thorough process of testing. The process of harmonizing standards has also been slow, often taking years to adopt, whereas technology may have moved on in the meantime. Since 1983, member states have had to notify the Commission in advance of any new standards they intend to introduce. A stand-still period has been imposed to allow time for the Commission to examine them, initially for three months, which can be extended up to twelve months. In addition, the procedure for complaints is being improved for those industries adversely affected by such barriers.

The EU has achieved agreement by issuing European standards for many products. It has abandoned the idea of trying to harmonize every detail of a particular product, and it has tried instead to establish minimum standards for health and safety, exemplified by a mass of items ranging from pressure vessels to toys, with many further proposals of essential requirements for items such as construction products and machine safety. Likewise, to remove technical barriers for foodstuffs, instead of complicated specifications on their composition, the EU's food harmonization is based on 'framework' directives for food labelling, additives, food for certain nutritional uses, and materials and articles in contact with food. Common standards will be of great benefit to European producers, but they will have to operate on the basis that the whole Community market is in fact their home market. Unless this happens, the major beneficiaries may well be outside suppliers such as Japan and the USA, since they much prefer to work to one standard rather than to 15 different national standards in the Community. The EU has accelerated the output rate of European standards; it has also added a new standards institute for telecommunications and incorporated wider consumer representation throughout in the formulation of European standards. Progress has also been made in testing and certification through the development of the 'CE' mark and in creating the European Organization for Testing and Certification.

There has been a new attempt to reduce national preferences for public contracts, since public purchasing accounts for up to 15 per cent of the EU's GDP. The contractual part of public purchasing, that is, public procurement, accounted for between 6.8 and 9.8 per cent of GDP and in the short term it is this which will be opened up, but in the long term the majority of public purchasing will be open to non-national suppliers (*European Economy* 1988). The reluctance to buy from outside suppliers has been aided by lack of proper advertising and by the complexity of tendering procedures. The bias in favour of national suppliers has continued, despite the adoption by the Council of directives on public works' contracting as long ago as 1971, and further directives in 1977 on public supply contracts. Directives apply to contracts above particular threshold levels; for example, ECU 200 000 for supply contracts for regional and local authorities which are subject only to EU rules, and ECU 1 million for public works contracts.

The exclusion of important sectors, such as transport, water, gas, electricity and telecommunications, was rectified in the 1990s to prevent the national industrial champion from preserving a monopoly of orders such as for power stations and telecommunications. The Utilities Directive applied not just to public but to private firms, partly as a consequence of increased privatization. The thresholds were set for utilities suppliers at ECU 400 000 and for telecommunications at ECU 600 000. National preferences had resulted in excess capacity and higher costs of European firms in these sectors.

Significant savings were estimated (ranging from ECU 8–19 billion) via three mechanisms. First, the static trade effect yields cost savings by buying from the cheapest supplier (ECU 3–8 billion). Second, the competition effect will reduce the prices charged by national producers in the face of foreign competition (saving ECU 1–3 billion). Finally, restructuring occurs as firms benefit from shared R&D costs (saving ECU 4–8 billion). These total gains are equivalent to 2–5 per cent of public purchasing, and exclude all the gains for private-sector purchases. They also exclude dynamic effects on innovation and growth and the relative strengthening of EU industry *vis-à-vis* the rest of the world.

In several technological sectors, discriminatory public purchasing coincides and reinforces separate national standards, such as telecommunications. For example, in telephone exchange switching equipment the Commission estimated that open procurement would reduce the price significantly per phone line towards the lower line costs in the USA, resulting in fewer Community suppliers. Open procurement will limit single tendering and lengthen the time period for bids. Also, better policing has been proposed to tackle non-compliance so that action can be instigated against offending purchasers. An attempt is being made to use European standards to define the technical specifications for contracts. For example, IT systems have been incompatible but Open Systems Interconnection (OSI) standards are being developed and in 1987 the EC adopted a decision requiring public purchasers to specify these standards when buying IT systems.

In opening up public procurement internally, the EU was divided over whether this should apply equally to public-sector purchases from outside the Community. The more protectionist-minded countries such as France and Italy preferred continued discrimination against others. Some compromise was required whereby public-sector purchases would occur mainly from internal EU sources if there were only small differences between external and internal prices; for example, up to 3 per cent cheaper than the best Community tender. This led to adverse reaction outside the EU, and a reciprocal agreement with the USA, whilst a WTO agreement in 1994 included multilateral procurement, though with significant omissions such as telecommunications.

*Microeconomic and macroeconomic effects*  The lack of a single internal market was estimated on average to have added some 15 per cent to total costs. The removal of unnecessary restrictions will result in microeconomic gains arising initially from the removal of the costly barriers affecting trade and production. The consequence is a significant reduction in costs; for example, removing barriers at frontiers could result in cost savings of ECU 8–9 billion and public-purchasing savings of ECU 20 billion could accrue. Studies of individual sectors have identified significant cost reductions and one of the few wholly Community-wide surveys resulted in an estimated fall in costs of 1.7 per cent for manufacturing industry. Further market-integration benefits accrue significantly from economies of scale (likely to reduce average cost by some 1.5 per cent). These economies of scale provide the largest single source of economic benefit and they arise very much as restructuring takes place. A further significant effect is increased competition which is reducing X-inefficiency and monopoly profits, with

*Table 3.1   Potential gains in economic welfare for the EU resulting
from completion of the internal market*

| | Billions ECU | % GDP |
|---|---|---|
| *Step 1* | | |
| Gains from removal of barriers affecting trade | 8–9 | 0.2–0.3 |
| *Step 2* | | |
| Gains from removal of barriers affecting overall production | 57–71 | 2.0–2.4 |
| Gains from removing barriers (sub-total) | 65–80 | 2.2–2.7 |
| *Step 3* | | |
| Gains from exploiting economies of scale more fully | 61 | 2.1 |
| *Step 4* | | |
| Gains from intensified competition reducing business inefficiencies and monopoly profits | 46 | 1.6 |
| Gains from market integration (sub-total) | 62*–107 | 2.1*–3.7 |
| Totals | | |
| For 7 member states at 1985 prices | 127–187 | 4.3–6.4 |
| For 12 member states at 1988 prices | 174–258 | 4.3–6.4 |
| Mid-point of above | 216 | 5.3 |

*Notes:*
\* This alternative estimate for the sum of steps 3 and 4 cannot be broken down between the two steps.

The ranges for certain lines represent the results of using alternative sources of information and methodologies. The 7 member states (Germany, France, Italy, United Kingdom, Benelux) account for 88% of the GDP of the EC(12). Extrapolation of the results in terms of the same share of GDP for the 7 and 12 member states is not likely to overestimate the total for the 12. The detailed figures in the table relate only to the 7 member states because the underlying studies mainly covered those countries.

*Source:*   Commission of EC, study of Directorate-General for Economic and Financial Affairs, in Cecchini (1988, p. 84).

monopolists losing the ability to engage in price discrimination between customers in different markets. Gains in economic welfare for seven countries have been recalculated upwards for the EC(12) and estimated at between ECU 174–258 billion. Taking the midpoint would yield gains of ECU 216 billion, equivalent to some 5.3 per cent of GDP (Cecchini 1988). The magnitude of these gains is shown in Table 3.1.

The sources of the gains in economic welfare were illustrated earlier in the customs union (Figures 3.3 and 3.4). Producers will gain since they will be able to lower costs through taking advantage of cheaper sources of EC component supplies and lower costs of financial services and distribution. The greatest benefits will arise when business reorganization permits greater concentration on major product lines, reaping economies of scale and often rationalization of a firm's operations on one site. However, consumers will gain more than producers since intense competition will drive down prices.

There has been a continuing wide dispersion of prices between national markets which has tended to increase slightly in those least open to competition. Whilst up to a quarter of the price differential may be attributed to different taxes, and recognizing the difficulty of comparing products because of qualitative differences, there still remains a large residual price differential. One measure of market fragmentation has been the continued practice by firms – for example, in the motor industry – of charging different prices between national markets; car prices have varied by up to 50 per cent, being cheapest in Belgium and dearest in Denmark. There have been even wider price variations for many other products, and in pharmaceuticals, for example, the widest dispersion was as high as 10 to 1. In an integrated market with resale arbitrage, firms would be forced by competition to charge similar and lower prices. Prices would tend to converge downwards towards the lowest price so that in the long run a common single price would prevail. A more conservative hypothesis would be one in which only prices above the Community average converge downwards towards that average. Estimates of potential gains for the latter convergence for the EC(9) were 2.1 per cent of GDP for goods and services, compared with 8.3 per cent for the extremely optimistic hypothesis that prices would converge on the minimum price (*European Economy* 1988, p. 123).

The price gains will vary, being limited in those sectors and countries that are already competitive and close to being a single market. For example, in the textiles and clothing industry most internal barriers have been dismantled and there have been massive imports. Hence prices of textiles and clothing may only fall by a further 0.5–1.5 per cent. In other sectors the scope for price reductions is far higher; for example, in financial services great gains will occur for consumers in Southern Europe. In pharmaceutical products, prices already tend to be low in Southern Europe, and therefore prices are likely to fall in other countries where prices have been controlled at higher levels to support domestic production and research. In addition, the range of consumer choice will continue to widen.

At the macroeconomic level, countries have found that attainment of their basic economic objectives is increasingly elusive. The attempt to squeeze out inflationary pressures tends to slow down economic growth, resulting in higher unemployment. The attraction of the single market is that it offers the opportunity to attain a better overall macroeconomic performance. Macroeconomic gains have been modelled, deriving from the primary microeconomic effects outlined earlier, and the secondary effects resulting from econometric models have been simulated for four areas. These are: the removal of customs barriers; public procurement; liberalization of financial services and capital markets; and finally, the supply-side effects based upon the strategic reactions of companies to their more competitive environment. These results are shown in Table 3.2.

For GDP the effects under each of the four headings have been aggregated, with particularly significant medium-term benefits in financial services and overall supply effects. The overall effect would be to raise GDP on average by 4.5 per cent, with a beneficial effect in creating 1.8 million new jobs. What is remarkable is that this would not be inflationary and there would be downward inflationary pressure. This would derive from the more favourable budgetary and trading balances. The general governmental budgetary position would improve, for example, through lower expenditure in public purchasing, while the Community's external balance would improve as its internal market measures make it more competitive *vis-à-vis* the rest of the world. In addition, there may well be some marginal trading benefits at the expense of outsiders, and these have given rise to fear by outsiders of a Fortress Europe problem. Some of the industrial consequences of inward overseas investment to minimize any displacement of imports are discussed in Chapter 5.

Some initial job losses may occur, such as the loss of jobs of customs collectors, and redundancies created through company restructuring and loss of market share by less competitive firms. Given that governments

*Table 3.2  Macroeconomic consequences of completion of the internal market: Community as a whole in the medium term*

| | Frontier controls | Public procurement | Financial services | Supply effects[1] | Total Average | Total Range |
|---|---|---|---|---|---|---|
| *Relative change (%)* | | | | | | |
| As % of GDP | 0.4 | 0.5 | 1.5 | 2.1 | 4.5 | 3.2 to 5.7 |
| Consumer prices | −1.0 | −1.4 | −1.4 | −2.3 | −6.1 | −4.5 to −7.7 |
| *Absolute change* | | | | | | |
| Employment (thousands) | 200 | 350 | 400 | 850 | 1800 | 1300 to 2300 |
| General government borrowing requirement as a % of GDP | 0.2 | 0.3 | 1.1 | 0.6 | 2.2 | 1.5 to 3.0 |
| External balance as a % of GDP | 0.2 | 0.1 | 0.3 | 0.4 | 1.0 | 0.7 to 1.3 |

*Note:*
[1] Scenario including the supply effects estimated by the consultants, the economies-of-scale phenomena (industry) and the competition effects (monopoly rents, X-inefficiency).

*Source:   European Economy*, no. 35, March 1988, p. 159.

are likely to achieve a more favourable macroeconomic trade-off between their conflicting policy objectives, they could use their better budgetary and trade position to reflate their economies. The effect of using some of this additional flexibility to expand their economies further could result in the creation of some 5 million new jobs, depending upon the amount of accompanying expansion. For example, to maintain external balance, some 4.4 million new jobs could be created, but with some deterioration in the external balance as many as 5.7 million jobs could result. These are shown in Table 3.3. Some economists (Baldwin 1989), drawing on the new growth theory and recognizing increased investment, thought that the Commission may even have significantly underestimated the expected gains. In practice this seems unlikely, and a major question mark hangs over the job-creating effects of the single market. No spatial distribution of these jobs was shown in the Cecchini Report (and the distributive regional dimension of the EU is discussed further in Chapter 7). In terms of winners and losers, countries with high intra-industry export/import ratios greater than 1.0, and with high employment in those sectors, would gain most, and these were located mostly in Northern Europe, especially Germany, rather than in Southern Europe.

The size of forecast gain by the Commission seems excessive, given that tariffs were removed long ago. Also, perhaps too much emphasis was given to the further gains from scale economies since many of these had also already been exploited in the customs union. In addition, one must recognize that the Commission studies of internal market gains are merely forecasts, based upon the programme being realized in full, and having built-in margins of error of ±30 per cent. Such forecasts could turn out to be over-optimistic with any slippage in implementing the proposals. Also, using slightly different assumptions, the gains in employment may be significantly reduced. For example, altering the Cecchini assumption that two-thirds of productivity gains are transmitted into real-wage increases to an assumption that all productivity gains are transmitted into real-wage increases removes the large job-creation effects from the single market. In addition, the sequence of interlinking steps from microeconomic benefits to macroeconomic employment gains rests upon a reflationary choice of action actually being taken. This will depend very much upon German economic policy decisions and the new framework of EU monetary and fiscal integration which is being developed (see Chapters 8 and 9).

Despite a transposition rate of internal market directives of 94 per cent by the beginning of 1998, the impact of the single market has been

*Table 3.3  Macroeconomic consequences of completion of the internal market accompanied by economic policy measures (medium-term estimates for EU(12))*

| Nature of economic policy | Room for manoeuvre used | Economic consequences | | | | |
|---|---|---|---|---|---|---|
| | | GDP as % | Consumer prices as % | Employment (in millions) | Public deficit as % point of GDP | External balance as % point of GDP |
| Without accompanying economic policy measures (from Table 3.2) | | 4.5 | -6.1 | 1.8 | 2.2 | 1.0 |
| With accompanying economic policy measures | Public finance | 7.5 | -4.3 | 5.7 | 0 | -0.5 |
| | External position | 6.5 | -4.9 | 4.4 | 0.7 | 0 |
| | Disinflation | 7.0 | -4.5 | 5.0 | 0.4 | -0.2 |

Margin of error: ± 30%

*Notes:*
The accompanying economic policy (public investment and reduction in direct taxation) is such that the room for manoeuvre created by completion of the internal market in respect of the public finance position (or in respect of the external balance or prices) is fully exploited.

It has been assumed, in this case, that the accompanying economic policy is so arranged as to exploit 30% of the room for manoeuvre created by the fall in consumer prices. Full use of that room for manoeuvre would give unrealistic results (sharp deterioration in the external balance in particular).

*Source: European Economy, no. 35, March 1988, p. 165.*

slower than assumed in the Cecchini Report, with a more gradual adjustment path (Mayes 1997, pp. 89–90). Some of the reasons for this include problems in achieving compliance, for example, with regard to public procurement where most countries (apart from those lacking industrial capacities) still tend to source most of their products nationally. This has been confirmed by a statistical analysis of the nationality of suppliers winning contracts in each member state (see Mayes 1997, p. 106). The directives have led to sufficient subsidiarity, as a result of which countries have controlled the effective implementation and enforcement of the procurement rules. Furthermore, it has been difficult for businesses in contesting cases to prove that they would have been able to win contracts without discrimination and to assess the monetary estimates of any loss.

The conflicting interpretations of the *ex ante* effects of the single market have continued into the *ex post* analysis. *Ex post* assessment has simulated the reality of the monde compared with the counterfactual anti-monde (excluding the single-market effects). Results in the *Single Market Review* in a general equilibrium model have shown beneficial aggregate effects (Commission 1998). The results, though smaller than in the Cecchini Report, are still incomplete and influenced by the time-scale of introduction of measures. Furthermore, there are implicit difficulties in separating the effects of the single-market changes from all the other changes occurring, including German reunification and business-cycle fluctuations, and so on. Nevertheless, results show that intra-trade has risen significantly, assisted by *ex post* cost savings from the removal of customs formalities of 1–1.5 per cent of trade costs. Trade has grown fastest for manufactured goods, and even more for financial services and telecommunications. Certainly a more competitive climate exists and prices have fallen, especially in sectors such as air transport and telecommunications, where there was restricted entry. Trends towards privatization and opening up competition in national markets have been reinforced by the single market. These beneficial microeconomic gains have fed through to the macroeconomic level, helping to reduce the rate of price inflation by around −1 per cent in 1994. Dampening price inflation was also assisted by restrictive economic policies to prepare for EMU. A significant rise in investment has underpinned the increase in GDP, though a main weakness was in job creation, which 1985–94 amounted to only 0.25–0.49 per cent of total employment. The consequence in the short term has unfortunately been unemployment, partly because of wage rigidities and insufficient movement of unemployed workers. The single market has seen significant rationalization, restructuring and company mergers, with a huge influx of FDI. While more *ex post* analysis is needed to confirm the size of economies of scale, the many changes occurring have proved positive, though only in the long term will it be possible to assess with more precision the full effects.

## UK trade in the EC

The removal of tariffs on trade between the UK and the EC led to a reorientation in the pattern of trade. In 1958 21.8 per cent of UK imports and 21.7 per cent of UK exports were with the EC; in 1973 32.8 per cent of UK imports and 32.3 per cent of UK exports were conducted with the EC (Cohen 1983, p. 23). By 1995, 55.3 per cent of UK imports and 59.8 per cent of UK exports were with the EC (Eurostat 1996). Initially the main problem was that imports from the EC tended to rise faster than UK exports to the Community. This was to be expected to some extent, given the diversion in UK imports of agricultural products towards Community suppliers. Although North Sea oil developed as a valuable export to the EU, in some respects, by pushing up the UK's exchange rate, this made it harder for the UK to export manufactured products.

A summary of UK transactions with the EC since 1973 has shown the UK generally to be in balance-of-payments deficit, and in relatively few years, such as 1980 and 1981, was the UK in small surplus in its current-account transactions with the Community. The general imbalance can be attributed mainly to the deficit on visible trade, but the UK has also been in small deficit on invisible trade with the EC, apart from a few years, such as 1981 to 1984. In 1986 the UK's deficit on invisibles was £783 million, and this can be attributed mainly to government transfers associated largely with the Community budget, which has offset the surplus on items such as private-sector financial services.

Of major concern has been the growing imbalance on UK trade in manufactures. In 1973 the EC took 31 per cent of the UK's total export of manufactures and provided 39 per cent of its imports of manufactures. By 1984, although the EC received 39 per cent of UK exports of manufactures, it supplied 50 per cent of UK imports of manufactured products. Over half the UK trade deficit with the EC in manufactured goods was accounted for by the UK's trade with West Germany (Dearden 1986). Unlike the UK, West Germany enjoyed a massive trade surplus, especially in its trade with the Community. West Germany's exports as a percentage of its GDP are not significantly different from the UK's, but the latter's imports as a percentage of GDP are far higher. Key sectors such as information technology, consumer electronics and motor vehicles have accounted for a large part of the UK current-account trade deficit. For example, by the mid-1980s over half of UK motor vehicles originating in the EC came from West Germany. The total UK trading imbalance in motor-industry products deteriorated in the 1980s and by 1989 motor vehicles accounted for just over one-third of the total deficit in manufactured goods. For the first time, trade in parts and accessories moved into a deficit in 1986 of £346 million. UK demand has exceeded its supply capabilities, and although foreign investment in the UK motor industry has helped to close the trade gap in motor vehicles, the latter will still remain too high unless the vehicles produced contain a greater domestic content.

The export–import ratio of the UK in its trade has been in deficit in most manufactured sectors. Apart from road vehicles, there have been deficits in, for example, machinery, iron and steel, and textiles, though the UK did have a surplus in a few sectors such as clothing and chemical products (Cohen 1983). The UK performance has been disappointing, given the promising position from which many of its industries started their trade with the EC. The UK, perhaps surprisingly, performed relatively badly in those sectors in which it was quite strong in the selected pre-entry year 1970–1 up to 1978–9 (Millington 1988, p. 71).

The EC itself has been split between the countries which generally hold a more liberal view of world-wide free trade, such as the UK, and those that are more protectionist. For example, in textiles, the EC on occasions has been forced to impose temporary restrictions on cloth imports, mainly in response to French and Italian producers, adversely affecting those British manufacturers that are stronger in other stages of textile processing. Similarly, in the motor industry those countries with a large indigenous industry, such as France and Italy, have pushed for more protectionist policies than the UK.

It would be wrong, however, to attribute all of the UK's trading problems solely to its membership of the EC. The UK's basic problem has been the low world income elasticity of demand for its exports and a high UK income elasticity of demand for world imports. Indeed, the UK's dilemma has been that it has not only been in deficit in its manufactured trade with the Community, but also with other developed countries. Furthermore, the export–import ratio for UK trade in manufactures with both Japan and North America has deteriorated far more than that with the EC. The pattern for the UK has been one of tending to sustain trading deficits in manufactures with major developed competitors, and to offset these partially by running a trading surplus on manufactures with less-developed countries. The UK would therefore suffer badly from any Fortress Europe consequences of the single market. Its trading imbalance in manufactures has resulted from ongoing microeconomic deficiencies, exacerbated by macroeconomic problems, such as a periodic overvalued exchange rate.

While UK industry has obtained export benefits in EC markets, the UK trade balance has not benefited sufficiently because of rising imports – though precise estimates of the trade balance vary according to the sources used (Wallace 1980). In the light of the massive decline in the UK's domestic manufacturing output, one conservative estimate is that it reduced this by at least £3 billion, about 1.5 per cent of GNP, and the effect could easily be twice as high (Winters 1987, p. 328). Despite the adverse effects on domestic unemployment, Winters has taken the optimistic view that the welfare benefits to users and consumers of manufactured products could be high enough to outweigh the losses to home producers.

Apart from the lack of competitiveness in manufactured trade, the UK also suffered initially from insufficient integration in sectors in which it is more competitively placed, such as financial services and air transport. Hence the extension of integration in these sectors was welcome, and during the UK's Presidency of the EC Council in 1986 it sought to consolidate integration in these sectors of the internal market where it could benefit from its comparative advantage. Financial services accounted for some 7 per cent of the EC's GDP, and the aim of the internal market was to go beyond the rights of establishment in other member states to the direct provision of these services. For example, an EC non-life insurance services directive provides cover irrespective of where the insurer is established (though transitional arrangements in Greece, Ireland, Portugal and Spain delayed its application until the end of 1992). Nevertheless, in opening up the market in financial services it was important for the UK to ensure that this did not have an adverse effect on those non-Community financial institutions that are already active in the 'City'. The UK also had to compete with other countries which began to enjoy a more liberal and less regulated financial framework. But overall the UK clearly enjoys a comparative advantage in particular sectors, such as insurance and Stock Exchange dealings.

London's position as the leading European financial centre was confirmed by its choice as the location for the new European Bank for Reconstruction and Development to channel financial aid to Eastern Europe. Unfortunately the next key decision to base the new European Central Bank in Frankfurt rather than London was a major blow to the UK and connected to its failure to see the single market extending to include monetary integration.

The single internal market is a source of new opportunities, but not without risks, and some manufacturing sectors may suffer from greater import penetration without these costs being outweighed by extra export sales. Some industries, such as textiles, have already reorganized after long exposure to stiff international competition, and other industries now face similar rationalization. If British business fails to involve itself more actively in European Standards bodies, problems will arise in working to new foreign technical standards. Once a harmonized standard has been agreed by a majority vote in the Community, then conflicting national standards have to be removed. Recently the UK has held the Secretariat of far fewer technical committees of the European Standardization Committee than either Germany or France.

The view that the internal market is attractive since it is largely costless in budgetary terms neglects other costs, such as those imposed on depressed areas. Many local authorities have made use of public purchasing to stimulate development by favouring local suppliers. They have also exercised a social influence over the employment practices of their suppliers. The opening up of public procurement policies is likely to be a further source of imports and to dilute local economic development policies.

The UK introduced a more active internal market publicity campaign than West Germany – the latter had already done well in industrial exports and was hesitant about opening up its protected service sector. Other countries, such as France, were quick to publicize '*quatre-vingt-douze*' (1992). In addition, Italian businessmen, in particular Carlo de Benedetti, the head of Olivetti, began to exploit the EC as a natural base for industrial growth. This was illustrated by his attempts to gain control of Belgium's Société Générale early in 1988. Parts of UK industry have similarly become even more vulnerable to foreign takeovers, whereas many continental countries are better protected against such incursions.

The single internal market will generate aggregate economic gains for the EC, and also for parts of the UK economy, such as high-tech industries and much of the service sector. (The importance of the service sector in terms of employment is shown in a 3-variable graph in Chapter 4.) Nevertheless, in the short term some of the changes will be uncomfortable and result in further job displacement in weaker industrial sectors.

*Dynamic effects on the UK economy* It was always hoped that there would be strong dynamic effects on British industry in the EC, arising primarily from the opportunities for greater economies of scale, a sharper competitive climate and faster growth; these have been further reinforced in the single internal market. There are some distinct examples of industries in which static and dynamic economies of scale have been reaped, but often the greatest gains have been made by continental producers in industries such as passenger cars, commercial vehicles and white goods (Owen 1983). Given the UK's relative decline in manufacturing industry, the truth about the dynamic effects may be closer to some of the early gloomy predictions (Kaldor 1971).

The benefits for consumers of lower prices from a process of 'Darwinian destruction' have to be set against some of the adverse effects on UK producers. Although some firms have been jolted into greater efficiency as a result of more competition, others have been unable to survive, resulting in a substantial loss of domestic capacity. Furthermore, excessive competition by lowering profits can inhibit some much-needed long-term investment. Nevertheless, it does appear that the heightened competitiveness in the Community may have helped to tackle the 'British disease', whereas earlier pessimists concluded that the main hope lay in spreading the disease to others!

The assumption that membership of the Community would automatically shift the UK on to a higher plateau of economic growth was over-optimistic. Certainly the UK has become a more attractive location for inward investment and its growth rate was good in 1973 – the year of entry into the Community – but the subsequent economic recession reduced economic growth rates. Between 1960 and 1972 the UK rate was only 2.9 per cent per annum, compared with 5.1 per cent in the EC. Since 1973, while there has been a convergence of the UK growth rate towards that of the EC, this has been at a much reduced level of aggregate economic growth. Between 1973 and 1986 the UK rate of economic growth was 1.9 per cent per annum compared with 2.2 per cent per annum in the EC. UK growth as a percentage of that in the EC rose from 57 per cent in 1960–72 to 82 per cent in 1973–86. If one assumes that outside the Community the UK had continued to grow at its pre-entry rate (57 per cent of that in the EC), then UK economic growth would have been only 1.3 per cent from 1973 to 1986, closing even further in the late 1980s (Johnson 1987). For example, in 1983–8, the total UK growth rate per annum was 3.6 per cent (compared with the EC average of 2.8 per cent), and growth per head of population was 3.4 per cent per annum in the UK (and 2.5 per cent per annum for the EC). Another result in line with this has shown that the EC accounted for about 30 per cent of the UK's economic growth rate from 1974 to 1981 (Marques Mendes 1987). Since the early 1980s the UK's comparative growth rate internationally has been much improved and the internal market has helped to reinforce its vibrant economy.

It is always difficult to disentangle the effects of the EC from other major changes taking place over the same period, of which perhaps the major one has been the production of North Sea oil. Although this has helped to loosen the overall balance-of-payments constraint for the UK, its effect in pushing up the exchange rate has aggravated the trading competitiveness of manufacturing industry. Hence the expansion in sectors such as oil has been partly offset by further de-industrialization. This has limited some of the projected dynamic gains from belonging to the Community.

The faster growth of manufacturing imports from the EC and elsewhere has clearly contributed to rising unemployment in the UK. Between 1980 and 1986 UK unemployment averaged 10.6 per cent, compared with 9.9 per cent in the EC. However, in the 1990s earlier UK liberalization measures enabled it to improve its relative economic position within the EU, in which unemployment rose rapidly with deflationary monetary policy in preparation for EMU. Nevertheless, the weaker economies, such as the UK with its structural problems of declining traditional industries in particular regions, have tended to suffer unduly from freer trade. Furthermore, Community membership may have added 0.75 per cent per annum to the UK inflation rate since 1973, largely because of applying the protectionist high-price CAP. Despite being already inflation-prone (the UK between 1960 and 1972 saw inflation average 4.5 per cent compared with 4 per cent in the EC), inflation accelerated, and between 1973 and 1986 it averaged 11.3 per cent in the UK, as against 9.6 per cent in the EC; hence UK inflation was 113 per cent that of the Community from 1973 to 1986 (Johnson 1987). The main inflationary bias has been given to food prices, since the removal of tariffs actually reduced the relative prices of industrial products.

# 4   Agriculture and fisheries

**The economic characteristics of agriculture**

Agriculture possesses distinctive characteristics: these result in short-run fluctuations in price, while in the long run agricultural prices tend to decline in real terms. The latter have necessitated movement of resources out of agriculture and into other sectors of the economy.

A free agricultural market, at the mercy of weather and climatic conditions, is likely to veer from good harvests to bad ones. The marked fluctuation in price is shown in Figure 4.1.

Reading along the supply curve: with a poor harvest, quantity $OQ_1$, shortages result in a high price $OP_1$. Quantity $OQ_2$ and price $OP_2$

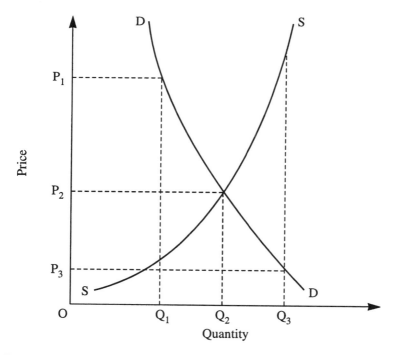

*Figure 4.1   Agricultural market*

provide the market equilibrium. A golden bumper harvest, quantity $OQ_3$, results in the low price $OP_3$. A difference between agriculture and many other markets is the relatively inelastic short-run supply and relatively inelastic demand. The steep slopes of these curves magnify the range of price fluctuations.

Why is agricultural supply so unstable and unpredictable? It takes a long period of time to adjust output, and the production of many joint products means that increasing output of one product in high demand may result in the surplus of another product. Agriculture, unlike many industrial sectors, is still characterized by smaller units, though farm size has risen and some sectors of agriculture approximate to factory production, as in poultry. Resources are often trapped in farming with investment in product-specific equipment. In the short run, farmers continue to produce as long as they can cover their low variable costs; for example, labour costs, in which there has been a much reduced labour force to remunerate. However, relative immobility has been intensified by an ageing farm population and a lack of better alternative jobs during a period of much slower economic growth.

Agriculture is still highly competitive, but some farmers may not be solely maximizing profits, but maximizing their satisfaction from family farming. Agriculture may respond less closely to market signals than economists would like. Some farmers choose a target income level and to maintain this they continue to produce in an attempt to offset falling prices: past experience has borne this out in various sectors. Even with the right price signals, policy-makers find it difficult to achieve the required output level; but with the wrong price signals, which have often been given in the EC, overproduction has been a major problem.

On the supply side, equilibrium is not achieved in some products. In the stable cobweb cycle a convergence towards equilibrium does not occur where supply and demand curves both have a relatively inelastic slope. In the divergent cobweb cycle, when supply is more elastic than demand, there is an explosively divergent outcome. While these lagged adjustments are based on simplified assumptions and assume that farmers never learn, the basic cycles have been well exemplified over the years in various sectors; for example, the recurrent pig cycle.

The other determinant of prices, demand, is also relatively inelastic. Both price and income elasticities are well below unity for agricultural foodstuffs; that is, a 1 per cent fall in price or rise in income results in a less than 1 per cent rise in demand. Since the 1950s food consumption rose only slowly in most EC countries. The population increase in the EC(12) rose only 0.7 per cent per annum in 1950–75, with a projected increase of only 0.3 per cent per annum in 1975–2000. Total food consumption in Western Europe was expected to rise by only about 0.6 per cent per annum in 1975–2000 (Duchêne et al. 1985, p. 81). The EC's agricultural consumption, especially after the recession in the 1970s, failed to keep pace with rising supply. Agriculture is inevitably a declining industry in terms of demand in mature, advanced economies, but paradoxically has been expanding in supply, with a sustained rate of productivity growth based on technological and biological change. The latter has recently taken a further leap forward in terms of genetically modified crops.

It is generally recognized that there is a need to shield agriculture from the completely free operation of market forces, though there are policy disagreements on the most appropriate measures to adopt. There is a danger that a search for stability and cushioning in the short term can aggravate the need for long-term adjustments. The EU is now confronted by this fundamental problem of major agricultural adjustment.

## The Common Agricultural Policy (CAP)

### National historical traditions
Historically, agriculture in the major continental countries has manifested widespread protectionism. In the nineteenth century, farmers in Germany, France and Italy resorted to protectionism and resisted change, whereas their counterparts in the UK, Denmark, the Netherlands and Belgium modernized and reorganized their farming systems. Cheap imports of grain from the new world were impeded by high tariffs in countries such as France and Germany. In the Netherlands and Denmark imports of cheap grain were used to adapt their agriculture and they began to specialize in the production and export of high-value dairy produce and meat.

Between the First and Second World Wars, especially in the 1930s, agricultural policies became highly protectionist as a result of the collapse of international markets due to the depression. Germany and Italy became even more concerned with promoting self-sufficiency. Germany realized the importance of this in reducing import dependence, since war disrupted outside agricultural supplies. In the 1940s feeding the population became the major agricultural priority. After the Second

World War, with scarce foreign currency reserves in Europe, countries continued to support domestic agriculture in order to improve their balance-of-payments position.

*Evolution of the CAP*

Essentially, the evolution of the CAP represented some continuity of the national agricultural policies by the major continental countries, particularly German policy, based on high prices. Because of a new Franco-German *rapprochement* at the heart of postwar integration, a balance had to be struck between the interests of the two countries. It was decided to adopt common policies for both the industrial and agricultural sectors. West German industry recovered strongly after 1945, based upon a liberal market approach with low tariff protection; it looked forward to increasing its share of industrial trade within the customs union and has become the dominant European industrial power. France as a large agricultural producer sought reciprocal benefits for its agriculture in the EC. The major food exporters, France, the Netherlands and Italy, sought to capture the German market, partly at the expense of non-European suppliers.

A decision to include agriculture was taken during the preliminary conference in 1955, since the removal of barriers to trade and industrial products *per se* would be insufficient, unworkable and incomplete. The Commission examined various agricultural systems before coming round to more interventionist policies; this reflected national political expediency. While efficient agricultural producers like the Dutch could have prospered with a less regulated CAP, their producers, especially of dairy products, gained substantially from higher prices.

The less efficient and high-cost countries – Germany, Belgium and Luxembourg – which were net importers, would only open up their markets if prices were set at a level sufficient to support their own farmers. To accommodate them, a range of product prices was agreed, with the first crucial prices being set for grain in 1964. Once a high price had been fixed for cereals it became necessary to set the prices of other products at comparable levels to maintain the right inter-product relationship. One of the important products was milk: its price was raised substantially to cover higher-cost producers. During the 1960s the CAP was extended to cover almost all agricultural products, with the few gaps being filled during the 1970s (see the final section of this chapter on the Common Fisheries Policy).

*Grand objectives*

The objectives of the CAP were laid down in Article 39 of the Treaty of Rome. The five aims were: to raise agricultural productivity; thereby to ensure a fair standard of living for the agricultural community; to stabilize markets; to assure availability of supplies; and to ensure that supplies reached consumers at reasonable prices. This was an ambitious list of highly desirable but sometimes conflicting principles. The consequence has been a failure to achieve some of these objectives because of insufficient policy instruments. Over-reliance on price support made it almost impossible to maintain reasonable prices for consumers; for example, many products can be purchased at much lower prices on the world markets.

Policy has been most successful in achieving the objective of secure supplies, indicated by a growing self-sufficiency in many products. However, full security of all supplies is neither desirable nor feasible, given the growing dependence on energy imports. It is of great importance to produce those products for which there are no close substitutes available on world markets. For other products it is prudent to buy them cheaply from the world markets, rather than to become over-conscious about security and build up massive surpluses. These surpluses have made price stabilization very difficult and though the Community has had some success in stabilizing markets, this has been at the expense of creating even more instability on world markets.

The EC has been far more concerned with raising production than productivity, but labour productivity has increased through large-scale drift from the land and mainly through greater inputs of capital. Environmentalists have become concerned about the excessive use of inputs such as fertilizers; they are also concerned about the destruction of hedgerows to create larger fields and the adverse effects on wildlife. Since the CAP was designed to benefit farmers, their incomes have risen, though the ratio of agricultural income per head to that of the economy as a whole remained relatively constant for many years (Van den Noort in Coffey 1983). There are problems in comparing agricultural incomes closely with incomes earned in other parts of the economy since farmers' incomes consist not only of a return on labour but also on capital and land, which yield capital gains; farmers also consume some of their own output. Finally, farmers do not incur the high costs of travelling to work, as do many industrial workers.

Apart from an uneven distribution of income, many farmers are dissatisfied on other counts: they complain that too many of the benefits are siphoned off by suppliers of farm inputs and the processors of their raw materials. Where the farmer has himself gained, the capital value of his farm has been driven up, making it more difficult for new entrants to agriculture. The relatively low pay of many farm workers has led to part-time working becoming the norm in some areas. Many part-time farmers work evenings and weekends on the farm, relying on wives and elderly parents to do the real work. In West Germany, for example, the majority of farmers are part-timers, supplementing their income substantially from other jobs.

*The system of common prices*

While the system of common prices differs from one product to another, a general account will provide a basic picture and understanding of the main elements in the CAP pricing policy. There are four key prices: target, threshold, intervention and world prices; these are shown in Figure 4.2. The target price (*prix indicatif*), $P_x$, is the internal wholesale price which should generally be obtainable, and it is important in determining other prices. This price is set for the main cereals and is based on the area which produces the lowest proportion of its own grain requirements and is the highest-cost area – this is Duisburg in the heavily industrialized Rhine–Ruhr area. For some other products slightly different price terminology is used, such as guide prices, basic prices and norm prices, though these correspond to the highest price shown in the diagram.

The next price in the diagram, the threshold price (*prix de seuil*) $P_t$, is important in relation to extra-EU trade, and more will be said about this later in relation to the world price. Other terminology analogous to the threshold price is also used, such as sluice-gate prices, reference prices and so on. The difference between the target price, $P_x$, and the threshold price, $P_t$, is accounted for by handling charges and transport costs; for example, for grains, the costs between Rotterdam and Duisburg.

The intervention price (*prix d'intervention*), $P_i$, is the important support price below which prices are not allowed to fall. The EU Farm Fund (EAGGF) buys up supplies as the price falls to this level; it is obliged to buy everything offered to it at the intervention price, providing the commodity meets the quality and quantity criteria laid down; for example quantity $Q–Q_1$ in the diagram. The intervention price for cereals has been based at Ormes, a city in the Paris basin, which has the maximum cereal surplus, and for rice the intervention centre is Vercelli in northern Italy. The intervention storage is carried

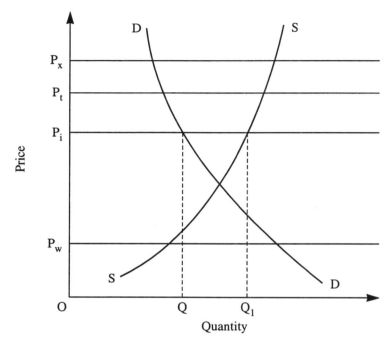

*Figure 4.2 Key agricultural prices*

out either directly by intervention agencies or by contracts with merchants to undertake the storage, with the merchants owning the cereals. Intervention prices have resulted in very effective and high price support for key products such as cereals and milk. In other products, such as fruit and vegetables, the price support is at a much lower level, while some products – eggs and poultry – have lacked internal support.

The world price, $P_w$, represents the price at which EU consumers would purchase their imports in a completely free market. The imposition of variable levies on imports raises the import price to the threshold level; this ensures that importers cannot undercut Community suppliers on price. For some products customs duties are levied, and for others in which the Community lacks indigenous supplies, such as oil and oil seeds, a deficiency payment system is in operation (how this works is discussed in a later section; for more details on specific products see Fennell 1988).

The Community, with its growing surplus of intervention stocks, has had to dispose of these on the world market at price $OP_w$. The export subsidy used is generally described as an export refund or restitution: in the diagram, $P_i - P_w$ = export restitution. A wide price gap has long existed between some Community and world product prices. In October 1986 EC intervention prices, compared with estimated representative world prices, were over twice as high for wheat, over three times as high for sugar and butter, and over nine times as high for skimmed milk powder (*Financial Times* 18 December 1986, p. 25).

For many continental countries the Common Wine Policy has been important, and its features have included price support; storage (and when ineffective, distillation has taken place); controls on planting and replanting; controls on imports of non-EC wine; and rules prohibiting blending of EC and imported wine. Measures have led to increased wine yields, but often poor quality, with much wine being unusable for human consumption and just produced for distillation. In addition, alcohol obtained from distillation is far more expensive than that produced from petrochemicals.

*Agricultural expenditure: the European Agricultural Guidance and Guarantee Fund (EAGGF)*

The EAGGF or Fonds Européen d'Orientation et Garantie Agricole (FEOGA) comprises two financial sections. The Guarantee section is concerned with support prices (as outlined earlier), and the Guidance section seeks to improve the structure of agriculture. Until 1966 the Guidance section expenditure could amount to one-third of the Guarantee section; but with Guarantee sums rising rapidly a ceiling was imposed. Financial support to the farmers in the EC escalated, and for the total of the four years 1986–9 total transfers associated with agricultural policies were $425 billion, whereas the USA over the same period spent $310 billion to support fewer farmers. Transfers comprise those for both consumers and taxpayers, and the former were far higher in the EC. In 1990 state subsidies to EC farmers were around $49 billion, with consumer subsidies of £85 billion in higher food prices (above prevailing world levels), compared with £47 billion federal subsidies to farmers in the USA, and only £28 billion as a subsidy to American consumers (*Financial Times* 2 November 1990). EAGGF expenditure is shown in Table 4.1.

Guarantee spending has swamped the tiny Guidance payments. While net expenditure was reduced by the receipt of ordinary levies and sugar

*Table 4.1  Budgetary expenditure on the Common Agricultural Policy*

| | Unit | 1994 | 1995 | 1996 | 1997[1] | 1998[2] |
|---|---|---|---|---|---|---|
| EU budget | Mn ECU | 59 909.1 | 65 498.1 | 80 456.5 | 80 088.0 | 81 433.6[6] |
| 1. EAGGF Guarantee | Mn ECU | 32 970.4 | 34 502.7 | 39 107.8 | 41 805.0 | 40 987.0 |
| – Plant products | Mn ECU | 21 852.8 | 22 959.3 | 24 980.1 | 27 082.0 | 26 697.0 |
| – Animal products | Mn ECU | 9 803.9 | 10 328.5 | 12 003.3 | 12 147.0 | 10 970.0 |
| – Ancillary expenditure | Mn ECU | 793.6 | 346.5 | 252.3 | 172.0 | 1 020.0 |
| – Set-aside and income aid[4] | Mn ECU | 30.0 | 36.3 | 19.5 | 10.0 | 3.0 |
| – Accompanying measures | Mn ECU | 490.1 | 832.1 | 1 852.3 | 1 889.0 | 2 297.0 |
| – Monetary reserve | Mn ECU | (1 000) | (500) | (500) | (500) | (500) |
| 2. EAGGF Guidance | Mn ECU | 3 335.4[5] | 3 609.1[5] | 3 934.5 | 4 239.6[3] | 4 390.6[5,6] |
| 3. Other agricultural expenditure | Mn ECU | 126.5 | 106.1 | 109.8 | 158.9 | 124.3 |
| 4. Total agricultural expenditure | Mn ECU | 35 682.5 | 38 217.9 | 43 152.1 | 46 203.5 | 45 501.9 |
| Changes under the Common Agricultural Policy: | Mn ECU | 2 304.5 | 2 160.7 | 2 023.8 | 2 239.4 | 1 856.6 |
| – ordinary levies | Mn ECU | 922.4 | 844.3 | 810.1 | 873.4 | 693.2 |
| – sugar levies | Mn ECU | 1 382.1 | 1 316.4 | 1 213.7 | 1 366.0 | 1 163.4 |
| Net cost of the CAP: | Mn ECU | 33 378.0 | 36 057.2 | 41 128.3 | 43 964.1 | 43 645.3 |
| – as % of GDP: | % | 0.5 | 0.46 | .. | .. | .. |
| – per head in the EU | ECU | 95.9 | 93.9 | .. | .. | .. |

*Notes:*
1  Payment appropriations entered in 1997 budget.
2  Appropriations entered in letter of amendment in 1998 preliminary draft budget.
3  Estimate 1997 budget outturn.
4  From 1994 the 'Set-aside' Chapter B1.40 will become item B1.106 and will be entered in Chapter B1.10 'Arable crops'.
5  Including amounts under the CIPs.
6  Draft budget, first reading.

*Source:*  European Commission, Directorate-General for Agriculture, *The Agricultural Situation in the European Union*, 1997 Report.

levies, these small sources of revenue lacked buoyancy and the early ideas of a self-financing agricultural policy soon had to be abandoned. The high level of expenditure in supporting prices can be attributed to the high prices set and to the fact that the EC expenditure replaced national expenditure on price support. For guidance expenditure the EAGGF pays only a proportion, with the remainder coming from national governments and, where relevant, the individual beneficiary. It would make more sense to raise expenditure on Guidance, but while there have been movements towards this, it can only be done prudently by reining back the level of price support. If the semblance of a common policy is to be maintained, it would be better for the Community to take over more of this Guidance expenditure and to limit the tendency of national governments to frustrate a *'communautaire'* policy by excessive aids to their own farmers – this is on the likely assumption that the EU wishes to continue with the basic principles of a common policy instead of shifting its financial costs to national exchequers.

Guidance expenditure takes place for a wide variety of schemes and projects and like Guarantee expenditure it has a direct regional impact (Moussis 1982, p. 215). Assistance should go mainly to those in need and it is important to ensure that Guidance expenditure does not add to existing farm surpluses. The Commission proposed in 1986 to pension off workers over 55 years of age, rejuvenating the workforce and adopting less capital-intensive production methods. However, elderly farmers do not have as much energy to produce surpluses as younger farmers with heavy borrowing, who may produce even greater quantities of unwanted food.

*Political pressures*

The political pressure exercised by the agricultural lobby – which means that more than a third of farmers' incomes is derived from subsidies – is totally disproportionate to the numbers employed in farming and to its share of GDP. National agricultural interest groups have been influential in France, seeking to exploit the full potential of its large land area, with French farm ministers continuing the passionate defence of French farming interests. Similarly in Germany, farming has tremendous political weight and the German Minister of Agriculture, Ertl, in power from 1969 to 1983, drew considerable support from farmers. Meanwhile, Helmut Kohl's reluctance to lose Christian Democrat support from farmers before the first postwar all-German elections late in 1990 delayed agricultural concessions in the GATT round of negotiations. In the smaller countries, with fewer farmers, but with significant upstream and downstream linkages, agricultural organization is often even stronger and more effective.

Since the EU represents aggregate national interests, interest-group activities have also moved upwards to the Community levels. The Federation of EU farming interests is the Comité des Organisations Professionelles Agricoles des Pays de la Communauté Economique Européenne (COPA). This has lobbied strongly in the various Community institutions and its influence has far exceeded that of consumer interests.

In setting farmers' incomes each year, the annual price review has generally raised prices to try to keep incomes on modern farms in line with average incomes in other sectors. Commission proposals, and particularly agreements by the Council of Ministers, have tended to bow to agricultural pressures. In the highly politicized decision-making process agriculture ministers are expected to defend their own farming interests vigorously, since they do not wish to be criticized for selling their own farmers short. Package deals have been stitched together and trade-offs made, but invariably a final agreement has only been possible by trading-up the settlement. It is only financial constraints that have restored a sense of realism to agricultural policy-making by the Council, along with some disquiet voiced by the European Parliament.

*Agricultural problems*

*Low farm incomes* The CAP includes a diversity of countries with differing levels of dependence on agriculture and a wide range of farm incomes. The percentage of the labour force employed in agriculture, relative to that employed in the industrial and service sectors, can be illustrated as in Figure 4.3 on a 3-variable graph. The movement over time has been one of diminished agricultural employment and growing convergence towards increasing reliance on tertiary activity.

The country most dependent on agriculture is Greece, and reading across the left-hand axis, Greece had 21 per cent of its labour force employed in agriculture; reading down the right-hand axis, 24 per cent of its labour force in industry; and reading up the horizontal axis, 55 per cent of its labour force in the service sector. These graphs are useful in illustrating any 3-variable distribution which sums to 100 per cent and each point shows the position of every member state in the EU(15). Southern European countries are shown to have relatively high depend-

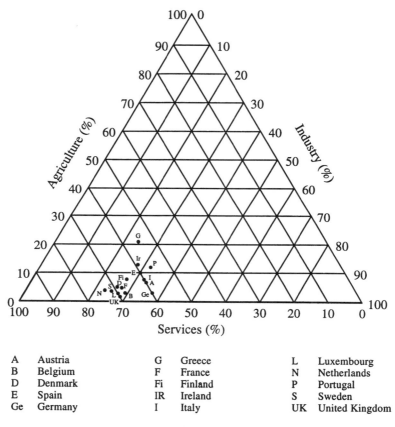

*Source*:   Drawn from percentages in Eurostat (1994).

*Figure 4.3*   *Percentage distribution of employment in agriculture,
industry and services, 1996*

ence on agriculture when measured in terms of employment. If this had
been illustrated alternatively in terms of agriculture's contribution to
GNP, it would have been lower, reflecting low agricultural productivity.
Future East European enlargement poses problems of greater agricultural dependence and would alter this graph significantly because of

high employment in both agriculture and industry, with marked under-development of the service sector. For example, Poland has large absolute and percentage dependence on agriculture, with some 28 per cent of its employment in agriculture, but because of particularly low productivity this produces only 6.5 per cent of its GDP.

Farm incomes are lowest in Southern Europe, which has suffered from generations of poor soil-conservation policies and lack of irrigation. Farmers in Southern Europe have tended to receive less generous support for their produce than have their counterparts in Northern Europe. In Northern Europe some beneficial specialization has occurred, raising incomes for cereal growers in areas such as central France and eastern England, and also for pig and poultry producers in close proximity to ports in the Netherlands through which animal feeding-stuffs can be imported cheaply. Spain has also begun to specialize successfully in supplying fruit and vegetables to Northern European markets. This is far more sensible than maintaining expensive glasshouse production in countries such as the Netherlands and trying to keep them competitive by subsidies on heating oils.

The policy of seeking to raise farm incomes has had paradoxical results, since the large number of small farmers who are most in need of welfare support have tended to receive least, whereas the smaller number of large and highly productive farms in least need of any such support have benefited the most. The attempt to raise farm incomes by increasing farm output prices has distorted the allocation of resources and failed to tackle the problem of low-income farmers effectively. More appropriate policies for the latter are by direct supplements to labour income.

Structural policies would help to create more viable and efficient farms. Though much progress has been made in increasing the average size of farm and in better production methods, many farms are still sub-optimal. More than half of the farms in the EU are less than 5 hectares (1 hectare = 2.4711 acres). At the end of the century there are still too many EU farms of modest size, even though total numbers employed in farming continue to decline (Eurostat 1996). Land fragmentation and scattered strips of land have restricted mechanization and the scope for economies of scale. Nevertheless, the optimum size of farm is still lower than the optimum unit in manufacturing industry, and well below the size of the large collective farms created in Eastern Europe. But there is a danger that larger units with greater capital investment will tend to intensify production with accompanying problems of surpluses and greater environmental damage. The alternative is one of persisting with the structure of many small farms, often on a part-time basis, and perhaps seeing as a positive rather than a negative virtue that they do not optimize output.

*Farm surpluses*   Agricultural output is far more variable and unpredictable than industrial output. Clearly underproduction as a result of a bad harvest would be catastrophic, particularly where countries were unable to purchase supplies on the world market. Overproduction, while less of a crisis than underproduction, has generated embarrassing surpluses which have tended to recur in some products. The main problem is not so much that of natural seasonal surpluses but of structural surpluses; these are the consequence of fixing prices artificially above their equilibrium level.

Technological progress has added further to the capacity of agriculture to produce in excess of demand. By the use of fertilizers and other techniques, farm yields have risen, because farmers have found that it costs almost as much to cultivate a field to produce one tonne per acre as to produce three tonnes. These techniques have been stimulated by high prices, though real prices for many products have actually fallen (Duchêne et al. 1985, p. 14). Indeed, for some years now agriculture has been subject to quite a strong cost/price squeeze which likewise has resulted in the need to raise yields. Expansionary technological forces are making the problem of surpluses a permanent feature of the agricultural landscape.

Overproduction has led to massive stocks, with a high value of products in public storage. The most costly stocks are of butter and skimmed milk powder. Since it is inconvenient to store fresh milk, surpluses are manifested in mountains of butter and skimmed milk powder. The actual worth of some of the stocks has been only about one-third of their book-value, since many of them deteriorated with age. In disposing of them one needs to think less in terms of the sunk costs of acquiring them and more in terms of their opportunity costs.

The EC(6) moved from a situation of 91 per cent self-sufficiency at its inception to one of overall self-sufficiency for the EC(10) after Greek enlargement. Furthermore, this actually understates the full rise in self-sufficiency, since UK entry into the EC depressed the Community's ratio of self-sufficiency. The EC(12) generated further overproduction of some products such as wine, though it is still in marginal deficit in products such as fresh fruit, citrus fruit, and oils and fats. The agricultural land area utilized in Spain is second only to that in France and its potential productive capacity has proved substantial, as agricultural prices for Spanish producers have risen to the higher levels in the EC. While the newer states may complement the northern members of the Community in some respects by importing more cereals and meat from them, in the long run the Iberian peninsula could become self-sufficient in grains. If additional surpluses do not arise, then it can only be due to the mixed blessing of inefficient farming, which is the case in Portugal.

Meanwhile, the incorporation of East Germany into the Community added further agricultural problems. Its farms, larger than in West Germany, were nonetheless inefficient because of overmanning and old unreliable machinery. Over time its agricultural efficiency is likely to rise, contributing to overproduction in some sectors. In sugar, for example, East Germany has received a generous quota, adding to the Community's existing surplus. Furthermore, when other countries, such as Poland and Hungary, join the EU, any future agricultural growth in Eastern Europe is likely to drive down world prices, increasing the cost of any export subsidies.

The EU has adopted a combination of internal and external measures to alleviate the problem of surpluses. Internally, it has destroyed products such as fruit and vegetables; in addition, some denaturing of products occurred in the past, rendering them unsuitable for human consumption and fit only for animal feed. Consumers prefer the surpluses to be sold domestically, and specific products, for example, butter and beef, have been subsidized for consumption by pensioners and families on low incomes.

The Community's external policies have consisted partly of selling off the surpluses cheaply to other countries. This has aroused almost as much emotional concern in the UK as the destruction of the surpluses, particularly when they have been exported to the Soviet Union. It is paradoxical that Soviet agriculture's main problem was one of under-production, whereas that of the EU has been overproduction. Other external policies are also controversial, especially the use of export subsidies to make products saleable on world markets. The only policy with any popular support, certainly on humanitarian grounds, is helping the needy people in the Third World. Yet even food aid in the long term may encourage a taste for different imported products and actually reduce the recipient's own agricultural output as prices are lowered. Compared with butter, products such as milk powder have higher nutritional value and are fairly cheap to store. The EU's aid policies have been motivated by a desire to remove its food surpluses, and critics of aid believe that a policy of assisting agricultural developments *per se* may be a more effective approach in less-developed countries (LDCs).

*Distortion of international trade*   The CAP has led to some alteration in the pattern of international trade. The EU's agricultural trade has gone through two phases. The first phase consisted of a massive growth of intra-trade in foodstuffs which rose more rapidly than extra-EC food imports. France and the Netherlands, more so than Italy, have increased their exports, largely to the main import markets of West Germany and the UK. But the Community market has become satiated as West Germany and the UK have increased their own levels of agricultural self-sufficiency.

In the second phase the Community, though still a major world importer, was transformed into a major world exporter of food, second only to the USA. In a few products the EC actually became the world's number one exporter (Duchêne et al. 1985, p. 55). However, since international trade in agricultural products represents only a small proportion of world production, major changes in the league table can occur based on rather marginal quantities. Expanding import markets for agricultural sales have opened up only slowly in Japan, the newly industrializing countries (NICs), the Organization of Petroleum Exporting Countries (OPEC) and in Eastern Europe. Both India and China have become net exporters of wheat, and many LDCs in great need of food have unfortunately lacked the foreign exchange to translate this into effective demand. World food consumption is failing to increase at a pace necessary to absorb the surpluses of temperate developed countries.

The EC's sales in international markets were only competitive by using large export subsidies, though other countries like the USA also maintain exports in other ways. In 1985 a third of EC appropriations were for export refunds since as a single transaction in many cases it was cheaper than storage. Efficient international suppliers in the rest of the world naturally resent any displacement of their own sales by the EC. They have seen the loss of many of their exports to the EC itself and this has then been compounded by displacement from other world import markets. EC exports of agricultural products to the rest of the world rose from an index of 100 in 1973 to 295 in 1986, whereas its imports from the rest of the world rose from an index of 100 in 1973 to 166 in 1986. EC policy runs counter to the whole purpose of free trade, which is to create beneficial international specialization on the basis of comparative advantage. EC policy has created a further adverse effect of greater instability in world market prices.

Temperate food producers, such as Australia and New Zealand, have been badly affected, despite some continuing special arrangements to mitigate the worst effects on the latter. The rules of GATT for agricultural trade have been inadequate; for example, the code obliging countries to avoid export subsidies which would lead to an inequitable share of world markets has been too imprecise. The challenge by more fair-minded exporters has led to a more effective GATT after the Uruguay Round. At meetings of the GATT International Dairy Agreement, Australia accused the EC of using secret subsidies. New Zealand has greatly cut back its own subsidies since 1984, with its milk producers, for example, surviving on a price only one-fifth of the level in the EC.

Both Canada and the USA have made complaints about EC exports eroding their sales of products such as wheat. The EC's world market share of wheat rose from 12 per cent in 1979–80 to 17 per cent in 1984–5. The Iberian enlargement led to further exports of wheat, corn and oil seeds. The USA demanded compensation and at the beginning of 1987 threatened to introduce a 200 per cent tariff on a range of European goods, including gin, brandy, white wine, blue cheese and endives. A compromise was reached, averting an open trade war between the two blocs. Nevertheless, it is difficult to reconcile the EC's concern with a managed market with the American preference for a freer market, even though the latter does not operate a policy based on a completely open market (Josling in Tsoukalis 1986).

The CAP has had adverse global effects on poorer countries in an even more vulnerable position; for example, in South America, Argentina derives approximately three-quarters of its export revenue from agriculture and is a major producer of maize and beef. The EC took temporary measures against Argentina during the Falklands crisis, but the long-term effects of the CAP have had a much more significant impact on the displacement of Argentinian products from the EC market.

Similarly, Brazil has failed to develop its export potential sufficiently to prevent a growing problem of financial indebtedness. The EC's sugar policy has been an additional factor in Brazil, seeking to convert sugar surpluses into fuel to reduce its import bill for energy. Despite favourable treatment of sugar imports from the Lomé countries, the EC's own high price and dumping of sugar on world markets has created major difficulties for producers such as Cuba, the Philippines, the Dominican

Republic and Thailand – the last also having a different complaint relating to the Community's policy on cereal substitutes. Despite sugar quotas for the EC's own producers, the CAP has shifted the price adjustment on to the residual world market. LDCs have tended to become net importers of food, not only because of the EC, but mainly because of their own inadequate agricultural policies, which result in low agricultural investment, with low domestic food prices being set in the interests of urban consumers.

*Reforms to the CAP*

Proposals for the reform of the CAP abound, but their application, though reducing the share of agricultural spending in the EU Budget, has often been cosmetic; they have fallen short of the fundamental root-and-branch changes that are necessary. The most significant early proposal for important structural reform was contained in the *Memorandum sur la réforme de l'agriculture dans la Communauté Economique Européenne*, more popularly known as the Mansholt Plan of 1968. Unfortunately, this proved too threatening and neither sufficient movement of labour from the land nor the significant reduction in the agricultural land area which it proposed took place. However, directives were introduced in 1972 dealing with farm modernization; cessation of farming and land re-allocation; and supply of guidance and training in new skills. Even so, the decade after enlargement in 1973 was largely wasted in terms of reform, since the rest of the EU had access to the large UK import market. Meanwhile the CAP gradually became outmoded and increasingly expensive as underproduction gave way more and more to overproduction in the 1980s.

The main policy weakness was excessive reliance largely upon one policy instrument of high prices, and reluctance directly to reduce these prices initially often resulted in weaker alternatives. For example, co-responsibility levies were applied to milk after 1977, but were generally too low to be effective. They operated on supply, to reduce price, and on demand, with the levy being used in an attempt to stimulate falling sales of milk. Quotas have also been introduced since they seem to cause least disturbance to the existing situation, but manage to reduce surpluses, dumping and budgetary costs. They have long been used for sugar beet and in 1984 were introduced for milk, but were set at too high a level and production continued to outrun consumption. In 1986 the Commission agreed on a further substantial reduction in milk quotas over a three-year period. It sought to make farmers individually responsible for keeping within their milk quotas to prevent those who were overproducing from incurring penalties of the super-levy. Quotas can be applied most easily in the case of the products mentioned, where there are a limited number of factories and dairies: their disadvantage is that when rigidly set they tend to freeze the existing pattern of production inefficiently. There is a danger of being forced to extend quotas elsewhere and ending up with an even more controlled and managed system.

Other suggestions floated were to go beyond quotas on outputs and to impose them also on inputs such as nitrogenous fertilizers. Quotas on the latter hit the operations of the larger and more efficient farms, though they fit in with a policy of cutting output without driving the small farmer out of existence. There is certainly less scorn being shown for a marginal return to low-input organic farming, though this can constitute only a small part of farming in the EU because of its higher costs.

There was a consolidation of agricultural reforms after the late 1980s, reflected, for example, in the proposals for stabilizers to limit financial support to a guaranteed output, beyond which price cuts would apply. This was agreed for the very important cereals market. Cereals are key products in which price reductions provide immense benefits to livestock producers. Further significant progress was made in the MacSharry reforms of 1992 and in the Uruguay Round of negotiations in which the EU agreed to reduce cereal prices towards world levels. Also important was the agreement by the EU to scale down the level of export subsidies and also to move towards a system of tariffication in which it would convert all its import barriers, particularly levies, into a fixed tariff as the only measure of protection. These were then to be reduced steadily.

A policy of continuing to lower farm prices was vital and Commission proposals leading up to the Berlin Summit in March 1999 were for another 20 per cent cut in cereal prices. This was lessened to only a 15 per cent fall in two stages of 7.5 per cent reduction in 2000 and 7.5 per cent in 2001. Dairy prices are to be cut by 15 per cent and production-limiting quotas to rise 1.5 per cent, but implementation has been delayed to 2005–6. Beef prices are to fall by 20 per cent over three years from the year 2000, and there will no longer be a guarantee to buy up meat, except when markets are weak. Price reductions clearly meant that there would have to be resort to some alternative income support for farmers, particularly for small farmers. Direct income payments are more equitable and are also of benefit to Southern Europe, which has more small farms. Unfortunately the thrust of policy in shifting support from the consumer through high prices towards the taxpayer seems unlikely to reduce the total cost of agricultural support.

The emphasis on setting land aside to take it out of cultivation is also a step in the right direction and was further reinforced for cereal production, with some 10 per cent of land to be compulsorily taken out of production each year up to 2006. However, set-aside is not free from problems; it has been used for many years in the USA with limited effects. Although output falls, this is not in direct proportion to the land set aside and may be negated if farmers leave their poorest land fallow and simply produce more intensively on their existing land. Also, after land has been fallow, fertility is increased when it is returned to production by rotation. Furthermore, if the land is used for grass and fodder crops, this simply transfers the arable problem to the livestock sector. It remains to be seen whether set-aside and changes which involve paying farmers to act more as park keepers in caring for the environment (but producing nothing) is a complete solution to the problem, but at least it is better than producing unwanted food.

There is increasing environmental awareness in agriculture, with the designation of environmentally sensitive areas (ESAs). These may help to preserve the much diminished wetland areas with their variety of wildlife; and by growing suitable trees such as willows, traditional rural crafts, for instance basket-making, can be revitalized. A policy of compensating farmers for the maintenance of landscapes and amenities is beneficial, though in few instances are farmers able to make sufficient income from the market, so continuing farm subsidies are necessary.

Incremental reforms have improved the CAP, but have led to dissatisfaction in new quarters, which now include farmers facing a price squeeze on their real incomes and also excessive bureaucracy and form-filling. It has certainly made agricultural policy even more bureaucratic (Nedergaard 1995). Furthermore, the overwhelming pressure for agricultural reform has come more from external than internal sources; for example, from the USA, the Cairns Group and, most recently, from the proposed enlargement of the EU to Eastern Europe. Enlargement would increase the EU land area by about half and approximately double the agricultural labour force, but only add about 100 million consumers, whose average purchasing power is around a third of that of existing EU consumers. The EU has recognized that the costs of the CAP would prove unbearable with such high benefits going to farmers in Eastern

Europe, where agricultural prices are generally low and would rise significantly. It would be undesirable to re-impose a planned interventionist and high-price agricultural policy which is contrary to all the market reforms in Eastern Europe. The EU would also be financing a system which East European economies cannot afford themselves. It is far better to follow the WTO in liberalizing trade, cutting prices and compensating EU farmers (and not farmers in Eastern Europe) by direct income aids. Hence the EU 'Agenda 2000' reforms represent further significant progress, though even these may fall short of being sufficiently radical. However, at least policies continue in the right direction of cumulative price reductions so that farmers recognize and respond to the new signals; there is also compulsory set-aside, extension of the dairy quota scheme, and direct income support, but subject to a clear ceiling.

While the EU seems determined to uphold the general principle of common financing, this has resulted in the major agricultural importing countries bearing a disproportionate share of the costs of the CAP. Yet any return to national financing is opposed by the major agricultural producing countries who argue that it would undermine the CAP. Furthermore, it is likely that richer members states would still choose to subsidize their agriculture heavily, but at least the support cost would be apparent nationally. The countries most affected by any re-nationalization of agricultural policy would be those in Southern Europe which lack the financial resources necessary to support their farmers.

The most welcome recognition is that rural development is not completely synonymous with the CAP, and that there is a need to focus more upon rural development *per se*. This includes, for example, the promotion of environmentally friendly small and medium-sized enterprises (SMEs) in rural areas and also the development of the rapidly growing tourism market. Such a policy is integrated increasingly via the Structural Funds, which are covered in Chapter 7.

### Green currencies and monetary compensatory amounts (MCAs)

Why did green currencies arise? The CAP was constructed on the basis of common prices, but unfortunately the international monetary system of fixed exchange rates began to collapse in the late 1960s. In August 1969 the French government decided to devalue the franc and this was followed in October 1969 by a revaluation of the Deutschmark. Both countries wished to retain the common price system of the CAP. France was not prepared to accept the inflationary effects of devaluation on its consumers, while Germany was concerned about the adverse effects of revaluation on its farmers and their loss of exports. Therefore it was decided to retain agricultural prices at their original levels by instituting a special new system.

The system adopted has been known as one of 'green currencies'. It might be questioned why a special procedure should apply to agricultural exchange rates and not to other products; for example, there is no 'black currency' for trading coal. The reason is that the Community has not tried to stabilize prices for coal with an intervention system; nor has coal over the years assumed the overriding importance of agriculture. It was decided that the difference between the new market rates of exchange and their original level (that is, green rates for agriculture) would temporarily be bridged by the use of monetary compensatory amounts (MCAs). This meant that in the case of France a negative MCA was applied, and a positive MCA for Germany.

MCAs were applied to agricultural products subject to the intervention mechanism and which would otherwise suffer from currency fluctuations. Initially the MCAs were financed by national governments, but in July 1972 (for trade with non-EC countries) and in January 1973 (for intra-EC trade) compulsory MCAs were introduced and financed by the EC. While the joint float of EC currencies in 1973 made the system more manageable, the first enlargement of the Community brought in new countries with representative (green) rates; also, there were still problems with EC countries not able to operate in the joint float.

Any assessment of the consequences of green currencies depends upon the extent to which one considers that agriculture should be insulated from exchange rate changes. Is there something distinctive about agriculture *per se*? Whereas industrialists in trading products can choose to trade at the new exchange rates, or to adjust domestic prices accordingly, farmers (without MCAs) face an immediate change in farm prices and in trading patterns. MCAs, by trying to freeze the original situation, have led to some misallocation of resources; for example, Germany's positive MCA system enabled its farmers to sell more products abroad, reducing inroads of inherently more efficient imports from other Community countries. German producers, benefiting from lower imported input costs, were able to raise agricultural self-sufficiency, much to the chagrin of countries such as France.

The MCA system was extremely complex, varying between products. It covered mainly those heavily traded products for which intervention prices existed (though there were exceptions to this, with poultry and eggs being included, despite absence of intervention prices, mainly because of their dependence on cereals, for which there are very significant intervention prices). The existence of MCAs added to the risks involved in trade since buyers preferred to purchase at fixed prices instead of having to carry the risk involved with an MCA; for example, the Community lost some long-term export contracts overseas by refusing to quote fixed prices.

Despite these criticisms of green currencies, they did offer some advantages, especially in the short term, in maintaining price stability, which would have been wrecked by floating currencies. MCAs helped to maintain a veneer of common prices, while at the same time conferring some freedom of manoeuvre on national governments – via devaluation or revaluation of their green currencies – to set prices to suit their own interests. The use of MCA adjustments sometimes helped to facilitate agreements at meetings of agricultural ministers; this was because any prudent price increases could be varied by national governments for their own farmers by MCA adjustments. Nevertheless, it was accepted that on balance in the revised agri-monetary system MCAs should be phased out in the long term.

### The UK and the CAP
Historically, the UK imported foodstuffs freely from the rest of the world, but during and immediately after the Second World War steps were taken to raise the level of domestic self-sufficiency. A distinctive system of deficiency payments to farmers was introduced to cover the difference between the realized market price which the farmer obtained on the open market and the higher guaranteed price. This system increased domestic production while at the same it enabled imports to continue relatively freely, giving consumers the benefit of low food prices. The system was financed out of general taxation, but rising budgetary costs led the government to introduce more selective policies, including guaranteed prices only for standard quantities of various products.

On joining the EC, the UK switched over to the Community system of farm support, though in some products, such as the sheep meat regime, the UK was allowed to operate a variant of the original deficiency payments system. But the Commission proposed in 1987 that this should be phased out as part of Community agricultural reform to limit costs.

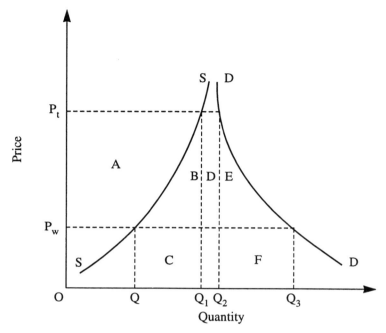

*Figure 4.4    Effects of the CAP*

Under the CAP, the main difference for the UK has been the fixing of a high target price, as shown in Figure 4.4.

The effect of setting a high price $OP_t$ induces more resources into agriculture, B+C, and enables a larger surplus to be reaped by existing producers, A. Whereas under the deficiency payments system consumers purchased foodstuffs at the world price, $OP_w$, under the CAP there is a loss of consumer satisfaction, E+F, since demand has fallen from $OQ_3$ to $OQ_2$. High prices have the unfortunate effects of raising supply and cutting demand, with resultant surpluses. While the levies on imports, D, are a source of revenue, they have been insufficient to finance the massive agricultural expenditure.

From the viewpoint of the UK, the import levies do not accrue directly to the British government, but form part of the Community's 'own resources'. Since the UK is still very dependent on imports of foodstuffs from outside the EC, it contributes disproportionately in levies. Likewise, substantial levies are collected by the Netherlands, since Rotterdam is the single biggest point of entry.

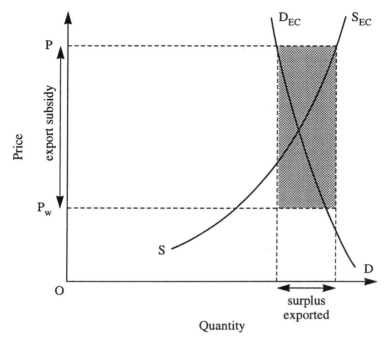

*Figure 4.5   The CAP and export surpluses*

Many Community countries are net exporters of foodstuffs and the total cost of subsidizing export surpluses is illustrated by the shaded area in Figure 4.5. Whereas in any national system the exporting country would have to bear the cost of this itself, in the Community it is financed from the 'own resources' provided by all EC members. This may be logical if one believes in a 'Community', but its consequence is that the UK contributes to financing the surpluses of other EC countries – the latter having less incentive to reduce such surpluses when they are not financing the full cost themselves.

Various estimates have been made of the budgetary costs to the UK arising from the CAP (Buckwell et al. 1982). In addition to the focus on budgetary costs, total costs to the UK are even higher when one adds the trade costs of buying at EC instead of world prices. Higher agricultural prices have led to a redistribution of benefits from consumers to producers and in the UK the losses have outweighed the benefits. Various studies have indicted a range of substantial costs to the UK (Whitby 1979; Buckwell et al. 1982; Hill 1984; El-Agraa 1994).

Much depends upon assumptions about what the scenario would be if the UK were not part of the Community. Would world prices still be lower than EC prices, and would any increase in UK demand on the world market be matched by increased supply? EC surpluses would be available on the world market, carrying export subsidies and other world producers could probably ensure sufficiently abundant supplies. UK consumers would gain most in welfare from free trade, though this would not be attractive to UK farmers and in reality such a policy seems less feasible than choosing between the CAP and some alternative system of farm support. The CAP has had a negative effect on the UK rate of economic growth (Marques Mendes 1987, p. 100). It has also had an inflationary effect on the UK economy and has added to the balance-of-payments costs by paying higher prices for food imports. Although the higher price for food has tended to dampen demand, this has again been at the expense of consumers.

The green currency system for sterling has been operated inconsistently, but in its early years it was operated in the interests of British consumers. The pound floated downwards so that it fell substantially below its 1973 representative 'green rate'. Negative MCAs were applied and a widening gap opened up between the market and the green rate for the pound. Other Community countries objected to making budgetary contributions to subsidize British consumers. This in some respects was absurd, given that some of the countries with budgetary complaints about excessive contributions, such as Germany, were benefiting in their trade from higher agricultural exports to the British market. A combination of pressures led to some devaluation of the green pound. The major change occurred when sterling became a petrocurrency and the exchange rate of the pound rose above the green rate. After that time, consumers suffered, but on the other hand British farmers welcomed the opportunity to raise output with positive MCAs. However, by the late 1980s British farmers again felt disadvantaged as the pound fell in value, but the green currency system held UK support prices down and pushed up MCA levies on British exports. A 10 per cent devaluation of the green pound generally raises consumer prices by less than 1 per cent, and at the same time provides a very significant increase in commodity support prices to UK farmers. After the pound left the ERM in 1992, British farmers enjoyed a boom period from more competitiveness, benefiting from rising income. But some sectors suffered and after 1996 beef producers were affected by the global export ban on British exports caused by the BSE crisis. Also, the rise again in the value of sterling contributed to growing recession in UK agriculture in the late 1990s. This was compounded further, for example, by the loss of export markets caused by the Russian crisis in 1998 which added to a significant loss of agricultural export markets, such as those for sheepskins.

Overall, UK farm output prior to the recession in the late 1990s grew at a faster rate than industrial output, and British farmers helped to bridge the trade gap left by the continuing poor performance of the manufacturing sector in the wake of de-industrialization. A higher level of agricultural investment was undertaken, raising farm incomes, despite the squeeze of high costs, price restraints, the imposition of quotas and the BSE crisis. The UK raised its agricultural self-sufficiency (apart from the BSE-induced problems leading to the contraction of the domestic beef industry), supplying more than 80 per cent of its temperate food needs, compared with just over 60 per cent in 1973. Instead of being a sizeable importer of grains, the UK had become one of the world's largest cereal exporters. Cereal farmers, located largely in eastern England, have benefited substantially, more so than livestock and dairy farmers on the poorer western upland areas of the UK.

In general, the CAP has been much criticized, particularly in the UK, for its adverse effects on consumers. Despite reforms, it contains many failings which have distorted resource allocation. Yet its central importance to the process of integration meant that policy changes tended to be marginal rather than substantial. It is now recognized that radical reform is imperative to avoid disintegration and becoming overwhelmed by the budgetary costs of eastern enlargement. Whilst the UK favours price cuts towards world levels, where the *quid pro quo* is enhanced direct income aid to smaller farmers, the main beneficiaries tend to be the more numerous smaller continental farmers rather than the larger and more efficient UK farmers.

## The Common Fisheries Policy (CFP)

Fisheries are included in the definition of agricultural products and in principle a common policy seems sensible since fish know no national boundaries. The market regime for the CAP included some market support for fish prices, and support buying, operated by producer organizations, has not proved too costly since as a net importer of fish the EU uses tariffs to raise the price. The main proponent of a common policy and of market support was France, worried about the impact of free imports on its own fishing industry. The introduction of the CFP before the first enlargement negotiations with other important fishing countries resulted in major problems. Norway objected to proposals for a CFP and opted out of the EC, pointing out that the four prospective applicants had a fishing catch nearly three times as high as that in the EC(6) (Nicholson and East 1987, p. 122). For the UK, the agreement incorporated in the Act of Accession to the EC reduced its inshore fishing limit.

The Law of the Sea Conference in 1975 resulted in coastal states having resource zones extending out to 200 miles or the median line. The EC extended its own fishing limits out to that distance at the beginning of 1977, creating an exclusive zone reserved for EU fishing. Both the UK and Ireland argued that the principle of equal access conflicted with their demands for domestic preference. But the UK was only successful in retrieving the 12-mile limit which had existed under the 1964 Fisheries Convention. Negotiations to reach an acceptable CFP proved difficult and protracted, despite the agreement in 1977 and the revised CFP introduced in January 1983 which was a 20-year agreement until 2002.

The concern of the CFP is to conserve and manage stocks, setting total allowable catches for species threatened by overfishing and then dividing them into national quotas. Each nation has to declare its catch and be open to inspection, with 'black' fish to be thrown back into the sea. Difficulties have arisen over proper verification and its enforcement in all Community countries, with much evasion of controls. The UK has tended to have stronger enforcement measures with regard to inspection than many other countries. Additional worries relate to overfishing, with too much industrial fishing by countries such as Denmark, and consequent adverse effects on fish stocks. Market organization has tried to provide an adequate level of income for fishermen and, in addition, finance has been provided to restructure the industry. To underpin restructuring, a special fund, the Financial Instrument for Fisheries Guidance (FIFG), has been established to provide extensive and comprehensive financial support.

For the UK, whereas the CAP generally yielded a golden harvest for British farmers – at least until quotas and recession in the late 1990s – under the CAP its fishing industry has declined. For example, between 1971 and 1980 its nominal catch of marine fish and shellfish fell, whereas that of the EC(10) rose over the same period (Macsween

1987). While the decline of the British fishing industry and its overcapacity may be attributed to other factors than just the CFP, the latter's principle of free access has added to its problems.

The origins of UK difficulties lay in the loss of distant fishing rights after the Icelandic victory in the cod war. International sympathies were with little Iceland, which was so dependent on fishing, and it could also call upon American goodwill because of the important NATO base located there. The UK lost the valuable white demersal fish (caught near the ocean floor), which were the traditional purchase of the British consumer. The UK started to land lower-price pelagic fish (caught near the surface), greatly reducing the value of domestic fish landings. Iceland's declaration of its own 200–mile limit led to a laying-up of British trawlers, with devastating effects in fishing areas such as the Humber ports, where much of the fish processing industry is based. Frozen-fish processors began to meet the UK's traditional taste for white fish much more from imports.

In the revised CFP, which was based on the historic pattern of fishing for each stock, the UK had to settle for less than its percentage share of Community fishing waters. Another difficulty for the UK has been that the EU has made agreements with outside countries so that it is now all Community fishing countries that obtain reciprocal concessions. The EU has signed fishery agreements with non-EU countries, whereas national agreements made by the UK before it joined the Community would probably have led to greater national benefits on a *quid pro quo* basis. Agreements have been signed with countries such as Norway, which share joint stocks with the Community; also with Canada in return for reduced import duties on Canadian fish. The EU has also purchased fishing concessions from less-developed countries, particularly in Africa.

The fishing industry has been whittled down in size, particularly in England, and its plight is a testimony to mismanagement when an island economy becomes a net importer of fish. Some of its problems have been common to all industries, such as rising fuel costs, high interest rates and periodic overvaluation of sterling. Fishermen have been squeezed by these elements, plus accompanying quotas and further new measures agreed in December 1990 to tie up boats for a given number of days each month. Dwindling fish stocks have arisen from overfishing and, despite limits on Spanish fishing rights in the Community pond for its first ten years of membership, disputes with France and the UK soon arose; for example, over the registration of Spanish vessels in the UK which thereby ate into the British fishing quota. The UK, in an attempt to limit 'quota-hopping' by the Spanish, sought to invoke a nationality clause against Spanish ownership of British vessels, but was eventually overruled by the European Court of Justice.

# 5   Industrial and technological policies

## Industrial problems and policies

What kind of progress has been made by the Community in developing a common industrial policy, and what form has this taken? Why is industry in the EU in general not as strong technologically, nor as efficient, as that in the USA and Japan? What can, and is, being done to remedy this? These are just a few of the questions to be examined in this chapter. It will become evident that even if the EU had not existed, it would have been necessary eventually to establish something like it, so that European industry could enjoy the benefits of a larger market to reap economies of scale and collaborate to reduce the costs of research and development.

Industrial policy creates the conditions in which industry can flourish, and its main concern has been to create a competitive and efficient industrial structure. In recent years this has been strengthened by privatization programmes switching less efficient and large nationalized industries from the public to the private sector and reducing barriers to new entrants. There are, however, continuing grounds for governmental intervention to improve industrial performance by correcting market failures, such as underinvestment in R&D. Government intervention has also been concerned with the social costs to the environment that are associated with industrial activities, but it is not intended here to focus on environmental issues, since these are covered in Chapter 6.

The more traditional concerns of industrial policy-makers have been with controlling monopolies, restrictive practices and mergers. But they have had to be tempered by a recognition that large firms are necessary in some sectors to compete technologically and efficiently with American and Japanese firms. Unfortunately, European policies have often tended to support national champions, failing to recognize that the Community has opened up opportunities to develop firms on a continental scale and to co-operate more closely.

Traditionally, monopoly has been condemned since it results in a misallocation of resources. Furthermore, because of the absence of competition, a high degree of 'X-inefficiency' may exist under the operation of monopoly. *Prima facie*, a strong legal anti-monopoly policy can be implemented on the basis of a highly concentrated industrial structure: the USA has favoured such an approach. However, the case against monopoly is not always conclusive, for various reasons. First, in practice oligopoly tends to prevail in most sectors rather than outright monopoly. In oligopoly, firms may either collude or compete, and both the number of firms and the kind of products being produced are influential in determining the behaviour of such firms. Second, large firms are able to benefit from economies of scale and can spend more on R&D. The EU requires companies to be of a sufficient size to compete with large international corporations. Therefore, in Europe there has been a less dogmatic policy towards large firms than in the USA. Instead of an outright condemnation of firms on the structural grounds of high concentration ratios, there has been a preference to use this as a guide, but then to go further by examining other aspects of behaviour such as conduct and performance.

## EU industrial competitiveness and policies to promote technology

*Concentration and competition policy*

*Concentration*    Industrial concentration is reflected in the growth of large firms which have come to dominate particular industries and national economies. Absolute industrial concentration is measured by the percentage share of indicators such as employment, output, sales and so on, held by the few largest firms. Somewhat different results emerge when these indicators are used; for example, in 1989 Europe's three largest firms in terms of number of employees were Siemens, Daimler-Benz and BAT Industries, each with over 300 000 employees. When the ranking was based on sales, the top three firms were Royal Dutch Shell, IRI and British Petroleum; and when based on stock market capitalization, the top three firms were Royal Dutch Shell, British Petroleum and BT (*Financial Times,* 19 December 1989). Since the behaviour of giant firms is likely to be influenced by, among other things, the total number of firms in the industry, then other measures, such as relative concentration, can take this into account. Often it is the same industries internationally which tend to be much more highly concentrated; for example, plotting industrial concentration ratios for West Germany, France and Italy has shown certain industrial similarities.

Although the extent of industrial concentration has increased in the national economies of member states, there are some factors restraining this. One of these has been the diversification of large companies into different sectors; for example, one of many firms involved in an extensive process of diversification in the late 1980s was Daimler-Benz, and the West German government overruled objection by its Cartel Office to its takeover of the Messerschmitt-Bölkow-Blohm (MBB) aerospace group. Giant companies have become much more significant in national economies, establishing themselves as conglomerates. However, their dominant share of specific industries has often been diluted by new entrants: these have either been other giant companies or – where entry barriers are sufficiently low – from the start-up of new small companies.

When measuring the level of industrial concentration the most crucial determinant is the size of market. The EU's '*nomenclature des industries établies dans les Communautés Européennes*' (NICE) adopted a three-digit classification – compared with the more detailed classification used in the USA (Jacquemin and de Jong 1977, p. 45). The degree of concentration is greater where the market is defined more narrowly; for example, a local market for a particular kind of product, such as a bottle or container, is more concentrated than if one uses the whole container market at a Community level. The creation of the Community and the steps towards a single internal market provide a major constraint on local or national monopoly power. Although firms have expanded the scale of their operations in the larger market – recently in particular by mergers and acquisitions – overall the problem of monopoly is less intense at Community level. For example, in the motor industry, Fiat is just one of many companies to complete virtually a national monopoly by swallowing smaller Italian firms. Yet the car market is highly competitive, partly because of overcapacity, with Volkswagen having overtaken Fiat as Europe's largest car producer.

*Competition policy* Competition policy has been covered by Treaty Articles 85–94. This section first focuses mainly on Article 85, relating to *restrictive agreements* or concerted practices between two or more enterprises. Then it gives attention to Article 86, which refers to abusive behaviour by monopolies or firms with market dominance.

The Community has favoured free competition, through the interplay of demand and supply, since this provides the basic ingredient for efficiency. Competition policy has provided the means whereby the Community has achieved and maintained its object of free internal trade. It has tried to prevent the erection of new trading barriers, and competition policy has applied not only when trade with other member states is actually affected, but also where there has been an adverse potential effect. In addition to free trade, the other pillar of the Community has been to maintain open competition, based upon consumer sovereignty. Anything that appreciably distorts open competition in member states is prohibited. EU policy takes precedence over national policy, though national policies have also been used and shown increasing convergence.

Minor exceptions to competition are permissible on grounds of efficiency under Article 85 (but were not applied to Article 86, nor explicitly to merger policy). The *de minimis* rule applies to agreements of minor importance where firms together have no more than 5 per cent of the market (and their aggregate turnover does not exceed ECU 200 million). Only minor exceptions have been made to the open competition policy; for example, where restrictive agreements are of minor importance and are encouraging co-operation between small and medium-sized enterprises, such as that in R&D. Likewise, some exceptions have been made in the public sector with the application of state aids being permissible for particular depressed regions and industries. However, the aim is to ensure that the aid is on a selective and transparent basis, so that aids do not distort competition.

In forming such a strong competition policy, particularly against restrictive practices, the Community was shaped by West German practice, which legislated against restrictive practice in 1957. The Commission has received firm support from the Court of Justice. Firms have to notify the Commission about any agreements and arrangements that they have made with other firms, and these are generally considered invalid unless the firms concerned account for only a small part of the market or there are some benefits available; for example, in improving the production or distribution of goods; in promoting technical and economic progress; in ensuring that a fair share of the benefits go to consumers, and so on. EU competition policy has been very tough, permitting fewer exemptions than the UK's range of gateways. But subsequently it did introduce several block exemptions for various agreements where the harmful effects are sufficiently counterbalanced by beneficial features; for example, relating to specialization between SMEs, R&D joint exploitation, exclusive distribution, exclusive purchasing, patent licensing, distributive agreements for automobiles, franchising and know-how licensing.

Generally, horizontal and vertical agreements between firms have violated competition – though this did not include non-binding agreements unless such concertation was followed by prohibitive practices (Mathijsen 1985, p. 70). Often, collusion is difficult to prove, like that of parallel price movements which may be quite coincidental, and has to be shown to arise from concertation which will be manifested by its repetitive occurrence. Apart from price agreements, cartels have often been established to share out markets such as the Dutch and Belgian cement markets (Swann 1995, p. 138). The EU is opposed to territorial market-sharing, examining cases in a range of sectors such as detergents in which Dutch and Belgian producers in particular had agreed not to sell in each other's territory. In other practices, such as exclusive dealings, these have been prohibited once geographical restrictions have been created (Mathijsen 1985, p. 178). Joint purchasing and joint selling agreements have also tended to be prohibitive under Article 85.

The temptation for firms to collude during recession has been enhanced in oligopolistic markets; for example, Shell, ICI, Hoechst and Montedipe in the mid-1980s held two-thirds of polypropylene sales (a key product used in the manufacture of a wide range of plastics). The companies argued that over the years they had made significant losses in this field, but the EU showed that they were in fact operating a cartel and fixing prices. In 1988 another cartel between PVC producers, again fixing prices and production quotas, resulted in the imposition of heavy fines. The companies appealed against these and eventually the European Court of Justice slashed them, with ICI's fine of £1.75 million being reduced by nearly £700 000 in 1999. Competition policy is effective in restraining companies from getting together, though one consequence of this has perhaps been a slower downward adjustment of surplus capacity than in Japan.

Concern about *dominant firms* goes back to the days of the ECSC when France was fearful of any renewed concentration of the German coal and steel industries. In the EC Article 86 has tackled different types of abuse by dominant firms; for example, firms such as Commercial Solvents, which controlled materials and refused to supply them freely to other firms. Other cases of some significance have included that of Hoffmann–La Roche, which was drawn to the Commission's attention by Stanley Adams, who was subsequently badly let down by the Commission. Hoffmann–La Roche dominated the market for vitamins, charging different prices in various markets and also giving fidelity rebates which were aggregated across all products.

The concept of dominance depends on how the product and the market are defined. One important case in this respect was that of

Continental Can, a large American multinational manufacturer of containers. It obtained a dominant position in the German market through a takeover, followed by a takeover of a large Dutch producer. This was likely to suppress competition in both markets. The German firm had a dominant position in the market for preserved meat and fish, and for metal caps for preservative jars. There was clearly more of a monopoly when the market was defined narrowly. The Court's judgement came out against the Commission's views about Continental Can creating a dominant position, but it did provide a precedent enabling the Commission to move into the field of scrutinizing mergers. Also, the Philip Morris tobacco case in 1987 opened up Article 85 where concentration occurred from agreements by companies, but excluded hostile takeovers.

The Commission's powers to control mergers were initially limited, allowing them to be challenged only after they had taken place. Since the pace of merger activity was increasing as a result of the SEM, Competition Commissioners pressed for greater controls on anti-competitive mergers. This resulted in 1990 in the Commission being empowered to examine large mergers between companies whose combined sales world-wide totalled ECU 5 billion (£3.5 billion) or more, and where at least two of the companies each had EC sales of ECU 250 million or more. Thus the Commission has to be notified by the companies involved where these thresholds apply, and failure to do so, or providing wrong information, could result in a fine of up to ECU 50 000 (£35 000). Should the companies press on with the merger, they can be fined up to 10 per cent of their aggregate turnover. The Commission is mainly concerned to prevent any adverse effect of mergers in reducing competition. Where the combined market share of the companies involved is less than 25 per cent, it is generally compatible with the common market, but above this (and especially above 40 per cent) it becomes more incompatible. Between these levels a dominant market position is judged by a reference to criteria such as market structure, actual or potential competition from inside or outside the EC, supply and demand, and barriers to market entry (*Financial Times,* 21 September 1990, p. 4).

There is concern in some countries, especially those with well-developed policies of their own, about ceding powers to a relatively slow-moving Commission. If the Commission fails to reach a decision in time, the merger goes ahead automatically. On the other hand, other critics have favoured giving the EU greater powers to examine mergers with a lower turnover figure and a Commission Green Paper in 1996 suggested turnover thresholds of ECU 2 billion (instead of the ECU 5 billion rule), and ECU 100 million (instead of the ECU 250 million rule). After some national governments invoked subsidiarity to limit EU control, the Commission formally proposed thresholds of ECU 3 billion and ECU 150 million respectively. It was necessary to ensure that countries that had few or no merger rules were constrained from leniently supporting domestic mergers to create national champions. It was felt in some quarters that it would be best to establish a completely independent agency, modelled perhaps on the German Kartellamt, seeing the Commission, despite its theoretical independence, as being open to national political pressures. Some early mergers may have been allowed to proceed because of such pressures; for example, a merger in 1988 between two Dutch coffee companies, Douwe Egberts and Van Nelle, created a near-monopoly in the Benelux market. Despite the merger control regulation since 1990, the majority of mergers have been allowed to proceed, and in 1990–5 only four were prohibited; for example, in the case of turbo-prop aircraft, the proposed merger between Aérospatial Alenia and De Havilland was prohibited, since it would have resulted in the firm having a dominant position controlling well over half the world market.

In its competition policy under Articles 85 and 86 the Commission has gone through various stages in its approach. These may include negative clearance (making sure agreements are not prohibited); where agreements do exist it obliges firms to put an end to infringements; and it can issue a declaration granting an exemption. When making investigations, the Commission has wide-ranging powers to enter premises and to examine records. Finally, extensive penalties or fines may be imposed: these include daily fines for failure to respond, larger fines for incorrect information and ultimately fines up to 10 per cent of the world annual turnover of the undertaking. In some cases these may even be extended to firms outside the EU, such as Switzerland, since the EU has claimed extra-territorial jurisdiction.

*State aids* cover any actions by any nation-state body that distort or threaten to distort competition by favouring certain national undertakings and adversely affecting trade with other nations. They are defined by the European Court of Justice as applying when firms would not be able to obtain the finance from private-capital markets, or if they could do so, it would be on less favourable terms. There is a wide range of state aids which are scrutinized closely where they are specific and provide unfair advantage to certain firms or goods compared with others.

In a first-best analysis or ideal world, since perfectly competitive markets provide the most efficient allocation of resources, subsidies would reduce economic welfare. However, in a second-best analysis, subsidies can be beneficial and may help to reduce a distortion elsewhere. Nevertheless, the presumption in the ECSC and EEC Treaties was to rule against them, apart from instances such as regional development, SMEs, R&D, the environment and restructuring, and so on. Unfortunately, state aids have proliferated, and were recognized after the Copenhagen Summit in 1978 as measures enabling adaptation to competition from the NICs, albeit interim measures. Since the White Paper on the internal market in 1985 there has been much tighter surveillance of state aids to make member states aware of the damaging effect of their national policies on other member states. Apart from seeking to ensure that they do not negate the gains from the SEM, they are also increasingly costly, especially for the countries in Southern Europe with high budgetary deficits and needing to comply with the fiscal criteria for EMU. The Commission can order a member state to recover from a recipient any illegal aid that has been given. Public enterprises are also subject to competition rules, though these are not as transparent as in the private sector. While privatization makes matters better, it is still necessary to ensure that these are sold at realistic prices which do not involve a subsidy to the private-sector purchaser.

*American and Japanese industrial challenge: inward investment*
Some of the companies that have taken fullest advantage of the large EU market have been overseas multinationals. The large market and the common external tariff to outsiders have encouraged the growth of inward foreign direct investment (FDI) partly for defensive reasons to offset trade diversion. The main sources of FDI have come from the USA and later from Japan. J.J. Servan-Schreiber in *The American Challenge* (1968) expressed concern, but by the mid-1970s the American challenge was being rebuffed (Heller and Willat 1975). The threat of American industrial hegemony has been reduced by the growth of large European companies, some of which have begun in recent years to invest on a large scale with takeovers in the USA itself. This trend has been stimulated by the fall in the value of the US dollar against European currencies, such as the D-mark.

The EU has had no common policy on FDI and hence countries that are in keen competition with each other recognize that if there is to be inward investment in Europe, they may as well provide the location for it rather than importing products from another country in which the new investment has been based. In the longer term, there is worry about adding to the danger of overcapacity in some sectors and indigenous industry being weakened from within rather than from without. Furthermore, new inward investment has received many subsidies in some instances; from the Community viewpoint it would be better if these were scrapped and the money directed instead to European industry.

The main source of FDI into the EU has come from the USA. Cumulative US investment in the EU has dwarfed that from Japan, partly because Japanese investment has been drawn to the US market itself and to investment closer to home in South-East Asia. The pace of Japanese investment in the EU has been activated by a rise in the value of the yen and protectionist pressures by the Community which have threatened to cut back on Japanese imports. Japanese investment has consisted of setting up overseas subsidiaries, often on green-field sites, making a significant presence felt in manufacturing sectors such as motor vehicles and financial services. In a few instances of collaborative deals, the Japanese have been criticized for stripping away the technical capabilities of their partners. The Japanese challenge caught some of Europe's major companies off-balance. For example, Philips compared with Hitachi had far too many factories; in 1984 it had 450 factories, whereas if it had been organized on a Japanese basis it would have had about 30. This led to new strategies at Philips of rationalization and focusing on its ten product divisions, spending more on R&D and spreading the costs of this by means of joint ventures. Despite Philips' strong record in VCRs and compact discs, it is the Japanese who have been most successful in turning VCRs into a mass market.

The Japanese move into the production of goods in the EU such as VCRs, electronic typewriters, photocopiers and microwave ovens was prompted by EU imposition of controls and anti-dumping duties. By the end of the 1980s there were over 500 Japanese factories in Western Europe, with the most popular location being the UK. France started to adopt a very pragmatic policy, with the Japanese being shaken by the Poitiers affair in 1982 when France insisted that all Japanese VCRs had to be routed through this customs post. EU trade-restraint measures have prompted an influx of Japanese companies, sometimes basic screwdriver factories without sufficient input of domestic skills. However, over time some Japanese companies have begun to exercise growing sourcing of local parts, with beneficial effects on local companies. The influx of investment from South-East Asia suffered a setback as a consequence of the Asian economic crisis in the late 1990s, with a few investments being liquidated. Also, in the new millennium the source of FDI is likely to be modified further, with a small amount of FDI from the emergent superpower of China.

## Industrial policy: declining industries and rationalization

*The European coal and steel community*    The coal industry's fortunes have fluctuated very much in the postwar period, with initial expansion to fuel Europe's industrial recovery giving way to contraction as greater energy choice emerged between different fuels in a competitive multi-fuel situation. The EU has pursued a low-cost energy policy, unlike that in agriculture. In the 1960s, as the Community enjoyed super-economic growth: it imported cheap oil on a large scale and also found it cheaper to purchase coal from some low-cost world suppliers. The EU recognized that it had to be as competitive as possible with other countries which were using cheap oil, such as Japan. While the energy policy chosen appeared judicious at that time from a macroeconomic perspective, at the microeconomic level it resulted in massive regional and structural decline in coal-mining areas. Whereas coal accounted for nearly two-thirds of primary energy consumption in 1960, between 1973 and 1985 its share fell to just under a quarter. While this contraction could be tackled satisfactorily when there was a buoyant growth in the economy by absorbing displaced workers into new industries, the decline became far more difficult to cushion during the 1970s and 1980s. During the 1990s this decline in employment continued because of rising productivity displacing workers; environmental policy to reduce sulphur emission in coal-fired power stations; and in the case of the UK, electricity privatization ending the contracts to purchase British coal.

At the macroeconomic level, the decision taken to rely on the import of oil led to problems as oil prices were raised by the OPEC cartel and balance-of-payments positions deteriorated in EU countries. The rather insecure and more high-cost oil imports moved the Community to agree to recognition of the benefits of indigenous energy supplies. Meanwhile, a slowing down in the rate of economic growth created by the energy crises reduced the demand growth for energy inputs. Oil prices have been volatile, and with the weakening of the OPEC cartel, prices have again become more competitive – this is desirable at the macro-level for oil importers, but is detrimental to the future of the coal industry in the Community.

The ECSC has made loans to both the coal and the iron and steel industry to finance investment projects, and for schemes of conversion and housing modernization and improvement (at a very low rate of interest); also, grants have been made to assist the redeployment of workers. The ECSC has been able to finance its expenditure partly from a levy imposed on sales of its products. Cheap and large loans are also available to firms prepared to move into coal and steel regions.

Unlike the coal industry, the steel industry experienced a longer period of economic expansion until the early 1970s, when it was hit very badly by depression. Traditional steel-making areas operating old-fashioned small-scale plants and in close proximity to local sources of ore have been closed down. The steel industry consists increasingly of giant integrated plants which have been constructed particularly at coastal sites, following Japanese practice which led the way in showing the tremendous cost advantages which could accrue from economies of scale. Also, there are mini-mills which are specialized and turn scrap into steel by melting it in arc furnaces. These have grown in significance and account for close to half of production in Italy and Spain. Mini-mills are lean and energy efficient, environmentally friendly through recycling, and customer-driven.

The reorganization of the steel industry has made conversion important to try to create and transform undertakings capable of absorbing redundant workers. To redeploy workers, emphasis has been given to resettlement allowances and to financing the acquisition of vocational training skills. Under the Davignon Plan the EU steel industry was greatly restructured and slimmed down to enhance its competitive efficiency. The Davignon system has operated with price and production quotas. During the 1980s European steel-makers removed millions of tonnes of excess capacity in their readjustment of productive capacity to lower demand. But those critical of such intervention pressed the Competition Commissioner to consider a repeal of the Paris Treaty which gave special powers to intervene in the steel industry. Mergers have consolidated the leading producers; for example, in Germany Krupp has merged with Thyssen, and British Steel has merged with Hoogovens in the Netherlands, creating Europe's largest steel and multi-metal maker.

*Industrial policy in the EEC*   Whereas the EU has a strong competition policy based upon Treaty requirements, it lacked the same legal basis for the development of an industrial policy (apart from coal and steel) until after the SEA and the Maastricht Treaty. The initial approach was market-oriented and generally non-interventionist. It was only in 1970 that the Community published the Colonna Report on Industrial Policy which mainly reflected a non-interventionist approach, trying to create a unified market. The many issues it was concerned with included the elimination of technical barriers to trade, harmonization of the legal, fiscal and financial frameworks, the encouragement of transnational mergers, greater technical collaboration and the control of multinationals, and so on (Arbuthnott and Edwards 1979, p. 92).

Over the years there has been a significant growth in merger activities, most of which tended to occur initially within member states. Where there were transfrontier mergers, many of these took place with foreign firms rather than with firms in other member states of the Union. European mergers were hampered by fiscal difficulties and sometimes legal restraints on mergers. The problem is that national mergers have tended to create national monopolies, while mergers with American or Japanese companies led to a fragmentation of European co-operation. A few major European cross-frontier links are of long duration; for example, between the UK and the Netherlands with Royal Dutch Shell (since 1907) and Unilever (since 1927). A successor to such mergers included Agfa-Gevaert (formed in 1964), though this was not a true European company but only consisted of 'Siamese twins' (Layton 1969). Some subsequent European mergers proved even less successful, such as the Dunlop–Pirelli merger in 1971. Despite some complementarity in markets, the marriage was dissolved in 1981 and several other company mergers have foundered over difficulties in blending together different styles of management.

Nevertheless, pressures on companies to combine have accelerated since the Single European Market in order to obtain economies of scale and to finance the costs of R&D. The more recent internationalization of stock markets and the lowering of barriers have stimulated further cross-national takeovers. These span the gamut of industries, even including agriculture where close Italian–French business links have been established. Policy-makers need to ensure that mergers are underpinned by efficiency gains rather than by the search for market power, since the latter reduces competition. Contestable markets are most desirable where large existing firms are threatened by new potential entrants.

A landmark in the EU's development of industrial policy was the Spinelli Report in 1973. It proposed new measures for industrial and technological policy, although these were still couched within the framework of a competition-oriented industrial policy. Among new measures were those for harmonization; freeing tenders; encouraging transnational enterprises; and helping small and medium-sized firms to co-operate or merge. Co-operation between SMEs, especially on R&D, does not fall foul of the anti-restrictive practices policy. A Business Co-operation Centre was created to help small firms to find partners, and the role of SMEs in nurturing enterprise is now implanted in EU industrial policy, inspired partly by their important role in the German economy. European Economic Interest Groups (EEIGs) have been created especially to help SMEs in R&D, and their main characteristic is that they are non-profit-making.

The recession during the 1970s provided a turning-point towards more interventionist policies. National governments came under pressure to help industries, and to avoid trading distortions. Many of these policies were taken over, though sometimes reluctantly, by the Community, in order to co-ordinate them, and to make the assistance transparent. This is well exemplified in industries such as steel and shipbuilding. In the shipbuilding industry national subsidies led to an agreement by the EC in 1986 to limit direct subsidies to a common standard percentage of costs on contracts. Overcapacity has manifested itself in many other sectors, such as the car industry, in which the Community market is close to saturation. The biggest producers have turned increasingly toward Eastern Europe for production link-ups and sales.

The EU has had to contend with industrial pressure placed on national governments for support and state aid. It is member states that have had stronger industrial instruments, such as those of finance, and a greater will to defend their own mature industries to protect employment. Furthermore, subsidiarity has reinforced industrial policy based on national plus regional/local level co-operation (Devine et al. 1996). The EU has sought to build up and strengthen its own instruments by increasing its R&D expenditure, founding the European Venture Capital Association (EVCA), a European Business Innovation Centre Network (EBN) and the Commission's own Small and Medium Enterprise (SME) Task Force. Emphasis on SMEs has found favourable support, especially in the UK, where all new Community regulatory proposals have to be assessed for their impact on business.

*The EU's lag in technology*
The pace of structural change has highlighted the need to replace the declining or sunset industries by new sunrise sectors. The future lies

with new high-tech sectors in which EU countries can utilize their high educational skills. Over time, the traditional down-market industries are likely to become the mainstay of the NICs. If the EU is to remain at the forefront of major industrial powers, then policies to promote technology, comparable with those of the USA and Japan, are imperative.

New technology is a mainspring of growth and lower inflation, even though its employment-creating effects are less clear-cut. Employment is most likely to increase when technology is devoted to creating and marketing successful new products, rather than to developing process technology which reduces the input of labour. Despite microeconomic readjustment and displacement of labour, historically the long-run impact of technology in aggregate has been to increase demand and employment opportunities. Japan over the years has enjoyed much lower unemployment than the EU, and those countries which lag in new technology gradually become less competitive and lose jobs. Therefore the EU has little alternative – despite the adverse short-term effects of technology – but to encourage the transition from declining industries to expanding new high-technology industries.

The EU does not manifest a general technological lag across all industries. Indeed, in some industries it is strong; for example, in chemicals and nuclear power. In addition, individual countries such as Germany are strong in specific areas such as industrial machinery, while the UK shows potential in biotechnology. The main problem for the EU is not so much technology *per se* but the managerial gap in applying this technology commercially (Sharp 1985, p. 291). The Community has lost market share in high-technology products and has a particular lag in electronics and information technology (IT). This is serious because it affects performance in the various sectors that use electronics and are currently experiencing phenomenal growth. European firms have been confined largely to national markets, failing to achieve adequate economies of scale, R&D and effective innovation. The EU has shown a poor performance in computers, consumer electronics, office equipment, integrated circuits and industrial automation; for example, in robotics European countries have lagged far behind Japan, with a high proportion of robots in the EU being imported (Harrop 1985). The EU has too few companies that are internationally competitive in IT.

The EU is losing ground in high-technology sectors (Jacquemin and Pench 1997, p. 180). This has been manifested over many years by an index of technological specialization, defined as the share of each bloc in world trade in high-technology products, divided by its share of world trade in manufactured products. The EU figure fell from 1.02 in 1963 to 0.88 in 1980, whereas Japan's rose from 0.56 in 1963 to 1.41 in 1980, surpassing the US figure of 1.20 in 1980 (Heertje 1983, p. 102). The EU has a deficit on its trade in high-technology products with both the USA and Japan.

Those countries that are most progressive in terms of innovation capture a larger share of world markets. They are able to keep one step ahead of the NICs, which use more outdated technology. What has been worrying the EU is that it has not been moving up market at a sufficient pace, nor providing sufficient diffusion of innovation quickly enough within the economy. Apart from the pressure by the NICs in the more down-market areas, the EU has been outpaced by Japan and it has failed to cut back on the existing technological gap with the USA. European companies have experienced an inadequate scale of operations in some sectors such as telecommunications because of national purchasing policies. US companies have benefited more from economies of scale, not only in terms of static efficiency and reducing costs of production, but also in terms of dynamic efficiency given the high threshold costs of financing R&D.

Measures to overcome EU disadvantages have focused particularly upon trying to improve competitiveness; the Competitiveness Advisory Group (CAG) was set up in 1995 and has produced several reports. These have highlighted the benefits from continued privatization, nurturing innovative SMEs, and the usefulness of benchmarking performance. European firms have also been at a disadvantage compared with their American counterparts in fields such as patents and trade marks. In order to avoid the costly procedure of applying for separate patent protection in each country, in 1978 the European Patent Convention provided for European patent protection through a single application. Unfortunately a defect was that litigation had to be conducted separately in each country. Instead of a collection of national payments, the EU proposed a single Community patent and specified that the judgement in a Community Patent Court in one member state would be effective throughout the Community. Similarly, progress has been made on trade marks, both in harmonizing them and in introducing a Community Trade Mark which results from a single application to a European Trade Marks Office. Trade marks are important in denoting the origin and quality of goods and it was wasteful for firms which previously had to protect them by making separate applications in each member state.

*Technological co-operation*

Co-operation helps to avoid wasteful duplication and is appropriate in the following conditions: where R&D costs are high; where high risk capital is involved; where some standardization of the product is acceptable; and where the partners are of fairly equal size. But project assessment needs to be an ongoing process to avoid becoming locked into non-viable commercial ventures. Some examples are given in the next section on the aerospace industry.

Since the early 1980s it has become imperative to widen Community funding of collaborative R&D efforts beyond industries such as coal, steel and nuclear power towards other key sectors. This has been done in various framework programmes, beginning with the first one from 1984 to 1987; the second from 1987 to 1991 was underpinned by the SEA, which accorded greater status to R&D policy and enabled specific programmes to be decided by qualified majority voting. The third framework programme from 1990 had an enhanced budget and over a third of its expenditure was concentrated on information and communication technologies. There were also new priorities, such as environmental research and biotechnology, with less emphasis being given to energy research. The fourth framework programme from 1994 continued to increase expenditure, but there have been divisions between member states over the size and pattern of R&D spending, and especially over the movement towards qualified majority voting in this field.

The finance is to support high-quality collaborative research and is not allocated on the basis of quotas, unlike regional funding. It supports basic research which is mainly pre-competitive (at the stage before products are developed for the marketplace) in order not to conflict with EU competition policy. The major form of research support is contracted research, in which the Community normally reimburses up to half of the project costs, the participants raising the rest themselves. In other instances, such as medical research, the EU merely reimburses the co-ordination costs but not the research costs. Finally, the Community carries out its own research in the Joint Research Centre.

The launching of the European Strategic Programme for Research and Development in Information Technology (ESPRIT) in 1983 was a major development. It was centred on five main areas: advanced microelectronics, software technology, advanced information processing, office systems and computer-integrated manufacture. It has been concerned with joint pre-competitive research, with the EU covering up to half the costs of the exercise and industry providing the remainder. Participants have included some leading European electronics companies which have been able to increase their linkages. By the late 1980s ESPRIT was the Community's most costly project, followed by the large JET (Joint European Torus) project. Despite ESPRIT and the JESSI (Joint European Submicron Silicon Initiative) in advanced microchips, the Community has struggled to create a more competitive and strong European electronics industry. The EU's market share for chips and electronic products has fallen, its trade deficit has widened and some of the leading electronics companies have experienced financial difficulties.

The Community has several other significant R&D programmes which have included Research and Development in Advanced Communications Technologies for Europe (RACE) – this has been complementary to ESPRIT and tried to lay the basis for Europe-wide broad-band communications networks in the 1990s. Other R&D programmes for industrial technologies have included Basic Research in Industrial Technologies for Europe (BRITE), launched in 1985, which sought to encourage advanced technology in traditional industries; and European Research in Advanced Materials (EURAM). There are many other acronyms which have gained currency in the new technological Community; for example, Forecasting and Assessment in Science and Technology (FAST); Community Programme for Education and Training in Technologies (COMETT); Biotechnology Research for Innovation, Development and Growth in Europe (BRIDGE); and also the Strategic Programme for Innovation and Technology Transfer (SPRINT).

Another major European research programme of a slightly different kind was the French-inspired EUREKA (European Research Co-ordination Agency). This covered all EC countries plus EFTA countries and Turkey. It was established in July 1985 to give Europe research resources on the same scale as the Strategic Defense Initiative in the USA. It was given no central Community financing, but drew on support from national governments. Both the number of and the funding for EUREKA projects have grown enormously to around ECU 1 billion annually (Midland Bank 1987). Projects are concerned with commercial products that have clear market applications, but with each country favouring particular projects; for example, Germany chose several that were of environmental interest. SMEs have also begun to play a more significant role in EUREKA. Essentially the co-operation is between companies to avoid a highly bureaucratic framework, and there is no automatic state funding. Many high-tech projects have been covered in the civilian sector, close to the marketplace. While many of the larger companies would probably co-operate anyway, EUREKA has induced smaller companies to co-operate much more with each other. The company-level approach, with mainly privately financed schemes, provided a marked contrast with other Community-level projects, such as BRITE, RACE and ESPRIT, in which the EU has met 50 per cent of the cost of projects (Dinkelspiel 1987).

The Community's R&D programme has been too small and in the 1980s accounted for only about 2.5 per cent of the EU's budget and only about 2 per cent of total public and private expenditure on R&D by the member states (Albert and Ball 1983). Since then R&D expenditure has crept steadily upwards so that it absorbs more funding than any other EU policies, apart from those of agriculture and structural funding. Ideally one would like to see R&D funding rising closer to half the EU Budget and half of member states' national spending on R&D. Unfortunately, the mobilization of interest groups has elevated agriculture at the expense of the EU's industrial future, which will revolve particularly around the centrality of a true information society. Since the late 1980s there has been some scaling down of the R&D devoted to the energy sector, so that other costly programmes such as electronics, advanced microchips and high-definition television could take up a larger share of R&D spending. But there have been criticisms that EU financial support has been spread too thinly; that companies become too dependent on financial support and trade protection (with the latter bringing greater competition by location within the EU). A policy of supporting indigenous EU firms thereby becomes more difficult, and some of the latter have turned increasingly towards non-EU links; for example, Siemens with IBM and Toshiba in memory chips and Daimler-Benz with Mitsubishi of Japan in electronics and aerospace. The major European countries with independent R&D strength, and which are making large contributions to the EU Budget, have become cautious about the amount and direction of R&D spending, stressing the need for it to be cost-effective. For example, the UK has sought to restrict expenditure, especially on non-commercially oriented projects, not only in the EU but also in the European Space Agency, yet these have been among the few areas of technological collaboration from which the UK derives a net benefit in the EU.

*Case study of the aerospace industry*

*Nature of the problem* EU co-operation in aerospace was not called for in the Treaty of Rome; the only indirect reference was related to a common transport policy (deemed to extend to air transport). Military affairs are not the preserve of the Community, since these are dealt with by NATO. Why has the EC regarded it as imperative to foster co-operation in aerospace projects? It is partly because these are an essential ingredient of its common industrial and technological policies.

National aircraft industries in Europe are too small to compete effectively on their own against the USA. The dominance of the USA has applied both to military aircraft, stimulated by massive defence expenditure, and to civil aircraft, based upon a large domestic market. Consequently, the country has benefited from economies of scale with long production runs and high productivity, offsetting the higher real wages in the USA (*vis-à vis* the Europeans). The American labour market is very flexible, tending to fluctuate in accordance with demand in terms of 'hire and fire' policies.

The USA accounted for 86 per cent of world aerospace output in 1967 and its share was still 62 per cent in 1987 (with Europe's share having risen from nearly 11 per cent to 27 per cent over the same period). Large scale of production is crucial, with the number of manufacturers diminishing as the size and development cost of aircraft increase. The three American giants in the aerospace industry have been Boeing, McDonnell-Douglas and Lockheed. Subsequent rationalization after the Boeing–McDonnell merger left the company even more firmly in the number one spot; for example, its aerospace sales in mid-1998 were estimated at $55 000 million, followed by Lockheed Martin at $25 500 million. This has put pressure on the British, German and French aerospace industries to merge: Aérospatiale has merged with Matra, and British Aerospace (BAe) with Marconi Electronic Systems. A merger between BAe and Daimler-Benz aerospace combined would have sales of $25 400 million (*Sunday Times Business* 18 October 1998, p. 10).

Some American aeroplanes have enjoyed outstanding success and profitability over the years; for example, the Boeing 727. Up to 1984, when production ended, 1831 had been ordered. Similarly up to 1986, 1732 McDonnell-Douglas DC9s were ordered. The production run of European planes has been lower, but the successful Fokker F-27 had 786 sales, and from 1969 over 421 F-28s were sold. American firms have been dominant throughout the aerospace industry from airframes to engines and from space rocketry to the simpler production of helicopters. In aero-engines, economies of scale are greater than in the production of airframes; hence the market has been dominated by even fewer firms, with American firms Pratt and Whitney and General Electric being world leaders, followed by Rolls-Royce in the UK. R&D costs are enormous, with the result that co-operation has been very much the key word in the industry, and an increasing amount of investment has been made into bigger engines to power the latest generation of wide-bodied aircraft. The commercial payback on engines is nearly twice as long as that for airframe manufacturers. To share out cost, lessen risks and tap new national markets, the big three have all developed international link-ups over the years. For example, General Electric with SNECMA in France, Pratt and Whitney with Daimler-Benz, and Rolls-Royce with BMW in Germany; also, Japanese companies have become minor participants. Finally, in helicopters, American firms have again been dominant, and to remain competitive European co-operation by Aérospatiale with Messerschmitt-Bölkow-Blohm (MBB) created a holding company, making it the world's second largest helicopter concern behind the US company Sikorsky. Also, in 1999 there was a merger between the British company GKN's Westland Helicopters with Agusta in Italy to strengthen further European helicopter production. There is both a large military market and a growing civil market, the latter exemplified by the use of helicopters in North Sea oil development.

*Policy options: independence or co-operation*   One example of an independent company approach was that of Dassault in France: it created the very successful Mirage range of military aircraft. However, even that company was forced to modify its policy, and its failure to agree on the Eurofighter left the company to develop its own fighter aircraft, the Rafale, in which project it sought to interest other European countries such as Belgium and Spain.

An independent policy can prove costly where the market is small and where costs rise excessively; hence co-operation has become the byword in all parts of the industry. Nevertheless, there have been notorious examples of commercial failures of co-operative projects. One such example was the bilateral Anglo-French Concorde project which had both economic and political origins. The UK government also hoped that the project might be helpful in its initial application to join the European Community.

No cost–benefit analysis was ever published for Concorde, though it was shown subsequently that the costs exceeded the benefits (Henderson 1977). The main benefits have been derived from technical 'spin-off' and from the prestige attached to the technical achievement *per se*. If some of these technical advances had never taken place, even if funds had been devoted to such research, then this 'X' element of aerospace co-operation would be invaluable. Many alleged economic benefits both to employment and to the balance of payments did not materialize, and there were also some significant social costs. While all investment decisions are risky, particularly in industries such as aerospace, cost–benefit analysis is essential before decisions are taken; otherwise there is a tendency for some political interest groups to push particular projects vigorously. Unfortunately, once under way they tend to acquire a momentum of their own, for fear of incurring cancellation charges. The escalation of costs and the small number of planes built means that Concorde was a major commercial mistake – though there have been others in other industries, such as the British Advanced Gas-Cooled Reactor in the nuclear industry.

Other types of co-operation have been multilateral in nature, including not only members of the EU but also other European countries, the USA and Japan. Those who support a European solution wish Europe to possess indigenous technology, seeking to exclude outsiders such as the USA. Whatever the type of co-operation, it is vital to secure a long production run to reap economies of scale. The learning curve means that the first aircraft in a series can cost four times as much as the 250th plane produced (see Figure 5.1).

Assume that production is at a limited national output $OQ_n$ on the long-run cost curve, $LAC_1$; then average cost is $OC_n$. If output increased to $OQ_m$, then average cost on $LAC_1$ would fall to $OC_1$. The small national European markets preclude production at such a low cost, though co-operation does enable the production of a higher combined output, $OQ_m$. Unfortunately, the long-run average cost curves are likely to be pushed to the right, because of the costs involved in drawing suitable partners together. They have to decide on a project that matches their different needs, and often the outcome is an over-elaborate and expensive compromise. In addition, the allocation of the work may not be based on comparative advantage but on an equitable distribution between the partners.

Figure 5.1 shows two different scenarios for long-run average cost. In the first of these, on $LAC_2$, co-operation is successful in reducing average

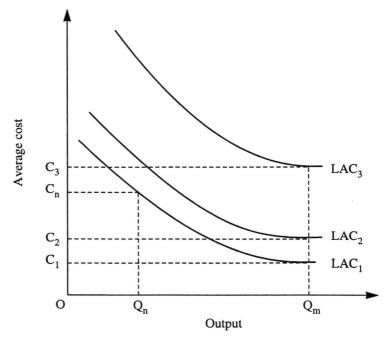

*Figure 5.1   Economies of scale in the aircraft industry*

costs to $OC_2$. This shows the expected reduction in average costs compared with national production. However, if political and bureaucratic influences result in an escalation of expenditure, and partners duplicate production, then a possible scenario is shown on $LAC_3$. In this situation average costs are even higher than in the original national markets! Furthermore, it is possible that the counterfactual is not domestic production but the purchase of aircraft at even lower cost from the USA. Some comparative estimates of alternative costs were made for the Tornado project relative to the F-14, F-15 and F-16 (Hartley 1982, p. 180).

As Tornado production eventually turned down, it became necessary to fill the gap with the new Eurofighter: the plan was originally signed in the mid-1980s for nearly 800 aircraft in total – about 260 each for the UK and Germany, 160 for Italy and 100 for Spain. It is Europe's largest defence programme, but escalating development costs led to doubts about Germany's real commitment to it, and its renegotiation led to a lower-cost plane, renamed the Eurofighter 2000, and a reduced

German order cut down to 150 planes. The initial partnership agreed had been 33 per cent each for the UK and Germany, 21 per cent for Italy and 13 per cent for Spain, but after renegotiation Germany's share was reduced to 21 per cent of the programme. The company set up to manage the venture is jointly owned by the aircraft-producing company in each of the four participating states: BAe, Alenia of Italy, Daimler Chrysler Aerospace (Dasa), and Casa in Spain, with Dasa and Casa deciding to merge in 1999. The production is allocated between the partners, with the UK responsible for building the front fuselage, plus half the right wing; Germany initially for the centre fuselage plus vertical fins; Spain: half of the fuselage plus half of the right wing; finally, Italy: left wing plus half of the aft fuselage. When deliveries start it will be the world's most advanced fighter aircraft and only the American F-22 will be superior, though much more costly. Eurofighter is designed as a highly agile, multi-role aircraft, using the latest technology; for example, high use of carbon-fibre composites, new high-speed engines and very advanced radar.

The main uncertainties relating to the Eurofighter include the huge escalation of costs, along with the slowness in bringing it into production; for example, each plane is costed at £35 million. Apart from some doubts about its technical capabilities *vis-à-vis* its French and American competitors, the ending of the cold war has removed the main enemy, the USSR. It will be important in order to compete on costs with the USA to secure substantial export orders, yet the previous Tornado combat aircraft failed to do this and obtained only one big overseas sale, in Saudi Arabia. If one assumes a similar export market to that of production, that is, just over 600 planes, and if the Eurofighter could get just over half of these, then this would push the production run successfully to around a thousand planes. The Eurofighter aircraft becomes available for export from 2005, with Greece being the first country to place an order for up to 80 Typhoons. There is also significant export potential to Eastern Europe as countries replace their ageing MiGs with new military capacity.

*The success of the Airbus*   Airbus Industrie was set up in 1970 after the signing of a Franco-German agreement in 1969 and an earlier agreement in 1967 which had also included the UK. The latter's ambivalence about the project resulted in only Hawker-Siddeley retaining a toe-hold, but subsequently the UK rejoined the project. Airbus is owned 37.9 per cent by Aérospatiale, 37.9 per cent by MBB (now

Daimler Chrysler Aerospace), 20 per cent by BAe, and 4.2 per cent by Casa of Spain. Specialization in production occurs, with, for example, BAe producing the wings, Dasa the fuselage and Aérospatiale the final assembly. Overemphasis by Airbus on *juste retour* restricted the attainment of full efficiency, and the loosely knit organization with weak central management failed to control costs effectively. Partners haggle for their share of the production, trying to charge the consortium as much as possible for their work, thereby adding to its costs. But Airbus was established as a grouping of mutual economic interests, and in taking that form under French law it maximized co-operation and minimized the amount of disclosure and tax payment. The structure adopted concealed subsidies received, much to the displeasure of the USA. The latter argued that they infringed the rules of GATT, keeping down the price of Airbuses and incurring massive losses. Airbus Industrie defied the USA over this, pointing to Federal Defense contracts which have helped to underpin American plane-makers. Eventually, Airbus agreed to remove production subsidies and to cut R&D subsidies radically. By the 1990s Airbus had started to move into profitability through revised accounting methods and successful sales, and was able to consider establishing a more normal company structure.

In 1970 aircraft manufacturers in the EC had less than a 4 per cent share of the civil market and only a 15 per cent share of the European market itself. By 1982 sales of the A-300 and A-310, as a proportion of total commercial twin-aisle jet sales, were 52 per cent. By the end of 1990 the A-320 had over 600 firm orders, which was the threshold level for its commercial return on invested funds. Airbus Industrie has optimistic forecasts for its share of new aircraft sales and by 1997 Airbus held 41.5 per cent of global orders for civil aircraft and Boeing held 58.5 per cent, which was the first time in its history that Boeing's market share had fallen below 60 per cent.

Success in aircraft production stems from producing a family of planes, and Airbus plans extended this with the A-330, a twin-engine short- to medium-range aircraft with 330 seats, and the A-340, a four-engine long-range aircraft with between 250 and 350 seats. Airbus has succeeded in outselling Boeing on some planes; with the A-330 and the A-340, by incorporating commonality for many parts, it will provide stronger competition across the product range for its American rivals. Meanwhile, Boeing, being behind Europe's A-330, was prompted to commit itself to the 777, defraying part of the cost by a small participation of Japanese producers in building part of the airframe.

Overall, Airbus has been particularly successful in denting the monopoly profits of Boeing. However, consumer benefits were partly restricted because of the weakened incentive of McDonnell-Douglas to compete with Boeing (Neven and Seabright 1995). Furthermore, while the production runs of the Airbus were similar to those of US firms, the development time (that is, for the project to go ahead from first delivery) was longer for Airbus (Martin and Hartley 1995). Problems exist in getting proper co-ordination, and where partners are not treated like sub-contractors, costs may be higher; similarly, costs rise in moving parts between split-site production. Nevertheless, European co-operation across a growing family of planes has provided a significant boost to Europe's civil aerospace and it is important that producers contain the tensions provided by threats to build outside the consortium.

**The UK's industrial dilemma**
The UK's relative industrial decline has given way to absolute decline in many sectors. It has concentrated too much on traditional down-market low-skill and low-technology sectors of production, retaining a higher market share of these than of the up-market areas. For example, in man-made fibres the UK retained a higher share of international rayon than synthetic fibre production, and whereas in the former its plant size in the mid-1980s was similar to that of the USA, its plant size for synthetic fibres was only about a third that of the USA and lower than that of Japan, Germany or Italy. The European man-made fibres industry sought to cut back its massive overcapacity, concentrating on higher-value fibres. The UK has lost ground in textiles to Germany, with the latter's efficient machinery and use of outward processing. Italy has also been a strong competitor in textile products, with its large successful woollen industry based on a flair for design, state enterprise and small firms operating on the fringe of the black economy.

It has been the same story in other industries, such as machine tools, in which product innovation in the UK has been lower than that of its major competitors. The UK lost ground not only to Japan but also to Italy and Germany, which were prominent in developing low-cost machining centres. Germany's strength has been derived from its highly trained, adaptable and multi-skilled workforce. The UK's main deficiency has been in too little investment in education and training, with insufficient engineering graduates and too little provision of basic training. Although the UK was in the forefront of the early application of numerical control in the aircraft industry, it failed to develop as strongly in computer numerical control because of weak upstream links with electronic suppliers and weak downstream links with the firms using machine tools.

UK industrial strategy has been one of increasing dependence on foreign direct investment (FDI). The UK has traditionally been a major source of outward as well as inward FDI. While the ideal would be indigenous industrial resurgence, this dependence on inward invest-ment has offered the only alternative and realistic way for the UK to recover its industrial dynamism, transforming its trade performance in key sectors such as the motor industry. The long dependence on Ameri-can companies has been supplemented by that of Japanese and German producers. With the increasing overcapacity in the industry and intense competition, parts of the Rover Group remain vulnerable to further contraction. But to maintain production in the UK the government offered aid of about £150 million in 1999 for £1.7 billion investment by BMW. The influx of FDI in different sectors has strengthened the trade balance; for example, in televisions the UK has a trade surplus, even though there are no indigenous producers since Ferguson was sold to the French firm of Thomson. In a very open economy, UK companies have been taken over more freely than those in continental Europe. In addition, there have been some highly desirable national brands which have been snapped up by foreign buyers. This applies not just to the motor industry, but also to many others, such as confectionery, with the Rowntree brands falling to the Swiss firm of Nestlé. However, there are dangers from particular types of overseas investment; for example, the sale of ICL to Fujitsu in 1990 marked the strategic loss of Britain's mainframe computer firm, and threatened its right to participate in joint European research projects. It left the British electronics industry in decline, with its main strength being in the lower added-value software sector. Meanwhile, it also contrasted markedly with the French policy of state support both for its own ailing computer-maker, Bull, and for Thomson, the struggling defence and consumer electronics group.

Technologically the UK has fared favourably compared with other countries in terms of the balance between patent receipts and payments and R&D spending; but its performance has declined relatively and the UK stock market forces companies to pursue short-term profitability at the expense of longer-term growth. Meanwhile there has been a maldistribution of technological effort, reflected in an overcommitment to military expenditure, including industries such as aerospace. Other industries have been starved of technological manpower, while new technology which might have been transferred to them has been locked away in defence establishments. This weakness has been recognized by government emphasis on new technology transfer trying to prise some commercial use out of the technology located in the Ministry of Defence. Private industrial R&D in the UK has been low in comparison with its major competitors, such as Germany. While research is important, the UK has often been less successful in the crucial development for the marketplace. Just one example of this is carbon-fibre technology, which was developed by the UK aerospace industry, yet Japan has subsequently dominated its production.

Since the end of the Second World War, given the massive British government outlay on aircraft launch aid, less than 10 per cent of its expenditure has been recovered. Despite a few successful planes and the strong position of Rolls-Royce engines, successive British governments have come round to the view that co-operation is essential on financial grounds. The dilemma is what form the co-operation should take, and whether it is to be predominantly with other countries in Europe or with the USA. For example, the Westland Helicopters affair in the 1980s reflected the continuing pull of American producers and the tension over British participation in European programmes.

The UK supports the principle of subsidiarity in R&D, failing at times to make EU funding fully additional. It has recognized that where international co-operation is critical in reducing the costs of R&D, projects need to be chosen judiciously; for example, it has learnt from past experience, such as the expensive commercial flop of Concorde. The multilateral Airbus project is more successful, though British government finance has been limited, despite new launch aid for participation in the A-330 and A-340 Airbuses. The UK has also favoured other forms of wider European-based co-operation such as EUREKA, since it is directed towards more privately funded activities and applied technology. The conditions for participation in co-operative products have to meet stringent criteria. These include increasingly regular evaluation; efficient administration; and an *à la carte* menu from which the UK can choose projects in which to participate.

# 6 Energy, transport and environmental policies

## Introduction

Whilst each of these policy areas can be treated separately, it seems sensible to bring them together in a single chapter since they are increasingly interconnected. For example, agriculture, industry, energy (production and consumption) and transport are major sources of environmental pollution. In recent years there has been increasing environmental concern about pollution from coal-burning power stations, while in transport there is increasing recognition that the continued growth of road transport needs to be limited in the interests of the environment. The EU's fifth environmental programme, 1993–2000, included emphasis on reducing consumption of non-renewable energy sources and also placed emphasis on more efficient and environmentally friendly transport policies.

Energy policy lay at the heart of integration in the ECSC and Euratom. Also, rail transport was significant in the ECSC, but transport, especially road transport, became more central when the EEC was established, though on environmental grounds rail has come back into favour. Environmental policy was not on the original agenda of the Community, but came later, after the early 1970s, and has grown significantly.

An economic strategy is critical for energy and transport, since these involve high investment costs over a long period of time for uncertain future returns. Underinvestment in EU energy projects results in critical and vulnerable overdependence on oil imports. Underinvestment in transport results in higher cost and inefficient distribution, which adversely affects economic performance. The level of investment determines economic success, while in turn rising GNP creates a demand for even more energy inputs and transport infrastructure. These have major environmental implications for the use of resources and effects on pollution. Policy choices are made on economic grounds, steered by intervention between different types of energy: coal, oil, gas, nuclear and renewables. Likewise, there are choices between different forms of transport: road, rail, water (sea and inland waterways) and air transport. Environmental considerations are increasingly taken into account, with governmental intervention to support renewable energy sources, though these currently constitute a minority of energy provision.

## Energy, transport and the environment

*Energy*

*Problems of the energy sector*    There is strong competition between different energy sources, and the EU has seen a continued movement from a mono-fuel economy (coal) to a bi-fuel economy (coal and oil) and towards a multi-fuel economy. There has been a significant change in the relative importance of different energy sources since the early days of the ECSC. For example, historically coal was the most important energy source, powering the first industrial revolution. Even where coal was not particularly competitive, as in Germany, utilities were obliged to buy coal from high-cost local suppliers. This policy was tolerated by the EC, especially post-1973 with the emphasis on security of supply. By the 1990s, with energy surpluses reappearing and the slump in demand, other countries, such as the UK (having privatized the industry), closed much of it down, including mines that were efficient by EU standards. This has also been reinforced by environmental concerns about the adverse effects of coal-burning power stations.

The competitive pressure on coal came originally from oil, which is more versatile, especially for transport. The oil industry has a highly oligopolistic structure and the companies are also highly integrated, especially vertically. Despite the bias towards private-sector ownership, a few state-controlled companies have existed, for example, in France, Italy and Portugal. Unlike the coal industry, where the EU has been largely self-sufficient (though it also imported coal at low prices from the rest of the world), oil has predominantly been imported. Although North Sea oil production has made a huge difference in this respect, especially for the UK and the Netherlands, profitability from extraction is far lower because of the much higher costs than in the desert of the Middle East. In the UK, only a small amount of oil has been found on land, and even its extraction has run into environmental opposition because of the intrusion of 'nodding donkeys' into rural environments.

The most dramatic growth in recent years has been in natural gas, which previously seemed set on a declining trend. The industry is dominated by large companies and has generally been in public owner-ship, apart from in the UK and Germany. There has been significant vertical integration, with the transmission companies which carry and import the gas being very prominent.

Electricity has grown very rapidly; its supply can be generated from a variety of primary energy sources. There is a choice between coal- or gas-fired stations (which are currently very much in vogue) and nuclear power. Gas-powered stations have been attractive in terms of cost be-cause of lower investment and short construction time. For example, for gas-generated electricity the investment constitutes about 20 per cent of the cost and the fuel cost is some 80 per cent. This contrasts with the huge financial risks resulting from the long period of return involved in heavy investment in coal, nuclear or hydroelectric power plants, in which most of the cost of electricity comes from capital investment and little from the fuel itself. The electricity sector in the past was organized on a national basis and under monopoly control. Despite some marginal continental links, such as those between the UK and France, they were mainly for emergencies, such as repairs, and peak demand. Lack of competition resulted in very different price levels, being lower in countries such as France, which rely heavily on nuclear supply. The single market has now been extended to electricity, with liberalization proposed in 1992 and the hope for full liberalization by 2005.

*Case for, and progress towards, a common energy policy*   The case for a common policy was to ensure that industries competed as much as possible on equal terms and that their products were competitive. Hence energy policy lay at the roots of the ECSC, which was mainly con-cerned with a competitive market; it was also important to ensure fair competition in the iron and steel industry, in which energy costs ac-count for a significant proportion of the value of the product. However, policy throughout has had to reconcile a competitive market with some intervention, which has taken place to deal with supply crises and to improve indigenous production potential. Euratom was likewise con-structed with a view to competition rather than regulation. Its main concern was in fostering extensive research into nuclear power, particu-larly in joint ventures. However, nuclear power has not developed as rapidly as expected. Although Euratom was established at the right time, after the Suez Crisis had raised oil prices, subsequently lower oil prices during the 1960s weakened Euratom. A further difficulty was that the French preferred national control. There have also been problems with European technology and a tendency for countries to use American pressurized water reactors (PWRs). Whilst nuclear power is competitive economically there are additional costs, incurred not just from building nuclear power stations but also from decommissioning older stations in the future. Nuclear accidents such as Chernobyl have shown the dangerous fallout and the environmental dilemma. Apart from the insidious environmental consequences locally for workers and residents, nuclear power scores on one important environmental aspect: it does not emit greenhouse gases.

The EEC Treaty which covered natural gas, electricity and crude oil was also oriented towards creating a competitive market. It was recognized that a competitive market was crucial in maintaining low-cost energy inputs to ensure the success of EU industry. This was particularly important to the heavy industrial users of energy. After the merger of the separate Communities, the Commission's first guidelines in 1968 towards a common energy policy continued this competitive approach. However, there has also been strong recognition of the need to reconcile this with security of supply, demonstrated by the growing dependence on oil imports after the Suez Crisis in 1956 which led to the closure of the Suez Canal. This encouraged a search for alternative energy supplies which were found in the Middle East and also in Nigeria, while Russia also entered the oil market as a big seller. The vulnerability of the EC was shown even more significantly during the 1970s; for example, in 1973, when the OPEC price rise showed its vulnerability to exploitation. OPEC used its new-found power politically as a way of exerting Arab pressure against Israel. In addition, it seized the opportunity to use its co-operative strength to improve its return. Furthermore, the countries in OPEC would be able to husband their reserves since the capital value of oil left under the ground would potentially provide an even better rate of return. The EC was highly vulnerable to outside actions and its response was initially fragmented, with the first cutting off of oil supplies to the Netherlands leaving the Community in disarray. Both the UK and France tried to do separate deals with individual Arab countries. It became necessary for Western Europe to create, if possible, sufficient monopsony power to match the OPEC monopoly. The aftermath of the oil crisis was economic stagflation and balance-of-payments deficits, though the latter were alleviated partly on the capital account since OPEC invested its new-found wealth back in to Western financial markets. While the increase in price naturally led to a significant reduction in demand, the fact is that demand for oil for some uses such as transport is fairly inelastic and therefore the bill for oil soared.

The oil crisis of the 1970s created a new focus on the need to create greater security of supply. This involved developing indigenous energy supplies more, notably nuclear power, and also providing Community funding for renewable energy sources such as wood, wind and water power, though it is recognized that these can only provide a small part of total energy supply. After a further crisis resulting from another hike in oil prices, action by the EC in 1979 reduced the coefficient between GNP and energy demand, which had been just over 1 in the 1960s to 0.7 or less by 1990.

The EC, despite some lack of co-ordination, proposed a new energy strategy, setting out not just forecasts but specific objectives for future energy supplies. These included an overall reduction in total energy consumption by pursuing more efficient energy use, involving cutting consumption losses and increasing R&D energy expenditure towards conservation. The EC also tried to change the composition of fuels, significantly reducing oil supply and raising the contribution of other energy sources, such as natural gas, nuclear energy, and temporarily reversing the decline of the coal industry. It also had a closer look at other renewable forms of energy, though these were essentially long-term. Initially the EC had to survive in the short run and hence undertook a variety of measures such as sharing supplies and stockpiling (raising oil-stock levels from 65 to 90 days of consumption). It considered introducing minimum stock levels for coal and nuclear fuels, and proposed that a minimum level of fuel stocks at power stations should be made compulsory. It also set a target of reducing oil consumption to a level of 40 per cent of primary energy consumption. The Community has been helped in its objectives of reducing energy consumption, particularly of oil, by the de-industrialization of major energy-intensive industries, and extra-EU import dependence has been reduced further by the availability of North Sea oil. Nevertheless, EU import dependence of just under half of gross consumption could rise to over two-thirds by 2020 (Commission 1996). The EU energy balance for 1990 and 1995 is shown in Table 6.1.

After the mid-1980s and the focus on enhanced competition through the SEM, there was further reinforcement of the original competitive orientation of energy policy; for example, by making prices more transparent. Despite significant progress, the EU only provided a framework

*Table 6.1*    *EU energy balance, 1990 and 1995*

| | Million tonnes oil equivalent | |
| --- | --- | --- |
| | 1990 | 1995 |
| <u>Primary production</u> | 706.99 | 707.74 |
| Solids | 209.86 | 133.33 |
| Oil | 117.46 | 134.13 |
| Gas | 137.31 | 162.33 |
| Nuclear | 181.31 | 205.21 |
| Renewable energy | 61.05 | 72.74 |
| <u>Net imports</u> | 646.23 | 697.34 |
| Solids | 88.68 | 106.04 |
| Oil | 462.73 | 475.31 |
| Natural gas | 92.49 | 114.74 |
| Electricity | 2.33 | 1.25 |

*Source*:    Commission, *European Energy to 2020*, Spring 1996.

of policy and failed to include a chapter on energy in the Maastricht Treaty, simply incorporating energy in its list of objectives and referring to it under the Environment title. The problems of reaching an effective common policy have occurred partly because each of the member states has different strengths and positions in each of the energy markets. Some, such as the Netherlands, are motivated by strength in oil and natural gas, whilst others, such as Italy, which was a relatively uninhibited importer of oil from third countries, are much more vulnerable and dependent on imports. Other countries with greater dependence on a high-cost coal industry tried to defend themselves by heavy import taxes on oil, but eventually had to contend with rationalization. This severely affected countries such as France and Belgium, leaving only the significant coal-producing countries of Germany and Spain, both heavily subsidized, and the UK, which enjoys a wealth of energy resources of all types. Given the difficulties of reaching rapid agreement about the problems, any progress is just as likely to occur outside as inside the EU; for example, via the International Energy Agency (an OECD body), which has also concluded agreements on similar policies such as reducing imported-oil consumption, stockpiling and sharing supplies. Both globally and in the EU, energy policy has had to be even more consistent with environmental concerns and these are the focus of a later section in this chapter.

## Transport

*Rationale for intervention*   Demand for transport has grown with increased movement of goods by businesses for sale and for deliveries, with some being engaged in 'just-in-time' production, with low stocks necessitating speedy delivery of parts. There is also much greater demand by the general public for better transport to facilitate movement. The transport sector has been dominated by governmental intervention for various reasons, since transport creates both positive and negative externalities. Positive externalities result from a transport infrastructure which, once provided, creates the facilities for goods and people to be moved around and from which all can benefit. But it also has some negative externalities in terms of congestion and pollution, especially with the massive growth of road transport. Hence the Commission has considered ways of internalizing costs by road pricing.

There is also the huge capital investment required in transport infrastructure, tending to involve large monopoly carriers, for example, in railways and airlines. These have been able to benefit from economies of scale, but the existence of state-owned monopoly carriers has conflicted with EU preference to move towards a more liberal competitive policy. In pursuing this, safeguards are built in for social obligations, such as subsidies for rail services to cater for specific socioeconomic benefits.

*The case for, and progress in, a common transport policy*   There was an explicit commitment in the Treaty of Rome to establish a common transport policy. This was because cheap transport is the means for opening up trade and specialization. It was necessary to prevent countries from maintaining transport under national control, creating discrimination against others and distorting international competition. The Dutch, in particular, lying at the heart of the EU, have been keenest on extending competition. It has been possible to accelerate the growth of trade by bringing down transport costs through promoting greater competition, so that transport costs become of diminishing significance in industrial location (Chisholm 1995 cites a variety of *ex ante* and *ex post* studies). Furthermore, transport costs often do not increase very much with distance since prices charged reflect uniform delivery prices quoted to customers irrespective of distance.

Despite the commitment to a common transport policy, progress was tortuous, especially in the early years, because of conflicting levels of state intervention. There was the Schaus Memorandum of 1961, followed in 1962 by an action programme to create a common transport policy on a competitive basis. The common transport policy has been concerned to eliminate discrimination between carriers on grounds of nationality and to avoid distortions in prices caused by frontier controls. However, some compromise was necessary in moving towards market prices by setting a price band, with maximum and minimum limits beyond which prices could not be driven. These limits were necessary because of the nature of supply and demand elasticities in which, for example, prices could be driven too low by excessive competition from commercial vehicle owners with their heavy fixed costs, probably without much increase in demand for carriage (particularly if the economy were in recession). The spread of prices was fixed at 23 per cent and later widened to around 45 per cent. Critical issues were whether the system should cover all forms of transport and be applied to both international and domestic transport, and whether it was to be a compulsory-rate bracket or merely for reference purposes. In practice there was a compulsory rate for international traffic for road and rail, with reference rates only for domestic traffic, and reference rates for international inland waterway traffic.

Road freight transport dominates domestic markets and has grown rapidly in international traffic. This has been assisted by deregulation of road haulage, and freedom of cabotage was set from 1997. Policy revolves around the general principle of getting users and polluters to pay, with operator prices to reflect all the true costs imposed on society. In other words, there is an attempt to internalize the external costs of congestion, accidents and pollution, with road transport responsible for most of these external costs. The aim is to get a better balance between road and rail, with railways being re-regulated to allow competitive access for international traffic.

For road freight operators it was also necessary for the Commission to harmonize the national quantitative and qualitative licensing systems for the carriage of goods to ensure that Community hauliers could transport goods across national boundaries without discrimination. It was also vital to ensure that carriers would no longer be operating uneconomically, returning home with empty vehicles because they had been unable to pick up another load. Progress was also made towards harmonizing the size of Euro-lorries, fuel taxation, and driving hours and working conditions by setting a maximum driving time enforced by the installation of tachographs in commercial vehicles.

*Acceleration and modal spread of policy*   Renewed impetus to the development of a successful transport policy was given by the recognition after the first enlargement of the EC that maritime and air transport would need to be included, and also by the actions taken by the European Parliament which took the Council of Ministers to the European Court of Justice (ECJ) in 1983 for failure to implement the common transport policy. In 1985 the Court ruled that the Council was violating the Treaty. A new push was given by the setting up of the Single European Market and by a new Article in the Treaty which laid down that SEM measures, including those for transport, would be implemented by majority vote.

The extension of the common transport policy to cover both shipping and civil aviation has also represented further significant progress. With regard to shipping and aviation, the issue of national carriers has been particularly contentious *vis-à-vis* that of promoting lower-cost operators. For example, in shipping the Community faced competition from low-cost fleets in Eastern Europe and LDCs. UNCTAD (United Nations Conference on Trade and Development) laid down a 40 : 40 : 20 split for liner trade between fleets of the countries of origin, of destination and of third-country fleets. The EU has applied this to trade with LDCs, but with a free-market low-cost approach to intra-EU trade and OECD trade. The entry of Greece, with its large competitive fleet, into the Community reinforced a more liberal approach. The EU also monitored port development, trying to ensure some control on excessive port subsidies, and has also encouraged safety programmes to fight oil pollution at sea, and so on.

Finally, it is air transport that has been the major new preoccupation of the EU in recent years. Air transport has grown rapidly in importance for tourist and business travel, plus the carriage of higher-value low-weight goods. Apart from charter travel, which offered very competitive prices, most air travel was highly regulated by the International Air Transport Authority (IATA) controlling prices and leading to a situation in which there was weak competition and a dominance of a few state-owned national carriers. Airlines agreed on routes and the division of revenue between the carriers, precluding competition from other foreign carriers. Pressures for change were created by the demonstration effect of competition from the more efficient and deregulated American carriers, though geographically Europe is smaller, with shorter trips, making other forms of transport highly competitive, particularly railways. The size of airline operator has also been smaller in Europe than in the USA. Apart from the US example, the UK and the Netherlands, with liberal preferences, privatized their state airlines and were competing for transatlantic business. They wished to see more competition created and their wishes ultimately prevailed.

Despite reservations, particularly by less efficient Mediterranean states such as Greece and Spain, which cross-subsidized loss-making routes (especially to islands), there were underlying developments underpinning EU changes in air transport. The opening up of air transport developed from qualified majority voting on transport policy after the SEA, which made it more difficult for governments to block progress. The SEM, with its neo-liberal agenda, also extended to air transport. Competition policy was also deemed to apply; for example, there was the European Court of Justice ruling in the case of Nouvelles Frontières in 1986, which was allowed to continue selling airline tickets at low prices.

Progress has been made in stages, and after 1987 airlines were given the right to continue further on outward flights; for example, British Airways could fly to Paris and then fly onwards to, say, Rome and other cities. On so-called 'thick' routes such as London–Paris, each side could designate an additional carrier, for example BA plus one other. After 1992 there was progressive opening of all intra-EU routes, including cabotage rights to fly onwards within the same internal market. Full cabotage, however, was postponed until 1997. In 1993 there was regulation on slot allocation and 1996 on ground handling. Competition rules have also been applied to abuses of dominant position and concerted practices, with Article 86 applied to dominant positions and Article 85 to anti-competitive agreements between airlines. In particular, the mergers between airlines and the support of state subsidies require very careful monitoring. Dominant airlines have had to abandon some routes, often with other smaller airlines flying them on their behalf.

*Trans-European Networks*  During the 1990s there was renewed emphasis on linking up the transport networks between member states. Funding has long been available for this from the European Investment

Bank (EIB), not just for grand schemes such as the Channel Tunnel, but also for many other transport projects. The acronym used for Trans-European Networks is TENs. The TENs action programme of 1990 was incorporated into the Maastricht Treaty, which provided the legal base for a common infrastructure policy. The Treaty also specifically earmarked Cohesion Funds for TENs, under which the Cohesion countries agreed not to reduce their own public expenditure on transport and the environment.

The focus on TENs has been driven by a variety of influences which, apart from reinforcing a competitive single market, include contributing to more balanced regional development which is vital in a large union. Between agreeing and ratifying the Maastricht Treaty, the TENs initiatives also became linked to the need to create employment opportunities reflected in proposals of the 1993 Delors White Paper on Competitiveness, Growth and Unemployment. To some extent it was akin to Keynesian public-works-type schemes, in which expenditure via the multiplier process could make inroads into very heavy unemployment through prioritizing construction and improvement of infrastructure.

The Essen European Council in December 1994 agreed on 14 priority TENs projects. These projects were important in reflecting some shift from road to rail transport. For example, they included many high-speed rail links, hoping to make rail travel more competitive with road and air traffic. Furthermore, transport expenditure and policy by the EU has also recognized the need to involve other countries with which trade is growing, such as the Central and East European Countries (CEECs), and which are also affected by positive and negative externalities. Proposals include a new east–west motorway, and later a north–south motorway from the Baltic to the Mediterranean.

### Environment

*The rationale of policy intervention*    There is a strong case for governmental intervention in environmental policy, since the assignment of property rights, though helpful, is not always feasible in many instances. It is important to ensure that market prices reflect the full costs of production, not only the marginal private costs (MPC) incurred by business, but also the marginal social costs (MSC) created by negative externalities in production or consumption.

Referring to Figure 6.1, in a free market, price would be OP and quantity OQ. Hence there is overproduction which creates excess pol-

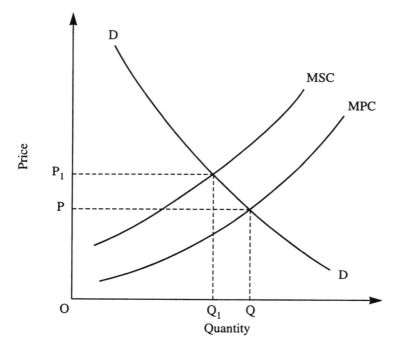

*Figure 6.1   Marginal social cost pricing*

lution. The optimum price environmentally is $OP_1$, leading to lower demand and hence lower output $OQ_1$. This can be achieved through imposing a tax which would be the difference between MPC and MSC at output $OQ_1$. Green taxes have been used widely, for example, in the motor industry by raising petrol prices and also having a differential between a higher price for leaded, compared with unleaded, petrol. Apart from imposing taxes, governments can impose production standards to reduce output to $OQ_1$, and reliance on standards has been the approach favoured by the EU.

The case for a common EU policy is that if one member state alone were to take action whilst other members states did not, and continued to allow firms to charge OP, this would make the environmentally conscious countries uncompetitive. Hence this reinforces the need for a common policy to maintain fair competition. However, there are other powerful reasons for the EU to become involved in a common environmental policy because of the cross-border nature of pollution in the rivers (such as the Rhine) and seas, and airborne pollution. If one country takes action alone, others would free-ride on the benefits. Therefore there developed a slow recognition that there was a strong underlying justification for the EU to be responsible mainly for environmental policy, and also to participate in a global forum to tackle the concerns with deterioration of the global environment. Meanwhile, future Central and East European enlargement of the EU will reinforce environmental policy further since there are even greater environmental problems. These have been left by heavy polluting industries which were formerly concerned with meeting planned output targets, with underpriced inputs and little concern with the adverse consequences of environmental degradation.

*Types of pollution and EU policy progress*   During the 1950s the main concern was with economic recovery and growth, and not so much with environmental issues. To the extent that problems were identified, they were seen more on a localized basis, such as the creation of smog through burning coal in industry and households. After the early 1970s there was much more global awareness of environmental issues – acid rain, global warming and depletion of the ozone layer. There was also recognition of the limits to growth that could result from resource depletion and pollution. Environmental policies were not covered in the Treaty of Rome, but only came on to the agenda after the Paris Summit in 1972. The First Action Programme in 1973 was concerned with trying to clear up pollution, especially on the basis of the 'polluter-pays' principle. This applies throughout to all types of pollution, including waste, where owners are required to finance the waste disposal. In the 1970s there was focus on issues such as dangerous substances; the chemical industry, for example, is subject to very stringent regulation. The Seveso incident in 1976 led to stronger efforts to prevent major industrial hazards, the control on the classification of dangerous substances and the transport and elimination of certain toxic substances. In relation to water regulation, a vast body of legislation has developed. A key question is whether to have quality standards or to impose emission standards for water pollution, with the latter being stricter in setting maximum quantities for the pollutants. The EU has given most priority to emission standards with limits set for dangerous substances, such as those in drinking water. Quality standards have also been set, with regular sampling, to improve drinking-water quality, and for bathing water, fishing water and urban waste water.

In 1981 DGXI was established for environmental policy. This created new impetus and in the early 1980s the Community's environmental policies broadened and extended beyond humans to include the protection of flora and fauna. There was much more focus on trying to prevent pollution; there was also resource management and environmental impact assessment, with the latter being proposed in 1980 and a directive implemented in 1985. EU policy has been extended to cover both noise pollution and pollution of the atmosphere. In the case of the former, both optional and binding standards exist. These apply to motor vehicles, motor cycles, construction plant equipment, household appliances, lawnmowers and aircraft. Member states cannot refuse to import products meeting these standards. The Community's policy towards atmospheric pollution developed following its ratification of the 1979 Geneva Convention on transboundary atmospheric pollution. Limit values were fixed for emission of certain polluting substances, and those by large plants. Directives were introduced for sulphur dioxide, nitrogen dioxide, lead, chlorofluorocarbons, carbon dioxide and other greenhouse gases. There have also been limitations imposed on polluting emissions, such as lead and benzene in petrol, sulphur content in gas and oil and emissions from motor vehicles.

After the SEA a further and significant step forward was made when articles relating to the environment were inserted into the Treaty and the supportive role of the EP was increased. The important principle of majority voting was introduced for all aspects of the single market (such as product harmonization), though environmental protection still required unanimity. The Maastricht Treaty firmed up the legal base of the SEA, which has provided for a massive growth of environmental legislation. The Amsterdam Treaty signed in 1997 enshrined the principle of sustainable development and further extended majority voting on environmental policy, but with unanimity still required on some aspects such as environmental taxation. Under Scandinavian influence particularly, member states can continue to introduce stricter national environmental legislation subject to approval by the Commission.

During the 1990s attention turned towards the environmental component in other policy areas, such as energy and transport (and agriculture), along with sustainable use of resources. Also, atmospheric pollution measures have been introduced to limit emissions from coal-burning power stations and from commercial vehicles and cars. In improving air quality some countries wanted limits on pollution, whilst others challenge the risk-assessment seeking target zones, and a few countries pressed for derogations to cater for their specific problems. The longer Fifth Action Programme (1993–2000) was important in promoting more market-based measures and also in supplementing existing financial expenditure through the Structural Funds by an additional Financial Instrument for the Environment. This also extends to other countries around the Mediterranean and the Baltic, and exceptionally to regional and global problems connected to international agreements. Policies have passed increasingly to the EU level, with notable developments including the 1990 directive on freedom of access to information on the environment, and the EU's general consultative forum on the environment which is consulted by the Commission. The EU also has an eco-label award scheme for non-dangerous products which meet eco-logical criteria; the label improves consumer information on these environmentally friendly products (Barrass and Madhavan 1996, pp. 217–18). The EU's focus on directives has allowed those states with existing environmental legislation to amend this, while others for which it has been new have virtually reproduced the text of the direc-tives. However, the directives have suffered from slow application, and more recently the EU has turned to the adoption of regulations that take effect more rapidly and apply directly throughout the Community. Mem-ber states are very active with environmental enforcement and implementation, plus national issues such as countryside use.

There has been strong environmental pressure from those member states with high national environmental standards, such as Denmark, the Netherlands and Germany. The influence of the Green Parties has been of growing significance; for example, with the Red–Green coali-tion in the Schröder government, which replaced the Kohl government in 1998. To ensure that environmental degradation is prevented and safeguarded, the EU follows the polluter-pays principle as much as possible. The EU insists on all projects being subjected to Environmen-tal Impact Assessment (EIA). During the 1990s the EU also established an Environmental Agency based in Copenhagen, whose main task has been to collect statistics and information, publish reports and monitor enforcement; it also covers several non-EU countries.

*Conflicting problems*   Despite great legislative progress, with many directives on environmental issues, policy progress has been constrained by conflicts with other objectives and interests. For example, there is a trade-off between environmental costs and economic growth (and em-ployment), even though in the long run there may be little alternative to environmental expenditure for sustainable growth to occur in the long term. In particular, many industries object to the imposition of extra costs arising from strong environmental pressure groups. For example, they attribute the additional costs being imposed on European industry to the strong environmental lobbying, particularly in Germany, which in turn is most able to benefit from its lead in new environmental technology. There is concern by the countries with weaker environmental standards, especially in Southern Europe and elsewhere, about the excessively high national standards, such as German or Danish laws on companies having to take back and recycle packaging. Companies in other member states fear that this will have an adverse effect on their own exports. The Commission has a difficult task in trying to harmonize environmental policy somewhere between the competing levels of minimum and maximum standards.

In the search for environmental improvement a difficult balance has had to be reached between the costs and the benefits. Some environmentalists would like to push to the extreme of eliminating nearly all pollution, while the general consensus is that the costs of trying to eliminate all pollution would be excessive and not feasible. Hence it is necessary to equate the marginal benefit from further pollution control with the marginal cost of creating an equilibrium outcome. There have also been some policy differences between the different DGs in the Commission, leading to conflict of views in environmental matters. Environmental policy effectiveness has been constrained by materialism and consumerism, with some member states and local governments being slow to implement directives because of local resistance and added costs. While the Maastricht Treaty ushered in majority voting on environmental matters, it also brought in the issue of subsidiarity which could unfortunately lead to even poorer compliance with legislation in countries lacking the will to conform fully to EU environmental policy.

**Policy problems in the UK**
The UK has had problems with some parts of all of these policies. For example, it has a very heavy dependence on energy, not just as a user but also as a producer. The UK has a wealth of alternative energy sources, making it the strongest energy supplier in the EU and hence shaping its preference for a more market-based approach to policies. Although having a large and efficient coal industry, particularly in Yorkshire and Nottinghamshire, it has been able to afford the luxury of closing down much of its industry, partly as a consequence of Thatcherite

policies aimed at lessening of power of the mining trade unions and also to prepare the industry for profitable privatization. For example, in the coal industry this led to a massive programme of pit closures, whereas less efficient German coal mines were kept open by subsidy. Furthermore, the UK's early lead in nuclear power was not consolidated because of problems in choice of reactor types and delays in construction of some new nuclear power stations. The most significant and unexpected development was the discovery of North Sea oil and gas, with the increase in world oil prices increasing the rate of exploration and, along with new technology, making production profitable despite the much higher costs of extraction at sea than in the Middle East.

With regard to transport the UK has been dependent on differing modes of transport, relying more on roads and maritime transport, and less on rail and inland waterways, than continental Europe. For example, the percentage of total goods transported by road in the UK in 1995 was up to 90 per cent which was higher than in nearly all other countries, apart from Sweden. The UK has also had a more liberal policy orientation compared with the more interventionist approach in many continental countries. In road transport, the haulage industry in the UK had harmonization problems and was initially reluctant to accept stricter limits on working hours which raised its costs, and the introduction of the tachograph, which measures conformity with the new driving limits, was an unpopular measure. Similarly, agreements on the harmonization of weights and dimensions for commercial vehicles involved particular problems of adjustment for domestic producers of such vehicles. Increasing the axle weight and tonnage of vehicles necessitated a derogation for the UK and Ireland with their lower size limits, but over the years the trend has been to carriage by bigger lorries. For the UK the introduction of the 40–tonne lorry weight for international journeys was delayed until 1999, although even bigger lorries can be used for the movement of railhead containers. The EU policy of granting commercial vehicle licences by quantity rather than quality was also out of line with UK practice.

Continental countries have provided greater governmental finance for rail transport, whereas the UK has adopted a more commercial approach, covering a higher proportion of its operating costs from revenue. The contrast in rail systems is now very marked, with new investment in high-speed trains in continental Europe, such as the French TGVs, contrasting strongly with the underinvestment in UK railways, outside the main east coast line. For example, the lack of a high-speed rail link to the Channel Tunnel can be compared unfavourably with the rapid speed of connection in France. At least in relation to airlines, the more liberal UK approach has spread in the EU, partly because of EU competition policy. However, there is still a constraint provided by greater state support for some continental airlines, compared with BA. While the EU has significantly affected UK transport policy, the UK has also been able to exercise some influence in the EU by pushing it towards a more liberal approach.

In relation to the environment, the UK has also faced significant problems, since it tended to have lower standards than many North European countries. The UK lacked the strong environmental party pressure from the Greens (partly because of the 'first past the post' electoral system in the UK). Because of its geographical position, it was also able to dispose of its effluent in its fast-flowing rivers and into the sea, hence opposing uniform continental emission standards. The UK was particularly concerned with the high costs of cleaning up the environment and the extension of the EU legal base to cover environmental matters; it would prefer subsidiarity to apply in many aspects of policy. While the UK has had no particular problem in relation to single-market aspects, directives extending to other areas, such as bathing-water and drinking-water quality, have met resistance because of the costs involved in complying with the very high standards imposed. The privatized water companies, which are in effect regional monopolies, have had to raise prices to consumers well above the general rate of inflation to finance the additional environmental investment costs. The UK was dilatory in complying with EU directives on both bathing and drinking water; for example, it was taken to the ECJ because of excessive nitrates in water. EU measures for a carbon dioxide tax in 1992 to reduce emissions contributing to global warming also posed particular problems for the UK and were blocked.

# 7 Regional and social problems and policies

## Tackling the core–periphery problem

### Economic characteristics of regions

The uneven pace of economic development and changing comparative advantage have resulted in spatial imbalance. There are centripetal forces based upon market size in which companies benefit from increasing returns to scale (Krugman 1998). Businesses that are concentrated at the core of the European Union market maximize sales and reduce transport costs, though the latter may be of diminished significance nowadays (Chisholm 1995). Businesses also reap economies of scale and benefit from all the linkages backwards and forwards with suppliers and customers. The central core area of the EU can be conceived as lying in north-west Europe in the golden triangle running from London to Paris and encompassing most of Belgium and much of the Netherlands. In addition, the so-called blue banana runs in the shape of a banana through the golden triangle down through West German cities such as Bonn and Frankfurt, through part of Switzerland and Austria and into northern Italy, including cities such as Milan (Williams 1996). The core still possesses important attributes such as converging transport networks, plentiful high-tech activities and a strong service sector, all of which are favourable to dynamic economic development. Capital cities dominate core areas and are in increasingly global competition with one another for specific roles, such as London and Frankfurt financially, Brussels as the political capital of the EU and Berlin as the new capital of the reunified Germany.

Less prosperous areas, on the other hand, comprise a multiplicity of problems, encompassing both industrial decline and a failure in some areas to take off even into successful industries. An example of the former is staple industries which were drawn in the past to locations on or near the coal fields and have since declined. Industrial areas with overspecialization and overconcentration on traditional industries (that is, with specialization and concentration location quotients greater than 1, where 1 is the national average) have declined, leading to regional and urban decay. The periphery of the EU is less industrialized and more rural, with a lower level of economic development. There is a dependence upon the supply of primary products of agriculture and fisheries. Agricultural problem areas comprise both underdeveloped areas and developed agricultural areas in which employment has inexorably declined. There are also border areas which have experienced problems resulting from their peripheral situation, though some of these have been lessened internally by the creation and enlargement of the EU. For instance, France has been able to open up its eastern border areas, while even its peripheral coastal regions have improved; for example, Brittany benefited from the development of the deep-water port at Roscoff, providing a link to the south-west of England. Both the EU and the Council of Europe have encouraged border area co-operation, in which a better transport network has been the key to linking up regions. German reunification, whilst accentuating regional differentials, has moved the border problem further east.

To what extent are free-market forces able to reduce regional divergence? Neo-classical economists have argued that there is a tendency towards the equalization of factor incomes spatially, given certain assumptions such as free mobility of labour and capital, equal technology, and so on. Yet factors are not perfectly mobile, and even on the assumption that they were, labour would have to emigrate from declining regions, and capital to flow into those declining regions. In a dynamic world, as neo-Keynesians have shown, capital has often been drawn towards regions that are already prosperous, since they offer high rates of return. Capital cities have provided a magnetic attraction, since economic advantages have been consolidated by being at the heart of cultural and political influences. Multinational companies have favoured proximity to such centres for their headquarters and decision-making. Firms have obtained external economies of scale from location in large urban areas. However, there has been a tendency in recent years for pleasant medium-sized towns, often located on the outer fringe of such areas, to attract new firms.

While dynamic growth effects may 'spill over' to benefit the less-developed regions, the latter are more likely to experience adverse 'backwash' effects, resulting in cumulative relative decline (Myrdal 1957). A polarization of resources occurs in which less-developed regions experience high rates of unemployment, de-industrialization, emigration of labour (often younger and enterprising people), and a run-down, shabby infrastructure. Therefore the free market *per se* fails to create convergence and any desirable balanced equilibrium between regions.

### Objectives of regional policy

Countries are concerned to reduce economic and social disparities that arise from the wide differences in rates of regional incomes and unemployment. Unfortunately regional policy is likely to be less effective when the overall level of unemployment is high, since this is a reflection of low demand and there are few firms wishing to expand and to relocate their activities. The absolute numbers unemployed are also high, even in the more prosperous city regions, though their percentage rate of unemployment is relatively low, with much of the unemployment being frictional and not of long duration, like that in the declining areas.

A higher rate of economic growth is a precondition for reducing unemployment and raising activity rates in the depressed regions. Nevertheless, the automatic link between growth and numbers employed may have weakened, with capital being substituted for labour; for example, there is high unemployment in Spain and Ireland despite much improved economic growth. However, it is still vital to raise the level of demand, particularly where labour supply is increasing rapidly. Whilst aggregate economic expansion creates inflationary pressures, balanced regional development helps to alleviate this, since demand can be channelled into areas with idle capital and redundant labour. This is less inflationary than pumping demand into regions that are already experiencing high demand and overheating, and are already running up against supply bottlenecks.

Firms are concerned in their decision-making with maximizing their private profits, but in so doing they fail to consider the social costs or benefits that would accrue to society from a more even distribution of economic activity. The preference of firms to locate in already congested cities imposes additional social costs. By relocating in the depressed and less-developed areas, social benefits could be increased. Furthermore, since many businesses are 'footloose', this can be done without adversely affecting their economic performance.

Politically, some central governments have become overloaded, making them more responsive to regional decentralization, particularly where this has coincided with demands for regional autonomy to meet different cultural and linguistic interests. To maintain national unity some countries have had to show more sensitive awareness to their regional differences; for example, in Belgium the government has tried to limit the tendency towards fragmentation between the French-speaking and declining Walloon area in the south and the more prosperous area of Flanders to the north. Spain has also had to grant increased autonomy to accommodate regional differences, especially for the Catalans and Basques.

## EU regional policy and the Structural Funds

### *The case for EU regional policy*
While the case for national regional policies is well established and accepted, is there also a case for a strong regional policy at Community level? If so, should the policy supplement national policies or replace them? The latter is what has happened with regard to the Guarantee section of the CAP. The case for an EU regional policy stems largely from the way in which a large free market tends to exacerbate regional problems.

The removal of trading barriers in the customs union has led to the contraction of less efficient industries and although new industries have emerged, these have often been attracted elsewhere, to the core areas. New industries perceive the economic advantages of locating at the heart of the EU market. The free mobility of factors of production in the common market has tended to increase the flow from the periphery to the core, particularly labour, though there has also been some encouraging evidence that capital has started to flow back towards the periphery to benefit from lower labour costs. However, some weaker regions still encounter difficulties in selling their products competitively, particularly when productivity is lower, yet workers receive nationally based wage rates or expect to receive rates of pay comparable to those in the prosperous areas of the Community for similar work. National collective bargaining, rather than local or regional bargaining, and also Community-wide pay comparability, tend to make regional labour markets rather inflexible. In addition, the operation of national and multinational companies in charging uniform prices wherever they are located is a further source of disequilibrating activity.

Further progress towards closer economic integration has also tended to reinforce regional problems; for example, the creation of the internal single market has not only accelerated existing flows of trade and factors, but also opened up the Community market for services: these have tended to be concentrated in the most developed EU regions. The best-placed regions in terms of location and economic structure have been favoured by the internal market, while the weaker regions have suffered from increased intra-EU competition and also from external trading competition where the EU has accommodated imports from LDCs which produce basic products even more competitively; for example, increased textile imports will continue to accelerate the contraction of traditional textile industries concentrated in many weaker regions.

Enlargement of the EU has brought in the peripheral European economies. This has widened regional divergences, especially in countries of Southern Europe with low levels of national income and with a high dependence on agriculture. In the EU(12) the regional disparities created were twice as high as in the USA in the case of GDP and three times as high in terms of unemployment. While the regional problems of the fourth enlargement in 1995 to the EU(15) were fewer, mainly involving remote and less-developed regions, the next enlargement to Eastern Europe will magnify regional differences even more. For example, apart from capital cities, East European economies constitute regional problems throughout in comparison with Western Europe. Meanwhile, renewed progress towards EMU with the locking together of national currencies in the euro has reduced the leeway for national authorities of the EU euro members (11 initially) to increase their industrial competitiveness by exchange-rate depreciation. The less competitive industries, which suffer most, tend to be those located in remote regions with high transport costs. Since EMU confers desirable monetary advantages, these should be used to tackle some of its disadvantageous regional effects by further strengthening EU regional policy.

### Regional policies
Different types of regional policy can be pursued, either by improving the working of market forces or by intervening with positive policies of incentives to encourage relocation by private firms and active relocation of some public-sector activities in the weaker regions. In addition, to try to force development towards such regions, restrictions may be imposed to curb expansion in the overdeveloped and congested areas.

*Labour mobility*   Unemployment and low wages result in outward migration, which is pulled into other areas where jobs are plentiful and wages are higher. There is a modified inverted U-curve relationship between migration propensity and average real per capita income (Hammar et al. 1997, p. 100). Massive labour migration occurred interregionally and internationally during the economic boom in the Community up to 1973. Labour emigrated from the Mezzogiorno to the north of Italy and also to the rapidly growing economies of West Germany and France. Free labour mobility became increasingly part of the creation of a common market, but despite legislation to promote this, it was hampered in practice by continuing obstacles. While demand for labour was high, the main inflow was sucked in from Southern Europe, where there was also a strong 'push' element. Some of these countries – Greece, Spain and Portugal – became full members of the Community in the 1980s, concentrating on exporting more goods to the Community, with some economic convergence, especially in Iberia, leading to a lessening of their outflows of labour.

Some proponents of labour mobility have argued that favourable allocative efficiency effects lead towards economic convergence between regions and countries. Areas receiving labour are able to meet their high labour demand, while areas losing labour may gain through the removal of surplus labour which was either unemployed or underemployed. In the host regions and countries much hinges upon whether the immigrant labour supply matches the demand, or whether it leads to a dynamic growth in which demand continues to expand faster than supply, with continuing inflationary consequences. Migrant labour has been exploited by low wage rates and long hours of work, since it is often weakly unionized. Businesses make higher profits from which they can finance a higher level of investment: this leads to the employment of both capital and labour as output rises, although some firms may prefer to continue with cheaper labour-intensive production methods.

The emigration of labour, though generally a more converging than diverging influence, is not the panacea for regional imbalance in areas which lose labour on such a large scale that they become depopulated and continue to decline. A policy of marginal labour movement is more appropriate where this creams off an overpopulated area. A reduction in outward migration may only partly reflect an improvement in regional performance, since it also reflects the lower demand in the core of the Community, resulting from periodic recessions. The number of migrants living in the Community has fallen back as a consequence of repatriation, with policies of return migration having been pursued in Germany and France (Dustmann 1996).

*Positive regional policy*   Instead of reducing excess labour supply by labour mobility, a positive regional policy aims to raise the level of demand for workers. In private-enterprise economies, inducements are given, mainly through subsidies and tax concessions on capital, to encourage firms to expand and to relocate in unemployment blackspots. A policy of subsidizing capital has encouraged a substitution of capital for labour, tending to swamp any additional significant output effect on the employment of labour. Often taxpayers' money has been given to multinational companies which have used their bargaining power to extract maximum subsidy between competing bidders.

Where new firms have been attracted, these have often been branch factories of large multinational companies which in recession have tended to be the first to face cutbacks. A lower propensity to invest during recession has resulted in a refocusing of regional policy towards indigenous expansion by smaller and medium-sized enterprises with technological potential within less-developed regions. This has been consolidated by attempts to link Community R&D programmes to such regions. But these policies are constrained by an existing over-concentration of R&D and innovation in the core regions; also, it is difficult to develop 'leading-edge' technologies in weaker regions, even though these can be applied not only to new industries but to revitalize traditional ones as well. To help weaker regions the Community has launched programmes such as Special Telecommunications Action for Regions (STAR) and Science and Technology for Regional Innovation and Development in Europe (STRIDE).

Proponents of highly interventionist-planning-style regional policies advocate greater state expenditure in less-developed areas; this consists of spending more on infrastructure and also of laying down specific guidelines to increase the level of nationalized industry spending in such regions. Member states have differed in their regional policy emphasis, with Italy providing one of the best examples of state enterprise. In contrast, Germany, with fewer regional problems prior to reunification, tended to place greater reliance on market forces of labour mobility and inducements to private enterprise.

Italian regional policy has gone through several different phases in trying to tackle its problem of regional dualism, with the underdevelopment of the Mezzogiorno. The Cassa per il Mezzogiorno was founded in 1950 and sought initially to improve agriculture and infrastructure. It then tried to force the pace of industrialization by laying down specific targets for investment by state enterprises. State firms were instructed to make 60 per cent of their total investment and 80 per cent of their new investment in the Mezzogiorno. While these targets were underachieved, Italy's positive use of investment via its large state holding companies acted as a catalyst in encouraging private-sector development in the south. It succeeded in doubling the percentage of national industrial investment in the Mezzogiorno from around 15 per cent of total investment in the early 1950s to about 30 per cent in the 1970s. But too much of this investment was in highly capital-intensive sectors yielding relatively few immediate jobs. The Mezzogiorno's share of Italian GDP (at just under a quarter) showed little change from 1951 to 1978 (Klaassen and Molle 1983).

Italy has found it difficult to narrow the gap between the so-called two Italys, with much success taking place in the so-called third and more central Italy, assisted by the successful links between SMEs. Cooperation reinforces the beneficial locational external economies of scale enabling the average cost curve to be displaced downwards for all the businesses located there. In the south, productivity per worker in both industry and agriculture remains well below that in the north. Average unemployment in southern regions such as Basilicata, Calabria and Sicily has often been over 20 per cent. A policy relying heavily on budgetary transfers and active state intervention has become less valid in an era of national budgetary constraints and a preferred role for privatization. The Italian model prevented further regional divergence and without it even faster emigration would have had to occur from the south. A real base has now been laid in the Mezzogiorno, despite some criticisms of its industrialization without real development and an overreliance on loss-making activities by state enterprises. Southern Italy compares favourably with similar Mediterranean countries such as Greece and Portugal in per capita income (*European Economy* 1993) and the changing focus of the Community towards southern Europe placed Southern Italy in a better position for future development. The Mezzogiorno was a priority for both the Italian government and also for EU aid-giving institutions, though special intervention for it was abolished after 1993.

*Negative regional policy*   Negative regional policy refers to measures to limit overexpansion in prosperous and congested areas. Such measures have been used by several countries, such as France and the UK, particularly in their capital cities. At a time of economic expansion these measures could be justified, although generally it is better to attract firms positively to depressed regions instead of preventing them from locating at their chosen site. Given the depressed economic conditions after the early 1970s, such restrictions lost much of their rationale. This was because investment had fallen, and preventing firms from investing in particular areas was likely to have two effects: either the firm might postpone its investment completely, or it might decide to locate in some other region to avoid the controls – this could be in another EU country or even in some other part of the world. A reluctance nationally to apply negative measures so strongly during recession left a gap in Community policy to control areas of overconcentration (Vanhove and Klaassen 1980, p. 452).

*The funding of EU policies*
National regional policies are still more significant in many respects than EU regional policies; for example, total regional expenditure by national governments has exceeded that by Community aid-giving bodies. Furthermore, Community-level funding by regional bodies was channelled for many years via national governments. The optimum assignment of powers between the EU, the member state and the region is a difficult one to determine precisely. National governments have sought to cling on as much as possible to their powers, often conceding to administrative regionalism mainly to access and channel EU regional funds. Even in those countries where regional powers are decentralized and there is a belief in political regionalism, such as Germany, EU regional policy initially tended to strengthen national control. However, the EU finally recognized the need to elevate the regional level of activity and to downgrade the national role if it were to create a more meaningful direct relationship between the Commission and the diversity of regions.

The rationale of Community regional policy is to ensure that regional assistance is channelled to those regions that have the most acute problems. However, the prosperous are reluctant to see income transferred to weaker regions. For example, in Germany the Finanzausgleich, which provides financial compensation, has been challenged by regions which thought they were either contributing too much or not receiving enough. Since regions are sometimes reluctant to accept national transfers when one might expect citizens to have some regard for the plight of their fellow citizens, there tends to be even less willingness to support transfers for weaker regions in other Community countries. Nevertheless, on equity grounds such transfers are justified since even the poorest areas of West Germany are still better off than the richest areas of Portugal and Greece.

A Community regional policy has had to be pursued to limit the excessive degree of support granted by countries at a national level to support their own weaker regions when such regions actually lie above the EU average on basic indicators, such as employment, income per head, and so on. Therefore the Community has had to control carefully the degree of support given by countries such as Germany to assist regions that are prosperous by European standards. The Belgian government, which was lavishing regional assistance widely to avoid cultural divisions, has similarly had to curtail the breadth of this assistance. Both the number of regions designated for regional aid and the level of aid have had to be reworked in such a way as to prevent non-needy areas from attracting an undue share of regional aid. EU regional policy has both co-ordinated national policies and offered structural aid in sectors such as iron and steel and agriculture. It then moved on, after the first enlargement, to the establishment of a specific Regional Development Fund.

*Regional funds: objectives and appraisal*
This section examines the following aid-giving bodies: the European Agricultural Guidance Fund (EAGF) and the Financial Instrument for Fisheries Guidance (FIFG); the European Investment Bank (EIB); the European Regional Development Fund (ERDF); and the Cohesion Fund. The European Social Fund (ESF) and its role in social policy are covered separately in a later section. It should be borne in mind that some schemes have been financed jointly, enhancing the value of the aid given.

Any appraisal of the Structural Funds is determined by their size and composition. Judgement about the effectiveness of expenditure is influenced by the level at which intervention occurs, in particular at a Community level, and by the extent to which policies contribute to economic objectives in strengthening regional structures or simply provide by transfer a social 'hand-out'. In addition, regional priorities have differed between agricultural and industrial areas. Some of the traditional industrial regions formed an association for Régions Européennes de Tradition Industrielle (RETI) to resist any further erosion of their regional assistance towards less-developed areas, such as those in the Mediterranean. Over the years the operation of the Structural Funds has been modified and improved with the establishment of enhanced concentration of resources and clearer priorities. After the Single European Act (Article 23) a new title was included in the Treaty on Economic and Social Cohesion.

The Commission proposed that budgetary resources for the Structural Funds should rise significantly in real terms. Furthermore, it focused its activities on specific objectives. These were to be achieved by supplementing existing activities with ERDF programmes determined on the basis of Community Support Frameworks. The first objective was to help less-developed regions to catch up (that is, those with per capita GDP less than 75 per cent of the Community average). Regions are based and defined on the Nomenclature of Territorial Units for Statistics (NUTS). Different levels are used, with the main focus being on NUTS level II. Up to 80 per cent of ERDF commitment appropriations were earmarked for Objective 1 regions, with particular emphasis on creating a proper infrastructure. The second Objective has been to assist conversion in declining industrial regions, and here NUTS level III applies. These regions were defined on the basis of high unemployment and de-industrialization. Objective 2 has had a smaller geographical and population coverage than Objective 1. Objectives 3 and 4 have been horizontal in nature, with Objective 3 to combat long-term unemployment and also now to facilitate the integration into working life of young people and those threatened from exclusion from the labour market. Objective 4, which used to consist of measures to help the occupational integration of young people, has been modified by incorporating young people into Objective 3, thus creating a new Objective 4 which facilitates adaptation to change by those already in employment but whose jobs are threatened. Objective 5a has been to speed up the adjustment of agricultural structures and has been tackled by the European Agricultural Guidance Fund and the Financial Instrument for Fisheries Guidance. Objective 5b is regional, laying down the general criteria of a low level of economic development involving features such as low agricultural income, high agricultural unemployment and depopulation. Table 7.1 shows the distribution of expenditure between these Objectives, with two-thirds to three-quarters being concentrated on Objective 1 regions. A new Objective 6 was introduced after the 1995 enlargement of the EU to include countries with a low population density (with fewer than eight people per square kilometre). Further modification is under way to change and reduce the number of Objectives, mainly to focus on all aspects of underdevelopment in Objective 1; Objective 2 to include all regions' restructuring; and Objective 3 to be for human resources.

*Table 7.1    Structural Funds financial allocation by Objective*

|  | 1989–93<br>% | 1994–99<br>% |
|---|---|---|
| Objective 1 | 63 | 74 |
| Objective 2 | 11 | 6 |
| Objectives 3 and 4 | 12 | 11 |
| Objective 5a | 10 | 4 |
| Objective 5b | 3 | 5 |
|  | 100 (rounded up) | 100 |

*Source*:    European Commission, DGVI.

The Commission approach has been based on complementing national measures, consultative partnership, and in particular greater use of programming (with the gradual disappearance of EU help to small projects). Procedures have been simplified with better co-ordination and an enhanced role by the EU. For example, Community Initiatives (CIs) have been introduced to deal with problems affecting several regions. Some 15 per cent of ERDF money was set aside for this in the 1990s, but to constrain expenditure growth and the mushrooming of CIs, proposals were made to reduce this to 5 per cent and to reduce the number of CIs to three fields: cross-border and transnational co-operation; rural development; and human resources (with particular attention to equal opportunities).

*The European Agricultural Guidance (and Guarantee) Fund and the Financial Instrument for Fisheries Guidance*    The EAG(G)F was developed to administer the CAP and, because of the high price support, most of the expenditure consisted of guaranteeing prices, with only a small proportion being concerned with guidance expenditure. CAP expenditure has helped all farmers, not only smaller farmers in very peripheral regions. It has proved neither a very efficient agricultural policy nor a very effective regional policy. Increasingly efforts were made to link the EAG(G)F more closely to regional policy; one indication of this was in 1974 when 150 million EUA were transferred from the Guidance section of the EAG(G)F to the European Regional Development Fund (Vanhove and Klaassen 1980, p. 422). The larger farms in the EU, operating in regions with favourable conditions, have gained most, especially those involved in grain and dairy production which have received very high price support. Although structural measures have been developed very much to favour those smaller farmers in Southern Europe, expenditure has been curtailed because of the undue weight to the Guarantee section of the Fund. Guidance expenditure has provided aid to Objective 1 regions that are lagging behind in development; to Objective 5a for agricultural structures in all regions, with no territorial limitations; and to Objective 5b, covering rural areas with particular limitations of unemployment, incomes and low population density and/or significant depopulation.

Structural measures have generally given farmers a minimum of 25 per cent of the total cost of projects for modernization of farms, rationalization, improvement of processing and marketing; help with movement of workers from the land, plus help for mountain and hill farming in less-favoured areas. Also, restructuring aid has been extended to the fishing industry via the Financial Instrument for Fisheries Guidance. The measures undertaken have tried to create a sustainable balance between resources and their exploitation and to develop economically viable enterprises. Assistance has been given to help redeployment operations, joint ventures and restructuring the fishing fleet.

While policies to assist declining sectors like agriculture are vital, they can only cushion its decline. They cannot maintain, let alone increase, agricultural employment in the future. Hence there is a need to develop related ancillary activities, such as tourism, food processing, marketing of local products and the establishment and development of small firms, especially in conjunction with part-time employment. The EU has also moved forward with Integrated Development Programmes, particularly in the Mediterranean. Many operations have been financed by LEADER, a French acronym (Liaison Entre Actions de Développement de l'Economie Rurale). Funds have been disbursed to local bodies to help grass-roots rural development. Projects have been wide-ranging, from environmental improvements to tele-cottages, and so on.

*The European Investment Bank (EIB)*   The EIB has been empowered to provide loans for projects which fall into the following categories: for developing less-developed regions; for modernizing or converting undertakings, or for developing fresh activities; and for projects of common interest to member states.

The Bank's capital has been subscribed by member states and increased after each enlargement; but most of its funds are raised on international capital markets at keen terms since it has a secure and high credit rating. In 1997 it denominated its borrowings in euros for the first time. The EIB is a very important source of long-term loans and has occasionally provided a guarantee for raising loans. Its loan terms depend upon the conditions prevailing on international capital markets and also on the projects themselves. Loans to industry are normally for a period of seven to 12 years and up to 20 years for infrastructure projects. Borrowing is at a fixed rate of interest and is a very useful source of funds for risky projects. Repayment of the loan may also include a period of grace before any repayment of the principal needs to be made.

The Bank has been of greater significance in terms of total lending than some of the other much-heralded and better-known funds. Table 7.2 shows the extent of EIB lending, of which about 90 per cent has occurred within the EU rather than in conjunction with the EU's European Development Fund (EDF).

An appraisal of the EIB's activities, especially from the viewpoint of a regional dimension, would point to some of the following deficiencies. The Bank is not concerned solely with regional imbalance but with other functions (as laid down at the beginning of this section). It has financed common projects of joint interest to Community countries, such as the Airbus project. Much of the expenditure on new industrial investment often occurs outside weaker regions. Although the EIB is concerned with financing improvements to the infrastructure, again much of this occurs in developed regions; for example, EIB lending for construction of the Channel Tunnel resulted in more investment in the south-east of England. If one wished to focus financial assistance purely on the problem regions, then the multi-purpose role of the Bank would have to be diminished. For those who favour a more interventionist and subsidized approach to regional development, the EIB would appear to be too much of a commercial institution, providing repayable loans and not grants (except when supplemented by a small subsidy from the ERDF).

The EIB is never a source of the whole finance of a project, but provides up to half of the cost, with the borrower having to obtain the remainder from other financial institutions. The Bank's lending is comparable with that of the World Bank, and was focused initially upon large projects. Some of these have been extremely capital-intensive,

*Table 7.2  EIB financing provided (contracts signed), 1959–89 (in million ECUs)*

| Years | Total | Within the Community | | | | Outside the Community | |
|---|---|---|---|---|---|---|---|
| | | Lending from EIB own resources | Loans under mandate and guarantees | Lending from NCI resources[1] | Lending from EIB own resources | Operations mounted from budgetary resources |
| 1959–72 | 2 836.7 | 2 340.1 | 110.1 | – | 155.7 | 230.8 |
| 1973–80 | 14 340.6 | 11 739.1 | 132.4 | 474.7 | 1 381.5 | 613.0 |
| 1981 | 3 531.4 | 2 523.8 | – | 539.9 | 377.9 | 89.8 |
| 1982 | 4 683.5 | 3 446.0 | – | 791.1 | 405.2 | 41.2 |
| 1983 | 5 921.8 | 4 145.9 | 97.6 | 1 199.6 | 426.0 | 52.7 |
| 1984 | 6 885.9 | 5 007.0 | – | 1 181.8 | 610.7 | 86.4 |
| 1985 | 7 181.5 | 5 640.7 | – | 883.7 | 581.3 | 75.9 |
| 1986 | 7 516.9 | 6 677.3 | – | 393.0 | 356.5 | 90.1 |
| 1987 | 7 778.0 | 6 965.1 | – | 425.2 | 184.4 | 203.3 |
| 1988 | 10 085.6 | 8 843.9 | 185.0 | 356.5 | 520.1 | 180.1 |
| 1989 | 12 246.1 | 11 555.9 | – | 78.3 | 485.9 | 126.0 |
| Total | 83 008.0 | 68 884.8 | 525.1 | 6 323.8 | 5 485.2 | 1 789.3 |

*Note:* [1] The New Community Instrument has operated since 1979, through which the Commission transfers money to the Bank for specific purposes.

*Source:* EIB *Annual Report, 1989* (1990).

with the consequence that, apart from workers employed in the initial building work, they have failed to mop up surplus labour. It was also argued that too much finance had been channelled into polluting industries, such as the chemical and nuclear power industries (Lewenhak 1982). With the benefit of hindsight, society is much more conscious of the environmental externalities associated with these industries. But in any energy investment a difficult choice has to be made between coal, oil, gas and nuclear power, with none of them being completely immune from some undesirable environmental impact.

The emphasis on financing large projects gradually diminished after the introduction in the late 1960s of a global loan system for allocating funds to financial intermediaries to on-lend to medium-sized firms. These intermediaries can be of many types, but are mainly banking institutions. As such, they are concerned primarily with the application of normal banking principles, especially with the capacity to repay loans. In some respects, from the perspective of promoting regional employment or steering funds to key sectors, they may be the wrong agents to act as intermediaries. At least global loans were a step forward and a recognition that financing big projects *per se* was a mistake.

Large projects in 'growth-pole' locations have not only provided few jobs but have often added to overcapacity, with the same vulnerability to decline as many traditional industries. Smaller and medium-sized firms, in contrast, have offered more potential for stable indigenous growth. By the mid-1980s, over half of the Bank's industrial investment was under the global loan system. However, this again was not as effective as expected in creating jobs, and it was suggested that more of its loans should be switched from manufacturing to the growing service sector.

The EIB has undoubtedly proved attractive to borrowers in countries which would have to pay high domestic interest rates and pay off loans over a short time period. But while EIB loans can make investments look more favourable, the Bank is a market-based institution and can only respond when there is a demand from borrowers. In a recession, when investment intentions are depressed, investment is low, and yet it is precisely at this time that investment needs to be stimulated. Investment is demand-determined and has tended to fall away during recession; to counter such cyclical decline the EIB has continued to innovate in its lending policy. The early 1990s saw the introduction of two new financing measures, the first particularly to finance capital infrastructure projects connected with the Trans-European Networks; but the second was the establishment of the new European Investment Fund (EIF) focused particularly on TENs and SMEs, with an interest rate subsidy for SMEs linked to job creation.

Some borrowers faced repayment problems, exacerbated by exchange rate changes, and to alleviate these, governments provided some element of protective compensation for borrowers. The British government felt that this had become too costly, and though some compensation was retained for loans to the public sector, it announced in 1985 that it was no longer willing to cover exchange-rate risks on small loans: this policy change was somewhat inconsistent with the overall strategy of helping small businesses.

*The European Regional Development Fund*    There was no explicit call for a common regional policy in the Treaty of Rome and it was only after the decision was taken to enlarge the Community that the ERDF was finally established in 1975. The ERDF (or FEDER – Fonds Européen de Développement Régional) has been assisted in its operation by two Committees comprising national officials: the Regional Policy Committee and the Fund Committee. The ERDF has provided grants for industry, services and crafts, and much of its investment has focused on infrastructure, such as transport, energy and water engineering projects. Infrastructure accounted for just over 80 per cent of ERDF financing in 1975–85. ERDF grants have normally been for half the investment costs and up to 55 per cent for projects of exceptional regional significance. For projects with a large investment cost, the rate of grant available falls and generally lies between 30 and 50 per cent. ERDF expenditure has been concentrated very heavily on a small number of regions relating to Objectives 1, 2 and 5b.

Originally there was a system of fixed national quotas for ERDF expenditure which handicapped its role (Moussis 1982, p. 221). There was a lack of sufficient discretion in allocating its finance, but in 1979 some improvements were made, including the concept of a small non-quota section of 5 per cent of ERDF finance which could apply outside the nationally designated areas. This provided additional flexibility, leading the Commission to propose an enlargement of the non-quota section up to 20 per cent of the ERDF and to concentrate this expenditure on a smaller number of regions defined according to Community criteria. Eventually agreement was reached on a system of flexible quota guidelines for each country, based on minimum and maximum levels. The total minimum expenditure was set at 88.63 per cent so that the Commission had discretion over the small remaining 12 per cent marginal expenditure of the ERDF's funds.

ERDF expenditure has grown, with the major beneficiaries over the years in absolute terms being Italy, the UK and Spain. Spain absorbed 23 per cent of the Structural Funds in 1994–9 and received about 30 per cent of ERDF grants, while Portugal, Greece and Ireland each obtained about 15 per cent of ERDF grants, though these constituted a larger share of their investment in GDP (Fuente and Vives 1995). The smaller economies have received significant injections of expenditure as a proportion of their GDP. Between 1975 and 1986 it was estimated by the Commission that ERDF expenditure created or maintained just over three-quarters of a million jobs, and most of those were newly created. The ERDF has moved to a preference for financing programmes rather than individual projects. It was hoped that this would improve co-ordination and coherence, reducing the time and effort spent in assessing each individual project. The programme approach has increased the role of the EU in regional policy. Programmes have been either Community programmes or national programmes of Community interest. There have also been Integrated Development Operations bringing all loans and grants together to concentrate on particular areas; finally, there have been Integrated Mediterranean Programmes.

*The Cohesion Fund*　The Cohesion Fund, which was set up to cater for member states with less than 90 per cent of EU per capita GDP, has been directed at Greece, Ireland, Portugal and Spain; it will naturally eventually cover all the new entrants in any future East European enlargement. There has been an even division of expenditure between transport and environmental projects. The focus has been mainly on projects or groups of projects. Cohesion funding has been conditional, based on the principle of Maastricht budgetary convergence. While this reduces additional expenditure, it is assumed that lower interest rates will bring about increased private-sector investment. Although the Cohesion Fund has had no explicit remit to create jobs, employment creation has been significant via the initial effects of construction (and demand-side effects), plus long-term supply-side benefits from these projects. However, it has been necessary to cap total expenditure so that no country is to receive in transfer more than 4 per cent of its national GDP from the Structural Funds and the Cohesion Fund combined.

*The effects of EU funding*   Funding outlays on the regions have risen significantly to account for a third of the Budget, with a greater concentration of expenditure, particularly on Southern Europe. Member states have turned more towards the EU as a potential source of regional funding as national regional expenditure has been pruned back severely in most North European countries. This has been reinforced by EU pressure to reduce state aids in richer member states. Studies have shown that incentives for investment in the productive sector by richer member states to help their own needy regions have been particularly detrimental to EU convergence (Martin 1998).

EU funding is not meant to be a permanent handout, but provides an initial Keynesian demand-side effect supported by stronger neo-classical supply-side benefits enabling regions to improve their economic performance. A wide range of support measures has been available, going beyond the normal national measures of infrastructure and productive business investment to include human resource development; environmental improvement; research; innovation and technology transfer; and small community development including health care (Keating and Loughlin 1997, p. 83).

Convergence has been slower than the standard neo-classical model of growth would predict, but structural funding has raised economic growth significantly in the Cohesion countries, especially Ireland, Spain and Portugal, as shown in Table 7.3. The GDP data show convergence when measured by purchasing power standards to take into account differences in price levels. The convergence in GDP 1986–96 in the four Cohesion countries was just over 10 per cent, with the most impressive progress in the new 'Celtic tiger' (Irish) economy. GDP is determined by the productivity of those in employment and also by the numbers employed. Both Ireland and Spain have largely closed the productivity gap, but still suffer from low employment rates. Portugal suffers mainly from low productivity, while Greece has done least well, having both low productivity and a low participation rate. There has been insufficient job creation in Objective 1 regions, especially in Greece and also in the south of Italy.

Overall, there has been some convergence in GDP per capita for the weakest countries and also for the poorest Objective 1 regions, which are found mainly in the Cohesion countries. By 1996 the bottom 10 regions (though changing their composition only slightly from 1986) had raised their GDP per head to half the EU average, while the bottom 25 regions had raised their GDP per head to 59 per cent of the EU

*Table 7.3  GDP per head of population in the Cohesion countries (PPS, EU = 100)*

|  | Ireland | Greece | Spain | Portugal |
|---|---|---|---|---|
| 1986 | 60.8 | 59.2 | 69.8 | 55.1 |
| 1990 | 71.1 | 57.4 | 74.1 | 58.5 |
| 1996 | 96.5 | 67.5 | 78.7 | 70.5 |
| 1999 (estimate) | 105.1 | 69.3 | 79.6 | 71.8 |

*Source*:  Eurostat, *calculations DGXVI*.

*Table 7.4  GDP per head and unemployment in the best- and worst-performing regions*

|  | Best-performing regions | | Worst-performing regions | |
|---|---|---|---|---|
|  | Top 10 | Top 25 | Bottom 10 | Bottom 25 |
|  | PPS, EU=100 | | PPS, EU=100 | |
| GDP per head (1986) | 153 | 138 | 41 | 52 |
| GDP per head (1996) | 158 | 143 | 50 | 59 |
|  | % | | % | |
| Unemployment (1987) | 2.2 | 3.1 | 23.9 | 20.1 |
| Unemployment (1997) | 3.6 | 4.2 | 28.1 | 23.7 |

*Sources*:  Eurostat, and Sixth Periodic Report on the social and economic situation and development of the regions of the European Union 1999.

average (see Table 7.4). More worryingly, the rate of unemployment worsened across EU regions, rising to 28.1 per cent in the 10 worst regions. There has been a failure to improve the rate of job creation sufficiently, especially in Objective 1 regions, though progress has been more satisfactory in Objective 2 and Objective 5b regions in reducing unemployment and diversifying economic activity.

The Structural Fund expenditure is supposed to be additional expenditure, promoting spending for specific purposes which the recipient would not have undertaken in the absence of a grant. Unfortunately, in some instances it has substituted for national government expenditure, going into general government funds. Although this fulfils the redistributive functions, at least for the poorest members states the resource allocation effect is lost. Structural funding expenditure should also be matched by member state contributions, which therefore means a bigger multiplier effect, though one has to recognize that some poorer member states, such as Greece, have struggled to come up with matching funding. This 50 per cent matching structural funding will prove even more difficult for the countries of Eastern Europe, whereas the 15 per cent Cohesion Fund co-financing is more tolerable.

The EU has altered the perception by regions of their own role and has had the effect of shifting countries from regionalization (that is, top-down regional policies) towards regionalism, characterized by decentralization in response to bottom-up pressure (Keating and Loughlin 1997). There are growing interregional links between regions in close proximity, or between those with similar or even with different problems. There is increased networking, not only within regions between the public and the private sector and other key groups, but networks are also being formed between Europe's regions. Not only have they learned from each other's experience, but also by making alliances they have been able to lobby more effectively for their distinctive regional differences from offices in Brussels. Cross-border co-operation between regions is a step on the road to much more co-ordinated regional planning which will also extend to much of Eastern Europe in this new millennium. In conclusion, while the elevation of the sub-national role by the EU Commission represents an important development in partnership, plus the enhanced voice via the Committee of the Regions, it will not displace the continuing dominance of the member state.

### Tackling social inequalities

*The range of social policy and the case for intervention*   Social and regional inequalities sometimes overlap, but there are also separate and persistent social differentials. Social policy encompasses a wide range of issues, and at national level it includes social security expenditure which subsidizes income, such as pensions, sickness and unemployment benefits. In addition, there is provision of commodity subsidies for major selected social services, such as health, education, housing, and so on. The rationale is to alleviate poverty and to lessen inequalities by redistributing income. However, it is recognized that there is some trade-off in which greater equality may impede economic growth through a loss of incentives to enterprise. Furthermore, given the need to contain an excessive growth of public expenditure, this has led to greater consideration of the role of the private sector in providing merit goods.

In the EU, social policy is much more narrowly defined in scope and concentrates primarily on labour-market issues. The EU lacks the will and budgetary finance to conduct more extensive social policy. Its role has been mainly to deal with the social consequences of restructuring that have emerged from increased market competition. For example, it has helped to protect workers' rights and has assisted workers who have become unemployed to retrain and/or move. There has also been concern to avoid unfair competition through employers skimping on health and safety conditions, or exploiting labour by preventing equal opportunities for women. Finally, with increased movement of capital there was concern by states with higher social standards over companies moving away to exploit lower standards of social protection in other member states. Although the Community has impinged upon educational and health matters, this has been marginal and often the by-product of other activities; for example, in promoting labour mobility, the EU has needed to involve itself educationally with the recognition of qualifications; or in industrial employment, there is the need to move on from specific health and safety requirements to a more general concern for citizens' health. From occasional meetings of Ministers of Education and Health, other EU issues have been taken on board. Yet essentially the conception of EU social policy is still far more limited than that more normally understood by social policy at a national level. Despite the rhetoric, social integration in the EU has been far outpaced by economic integration, with only piecemeal and fragmentary social policies, constrained by considerations of subsidiarity.

*The early development of social policy*   The foundations of EU social policy can be found in the various Treaties which contain a general commitment to improving living and working conditions. The ECSC covered such matters as unemployment compensation, retraining, health and safety, and housing. But overall, like the subsequent Spaak Committee, it felt no need for a common social policy. Thus in the Treaty of Rome there were few precise commitments and no definite timetable drawn up for action. However, the French were worried about the high level of social charges borne by their employers. They fretted that these would erode French industrial competitiveness unless some harmonization occurred. Though generally unsuccessful in its demands, France did manage to engage other member states to introduce equal pay for men and women, via Article 119 of the Treaty of Rome. Other Treaty clauses on holidays and overtime pay were gradually overtaken by events.

Gender inequalities in the labour market manifest themselves for women in terms of lower pay and horizontal employment concentration into a limited range of occupations, with a vertical clustering into lower grades. Proneness to unemployment arises from insufficient training, leaving the labour market to have children, and locational movements brought about by husbands' job changes. Women, like migrants, have been used as the most flexible marginal element in the labour market. They have been attracted increasingly into employment by higher pay, smaller family size and new labour-saving technology in the home. Negative influences on their participation have been higher earnings for husbands and higher unemployment. While part of the gender inequalities can be attributed to supply-side differences, such as education and training, even after standardizing for these, a significant level of discrimination still remains.

The many EC directives to tackle inequality have included the following: equal pay, 1975; equal opportunities in employment, recruitment, promotion and training, 1976; equal treatment for men and women in social security, 1978 (and 1986). Various action programmes have increasingly recognized the links between employment and child care, and in 1982 a directive was presented on parental leave (which the Council was unable to approve until 1992). The EC has also sought to protect women's maternity leave so that they can return to their jobs and have the incentive to train. Judgements by the European Court of Justice have clarified and consolidated equal opportunities legislation. The main limitation of gender policies was to focus upon women merely as workers rather than citizens, neglecting societal causes of gender inequality.

Another significant policy achievement in the context of making the market operate more efficiently was in promoting intra-EC labour migration. From the 1960s this was to a large extent from Italy, which was concerned with social security provisions and protection of working rights for migrants. However, especially from the 1970s, there was a desire to go further in social policy, with some favouring a more redistributive system. In the early 1970s social policy was extended and the Paris Summit Conference of 1972 called for a Social Action Programme to be formulated. Its priorities were to create full and better employment; improvement of living and working conditions; and participation by employees in the process of decision-making. There was in addition a statement of many other proposals, producing a worthy list of desirable social developments (Shanks 1977).

Implementing new developments was constrained by the background of a worsening economic climate, and though there were plenty of Commission proposals, most of them failed to obtain backing from the Council. However, new developments did include the Council decision to establish a European Centre for the Development of Vocational Training (CEDEFOP) which began in 1977 in Berlin (and moved in 1994 to Greece). In 1975 a Foundation for the Improvement of Living and Working Conditions was established in Dublin, and the Council also supported a project of the European Trade Union Confederation to establish a European Trade Union Institute.

*Renewed impetus from the SEA and the Social Charter*   Initiatives by the Commission in the 1980s were linked to other developments such as that of a People's Europe and the internal market programme. While the single market was concerned essentially with economic matters, proponents of social policy took advantage of its approach to setting minimum standards since this was easier than the slow search for harmonization. Qualified majority voting introduced into the SEA provided additional momentum and reduced opposition. The Social Charter on workers' rights in 1989 was a political declaration and not a legally binding document, though its proposals were taken up by others to form the basis for the social chapter in the Maastricht Treaty which provided for increased qualified majority voting.

The Community has sought to consolidate basic social rights whose pillars are already enshrined in standards laid down by the UN, the ILO (International Labour Organization) and the Council of Europe. Early in 1989 the Economic and Social Committee (ESC) adopted a favourable position on this, followed in late 1989 by Commission proposals for the implementation of a Community Charter of Basic Social Rights for workers. These were grouped under various headings, and in some matters, such as freedom of association and collective bargaining, the Commission did not propose any initiatives since it regarded these as matters for employers and unions in member states. In other areas the Commission limited its 50 proposals which comprise the Social Charter mainly to directives or regulations, which would be introduced by 1992. Some of the directives were amendments to existing ones, but others were more controversial. In the 1990s these included the Working Time Directive and the Directive on Pregnant Women at Work. This directive on maternity was based on both health and safety grounds and those of endorsing equal opportunities. It had the strong support of the Commission and the European Parliament which wanted to go beyond 14 weeks' paid maternity leave, though the Commission stuck to 14 weeks (Armstrong and Bulmer 1998).

EU labour market policy also extends to monitoring market trends in both employment and unemployment. For example, its Local Employment Development Action (LEDA) programme has identified and publicized successful local responses to employment problems. Other research has identified successful programmes or projects for long-term unemployed adults and for young people. Meanwhile, a long-established European system for the international clearance of vacancies and applications for employment (SEDOC) has been improved.

The Commission has sought to establish basic levels of employment and remuneration, being concerned to minimize problems such as social dumping; for example, it has expressed an opinion in favour of a minimum income level. Improvement of living and working conditions has also been tackled by directives to safeguard workers' rights in the event of transfer of firms or establishments, redundancies and insolvency of employers. The Commission's recommendations in the Social Charter were to impose minimum rules on the maximum duration of work, rest periods, holidays, amount of overtime by night work, weekend work, and so on; also, to protect children and adolescents. The EU directive guarantees a maximum working week of not more than 48 hours; a minimum rest period of 11 consecutive hours; a rest break of 24 hours a week; paid annual holidays of four weeks; and new special protection of night and shift workers, including requirements for medical health checks.

Health and safety measures have been promoted over many years, originating from the very dangerous and hazardous conditions in the coal and steel and nuclear industries. Health and safety was also part of the 1974 social action programme. Since the SEA there has been even more progress from the late 1980s, with health and safety being the first to come under qualified majority voting; in addition, there has been the setting of more general minimum standards. The European Court of Justice has also provided supportive judgements, such as that relating to the case of an insolvent employer who still has responsibility for any damages in respect of health and safety. Health and safety issues have also broadened from narrow concern with occupational diseases or work safety to broader social concerns, such as alcoholism, drug abuse and Aids.

The interests of disadvantaged groups, such as the elderly and the disabled, have also been considered so they can lead as independent a life as possible. For example, proposals have been made for an over-60s card; for the exchange of information on technical aids for the disabled; and for the continuation of the Helios Action Programme for the disabled.

Constraints on implementing some aspects of the Social Charter in the form of an action programme have arisen from different practices between the member states. In addition, a key concern is: to what extent is the setting of some minimum standards, which are an improvement on equity grounds, offset by higher unemployment if companies relocate outside the EU? For example, besides the NICs, there is now the attraction of location in low-cost countries in Eastern Europe. It is important for the Community to explore fully whether more extensive social policies are a natural complement to the internal market, or significantly detract from it by confronting businesses with higher labour costs. In small businesses which tend to be labour-intensive, the consequence in competitive markets is that of higher unemployment. This partially offsets further benefits from the internal market in reducing other costs, such as capital through lower and convergent interest rates, and lower cost through economies of scale. In a Community where macroeconomic policies are being increasingly integrated, it may be preferable economically to leave the labour market relatively free to perform the main mechanism of economic adjustment.

*Worker participation proposals*   The EU is keen on participation by the social partners at all levels, for example, in the EU itself via the ESC and in industrial relations. From the beginning of the 1970s there have been various proposals, especially under German influence, to extend worker participation along similar co-determination lines to those in Germany. Progress has been slow and limited to company board level, with difficulties in agreeing on the precise level of worker representation on company boards. The Davignon Report in the late 1990s suggested a 20 per cent level of worker representation. The EU has found it easier to make progress at the lower level, and one significant achievement was the European Works Councils Directive. This became possible in 1994 by targeting multinationals and by shifting the directive from its original Treaty base which required unanimity to the new social policy procedure established after Maastricht. The EWC Directive eventually overcame the opposition of European employers (UNICE), much to the surprise of those who had predicted the continuing power of capitalists to prevent the growth of European Works Councils (see the debate between Knutsen and Streeck in Knutsen 1997). The EWC Directive applies to undertakings in the Community with at least 1000 employees within participating states and with at least 150 employees in each of two or more participating countries. The thresholds for the size for the workforce are based on the average number of employees, including part-time employees.

Most European Works Councils are group-wide, though some are divisional. They nearly all cover economic and financial information, employment, social structure and restructuring, and some go on to other matters such as health and safety, working hours and conditions, training, equal opportunities, the environment, and new technology. There has also been close trade union involvement, including nominating employee representatives, with women tending to be significantly underrepresented. The EWC Directive, the successor of Vredeling, represented very much a dilution of his original proposals. The directive is limited to information mainly on essential aspects of the company, and consultation is only allowed where management action would have serious consequences for employees.

*Education and training programmes*   There has been continued commitment to raise skill levels via educational training schemes. For example, 1976 saw the first Community Action Programme in education, establishing EURYDICE on educational information and exchange. It was also agreed to organize study visits for educational specialists under the ARION programme. Meanwhile, the COMETT programme has provided support for transnational training, partnership and mobility between universities and industry and technology; EUROTECHNET has dealt with vocational training for technological change for workers in industry. The PETRA programme has backed the training of young people to follow a course of vocational training for at least a year. Its successor, LEONARDO, has encouraged high-quality vocational training, supporting life-long learning and trans-European projects. The EU over the years has sought to establish comparability of vocational training in many sectors. CEDEFOP promotes the development of vocational training through information, research and co-operation. A programme relevant to new equal opportunities for women has the acronym NOW. Exchanges of young workers are encouraged (including those with Eastern Europe), while student mobility and inter-university co-operation in higher education have been fostered by ERASMUS and SOCRATES. The LINGUA scheme has also improved foreign-language teaching.

*The European Social Fund (ESF)*   The ESF has been in operation since 1958 and this section will signpost its changing direction and emphasis. Originally it was not a proper instrument of positive regional policy, being concerned mainly with fostering labour mobility and in particular concentrating its expenditure on vocational training and re-training workers. In the early years West Germany, which was actively carrying out training and resettlement, was a major beneficiary.

A major turning-point in ESF activities occurred after 1972 when the fund was reformed with increased finance. This focused to a high degree on less-developed regions. The incidence of unemployment has risen, in particular affecting young people seeking to join the labour market for the first time, but also the duration of unemployment is even greater among older workers, as long-term unemployment has become firmly entrenched. Hence the ESF targets its expenditure increasingly on those two groups. In some years around half of those unemployed had been unemployed for over a year, and the Commission has aimed to reduce this proportion. However, ESF financial assistance has reached too small a percentage of the long-term unemployed; in addition, ESF help for vocational training for the unemployed has been only a small percentage of national expenditure. The fund also provides assistance to many other disadvantaged groups: migrant workers, the disabled, women returning to employment and often requiring retraining, and workers adversely affected by new technology. This last has become a major preoccupation of the Community, to improve technological performance, with the ESF insisting that all its training projects need to include a minimum amount of time devoted to new technology.

The ESF has recognized the regional dimension of its activities by allocating increased funds to help those in areas of high unemployment. During the 1990s the ESF was integrated into structural funding to increase cohesion, particularly in lagging regions. In addition, Objectives 3 and 4 were redefined, with Objective 3 covering all those unemployed and socially excluded. A new Objective 4 recognizes that even those already in employment need anticipative help to facilitate adaptation to industrial change.

The ESF is concerned with a very narrow interpretation of social policy. This focuses mainly on employment/unemployment and training rather than displaying the usual extensive concern of social policy with health and welfare. The ESF has operated in a slow and cumbersome manner, with excess pressure on its resources leading to delays in payment and uncertainty about funding. The Fund concentrates on supply-side labour-market measures which are complementary to ERDF demand-side measures. The ESF finances mainly the running costs of schemes and not the capital costs, whereas the ERDF finances subsidies to capital costs of investment. Unfortunately, as in the case of the ERDF, much of the funding (apart from innovatory expenditure) has been treated not as additional money but has gone into financing existing government training schemes.

The main problem in the EU is the continuing high level of aggregate unemployment and its uneven distribution which adversely affects the welfare of its citizens. EU unemployment rose from a low average of 2.2 per cent in the 1960s to 4.0 per cent in the 1970s, 9.0 per cent in the 1980s and over 10 per cent after 1993. Community problems have deepened and extended beyond concerns about whether workers are deriving sufficient job satisfaction, or are participating enough in their firms. The ESF has played a useful role in tackling the half of unemployment which is structural and reflected by long-term unemployment of over 12 months; it has helped the disadvantaged back into the labour market through counselling and training. It has become integrated into achievement of Structural Fund objectives, seeking to address supply-side problems. However, more radical measures by the EU to redistribute income would necessitate Community-wide payments of unemployment benefits, and neither the level of budgetary finance nor the common will to do this has existed.

**Inequalities in the UK**

The UK has suffered from three particular problems. As the first European country to industrialize, it also became the first to de-industrialize. Its overcommitment to staple industries and their subsequent decline resulted in de-industrialization, with very severe effects on traditional regions. The second problem is that the rate of economic growth in the UK has been considerably lower than in other EU countries in the postwar years. Although during the 1980s and 1990s the UK relative rate of economic growth *vis-à-vis* its continental neighbours greatly improved, much of the growth was in the tertiary sector. Third, the UK economy lies on the periphery of the Community's core area. Whereas the UK's location was central for trade with the Americas, the reorientation of trade towards the central areas of the Community has inevitably intensified the problem of regional imbalance.

The north–south divide has become very pronounced in the UK. The south-east of England and East Anglia have prospered, with most of the service jobs being created in the south (while traditional manufacturing jobs concentrated in the north have declined). The sun-belt area stretching down the motorway from Cambridge to Bristol reflects a growing concentration of high-technology sectors such as electronics. Infrastructure demands in the south-east have been high; for example, the building of the Channel Tunnel has strengthened and reinforced its position *vis-à-vis* the more depressed northern regions, handicapped by insufficient new rail infrastructure. However, the Channel Tunnel has also been highly beneficial for the depressed French region of Nord Pas de Calais.

Rank positions of regions for the EC(15) based on comparative GDP per capita (purchasing power parity) had Greater London continuing as the UK's best-placed region, standing at 140, in relation to the best-placed German region of Hamburg, 192 (Commission 1999). Regional performance is closely related to national performance, with the prosperous regions tending to lie very much in the core, such as in West Germany. The poorer regions are more on the periphery, including the UK, Ireland and Southern Europe. These will be joined with future enlargement by Eastern Europe, which will squeeze the regional funding and will limit further the regional funding for the UK, which has a much higher GDP per capita and lower unemployment. Whilst EU regional funding has proved significant in smaller economies such as Ireland, with substantial transfers per head of population, in the UK its overall impact has been less impressive. Most help to the UK has been for its Objective 2 industrial regions, and it has retained a safety net under these, despite its lower unemployment. Its Objective 1 regions have altered, with Northern Ireland and the Scottish Highlands and Islands being replaced in the new millennium by Cornwall, West Wales and the valleys, South Yorkshire and a continuance of Objective 1 status for Merseyside.

Given the magnitude of regional problems in the UK, it seemed paradoxical during the 1980s for the government to cut regional expenditure. However, its philosophy was geared more to cutting the high costs of job creation, especially in capital-intensive sectors. It was felt that regional policy was mainly redistributing employment instead of creating many new jobs. The assisted areas were reduced to cover a smaller percentage of the working population and there was also a switch from automatic investment grants to selective grants, linking assistance more directly to job creation. There was fairly centralized control of policy during the long years of Conservative government, but since the election of a new Labour government in May 1997 there has been increased commitment to devolution in the UK.

Because of the inadequate level of UK regional funding, depressed regions have had to tap EU regional funds. However, a full comparison of EU regional transfers showed a predominant agricultural imprint, so that between 1973 and the end of 1986 the UK received £8632 million from the EAGGF, compared with only £1600 million from the ESF and £1519 million from the ERDF. A regional breakdown of ERDF commitments 1975–86 showed that Scotland received nearly a quarter of these, with 15 per cent each going to Wales and to the north of England, nearly 14 per cent to north-west England and 10 per cent to Northern Ireland.

Awareness of the ERDF has been high, and local authorities have used ERDF grants as a substitute for loans on which they would have to pay interest. Many local authorities have appointed liaison officers to tap the Structural Funds, and this is worthwhile as long as the inflow of funds exceeds the additional costs of employing them. Applications have been rejected where they have not been fully documented or where they have not met the formal conditions on assisted areas, costs, number of jobs created, and so on. The House of Lords concluded gloomily that the Regional Fund caused very little to happen that would not have happened anyway, and that the principle of additionality was largely disregarded in practice (House of Lords 1984).

The European Social Fund was at first a less well-known source of regional support. However, in some ways the ESF offered fertile ground for applications since there were no national quotas – unlike the ERDF. While the ESF has played a valuable role in underpinning training schemes and helping the unemployed, especially in depressed regions, other aspects of EU social policy had a mixed reaction in the UK. The Conservatives and business interests opposed excessive intervention and corporatism in the labour market. This is because such moves were at variance with the neo-liberal deregulation of the British labour market in the 1980s, which was successful in job creation, especially by small businesses, though many jobs were low paid. There was also concern that some directives were presented as health and safety measures which only required a majority vote, whereas as employment measures they would need unanimity and could therefore be blocked. The Conservative government blocked costly social measures and opted out of many social policies. It used its discretion to minimize the effects of directives, such as that on maternity leave, by excluding very low-paid women and ensuring that the costs did not fall on the UK government.

The UK has a more flexible labour market with a higher percentage of part-time employees, a higher percentage participation rate of young people (aged 15 to 17), and also a higher percentage of workers working longer hours than in continental Europe. The UK labour market has relied mainly on collective bargaining; industrial co-determination never took off in the UK, with the failure to implement the Bullock Committee Report on Industrial Democracy in 1977. In the UK, multinational corporations also play a very significant role and have been attracted by location in a low-cost flexible labour market. It can be seen, therefore, why the Conservative government preferred an opt-out from the Maastricht Treaty provisions on social policy since they opposed more majority voting and any move towards a European model of social policy. The decision by the new Labour government to end the UK opt-out and also to go further in terms of labour-market intervention, with the introduction of a national minimum wage, has moved the UK to closer policy integration in this sector – albeit with potentially adverse future effects on employment.

# 8 Monetary integration

### Characteristics of the international monetary system: fixed and floating exchange rates

The growth of trade between countries requires a system for currency exchange and essentially the choice is between some kind of fixed or floating mechanism. In the early postwar years the international economy opted for a system of fixed exchange rates, after the traumatic experience of the 1930s. This new international mechanism was very much an Anglo-American creation and led to the setting up of the International Monetary Fund (IMF). It was based upon a fixed exchange rate system in which the dollar was fixed in relation to gold, and the dollar as the pivot of the system was fixed in relation to other international currencies. Where countries experienced disequilibrium, financial assistance was forthcoming from the IMF, and when countries reached a position of fundamental disequilibrium they were expected to adjust their exchange rates.

The fixed exchange rate system served the international economy well in providing the certainty and stability needed by traders and investors. It provided a 'known element' in an uncertain world where there are too many variables. Nevertheless, it ran into specific difficulties since there was a misinterpretation of IMF rules, and countries in fundamental disequilibrium sought tenaciously to defend the parity of their currencies. The countries with balance-of-payments deficits were reluctant to accept the political consequences of devaluing their currencies. They had sizeable reserves trying to ward off speculation, but usually succumbed eventually. Problems were compounded by the lack of equivalent pressure on countries with balance-of-payments surpluses to revalue their currencies, and though one country's balance-of-payments deficit is matched by another country's balance-of-payments surplus, the countries in surplus did not rush to revalue for fear of making the task of their exporters too difficult.

The international monetary system was undermined by growing balance-of-payments deficits in the USA and a greater reluctance by other countries to hold dollars. This led ultimately to a crisis at the beginning of the 1970s with the break from gold and the devaluation of the dollar.

Massive speculation and increasing divergence between national rates of inflation and economic performance brought the fixed exchange rate system to a state of collapse. Thus in the early 1970s the international economy moved over, with great enthusiasm, to a regime of floating exchange rates.

Floating the exchange rate seemed to offer an additional policy instrument, instead of being a policy target of economic management, enabling countries to pursue their own domestic economic policies. It was assumed that any balance-of-payments deficit/surplus would be adjusted automatically by appropriate exchange rate changes. It was assumed that markets were more likely to arrive at the 'right' exchange rate than were governments in administering a fixed rate – even if such a rate were fixed at the correct level to begin with, the reluctance to alter it meant that it soon became the wrong rate of exchange. Countries would no longer need to hold massive reserves to defend their exchange rates, so floating exchange rates could help to alleviate the shortage of international liquidity. To the extent that there were uncertainties about exchange rates, for a small cost traders and investors could protect themselves in forward markets.

Like most fundamental changes, the claims made were far in excess of what could be delivered by a floating exchange rate. While firms can protect themselves against exchange-rate fluctuations, the uncertainty and costs are a particular handicap to smaller firms in international trade. The system generally has been characterized by even more marked instability of currencies than of commodity prices, though less volatile than share prices. Exchange rates have fluctuated wildly in the short term and in the long term have still failed to settle at the correct levels, exemplified by the misalignment of sterling, particularly from 1979 to 1981, and the dollar from 1981 to 1985. Countries have found it difficult to withstand the sheer volume of capital movements as speculative capital has flowed in and then out of their currencies. In countries with depreciating currencies, a nominal fall in exchange rate was not translated into the same effective exchange-rate fall since it stoked up inflationary pressures. This resulted inevitably in the need for other policy instruments to be used, negating the very freedom which floating exchange rates were supposed to confer on domestic policy-makers. In countries with appreciating currencies, such as Germany, this has not markedly affected their trade performance, partly because their specialization has been in exporting goods such as capital equipment, where price is less important than the technical capacity of machines which are well designed, reliable and delivered on time.

Floating exchange rates have failed to live up to expectations and have imposed significant costs. These include: adjustment costs of temporary misalignments; greater uncertainty in trading products, which has contributed to a slowdown in capital formation; a rise in protectionism by countries whose exchange rates have been pushed up too far; and an additional increase in world inflation. Furthermore, any substantial degree of national monetary autonomy has been something of a 'myth' (Tsoukalis 1986). Yet the great overhang of mobile capital has precluded a full return to international fixed exchange rates, though it has led to suggestions for a tax to dampen excessive capital mobility. What occurred was an attempt to create some exchange-rate stability between the major blocs, and in particular within the EU via the European Monetary System (EMS): in other words, to try to obtain internationally the best of both worlds from a blend of flexible and fixed rates and ultimately complete fixity.

To deal with the problems of international exchange-rate management since the mid-1970s the Group of Five, subsequently expanded to the Group of Seven (G7), has, among other things, tried to create greater exchange-rate stability. For example, significant summit meetings were held at Versailles in 1982 which strengthened multinational surveillance of exchange rates, followed in 1985 by the Plaza Agreement to reduce the overvaluation of the US dollar, while the Louvre Accord in 1987 tried to stabilize the value of the dollar. It would appear, therefore, both at a European and wider international level, that business required greater stability of exchange rates.

## Economic and Monetary Union (EMU) and the European Monetary System (EMS)

### *Characteristics of optimum currency areas*
An optimum currency area (OCA) is a group of countries linked together through fixed exchange rates. Major academic contributions were made in this field during the 1960s and 1970s. They provided a useful background to consideration of the viability of EMU, even though this goes further than OCAs in seeking common economic policies and ultimately a common currency.

The ability to create and maintain an OCA is based essentially upon the extent to which there are forces leading to convergence within the area, without necessitating an adjustment of the exchange rate. A key criterion used to justify an OCA was that of factor mobility (Mundell 1961). His pioneering theory is open to criticism on the grounds that the direction of factor flows is ambiguous, since capital may flow more to the dynamic region while labour may be relatively immobile and reluctant to move from the depressed region. Impediments still remain to the free mobility of labour in terms of linguistic difficulties, lack of skills, shortage of finance, and so on. Although the EU has free labour mobility, much of the immigration has arrived from non-EU countries. However, the amount of capital mobility has increased significantly since the 1960s, with a growing trend currently towards the integration of capital markets.

A subsequent contribution stressed the importance of 'openness' in the economy (McKinnon 1963). Highly open economies which are very dependent on trade will be able to rely on fiscal and monetary policies without needing to alter their exchange rates. Highly open economies have a high marginal propensity both to import and to export products. Where a balance-of-payments deficit exists, then deflation can rectify this, with only a small amount of deflation being required to restore a balance-of-payments equilibrium since much of the cut-back in expenditure will be on reduced imports. Countries will also prefer fixed exchange rates and eschew floating exchange rates where currency depreciation is highly inflationary (and workers do not have money illusion which would spark off wage inflationary pressure again). However, note that for stronger countries fixed exchange rates are more inflationary than allowing the exchange rate to appreciate in value.

EU countries have become much more open with the removal of intra-Community trading barriers: intra-EU imports and exports as a percentage of GDP more than doubled between 1960 and 1985. Intra-trade is particularly high for the Benelux countries, though lower for the UK. From the latter one may infer that the UK was correct in not wanting to join the EMS exchange rate mechanism (ERM), though in fact its growing trade with the Community means that there is not now a large difference between UK intra-trade with the EU compared with that conducted by other countries, such as Italy and France, with the Community.

Another criterion for an OCA which has been enunciated has been that of diversification (Kenen 1969). Highly diversified economies will be able to manage without having to rely on exchange rate changes, since if demand in one export sector falls, the effect will be small – assuming again a high mobility of labour and capital into other sectors. Although in a depression most export industries might be seriously affected, the larger economies in the Community are sufficiently diversified to withstand this to a greater extent than the smaller economies. It can be seen in examining individual EU economies that some countries may be prime members of an OCA on particular criteria, but not on others (Presley and Dennis 1976). For example, the Benelux countries are highly open, but they are much less diversified than the economies of the larger member states of the Community.

A far more important problem which has beset economies has been that of inflation, and it has been argued that a similar national propensity to inflate should be used as the main criterion for an OCA (Magnifico 1973, pp. 43–81). Inflation rates diverge since countries have different preferences and a different trade-off between unemployment and inflation. In any kind of monetary union some of the countries have to sacrifice their preferences, either conforming to one preference – usually that of the dominant country – or agreeing between themselves on a common objective. Greater problems arise where countries have different trade-offs, since even if they were to agree on the same unemployment preference, countries with Phillips curves closer to the origin, such as Germany, have lower inflation. Institutional labour-market practices partly underlie its lower wage-pushfulness; for example, its industrial unions and system of co-determination (*Mitbestimmung*).

Since the Phillips curve trade-off has partly broken down, it has been argued that any success in reducing unemployment can only be temporary; hence governments have little choice except to aim for price stability. This led to more persuasive views on the prospects for EMU (Presley and Dennis 1976). However, the monetarist approach of controlling the rate of growth of the money supply to create lower and convergent inflation has run into problems in defining and controlling money supply satisfactorily.

Where the four criteria for an OCA exist, then the case for EMU is strong, but there are difficulties in overcoming all of these obstacles. The USA provides a shining example to which the EU aspires, in which the dollar totally fulfils the true functions of money across a large geographical group of states. Furthermore, it has been argued that any misgivings one might harbour about abandoning the independent use of one's own exchange rate is misplaced where a complete union exists, that is, with economic policy co-ordination, a pool of foreign exchange reserves and a common Central Bank (El-Agraa 1994). However, where workers do suffer from money illusion, where only a pseudo-union exists (that is, incomplete EMU) and where there are different trade elasticities, it may still be argued that a multiplicity of currencies provides the most flexible adjustment to tackle regional disparities.

*The case for monetary union*
Monetary union comprises the essential ingredients of fixed exchange rates and the integration of capital markets, with complete union involving a single currency and a single monetary policy. The case for monetary union focuses more positively on all the benefits from monetary integration. It is also closely tied up with the CAP since changing exchange rates result in changing prices and incomes for farmers (see Chapter 4 on agriculture, and in particular the section on MCAs which were introduced to try to insulate agriculture from the consequences of these exchange rate alterations). Just as agriculture and monetary integration are closely linked, likewise other chapters show how monetary union needs integration in other spheres, such as regional and budgetary policies. Although MCAs helped to hold the CAP together, they resulted in various complications, misallocating resources by encouraging further high-cost production in countries such as West Germany. France was particularly upset to see West Germany adding further agricultural gains to its existing large industrial benefits. The issue of MCAs was a source of disruption in the general cosy relationship between Schmidt and Giscard d'Estaing in March 1979.

By 1979 the EC had become increasingly disenchanted with the volatile system of floating exchange rates. It was also very concerned about the need to offer some alternative to the increasing problems affecting the US dollar. Apart from the traditional concern about the dominance of the dollar and 'dollar imperialism' which has often been expressed by countries such as France, there was growing recognition over time that the USA's economic situation was deteriorating. The USA shared the problem of many other countries in terms of rising costs of imported energy, and a high propensity to import goods from countries such as Japan. But what constitutes a special and continuous long-term burden to the USA is its very high defence expenditure. The likelihood of a continuing balance-of-payments deficit in the USA makes holders of dollars keen to switch into other reserve currencies. Other national currencies have been reluctant or unable to fulfil this role; hence countries such as Germany, fearful of a rush of dollars driving up the value of the D-mark in an excessive and unstable way, have sought to develop a common EU monetary position.

There are positive financial benefits which accrue from having fixity of exchange rates and eventually a single currency. The flow of goods and capital is facilitated and there are economies in the amount of reserve holdings since these are pooled. When one moves on from fixed exchange rates to the eventual outcome of a single EU currency, then money can fully perform its function as a medium of exchange by eliminating the costs of money conversion. Markets will operate far more efficiently. In addition, if the currency becomes a key currency, which is highly likely, then, as with the dollar, benefits arise from seigniorage. Thus holders are prepared to hold that currency without pressing to exchange it, enabling the Union, if it wishes, to run a balance-of-payments deficit.

Some of the advantages to the EU from having a single currency have been estimated, though not as comprehensively as those accruing from the single market. Transaction-cost savings range from ECU 13.1 billion to ECU 19.2 billion (see Table 8.1). They amount to around 0.5 per cent of EU GDP and are in excess of the gains from removing border controls of around 0.25 per cent of EU GDP. However, like

*Table 8.1　Cost savings on intra-EC settlements by a single currency*

|  | Billion ECU 1990 Estimated range | |
|---|---|---|
| 1.　*Financial transaction costs* | | |
| 　　Bank transfers | 6.4 | 10.6 |
| 　　Banknotes, eurocheques, travellers' | | |
| 　　　cheques, credit cards | 1.8 | 2.5 |
| Total | 8.2 | 13.1 |
| 2.　*In-house costs* | 3.6 | 4.8 |
| 3.　*Reduction of cross-border payment costs* | 1.3 | 1.3 |
| Total | 13.1 | 19.2 |

*Note*:　Exchange transaction costs associated with several sources of in-house costs are not included in this table.

*Source*:　'One Market, One Money', *European Economy*, no. 49, October 1990.

border controls, their removal will be of greatest benefit to SMEs and small open economies. The single market needs to go hand in hand with EMU, and when all goods are priced in the same currency – so that consumers can easily compare prices – that will further reinforce the trend towards price convergence. Microeconomic benefits are enormous, but even at the macroeconomic level there are also some gains from a monetarist perspective. Dynamic benefits will be reaped as the anti-inflationary credibility and visibility of a single currency lead agents to modify their wage- and price-setting in a more disciplined way. This will increase business confidence, investment and the rate of economic growth in the Community.

*The winding road to EMU*

EMU was not mentioned explicitly in the Treaty of Rome and it did not provide for fixed and immutable exchange rates, though Articles 103–9 did set down the principles of unrestricted currency convertibility, abolition of restrictions on capital movements, and the co-ordination of economic policy. To facilitate co-ordination a Monetary Committee was established in 1958 and a Short-Term Economic Policy Committee in 1960. In 1964 there was formed a Committee of Governors of Central Banks, a Budgetary Policy Committee and a Medium-Term Policy Committee – these Committees were later merged into a new Economic Policy Committee.

While exchange rates remained fixed there was little point in initiating EMU and it was only when pressures built up in the late 1960s for exchange rate adjustments that the issue assumed some urgency. The devaluation of sterling in 1967 was followed in 1969 by the devaluation of the French franc and the revaluation of the D-mark. There was concern to prevent countries from resorting once again to protectionist measures, since France, for example, had introduced import controls in the immediate aftermath of the 1968 crisis.

In 1965 and 1969 both P. Werner and R. Barre came up with proposals for monetary reform, with the latter proposing, among other things, a system of monetary support and financial assistance to help economies experiencing balance-of-payments deficits. Both these personalities were to be influential over the next few years in shaping EMU, after the decision to introduce it at the European Summit in late 1969, under the leadership of Brandt and Pompidou.

While member states were persuaded of the benefits of EMU, there were significant differences in perspective, and to reconcile these a working party was established under P. Werner. The differences were largely between France and Germany, but alongside the French were Belgium and Luxembourg, while the German view was shared by the Dutch and sometimes by the Italians. These different perspectives have been given the label 'Monetarist versus Economist'. The monetarist position was to favour a commitment to fixed exchange rates and pooling reserves along the lines of the second Barre Plan, published in March 1970. The competing economist strategy was not to rush ahead with monetary union since this was 'putting the cart before the horse' before economic co-ordination had been achieved. The West German approach was enshrined in the Schiller Plan in March 1970. This detailed Plan divided the progress towards EMU into clear stages and it was only in the final stage that a common currency was to be introduced. West Germany has been concerned to persuade other countries to reduce their excessive rates of inflation, since under a fixed exchange rate system it felt that it was importing inflation from others. A greater co-ordination of macroeconomic policies, in particular to reduce wide national disparities in rates of inflation, has been an ongoing concern of Germany.

The Werner Committee had to resolve these different perspectives, coming up with a compromise described as one of 'parallelism' (Kruse 1980, pp. 70–5); that is, parallel advance on both fronts in co-ordinating economic policy and moving forward by narrowing exchange rate margins, integrating capital markets and finally establishing a common currency and a single Central Bank. In March 1971 EMU was born and a stage-by-stage timetable was over-optimistically drawn up for its full achievement by 1980.

The main outcome was the creation of the 'snake' in 1972. The international monetary order had already been shaken by the devaluation of the dollar and the Smithsonian Agreement in December 1971, after which there was a widening of the margins of currency fluctuations which had existed during the postwar period. The original ±1 per cent margin (a band of 2 per cent) was now widened internationally to ±2.25 per cent (a band of 4.5 per cent). EC countries themselves decided to limit the range of their own member currencies to a band of 2.25 per cent, hence the band for the snake was half the width of the 4.5 per cent 'tunnel'.

In preparation for the first enlargement of the Community, the UK, Denmark and Ireland were to be included. However, in June 1972 speculation drove both sterling and the Irish pound from the snake and the tunnel, followed a few days later by the Danish krone – though Denmark was able to rejoin the scheme later that year. Italy withdrew from it at the beginning of 1973 and in spring 1973 the international fixed exchange rate mechanism collapsed and was replaced by one of floating exchange rates. Although the snake continued between those EC countries that were able to participate, the system floated in relation to other currencies, and thus the snake ceased to be 'in the tunnel'. Between 1973 and 1978 there were widespread currency realignments and further departures from the snake: for example, by France on two occasions, 1974 and 1976; and Sweden, which had participated, withdrew in 1977. These have been described quite aptly as 'les vicissitudes du serpent monétaire' (Moussis 1982, pp. 60–4).

The official target to achieve EMU by 1980 was dropped, but that did not prevent a plethora of new reports making further suggestions and recommendations. In 1974 Fourcade made a French proposal for a larger snake – a boa – which would have wider margins and allow countries to withdraw and re-enter the system. In 1975 a study group chaired by Marjolin reached the pessimistic conclusion that the prospects for EMU had been destroyed by discordant economic and monetary policies. Yet reports continued to circulate, with a group of prominent economists in 1975 suggesting the issue of a parallel currency – the Europa – for private use. A Belgian proposal by Tindemans in 1976 sought to strengthen the snake and suggested that a parallel currency might help. It also recommended greater co-ordination of economic policies, though it fell short of any target or deadlines for EMU. This was followed in the same year by a Dutch proposal (Duisenberg chairing the Council of Ministers) that European currencies ought to come closer together and that economic co-ordination might be improved by the creation of 'target zones'.

Despite adverse economic circumstances, a series of reports and favourable public opinion provided continued momentum; for example, Eurobarometer surveys recorded public opinion in favour of a European currency. There was greater support for a European currency to replace weaker national currencies in countries such as Italy than in those with stronger currencies, such as West Germany. Although the ambitious goal of EMU was postponed, the Community made a renewed and modest start again via the EMS.

*Political initiatives to launch EMS membership*
The political initiative for the EMS was taken by Roy Jenkins in his capacity as President of the EC Commission. He argued in a speech in

Florence in October 1977 that in the new situation of high inflation and high unemployment, the EMS could help to alleviate both macroeconomic problems. This reflected the new economic analysis starting from lower inflation, from which would come lower unemployment. This approach differed from and contradicted the original Phillips curve analysis in which inflation was inversely related to the level of unemployment.

The Community was in much need of redirection and the choice of the EMS was timely and appealed to West Germany, which Jenkins courted in his speech in Bonn in December 1977. His ideas were well received since it was clear that the dollar faced major problems and there was an international currency vacuum which could only be filled by a West German monetary initiative. In the past West Germany had accepted American monetary initiatives and American hegemony, showing a marked absence of responsibility for the international monetary system. The EMS provided it with a historic opportunity to take the leading role, since it would gain very much both at an international level and also domestically from greater currency stability. West Germany was concerned about the damaging effects of overvaluation of the D-mark which were eroding its export competitiveness, and hoped that in the EMS it would be able to depress the value of the mark. Chancellor Schmidt became a major instigator of the EMS, but he had to contend with some internal scepticism; for example, there was concern about West Germany becoming more prone to inflation in the EMS, whereas with the floating D-mark, currency appreciation dampened inflation. There was also worry about the degree to which West Germany would have to support weaker currencies and weaker economies. Nevertheless, on balance the EMS seemed favourable and by co-operating with other EC countries West Germany hoped to reduce the pressure on key currencies such as the mark and the dollar.

The next crucial step was to engage the support of Giscard d'Estaing in France, since Franco-German co-operation has formed the heart of Community developments. Politically France wished to remain shoulder to shoulder with West Germany in the first division of world powers, rather than head the second division. It offered France an opportunity to avoid a continual slide in the value of the franc, while a stronger franc would help the French to pursue an effective anti-inflationary strategy. It was naturally important to enlist other countries into membership of the EMS, though if that proved impossible then at least the range of credit facilities to support weaker members would not be dispersed so widely. It would be those weaker members that would enter the lower division of a two-tier Community.

Weaker countries, such as Italy, responded positively to avoid confirming its position in the second tier. Since Italy had taken the decision to become a founder member of earlier bodies such as the ECSC at a time when its steel industry could have been swamped by more competitive imports, it recognized the benefits of being in at the beginning of any new developments – in particular if special arrangements could be made. Italy also hoped that strict monetary obligations inherent in the system would be more effective than internal exhortations for restraint in dampening inflationary pressure. While Italy would have welcomed a really fundamental restructuring of the Budget and the CAP to provide a greater transfer of resources, after a pause for reflection it joined the EMS. It did so on the basis of guiding the lira downwards to an undervalued level and operating with wide margins of ±6 per cent (but later conformed to the standard ±2.25 per cent, having gained sufficient anti-inflationary credibility to dismantle its wage-indexation system – the Scala Mobile – in the 1980s).

The entry of the three major EC countries into the EMS was accompanied by the smaller countries which fully joined the system. They were enthusiastic, since small countries often manifest an even greater dependence upon trade as a percentage of GNP, and with high imports currency depreciation creates inflationary instability. The Dutch have shared a close identity of interest with Germany. Belgian influence was reflected by personalities such as Tindemans and van Ypersele who sought to reconcile the perspectives of different countries in a search for compromise and agreement. Denmark was also concerned with monetary discipline, though often less successful in actually achieving low inflation and currency stability.

The Irish decision to join the EMS manifested a resurgence of political confidence in seizing the opportunity to break free from its historic satellite currency link with sterling. In the past the Irish punt has been dragged down by successive devaluations of sterling, but there was now concern that the punt might appreciate in relation to sterling, adversely affecting Irish trade. In practice the opposite has occurred and since 1979 the punt has depreciated against sterling. While this has favoured Irish trade, the pattern of its trade has diversified towards other EC countries. Ireland has welcomed this and felt that in the traditional currency arrangements of the British Isles, its economic fortunes were tied too closely to the slow-growing and inflation-prone UK economy.

The balance between the two economies was maintained very much by the drain of free factor movements and by high interest rates in Ireland. In joining the EMS Ireland gained financial assistance, confident that if or when the UK decided to join, it would have illustrated its political and monetary independence from the UK. Having benefited so much from the CAP, it saw little to be gained by acceding to British requests for the EMS to be linked with agricultural and budgetary reform.

### EMS: the mechanics of operation and the ECU

The design and mechanics of the EMS differed from those of its predecessor, the snake, in various ways. A most important and central new creation was the European Currency Unit (ECU) which replaced the earlier units of account which were used by the Community. Apart from its book-keeping function, the ECU acted as the denominator for the ERM; it provided the basis of the divergence indicator; it was the denominator for operations in both the intervention and credit mechanism; it was also accepted as a means of settlement between monetary authorities in the Community.

The ECU was composed of a fixed amount of each Community currency in its 'basket', whose individual percentage share was based on the country's respective GDP, trade and short-term credit quotas. While the weight of ECU currencies in the basket was fixed, changes in market exchange rates resulted in an increasing weight of appreciating currencies, and the falling weight of depreciating currencies such as sterling. To avoid the risk that the ECU might become overdominated by the strongest currency in the basket, arrangements were made for the shares of the ECU basket to be examined if the weight of one currency changed by 25 per cent or more; it was also agreed that the composition of the basket would normally be re-examined every five years. The composition of the ECU is shown in Table 8.2.

The drachma was incorporated, with a very low share of the ECU, but a high rate of inflation in Greece was an obstacle to its participation in the exchange rate mechanism. In contrast, the Spanish Prime Minister, Felipe Gonzalez, drove down the rate of inflation so that Spain could participate in the ERM. At first the peseta shadowed the D-mark and then in June 1989 Spain joined the ERM on a wide band of ±6 per cent. The peseta accounted for just over 5 per cent of the ECU, and it performed strongly in 1990, supported by high interest rates.

*Table 8.2 Composition of the ECU*

| Currencies | Amounts of national currencies | | % share of currencies in the basket | |
|---|---|---|---|---|
| | in the original ECU basket 13 March 1979 | in the revised ECU basket, October 1990 | 13 March 1979 | October 1990 |
| German mark | 0.828 | 0.6242 | 32.98 | 30.4 |
| Pound sterling | 0.0885 | 0.08784 | 13.34 | 12.6 |
| French franc | 1.15 | 1.332 | 19.83 | 19.3 |
| Italian lira | 109.0 | 151.8 | 9.50 | 9.9 |
| Dutch guilder | 0.286 | 0.2198 | 10.51 | 9.5 |
| Belgian franc | 3.66 ⎫ | 3.431 | 9.63 | 8.5 |
| Luxembourg franc | 0.14 ⎭ | | | |
| Danish krone | 0.217 | 0.1976 | 3.06 | 2.5 |
| Irish punt | 0.00759 | 0.008552 | 1.15 | 1.1 |
| Greek drachma | – | 1.44 | – | 0.7 |
| Spanish peseta | – | 6.885 | – | 5.2 |
| Portuguese escudo | – | 1.393 | – | 0.8 |
| | | | 100.0 | 100.0 |

*Sources*: European Documentation, *The ECU*, Luxembourg; *Lloyds Bank Economic Bulletin*, no. 143, November 1990.

*The ECU, the Exchange Rate Mechanism and the divergence indicator* Each currency participating in the EMS had a central rate expressed in ECUs: this was derived from the rates ruling in the snake, while for others it was based on those existing on 12 March 1979. From these central rates a grid of cross-parities was derived for each pair of currencies in the system. Around these parities margins of ±2.25 per cent were allowed, and for weaker currencies, such as Italy, a wider margin of ±6.0 per cent was agreed. Intervention occurred to enable currencies to operate within these parities. There was much discussion about whether the intervention should be based on the bilateral grid or on the deviation of a currency in relation to the ECU. There were various technical objections to the use of the latter (Ypersele and Koeune 1985, pp. 48–9). Some concern was expressed, for example, that the divergence of one currency against the ECU would not necessarily be accompanied by the divergence of another currency in the opposite direction, and this would make it difficult to decide which currency to use for intervention purposes. It was decided, therefore, after the 'Belgian compromise', partially to use an ECU-based divergence indicator from which there would be a presumption to act, but that the bilateral grid would provide the automatic intervention. Thus the Central Bank of the country whose currency had appreciated to its full margin would buy the currency of the weak country which had depreciated, and the latter's Central Bank would sell the strong currency.

Both the ECU and the innovation of the divergence indicator constitute major differences from the earlier snake system, with the ECU having proved more important than the divergence indicator. The maximum divergence spread of a given currency against the ECU is ±2.25 per cent and the divergence is set at 75 per cent of this spread. Some observers may be puzzled as to why the variations are not precisely three-quarters of this; this can be explained by each country's currency being a fixed part of the ECU basket. The formula to calculate the divergence limit is ±2.25 per cent multiplied by $(1-w)$, where $w$ is the weight of the currency for which the divergence spread is being calculated. The greater the weight of the currency, the smaller is its maximum spread. Thus West Germany has the lowest percentage divergence limit. When the D-mark was 37.38 per cent of the ECU, the market ECU rate of the mark rose by 2.25 per cent × $(1.00 - 0.3738)$ of this; that is, by 1.40895 per cent. The divergence indicator is three-quarters of this; that is, 1.0567. Italy had the widest divergence limit because of the ±6 per cent applied to the lira.

In general, a currency will reach its divergence threshold before reaching its bilateral limit against another currency; but it is possible for it to reach its bilateral limit first when two currencies are at opposite poles, and all the other currencies are fairly stable. When a currency crosses its divergence threshold the authorities are expected to correct the situation by various policies; these include diversified intervention in different currencies to provide a better spread in the burden of intervention between EMS currencies; also, by domestic policies, in particular interest rate changes, plus other measures such as incomes policy. Finally, changes in central rates may be made, but to ensure that these do not occur too frequently and are not carried out unilaterally, extensive financial assistance is provided so that countries can fulfil their EMS obligations. This financial assistance was more extensive than that available under the snake, in spite of Germany's attempts to limit the amount. Short-term finance was made available for 45 days, compared with 30 days under the snake. In the EMS, short-term financial support was offered for nine months and medium-term financial assistance for a period of between two and five years. Measures were also introduced to strengthen the economies of weaker member states. While the full demands of Italy and Ireland, in particular for large grants, could not be met, it was agreed that loans would be made available which could receive interest-rate subsidies from bodies like the EIB.

Various recommendations were made on ways to strengthen the EMS: these could include some indicator of convergence measures, rather like the divergence indicator, with an expectation that the Commission would be obliged to issue warnings to members to take appropriate action. More concrete developments included a restatement of the objective of EMU in Article 20 of the Single European Act. In addition, in September 1987 European finance ministers agreed on new measures to defend currencies in the EMS, before the weaker ones reached their floor. They also agreed on an increase in the short-term credits available to defend currencies, to extend the repayment period and to allow greater repayments in ECUs rather than West German marks.

The financial support available was derived from countries depositing part of their gold and dollar holdings with the European Monetary Co-operation Fund (EMCF) and the countries concerned were credited with ECUs. It was intended that the EMCF would be turned within two years into the European Monetary Fund (EMF) and that there would be full use of the ECU as a reserve asset and means of settlement. However, the transition to this second phase had to be delayed and the Community has faced real problems throughout in adhering to its timetable for EMU.

*The ECU's attractiveness to users*  The ECU carried out some of the functions of money, but not the key medium of exchange role, and there were no ECU notes or coins circulating in member states. Belgium made a start in 1987 by minting commemorative ECU coins. Other progressive steps were suggested, such as the issue of a limited amount of ECUs to be used by tourists and migrant frontier workers to save them the costs of currency conversion; also, that ECU postage stamps could be introduced.

The ECU still offered many benefits in its usage, not merely as a standard unit of account for the operation of the Community, but also for private-sector activities. Since the ECU comprised a weighted average of EC currencies, each member currency deviated less against the ECU than against other member currencies, hence reducing exchange-rate risks. Indeed, the private sector made wide use of the ECU, with some multinational companies, such as the French company Saint-Gobain, drawing up their financial accounts in ECUs, and others such as Alcatel settling all intra-company transactions in ECUs. The ECU was also used increasingly in addition to dollars by airlines for settling their accounts. More European joint ventures in Eastern Europe were denominated in ECUs. Elsewhere some bodies in distant countries started to use ECUs, and the Wheat Board in Australia denominated contracts in ECUs. Some European countries opted to invoice customers in ECUs since it reduced exposure to adverse exchange-rate movements. In Italy nearly a third of companies sampled claimed to have done this; for example, in 1986 about $1 billion worth of Italy's exports were invoiced in ECUs.

Both savers and borrowers recognized the advantages of operating through ECUs instead of national currencies. They received a more stable return, avoiding the unforeseen effects of volatile changes in national exchange rates. Money placed in ECUs earned a weighted average of member countries' interest rates. Savers were quickly able to open ECU accounts for fairly small amounts in Belgium and Luxembourg, though West Germany initially restricted the opening of such accounts as it was opposed to any kind of index-linked savings, classing the ECU in that category. By 1987 West Germany showed some inclination to relax its opposition to ECU accounts, provided other countries in return would ease their controls on the movement of capital. Savers living in strong-currency countries received a higher interest rate in ECUs (though they risked accepting some depreciation against their own currency). Savers living in weak-currency countries and investing in ECUs were better protected against losses by depreciation. Some savers in Belgium, Italy and France became enthusiastic about ECUs.

The ECU offered advantages to borrowers and it grew to become one of the major bond-issuing currencies, along with the dollar, D-mark, sterling and special drawing right (SDR). The composition of the SDR basket was simplified but was so dominated by the dollar that the ECU was favoured by investors looking for a dollar alternative. By using ECUs borrowers in weak-currency countries were able to raise capital abroad more easily and at a lower interest rate than at home.

A strategy for developing the ECU was drawn up, commissioned by the Association for the Monetary Union of Europe: this was established originally under the auspices of Helmut Schmidt and Giscard d'Estaing. There is strong business support which is keen on a single currency – though banks will be affected by losing their profitable foreign-exchange activities. To accelerate use of the ECU a clear timetable of developments was recommended for both public- and private-sector institutions during the 1990s. These initially included enhanced information about the ECU; removing administrative barriers to its usage; and banks offering the full range of ECU services. That was to be followed by additional measures, such as insurance companies marketing ECU policies, companies recording their Stock Exchange accounts in ECUs and also being allowed to issue share capital in ECUs. Some businesses, such as the travel trade, were naturally likely to move towards ECU pricing. Later, commodity trade could be denominated in ECUs, and companies encouraged to pay taxes in ECUs, invoice in ECUs and record their accounts in ECUs. Finally, machines were to be converted and prices quoted in ECUs so that the EU would attain a single currency.

### Evaluating the performance of the EMS

Any evaluation is limited by the difficulty of determining what the situation would have been like without the EMS; also, there are many facets of the EMS. In addition, much depends upon which end of the exchange-rate spectrum one prefers, since if the aim is exchange-rate fixity, then some would argue that the system has been too flexible, with overuse of adjustment in central rates. Nevertheless, the general experience of currencies operating outside the EMS has been one of far greater volatility in exchange rates.

Overall, the EMS is recognized as being fairly successful, despite early misgivings by those who preferred monetary union to take place through the introduction of a European parallel currency (Zis 1984, pp. 59–60). After the two devaluations of the Danish krone late in 1979, along with a small revaluation of the West German mark, no currency realignments were necessary in 1980. Circumstances were favourable, partly because weaker currencies, such as the lira, had entered the EMS at low central exchange-rate levels, and with a wider margin for the lira. Italy survived without having to devalue until October 1981. West Germany continued to control its inflation with greater success than other countries, though the rise in oil prices severely affected its balance of payments, creating a massive external deficit in 1980. Apart from the D-mark weakening in 1980 against the EMS currencies, it also weakened against the dollar: this helped to take some of the speculative pressure off the mark as buyers purchased dollars. Indeed, longer-term problems have arisen when the dollar has weakened, and investors have switched into the mark, driving up its value. In the medium and long term, the lower rate of inflation in West Germany has caused pressure for further revaluation *vis-à-vis* other EMS currencies.

Table 8.3 shows the changes in EMS central rates. Between 1981 and 1983 five currency realignments occurred; these mainly affected the franc and lira in devaluations and to a lesser extent the Danish krone and the Irish punt. These currency realignments resulted in agreed changes which were conducted quite swiftly and without major panic of the kind which had existed under the fixed exchange-rate system of Bretton Woods. The alignments also resulted in more symmetry, with the stronger currencies also experiencing revaluation at the same time. The main revaluations have been to the West German mark and to a lesser extent to the Dutch guilder. The exchange-rate adjustments were usually accompanied by internal domestic policies to make the currency changes more effective and conducive to the maintenance of durable equilibrium.

There were no EMS currency alignments in 1984 and only one in 1985 – a significant depreciation of the Italian lira. April 1986 marked the ninth alignment in EMS, triggered mainly by weakness of the French franc, since French inflation had reduced the competitiveness of its manufactured goods. France had sought a larger devaluation than that eventually agreed upon; a collective package emerged in which there were accompanying currency readjustments, with the usual revaluations of the D-mark and the Dutch guilder. Italy's decision not to devalue the lira in 1986 aroused some misgivings by Italian businessmen fearing loss of competitiveness, which left the Italian lira vulnerable to a later devaluation.

The French franc and the German mark came under strong speculative pressure in January 1987, resulting in another realignment of the EMS. This became necessary because a weakening of the US dollar led to a flow of money towards the D-mark. The French government suggested that it was mainly a German problem and this was reflected by the revaluation of the D-mark by 3 per cent (along with the Dutch guilder), while leaving the French franc unchanged. West Germany bowed to speculative pressure, preferring the anti-inflationary effects of

*Table 8.3   Changes in EMS central rates: dates of realignments (%)*

| | Belg./Lux. franc | Danish krone | German mark | French franc | Irish punt | Italian lira | Dutch guilder | Spanish peseta | Portuguese escudo |
|---|---|---|---|---|---|---|---|---|---|
| 1979: 24/9 | – | –2.9 | +2.0 | – | – | – | – | | |
| 1979: 31/11 | – | –4.8 | – | – | – | – | – | | |
| 1981: 2/3 | – | – | – | – | – | –6.0 | – | | |
| 1981: 5/10 | – | –3.0 | +5.5 | –3.0 | – | –3.0 | +5.5 | | |
| 1982: 22/2 | –8.5 | –3.0 | | | | | | | |
| 1982: 14/6 | – | | +4.25 | –5.75 | – | –2.75 | +4.25 | | |
| 1983: 21/3 | +1.5 | +2.5 | +5.5 | –2.5 | –3.5 | –2.5 | +3.5 | | |
| 1985: 21/7 | +2.0 | +2.0 | +2.0 | +2.0 | +2.0 | –6.0 | +2.0 | | |
| 1986: 7/4 | +1.0 | +1.0 | +3.0 | –3.0 | – | – | +3.0 | | |
| 1986: 4/8 | – | – | – | – | –8.0 | – | – | | |
| 1987: 12/1 | +2.0 | – | +3.0 | – | – | – | +3.0 | | |
| 1989: 19/6 | Entry of Spanish peseta | | | | | | | | |
| 1990: 8/10 | Entry of UK pound | | | | | | | | |
| 1990: 1/1 | – | | – | – | – | –3.7 | – | | |
| 1992: 6/4 | Entry of Portuguese escudo | | | | | | | | |
| 1992: 14/9 | +3.5 | +3.5 | +3.5 | +3.5 | –3.5 | –3.5 | +3.5 | – | – |
| 1992: 17/9 | Departure of UK pound: Italian lira suspended | | | | | | | –5.0 | –6.0 |
| 1992: 23/11 | | | | | | | | –6.0 | – |
| 1993: 1/2 | – | | – | – | –10.0 | – | – | – | –6.5 |
| 1993: 14/5 | | | | | | | | | |
| 1993: 2/8 | Widening of bands to ±15% for all ERM members | | | | | | | | |
| 1995: 1/1 | Entry of Austria | | | | | | | | |
| 1995: 5/3 | | | | | | | | | –3.5 |

*Source:   Financial Times,* 1979–95.

revaluation to reducing interest rates or increasing domestic expenditure. To limit the full manifestation of French weaknesses, other countries which preferred to revalue in January 1987 had their requests refused. A growing balance-of-payments deficit by some countries with West Germany, which could have turned the system further towards a crawling-peg mechanism, was alleviated partly by the reduction in the united Germany's external balance.

There was some loosening of exchange controls under the EMS during the 1980s. These were the first significant movements since 1962 when the EC removed foreign-exchange restrictions linked to trade and individual change in residence, but not those dealing with share placements, short-term investment and individual investment across borders. In November 1986 EC finance ministers agreed on a package obliging members to remove exchange controls on long-term credit and on buying and selling unlisted securities, unit trusts and other mutual funds. A full removal of control on capital movements became the target for 1992. However, there was a danger that fully mobile capital flows – given continuing divergences in economic performance – could destabilize the exchange-rate mechanism.

Resorts to currency alignments in the EMS were less frequent than critics predicted and they were agreed collectively, so the onus did not fall solely on the weaker countries to devalue. There has been more stability in the exchange rate between EMS countries and a significant reduction in exchange-rate variability (both nominal and real) compared with the average of outside countries (Gros and Thygesen 1992, pp. 102–7). For example, other currencies such as sterling and the dollar have been much more volatile. There was greater convergence in the level of interest rates, since a genuine commitment of a weaker currency to exchange-rate fixity enabled its interest-rate differential to fall towards the German level. There was some consensus on the need to bring down the rate of inflation, and the average growth rates of monetary aggregates fell after 1979 and inflation differentials narrowed.

During the period 1983–9, the average rate of inflation for the EC(12) was 4.1 per cent per annum, but 3.2 per cent per annum for members of the ERM. Table 8.4 shows inflation ranging from an average of 1.0 per cent per annum for the Netherlands to 5.9 per cent per annum in Italy. Spain became a potential member with an inflation rate of 6.5 per cent, but the double-digit inflation of Greece and Portugal precluded entry to the ERM – though their unemployment was below the EC average. The average rate of unemployment in the Community

Table 8.4  *EC macroeconomic performance, 1983–9*

| % | Belg. | Den. | Ger. | Gre. | Spa. | Fra. | Ire. | Ita. | Lux. | Neth. | Port. | UK | EC(12) |
|---|---|---|---|---|---|---|---|---|---|---|---|---|---|
| Annual average | | | | | | | | | | | | | |
| Total economic growth[1] | 2.2 | 2.1 | 2.5 | 2.1 | 3.6 | 2.1 | 3.0 | 3.0 | 4.1 | 2.3 | 2.8 | 3.6 | 2.8 |
| Inflation | 4.1 | 4.0 | 1.2 | 16.3 | 6.5 | 3.3 | 3.8 | 5.9 | 2.1 | 1.0 | 12.3 | 4.6 | 5.4 |
| Unemployment[2] | 11.3 | 7.0 | 6.7 | 8.5 | 20.1 | 10.1 | 17.6 | 10.2 | 2.6 | 10.4 | 7.2 | 10.0 | 10.3 |

*Notes:*
[1] GDP market prices (at constant prices)
[2] Unemployment average, 1984–89

*Source:*  Calculated from Eurostat (1990).

215

remained stubbornly high (averaging just over 10 per cent per annum). The sacrifice rate (the reduction in inflation created by a 1 per cent increase in unemployment) was measured for the EMS (minus Germany) at a 1.8 per cent reduction in inflation for a 1 per cent rise in unemployment (Gros and Thygesen 1992). Although better than for the non-EMS countries where inflation and unemployment rose, the result was not robust, and some non-EC countries have been able to maintain a much better unemployment record. Without lower inflation really succeeding in securing a faster rate of economic growth to bring down unemployment, some countries were under severe pressure to reflate their economies. For example, the tolerable trade-off between unemployment and inflation in Luxembourg, Germany and the Netherlands contrasted with an unfavourable trade-off in countries such as Ireland and Spain, with about one in five out of work. Ultimately some countries' preferences and priorities are pushed by political and social pressure towards the reduction of unemployment instead of a relentless pursuit of anti-inflationary policies *per se*.

### The ERM crises, 1992–3
The exchange-rate stability under the EMS came under a severe speculative challenge which was mounted because of doubts about the timetable of progression to EMU. For example, the Danish referendum contributed to this uncertainty. There was speculative pressure on weaker currencies such as the Italian lira, whose inflation rate became excessive, and this led to a devaluation of the lira. However, perhaps the major source of the problem was German reunification, which placed great strain on the role of the D-mark as the anchor currency of the ERM. The massive budgetary transfers to Eastern Germany led to an increase in German inflation and the Bundesbank responded by raising its interest rate. This meant that other countries could only maintain their ERM parities by raising their interest rates, creating heavy unemployment. Speculators doubted the will of countries to persist with continued deflation, and the removal of capital controls led to massive speculation. The outcome was a series of violent currency realignments, in which central banks incurred huge losses. The lira and sterling were ejected from the system and the ERM bands of fluctuation were widened to ±15 per cent.

### Stages of development towards convergence
The process of EMU was given an élite impetus by central bankers who participated in the Delors Report in 1988/89 and this provided the

general path of three phases which underpinned the Maastricht Treaty progress to EMU. The first phase, from the beginning of July 1990, was to achieve closer co-operation within the existing EMS and greater macroeconomic convergence. However, after the Rome Summit the aim of getting all 12 EC currencies into stage 1 before proceeding further was diluted in favour of a vaguer objective of securing the greatest possible number of currencies in the ERM. It provided for exceptions which applied to weaker countries such as Greece.

The first stage of monetary integration also entailed making full progress to free capital mobility by removing exchange controls. When the EMS was established in 1979 all countries, except West Germany, the Netherlands and the UK, used tight controls on capital movements. Other countries, such as France, Italy and Belgium, gradually liberalized their capital flows, with Spain and Ireland moving into line by 1992 and Portugal and Greece by 1994. It has been recognized that capital controls tend to postpone eventual and more desirable long-run structural changes, and as economies converge there will be less need to resort to such controls. They also fit uneasily into the greater deregulation of financial markets.

The policy of setting target dates for various stages of EMU continued in order to maintain momentum. The second stage began on 1 January 1994; it involved the creation of new institutions, in particular the European Monetary Institute (EMI), located in Frankfurt, and this was the precursor of a new European Central Bank (ECB). The EMI sought to co-ordinate national monetary policies, moving towards a common monetary policy. It oversaw the operation of the ERM and also took over the tasks of the European Monetary Co-operation Fund. National Central Banks (NCBs) were made independent to reinforce their anti-inflationary resolve by avoiding governmental political intervention. Progress towards NCB independence and convergence was monitored in EMI reports to ensure compatibility with the Treaty.

Various convergence criteria were established in stage 2 before progress could be made to the final stage of EMU. Inflation was not to be more than 1.5 per cent above that of the three best-performing states. Another convergence criterion, again to keep a watchful long-term eye on inflationary expectations, was that long-term interest rates were to be kept within 2 per cent of the three lowest member states. The normal fluctuation margins of ±2.25 per cent without devaluation for two years had been thrown into disarray by currency speculation, but widening the band created opportunities for greater exchange-rate durability. The

*Table 8.5   Economic indicators and the Maastricht Treaty convergence criteria (excluding the exchange-rate criterion)*

| | | HICP inflation[1] | Long-term interest rate[3] | General government surplus (+) or deficit (−)[2] | General government gross debt[2] |
|---|---|---|---|---|---|
| Belgium | 1996 | 1.8 | 6.5 | −3.2 | 126.9 |
| | 1997[4] | 1.4 | 5.7 | † −2.1 | 122.2 |
| | 1998[5] | – | – | † −1.7 | 118.1 |
| Denmark[1] | 1996 | 2.1 | 7.2 | † −0.7 | 70.6 |
| | 1997[4] | 1.9 | 6.2 | † 0.7 | 65.1 |
| | 1998[5] | – | – | † 1.1 | 59.5 † |
| Germany | 1996 | 1.2 | 6.2 | −3.4 | 60.4 |
| | 1997[4] | 1.4 | 5.6 | † −2.7 | 61.3 |
| | 1998[5] | – | – | † −2.5 | 61.2 |
| Greece | 1996 | 7.9 | 14.4 | −7.5 | 111.6 |
| | 1997[4] | 5.2 | 9.8 | −4.0 | 108.7 |
| | 1998[5] | – | – | † −2.2 | 107.7 |
| Spain | 1996 | 3.6 | 8.7 | −4.6 | 70.1 |
| | 1997[4] | 1.8 | 6.3 | † −2.6 | 68.8 |
| | 1998[5] | – | – | † −2.2 | 67.4 |
| France | 1996 | 2.1 | 6.3 | −4.1 | 55.7 † |
| | 1997[4] | ** 1.2 | ** 5.5 | † −3.0 | 58.0 † |
| | 1998[5] | – | – | † −2.9 | 58.1 † |
| Ireland | 1996 | 2.2 | 7.3 | † −0.4 | 72.7 |
| | 1997[4] | *** 1.2 | *** 6.2 | † 0.9 | 66.3 |
| | 1998[5] | – | – | † 1.1 | 59.5 † |
| Italy | 1996 | 4.0 | 9.4 | −6.7 | 124.0 |
| | 1997[4] | 1.8 | 6.7 | † −2.7 | 121.6 |
| | 1998[5] | – | – | † −2.5 | 118.1 |
| Luxembourg | 1996 | *** 1.2 | *** 6.3 | † 2.5 | 6.6 † |
| | 1997[4] | 1.4 | 5.6 | † 1.7 | 6.7 † |
| | 1998[5] | – | – | † 1.0 | 7.1 † |

| Country | Year | HICP inflation | | Long-term interest rate | | Deficit | | Gross debt |
|---|---|---|---|---|---|---|---|---|
| Netherlands | 1996 | 1.4 | | 6.2 | | -2.3 | † | 77.2 |
| | 1997[4] | 1.8 | | 5.5 | | -1.4 | † | 72.1 |
| | 1998[5] | – | | – | | -1.6 | † | 70.0 |
| Austria | 1996 | 1.8 | | 6.3 | | -4.0 | | 69.5 |
| | 1997[4] | 1.1 | * | 5.6 | | -2.5 | † | 66.1 |
| | 1998[5] | – | | – | | -2.3 | † | 64.7 |
| Portugal | 1996 | 2.9 | | 8.6 | | -3.2 | | 65.0 |
| | 1997[4] | 1.8 | | 6.2 | | -2.5 | † | 62.0 |
| | 1998[5] | – | | – | | -2.2 | † | 60.0 |
| Finland | 1996 | 1.1 | ** | 7.1 | ** | -3.3 | | 57.6 † |
| | 1997[4] | 1.3 | | 5.9 | | -0.9 | † | 55.8 † |
| | 1998[5] | – | | – | | 0.3 | † | 53.6 † |
| Sweden | 1996 | 0.8 | * | 8.0 | * | -3.5 | | 76.7 |
| | 1997[4] | 1.9 | | 6.5 | | -0.8 | † | 76.6 |
| | 1998[5] | – | | – | | 0.5 | † | 74.1 |
| United Kingdom[4] | 1996 | 2.5 | | 7.9 | | -4.8 | | 54.7 † |
| | 1997 | 1.8 | | 7.0 | | -1.9 | † | 53.4 † |
| | 1998[5] | – | | – | | -0.6 | † | 52.3 † |

*Notes:*

\* ** *** First, second- and third-best performer in terms of price stability.

† General government deficit not exceeding 3% of GDP; general government gross debt not exceeding 60% of GDP.

1 Annual percentage changes.

2 As a percentage of GDP.

3 In percentages.

4 Data for HICP inflation and long-term interest rate refer to the 12-month period ending January 1998; European Commission (spring 1998 forecasts) for general government surplus or deficit and general government gross debt.

5 European Commission projections (spring 1998 forecasts) for general government surplus or deficit and general government gross debt.

*Source:* European Monetary Institute, 1998.

final criteria involved a national budget deficit less than 3 per cent of GDP and the ratio of government debt to GDP not exceeding 60 per cent. The Commission could be tolerant provided the ratios were moving towards these levels. Despite high unemployment, governments pressed on towards these targets and by a combination of strong policies and some fudging, the targets were largely achieved, as shown in Table 8.5.

On inflation, the Harmonized Index of Consumer Prices (HICP) showed the three best countries were: Austria (1.1 per cent), France (1.2 per cent), and Ireland (1.2 per cent), and adding 1.5 per cent to the average of 1.2 per cent, the reference value was 2.7 per cent. Only Greece failed on this. On long-term interest rates 14 countries were below the reference value. The lowest interest rates were: 5.6 per cent (Austria), 5.5 per cent (France), 6.2 per cent (Ireland), and adding 2 per cent to the average 5.8 per cent, the reference level was 7.8 per cent. With regard to the exchange rate – March 1996 to February 1998 – ten currencies were in the ERM for two years, but Finland and Italy for a shorter period of time. With regard to the fiscal surplus, three countries were in surplus in 1997 – Denmark, Ireland and Luxembourg – and 11 had deficits below 3 per cent. Again, only Greece was above this. The main weakness was in general government gross debt, and though privatization and expenditure cuts had helped to reduce this, three countries were still above 100 per cent: Belgium, Greece and Italy.

The third stage of EMU, originally for some time in 1997 but ultimately delayed to 1999, was the replacement of locked currencies by a single currency (the euro) and a single monetary policy (rather than the British preference for a common currency alongside national currencies).

*The reality of the ECB and the euro*
In May 1998 the European Council invited the large majority of countries (11) which were able to meet the Maastricht convergence conditions to join the EMU. The four non-members were the UK, Denmark, Sweden, which all opted out, and Greece, which alone failed to meet the convergence conditions.

The ECB or Eurofed ensures a common monetary policy, and governments have to follow precise targets on public debt and the way in which public deficits are financed. Ceding financial power to a new central financial body is seen to be more effective and efficient than continuing weakly co-ordinated policies by existing NCBs. The constitution of a new ECB was much contested, especially in relation to whether it was to be independent or politically accountable. Germany naturally favoured an independent central bank, modelled on the Bundesbank. This, like the Swiss Central Bank, has been very successful in delivering monetary stability and low inflation. While Germany argued that an ECB agreed by the governments of the EC would provide a sufficient democratic base, others, such as France and the UK, stressed the need for political accountability by any new ECB. Yet despite UK delaying tactics on EMU and political union, benefits from having a more independent central bank for the Bank of England were recognized by the Chancellor of the Exchequer, Nigel Lawson, and introduced by his later Labour successor, Gordon Brown. Any new ECB could have been a close replica of the Dutch Central Bank, in which the government can ultimately override the Bank, and if it objects, the government has to publish the Bank's argument along with its own reasons for ignoring it. In practice the new ECB was much closer to the model of the Bundesbank since Germany needed to be reassured about the maintenance of price stability which was enshrined in its statutes, with a high degree of independence from finance ministers.

The European System of Central Banks (ESCB) involves the National Central Banks (NCBs) and the European Central Bank (ECB). The ECB is dominant in policy-making and has exclusive authorization and control of currency issue. Most monetary operations are decentralized to the NCBs. The ESCB's main instrument of control is open-market operations plus other instruments undertaken at the initiative of the ECB.

The ECB has in its statutes the goal of price stability, whereas the US Federal Reserve Bank also has to consider output and employment as well as inflation. For inflation, no numerical target is set, whereas the ECB has set a tight limit at less than 2 per cent per annum. There are also concerns about the undemocratic nature of the ECB in setting the targets and implementing them. In the UK, for example, the Chancellor of the Exchequer sets the inflation targets, leaving the implementation to the Bank of England – the latter is also more open in publishing its minutes. The ECB Governing Council with its six Executive Board Members and 11 NCB Governors is unwieldy and unaccountable; it cannot take instructions from the EU or from governments of member states. Also, ECB proceedings are to be confidential (whereas in the USA the Federal Reserve Bank is accountable to Congress, with periodic questions). The ECB will need to rely more on rules than discretionary policy in order to establish its credentials.

Central banks carry out two main functions: monetary policy to affect inflation and interest rates, and banking policy, which is financial assistance and regulatory and supervisory action. The ECB has elevated the monetary function of stable prices, tending to neglect banking policy. There is no explicit reference to an ECB role in the role of lender of last resort and in supporting the banking system, despite a general pooling of reserves. Hence support rests more with NCBs, yet there is a case for the ECB taking on this role because of the increased financial risks created through greater competition between financial institutions and the risks of failure and collapse. Although single-market policy dealt with minimum harmonization of prudential standards, mutual recognition of national laws, and home-country control, it has been argued that this is insufficient (Lossani 1998).

The Growth and Stability Pact was finalized during the June 1997 European Council meeting in Amsterdam and adds credibility to the euro by imposing rules which limit national fiscal policy, thus avoiding a collision between monetary and fiscal policy which would result in ever-increasing interest rates by the ECB. It provides surveillance in order to give an early warning when the 3 per cent reference value for budget deficits is at risk. Where countries breach this, they have to face sanctions of a fixed element equal to 0.2 per cent of GDP, plus a variable element equal to one-tenth of the difference between the deficit rate and the 3 per cent reference level. To begin with, the sanctions would be of a non-interest-bearing deposit; only later would fines be imposed.

However, it is likely to be some time before fines are triggered, and there are escape clauses, such as severe recession, exceeding a 2 per cent annual output loss and also some discretion for output declining between 0.75 per cent and 2.0 per cent (Artis and Winkler 1998). In recession unemployment rises quickly and governments would be unable to act early and counter-cyclically to deal with this without fines until a large 2 per cent fall in output occurred. Fines will probably be a strong weapon, held in reserve to discipline errant governments. Since decisions are taken by qualified majority voting, it is possible for a blocking minority to emerge against the imposition of sanctions. The growth element of the Pact, which was added largely at French insistence, is less evident than the German emphasis on fiscal stability.

The right policy balance between monetary and fiscal policy is difficult and in some respects fiscal policy may not be sufficiently flexible. For example, if the new millennium ushers in not inflation but deflation, in the wake of the Asian crisis, ECB policy may prove unsuitable, especially for countries with high unemployment. Focus has been placed increasingly on tackling unemployment by supply-side reforms, but where there is cyclical unemployment as a consequence of deficient demand an economic policy stimulus is desirable. The interest rate set by the ECB started off at 3 per cent and Wim Duisenberg, President of the ECB, was determined to maintain credibility and independence from politicians. However, in April 1999, to counter the recession in Euroland, a decisive cut of 0.5 per cent was made in an attempt to stimulate flagging economies, without precipitating unwarranted inflation (since price stability is the whole *raison d'être* of the ECB).

Business is now conducted in euros, with credit-card and cheque transactions taking place, though notes and coins will only replace national currencies in the first half of 2002. The euro is a momentous development, comparable with the creation of the US dollar in 1792. The euro should prove a popular and stable currency since the ECB has prioritized low inflation. If EMU is successful, it will create unstoppable political union, whereas historically in other European countries, such as Germany and the UK, political union preceded monetary union.

### UK ambivalence towards the EMS and EMU
There are some similarities between the UK's attitude to the formation of the EMS and the formation of the EC in the 1950s. The UK thought that there was a distinct possibility of both ventures foundering, and therefore it avoided the risks inherent in being a positive founder member. Thus sterling, though part of the ECU, did not participate in the ERM for a period of 11 years (March 1979 to October 1990). Evidence suggests that the UK's policy approach was short-sighted since both the EC and then the EMS 'took off' successfully. The UK belatedly joined the EC and always tends to be one step behind, participating eventually in the evolving stages of EC integration. To join later always implies reluctance, a lack of real commitment and a loss of political goodwill. Furthermore, it appeared an anomaly to belong to the EC and not to belong fully to the EMS exchange-rate mechanism. The UK has preferred to see EMU as part of a looser form of *à la carte* integration. But on balance the EMS does not seem to manifest such adverse features as those associated with aspects of sectoral integration which the UK has entered into, such as the CAP.

The UK attitude to the EMS was to lay down such stringent bargaining conditions for its membership that there was little likelihood of them being accepted. For example, the list of conditions in the Green Paper on the European Monetary System in 1978 may have been desirable, but there was no prospect of satisfying them all. The UK had doubts whether the weaker countries which had dropped out of the snake would be able to stay in. With the UK's tendency for wage inflation to outstrip productivity, it felt there was a need for exchange-rate depreciation as a crucial policy instrument. There was a desire not to operate under an overvalued exchange rate, necessitating the imposition of deflationary domestic policies. In practice, however, non-participation in the ERM actually resulted in an overvalued exchange rate during the early 1980s!

The Labour government, already split in the past on the issue of the EC, simply lacked the confidence, support and vision to move forward in the process of European integration. It tried to link the introduction of the EMS to budgetary reform, though any progress on both fronts simultaneously was difficult. The UK also expressed concern about adverse effects of the EMS on the dollar, seeming to show even more concern about this than the Americans themselves. Nevertheless, there was general hostility to the EMS from other quarters in the UK; for example, the National Institute of Economic and Social Research agreed with most economists who had submitted evidence against the EMS to the House of Commons Committee which examined this in November 1978. Of even more emphatic influence was the opposition of the Treasury, though it had participated through Mr Cousins in the detailed discussions with Dr Schulmann and M. Clappier, the German and French representatives, about the precise construction of the EMS (Ludlow 1982).

The Labour government underestimated the unstoppable political momentum by the West German and French leaders towards the establishment of the EMS. They had become increasingly disillusioned with the UK's attitude and it was really only a desire of France to reduce the excessive weight of the D-mark in the ECU that helped to prevent the UK's total exclusion from the EMS. The UK settled for an intermediate position, opting out of the ERM. Yet by joining this the UK could have prevented the currency split with Ireland; it could have pressed to join with wider margins, like the lira; and could also have benefited from the financial aid available.

*Mrs Thatcher and the EMS*    While the reluctance of the Labour Party to embrace the EMS was understandable, the lack of enthusiasm of the

Thatcher governments required a somewhat different explanation. The predilection of the Conservative government for market forces was applied to the foreign-exchange market, taking the view that the market was more likely than intervention to create the right exchange rate for sterling. The government removed exchange controls, resulting in an outflow of capital, and this appeared judicious in an attempt to restrain the rising value of sterling (as a petro-currency), even though the combination of both effects was to have a devastating impact on UK unemployment in the early 1980s. The Thatcher government also decided initially to introduce a Medium-Term Financial Strategy in which it sought to achieve its anti-inflationary strategy by using monetary targets instead of by using an exchange-rate target. However, by 1986 the UK had started to move away from its main reliance upon money-supply targets; this was because of the problems in attaining them successfully. Their defects are that more deposits are now held outside the banking system; also, the development of sophisticated corporate financial transactions means that a single act of borrowing may often be counted several times. Hence there was some recognition that instead of a money-supply target there could be gains from pursuing an exchange-rate target, yet the UK still did not join the ERM.

A major obstacle to UK participation is the distinctive nature of the economy as a significant oil producer – though the Netherlands has not found near self-sufficiency in energy any barrier to membership of the EMS. But the UK's dependence upon world oil prices had made sterling a volatile petro-currency which fluctuates widely, making it difficult to contain within the ERM. A continuous fall in world oil prices – brought about by the failure of OPEC to maintain a cohesive cartel – would lead to a long-run decline in the value of sterling. There is concern about the opposite effect of a change in oil prices on sterling and the D-mark. Both sterling and the D-mark have been used as reserve currencies, with the D-mark tending to eclipse sterling.

Any durable participation of the UK in EMU is dependent on the UK reducing its rate of inflation towards the lower German level on a permanent basis. Much depends, therefore, upon the willingness of the UK to pursue the same preference of low inflation, and also its ability to achieve this successfully. Under Conservative governments economic policy brought down the rate of inflation to a level which would have been compatible with its membership of the EMS by the mid-1980s. Given this, it was surprising that the UK postponed entry into the ERM for another five years. In addition, sterling began to shadow the D-mark and it was understood that a secret target zone for the movement of sterling against the D-mark had been agreed between the two countries around the time of the Group of Five meeting in Paris in February 1987. The central target rate for sterling was believed to be about 2.90 D-marks, but the successful managed float of sterling against the D-mark was finally breached in March 1988 when sterling was uncapped, amidst disagreement between Mrs Thatcher and the Chancellor of the Exchequer over interest-rate policy.

*Belated entry into the ERM and early exit*   Pressure on the UK to join the ERM increased with the inclusion of monetary articles in the SEA and the proposals for full capital mobility. Jacques Delors threatened that progress on this front could not occur if some countries would not conform to the monetary discipline of the EMS. The UK confirmed at the Madrid Summit in June 1989 that if certain conditions were met it would join the ERM. These comprised: a sharp fall in the UK's rate of inflation; completion of the single European market; the full implementation of a free market in financial services; the abolition of all exchange controls; and the strengthening of the Community's competition policy. Many of these conditions were aimed at the rest of the Community, but the one key condition applicable to the UK was to achieve a sharp fall in its rate of inflation.

The ERM continued to be a divisive issue in 1989; Sir Alan Walters judged the EMS to be 'a half-baked scheme'. His controversial role as Mrs Thatcher's economic adviser and his difference in view from the Chancellor of the Exchequer, Nigel Lawson, finally led to the resignation of both men in October 1989. On economic grounds Walters's criticism of the EMS was that it would force interest rates down too much in high-inflation countries, such as the UK. Nigel Lawson, despite his innovative fiscal policy, failed to achieve entry into the ERM when it would have been most desirable, such as in 1985 when UK inflation was running at the low EC average of just over 5 per cent.

A groundswell of pro-ERM views helped to reinforce the more positive position of John Major in his short period as Chancellor of the Exchequer. For example, the National Institute of Economic and Social Research came round to the view that if the UK had joined the ERM, then inflation would have been much lower from the mid-1980s onwards, and membership would enable the achievement of price stability by 1992 (NIESR 1989). British business also advocated membership of the ERM to stimulate exports, arguing that it would reduce the costs of hedging against exchange-rate movements. It was also necessary to consolidate London's role as Europe's leading financial centre, to keep it well ahead of cities such as Paris and Frankfurt.

The economic arguments for ERM membership, of lower inflation and greater nominal exchange rate stability, were strengthened by the constellation of political changes in 1989–90. John Major was in a strong position since the government did not wish to lose another Chancellor, and he continued Nigel Lawson's path towards membership of the ERM. In November 1989 the government published its *Evolutionary Approach to Economic and Monetary Union*. It approved of stage 1 of the Delors Report, but disagreed with stages 2 and 3, proposing instead to build upon Lawson's earlier ideas of competing currencies. To have any influence on these later stages, some concession had to be made by joining the ERM. Since the timing of entry was less ripe economically than at certain points in the past, it meant engineering an appropriate dilution of the Madrid conditions regarding the UK's rate of inflation. The criterion was modified by notionally lowering the underlying rate of inflation by excluding mortgage rates and the community charge, and focusing on the future downward trend in inflation towards the EC level. Furthermore, since there were wide disparities in rates of inflation when countries first joined the ERM, the argument changed to one of the ERM itself leading to convergence. In other words, the causal link shifted to one of membership of the ERM not being conditional on a preceding low and immediately converging rate of inflation, but rather that the ERM would by itself subsequently drive down UK inflation, converging to the level in the EC.

The concern of Walters about the danger of lower interest rates overheating the British economy gave way to an opposite need to limit recession in 1990–1. But the latter was aggravated by a higher exchange rate and deflationary convergence towards the lower West German rate of inflation, since these tended to outweigh any expansionist effect of lower interest rates – especially if the latter were partly offset by a tighter fiscal policy. The government in late 1990 found itself increasingly 'boxed in', seeking to achieve its prime economic target of lower inflation, and constrained by the electoral cycle of needing to manifest success by the beginning of 1992. In some respects the government had allowed the economy to become overheated in 1988, following its re-election in 1987 and the lowering of interest rates to avoid an economic decline after the Stock Market collapse in autumn 1987. From February 1987 to March 1988 the informal fixing of the pound against the D-mark and the strengthening of the pound had led to a sharp reduction in interest rates. Dampening this overexpansion had resulted by the end of 1990 in stagflation, but with membership of the ERM being seen as economically and politically expedient. Some financial commentators, such Samuel Brittan of *The Financial Times*, have long awaited the discipline which membership of the ERM would impose on the UK to dampen its rate of inflation.

The Chancellor of the Exchequer was ready to exploit the first window of opportunity to join the ERM in order to influence the subsequent stages of evolution to EMU. For example, in June 1990 John Major, addressing an Anglo-German audience, seized the initiative in proposing a hard ECU, operating alongside national currencies. His pragmatic proposal was derived from Sir Michael Butler's plan based upon the hard ECU circulating in parallel alongside national currencies. The hard ECU would be guaranteed never to be devalued and it was proposed that it should be managed by a new European Monetary Fund. Whether a single currency then evolved would depend in the British view upon market choice.

On 5 October 1990 the government set a positive mood for the start of the Conservative Party conference by announcing that sterling would finally enter the ERM on 8 October. This stripped the Opposition Parties of their own economic platforms on this issue. The government opted for a high exchange-rate level: £1=DM2.95.

British business, while desiring exchange-rate stability, is hampered by a high exchange rate, unless it pressures companies into resisting excessive wage awards on the basis of the very visible adverse effects that these would have in raising domestic unemployment. But business welcomed the accompanying initial 1 per cent reduction in interest rates. For the government the ERM appeared to offer a way out of their political dilemma of how to reduce excessively high mortgage interest rates, as a Party committed to raising private home ownership.

Some degree of flexibility was provided by opting for a wide band of ±6 per cent, previously enjoyed by Italy and subsequently by Spain. The choice was sensible given the difficulty in setting the right central rate, compounded by exogenous shocks, such as oil price effects, for example, following the invasion of Kuwait by Iraq. Theoretically the pound would trade against the D-mark between DM2.78 and DM3.13, but during 1990 the Spanish peseta was very strong, being some 3.5 per cent above its central rate against the D-mark, while the pound was about 1.25 per cent below its central parity against the peseta. Hence the pound could not drop by more than 4.75 per cent before hitting its limit against the peseta. The pound was also limited in its movement against the ECU and if sterling were to rise 6 per cent against all other EMS currencies, its rise against the ECU would be only 5.25 per cent; this is because the pound constituted one-eighth of the ECU basket. If the pound could not stay high enough, then devaluation would be necessary; for example, the pound fell during the 1980s on average by just over 5 per cent a year against the D-mark, and the new range of downward adjustment for the pound in the ERM would accommodate a similar depreciation.

The UK's inflationary problems, *vis-à-vis* countries such as Germany, arise from several sources. For example, strongly decentralized pay-bargaining in the UK was encouraged by governments during the 1980s and 1990s. In many European countries industry-level bargaining often occurs based upon national economic activity. UK annual bargaining creates leap-frogging and would be better if it were synchronized in the first quarter of the year, with longer-term agreements. British unions also preferred to link pay claims to high past annual rates of inflation, instead of accepting the lower projected governmental inflation rate within the ERM. A shortage of skilled labour in key sectors also contributes to persistent inflationary pay awards. In addition, despite privatization, there is still a large public sector not subjected to the same visible exchange-rate constraint faced by private companies exposed to international competition. Meanwhile, financial profligacy after the abandonment of monetarism and financial deregulation in the late 1980s had led to a massive growth in credit, significantly larger than in West Germany, in spite of higher UK interest rates.

In entering the ERM at a high rate of exchange, everything hinged on dampening inflationary pressures, otherwise the British economy would experience mounting unemployment; for example, its chronic balance-of-payments deficit was exacerbated by price uncompetitiveness. Although inflationary pressures increased in Germany as a consequence of reunification, and of the expenditure required to sustain the eastern part of Germany, the Bundesbank commitment to a restrictive monetary policy of raising interest rates was to undermine the ERM. Hence the UK blamed the Bundesbank for high interest rates and for its reluctance to support the pound sufficiently when it came under speculative pressure in the currency markets. However, the failure of the UK to remain in the ERM was also partly a consequence of the UK's unwillingness to raise interest rates early enough because it was already in recession. It was concerned because of the very severe economic costs already being imposed upon the real economy in terms of depressed output and high unemployment. Membership of the ERM failed to bring down interest rates rapidly, as some economists had forecast, compounding recession because of the UK's underlying weaknesses.

While devaluation is not the solution to fundamental economic problems, it can be beneficial; for example, UK economic growth improved markedly after the 30 per cent fall in the pound against the D-mark between July 1985 and February 1987. British unemployment started to fall in 1986, whereas unemployment in France and Italy rose eventually above the UK level. Likewise, after the exit of the pound from the ERM in 1992, UK unemployment fell rapidly as its trade situation improved, whereas the opposite happened in Germany, which became less competitive and succumbed to very heavy unemployment, with over four million people out of work.

*The UK and the euro*    Successive UK governments have had to evaluate the benefits and costs of European monetary integration. A single currency enhances trade and consolidates single-market gains from greater competition between firms and stronger price transparency. The ECB based on the Bundesbank prioritizes low inflation, providing greater credibility than the Bank of England, with a poorer record in the past on inflation. Furthermore, even with an independent central bank, it will take time to acquire a good anti-inflation reputation. A lower rate of inflation reduces interest rates (partly because there is no need to raise them to protect national currency holders from the risk of exchange-rate depreciation). Lower inflation and a lower interest rate increase investment, since they provide a more certain world for business in the large single market.

Despite the immense benefits, UK governments have continued with a 'wait and see' policy. The Labour Chancellor of the Exchequer, Gordon Brown, has continued this by setting five general tests that must be met before entry to the euro. Are business cycles compatible, and has the UK economy achieved sustainable convergence with the economies of the single currency? Is there sufficient flexibility in the operation of the Stability Pact and in the UK economy to adapt to change and other unexpected economic events? Will the single currency create better conditions for businesses to make long-term decisions to invest in the UK? What impact would membership have on the UK financial services industry? Finally, will the euro be good for employment?

The UK economy, having enjoyed several years of better growth and lower unemployment than continental Europe in the late 1990s, was at a different point in the European business cycle. Continental economies are pulling out of recession, especially peripheral countries, and benefiting from lower interest rates. There is concern that a single interest-rate policy will not fit the different economies in Euroland (11), let alone the very different UK economy. For example, the Irish economy has achieved super-economic growth in recent years, but the low single-interest rate may lead to overheating. In the UK monetary policy also has a powerful transmission mechanism because of the importance of owner-occupation and variable-rate mortgages. In this context the lure of lower continental interest rates is strong, but precluded largely because of the currency risk of borrowing and having to repay in euros.

Despite non-membership of the euro by the UK until after a referendum early in the new millennium, the likelihood is still one of a creeping usage of the euro. For example, British business in its continental trade is pricing, and invoicing customers and suppliers, in euros. In addition, the City of London has had to be in the forefront of adaptation in its battle to retain its premier position as Europe's leading financial centre. There are conflicting views about the effects on the City by the UK remaining outside the euro. Savings accounts in euros will probably remain unpopular, depending on the UK interest-rate differential *vis-à-vis* the currency level of the pound against the euro. However, there may be some attraction in being paid in euros, which would lead to benefits from cheaper euro-mortgages.

Even out of the euro the UK has had to incur some preparatory costs in order to be ready. The immediate effect of the euro was to make the UK less competitive since business still incurred the transaction costs and also faced increased price competition through greater transparency in euro-pricing. There is concern, too, that the traditionally volatile pound (partly affected by oil prices, and so on) could face increased speculative pressure now that the other 11 national European currencies have been replaced by the euro. Initially, in the early months the euro depreciated against the pound. However, a continuing worry that the 'outs' might ultimately secure a competitive advantage will reinforce pressure on them to rejoin a fixed exchange-rate system linked to the euro. Finally, there is economic and political uncertainty caused by government in expecting business to prepare for entry, before they know that this is definite. Furthermore, there could still be a 'sting in the tail' should voters in England reject the euro and voters in Scotland endorse it, given Scotland's devolved parliament.

# 9 Fiscal policy: taxation and the EU Budget

## Fiscal policy issues

The term fiscal policy covers a wide range of public-finance issues relating to both taxation and government expenditure. One of its main concerns has been with the allocation of resources since public goods have to be provided collectively. However, in recent years most EU countries have become concerned about the excessive size of the public sector, cutting the public-sector borrowing requirement and trying to make room for the growth of the private sector. Even those countries which could indulge in high public expenditure in the past from energy revenue, such as the Netherlands and the UK, have had to moderate the level of public expenditure.

The concern of fiscal policy with macroeconomic stabilization has been the outcome of Keynesian economics. However, over recent years scepticism has emerged about the effectiveness of Keynesian demand-management policies when the outcome was invariably large budget deficits – such policies proved highly inflationary. Fine-tuning of the economy has been partly displaced in recent years by greater emphasis on budgetary balance and by using tax cuts as more a supply-side than a demand-side policy. Successful economies, as in West Germany, have been run along more orthodox lines, being less preoccupied with Keynesian macroeconomic stabilization policies, giving greater priority to monetary policy, within which at a microeconomic level freely competitive market forces could operate. Germany is the dominant economy in the Community and the pivotal force, so that economic policy in the EU is influenced very much by the German example.

National governments have traditionally used fiscal policy to create a more equitable distribution of income by designing progressive taxation in terms of ability to pay, while trying to ensure that on the expenditure side benefits go mainly to the poor. Such policies have not always been successful, with often high marginal tax rates existing not only for the higher-paid groups but also for some of the low-income groups because of the poverty trap. Meanwhile, expenditure policies have often included indiscriminate subsidies going to all groups, not only to the poor.

This chapter will focus on tax harmonization and in particular on the role of the Community Budget. Given the functions of national budgets, is the role of the Community Budget to carry out these same functions? What kind of activities does it carry out? Has it a macroeconomic stabilization role? How has it affected the distribution of income? The Budget is still very much concerned with financing the allocation of resources, rather than playing a major role in economic stabilization and the redistribution of income. Deciding on the appropriate level of budgetary powers and activities is difficult and, in the USA and Germany, for example, is highly decentralized. In the latter, the balance between national and regional provision tends towards the subnational level represented by the Länder. It is an even more difficult problem for the EU since its federal nature could be enhanced with a larger budget, but those countries contributing disproportionately to its finance remain lukewarm. Nevertheless, there is scope for transferring to the Community level some activities currently financed at a national level.

Since national budgets are far bigger than the Community Budget, to what extent is some co-ordination of the former necessary, or can these be left as the independent element for national macroeconomic adjustment? Some co-ordination of budgetary policy has occurred, especially since the Convergence Decision of the Council in 1974 to establish target guidelines for budgetary policies. This has been reinforced far more as part of EMU. The interdependence of Community economies has continued to grow and therefore macroeconomic policies have large spillover effects on other member states. For example, those economists whose prime concern is with unemployment are worried about the dangers of countries (already committed to restrictive German monetary policy exemplified within the EMS and EMU) adopting tighter fiscal policies than would be desirable for the EU as a whole. German emphasis on fiscal stability has led to provision for fines where countries have excessive deficits and are not in severe recession. EU fiscal co-operation may become too tight, preventing early counter-cyclical action.

## Tax harmonization and the Community Budget

### *The rationale of fiscal harmonization*

Fiscal harmonization is bound up with the achievement of the customs union, the Common Market and the Economic and Political Union. The first phase of removing customs frontiers remained incomplete, despite the elimination of intra-tariffs, since different rates of indirect taxation resulted in a continuing fiscal frontier. The creation of a single market has had to take this difficult problem on board.

The different excise duties levied on products such as wine and tobacco (plus tobacco monopolies in France and Italy) have distorted competition. Despite proposals to harmonize these, substantial differences have remained, since each country has been reluctant to relinquish its choice on the appropriate level of national taxation for these products on health grounds. Even assuming the same tax levels could be agreed, there would still be different tax yields according to the different patterns of consumption. Furthermore, countries' revenue requirements vary and are higher where these have to satisfy high public expenditure.

The creation of a free flow of factors of production within the Common Market led the EU to address particularly the issue of capital mobility, steering clear of any harmonization of direct taxation on labour. Finally, as more positive integration has occurred in different sectors, further tax harmonization has become necessary. For example, in agriculture, differences in value-added tax (VAT) in the early 1980s meant that farmers in the UK and Denmark, unlike those in other members states, could not claim back a percentage of VAT which had been paid on factors of production.

The aim of the Community is not to standardize everything but to harmonize taxation as a means of achieving other objectives. But countries that have relinquished many important national economic policy instruments already as a consequence of integration are naturally wary of any erosion of an independent fiscal policy to manage their economies. For example, EU members have surrendered their own national trade policies and most countries have largely given up their independent exchange rate policies within the EMU. Furthermore, continued integration within EMU will diminish the use of national monetary policy. Therefore it is important for economies to possess some key independent policy instruments, such as that of direct taxation. Nevertheless, tax harmonization has assumed added urgency since it is part and parcel of financing the revenue of the Community Budget. Meanwhile, progress towards integration in other areas such as EMU and the single internal market is facilitated by a large redistributive budgetary expenditure to help poorer countries.

## Types of taxes

The EC has sought to promote the harmonization of three taxes: value added tax, excise duties and corporation tax. It has not proposed to harmonize income tax, since labour is less mobile than capital; hence direct taxation provides the major independent policy instrument for national governments to use in managing their economies. However, it is intended that the overall fiscal stance between countries will be co-ordinated.

*Value added tax (VAT)*   Value added tax or *taxe sur la valeur ajoutée* has been applied in France since 1954. The Neumark Report in 1963 recommended VAT and it was decided to introduce this as the sales tax for the Community by a Council directive in April 1967. It was proposed that other member states which were operating different systems would change over to VAT by 1 January 1971; but extensions were necessary for Belgium and Italy and the latter did not introduce VAT until early 1973. The issue became tied up inextricably with Italy's other tax reforms and both the Mezzogiorno and export industries opposed VAT since under the existing turnover tax large rebates were possible. Other countries were much keener to introduce VAT, for example, West Germany, even though their cumulative multi-cascade tax benefited exporters by generous rebates.

The disadvantages of cascade taxes (that is, taxes on total value), compared with VAT, were that they encouraged vertical integration of production by firms purely to minimize their tax payments. For example, assume three stages in production with the value of the product (excluding tax) at the end of the stages being £1000 (stage 1), £2000 (stage 2) and £3000 (stage 3). Assume a 10 per cent cascade tax applied at each stage; hence tax payment would be £100 (stage 1), £200 (stage 2) and £300 (stage 3), making the total tax payable £600. To reduce the tax bill, businesses engaged in vertical integration in order to pay only £300 tax on the total value of £3000. VAT is neutral with regard to the structure of economic activity. The tax is paid not on the total value at each stage but on the added value; hence a 10 per cent VAT would yield £100 (stage 1), £100 (stage 2) and £100 (stage 3); that is, £300 VAT payable. Only in the case of the business being integrated is the cascade tax and the VAT bill the same. Without such integration a cumulative cascade tax yields more than VAT; in the example used, a 5 per cent cascade tax would have yielded the same as a 10 per cent VAT.

The replacement of cascade taxes by VAT removed the incentive for the kind of integration that offered no economic gains apart from saving tax. Cascade taxes, in encouraging integration, increased monopoly structure (even though the latter is more likely to occur with horizontal than with vertical integration). 'Le remplacement des taxes cumulatives à cascade par la taxe à la valeur ajoutée a eliminé la source principale des discriminations au sens des articles 95 et 96 du traité CEE' (Moussis 1982, p. 319).

A distinct advantage of VAT for the tax authorities is that it is difficult to evade since businesses have to make sure on invoices that tax has been paid at the previous stage of production so that their own tax payment is correct. VAT is also more favourable to fair trade than cascade taxes since the latter were often generously rebated for export, providing exporters with a hidden subsidy because of uncertainty about the exact amounts of tax that had to be paid at each stage. With VAT the taxes rebated are clear, but VAT applied at the destination by the importing country unfortunately means the existence of a fiscal frontier. If VAT were harmonized, then exports could take place smoothly from the country of origin.

The use of jurisdictional terms such as 'destination' and 'origin' is worth clarifying, though fuller details can be found elsewhere (Robson 1998, pp. 167–9). Where the destination principle is applied on all products in the country where they are consumed, both domestic and imported products face the same tax, while domestically produced goods for export are exempt from the tax. Under the origin principle, the taxes are imposed on the domestic production of all goods whether exported or not, and are not imposed on imports. Apart from the existence of a fiscal frontier with the destination principle, this is preferable where VAT rates have not been harmonized.

VAT is a general tax levied at all stages of production and distribution covering services (when the services affect the final price of goods) and consumer goods. Several directives have been introduced, such as the Sixth Directive in 1977 which was important in introducing a uniform basis for VAT. This sought to establish a common list of taxable activities and a common list of exemptions. This was necessary since the collection of the EU's own resources from VAT receipts to finance the Community Budget can only be equitable if all countries have the same basis of assessment. Hence the VAT payable to the EU Budget is based on a common notional structure, but has allowed countries to continue with their own existing VAT rates and their existing derogations.

*Table 9.1*   *Rates of VAT in member states as applicable from 1 January 1994 (%)*

|             | VAT %                                          |
|-------------|------------------------------------------------|
| Austria     | 10, 12, 20                                      |
| Belgium     | 1, 6, 12, 20.5                                   |
| Denmark     | 25                                              |
| Finland     | 6, 12, 17, 22                                    |
| France      | 2.1, 5.5, 18.6                                   |
| Germany     | 7, 15                                           |
| Greece      | 4, 8, 18 (Note the 25 and 36 rates abolished)   |
| Ireland     | 0, 2.3, 10, 12.5, 21                             |
| Italy       | 4, 9, 13, 19                                     |
| Luxembourg  | 3, 6, 12, 15                                     |
| Netherlands | 0, 6, 17.5                                       |
| Portugal    | 5, 16, 30                                        |
| Spain       | 3, 6, 15                                         |
| Sweden      | 12, 21, 25                                       |
| UK          | 0, 17.5                                          |

*Note*:   See individual country for categories covered and exemptions

*Source*:   European Commission, *Inventory of Taxes Levied in the Member States of the European Union*, 1996, Luxembourg.

The differences in the rates of VAT charged and also in the number of rates used in particular countries are shown in Table 9.1.

Denmark and Sweden have had very high rates of both direct and indirect taxation, and the latter is also high in Finland and Ireland. Portugal has been one of several countries which has had a luxury rate of taxation. Greece also chose several rates of VAT, though it delayed their introduction initially because of its primitive book-keeping methods and worries that it would raise Greek payments to the Community Budget. However, VAT replaced nearly half of the 500 indirect taxes existing in Greece.

Progress in harmonizing both the number and level of VAT rates has been constrained by two particular problems. First, member states using VAT as part of their economic policy are sometimes concerned about any inflationary effects from raising the rate – France has in the past suspended VAT on the retail sale of beef to keep down the rate of inflation. Second, countries differ in the extent to which they wish to define and tax products as luxuries or essentials. The latter may carry only low rates of VAT, be zero-rated or exempt from VAT. Those that are zero-rated are generally treated better than those that are exempt, since the latter are only exempt at their particular stage of production and they will have been charged VAT on the goods which have been bought in for processing or for resale.

Steps to equalize rates of VAT would have major budgetary implications for those countries heavily dependent upon VAT receipts, resulting in a budgetary shortfall. The Rogalla Report by the European Parliament in 1983 called for a standstill on any further widening of tax rates and a dual rate of VAT. However, to remove tax frontiers as part of the internal market programme Lord Cockfield's proposals in 1987 were to approximate VAT in two bands; a standard band between 14 and 20 per cent and a lower band from 4 to 9 per cent. The latter would apply to foodstuffs; energy products for heating and lighting; water supplies; pharmaceutical products; books, newspapers and periodicals; and passenger transport. These ranges are flexible since wide disparities are workable in local taxes in the USA, while taxes account for only a small part of the widely differing levels of consumer prices that exist. The ultimate goal was the removal of fiscal frontiers by 1992 and the Commission proposed a standard legal minimum rate of 15 per cent VAT from that date. However, an origin system would mean major exporting countries such as Germany benefiting tax-wise, unless some system of inter-country tax redistribution were provided to assist the losing high-import countries. Hence the destination system was retained for an interim period from 1993, and instead of collecting tax at the frontier the authorities collect it later, internally, when tax declarations are made.

*Excise duties*   The five main excise duties are on beer, wine, spirits, tobacco and mineral oils. These account for most of the excise receipts, though there are variations between member countries; for example, Denmark has a high and important excise duty on cars, whilst Italy has numerous minor excise duties on products such as sugar, coffee, salt and matches. The imposition of excise duties can be based on the value, weight, quality or strength of a product. Excise duties are levied on products with a low price elasticity of demand, and the excise duty is usually shifted forward to the consumer. They represent a significant revenue-raising element for governments since the five main excise duties account for up to 25 per cent of consumer spending.

Excise duties both reflect and influence patterns of production and consumption; for example, wine-producing countries tend to have no or only very low excise duties. Members of the EC(6) have tended to have lower excise duties, not only on wine but also on other alcohol and cigarettes, than those of the Northern European entrants to the EC (the UK, Ireland and Denmark). There have been very wide differences in excise duties, in particular between highly rated Denmark and the much lower rate in France. They reflect different governmental approaches to matters such as health, and in addition can be sources of tacit protectionism. Excise duties levied on mineral oils, though narrower between EC countries than other excise duties, have widespread effects since they are important inputs for many industries.

Tobacco taxation has constituted a high percentage of the final product price, but the basis of the taxation has differed; for example, some countries, such as the UK, Ireland and Denmark, used specific duties based on tobacco content, whereas others relied more upon *ad valorem* taxes. The latter, favoured by countries such as Italy and France, tended to discriminate against more expensive and higher-quality imported tobacco. From the early 1970s the EC agreed to limit the range of tobacco taxation. In 1978 the EC changed the system for tobacco, abolishing duties on raw tobacco leaf, and a new sales tax was introduced at the manufacturing level, combined with a specific tax per cigarette as well as VAT.

In general, rates of excise duties have varied more widely than VAT rates and, unlike the latter, excise duties are normally imposed in one operation at an early stage in the production process. It was suggested that some consideration might be given to replacing excise duties by special VAT rates (Coffey 1983). However, this has not occurred and the EC opted, unlike its original VAT proposals, to retain the destination principle for excise duties. To abolish tax frontiers, therefore, it decided to adopt a Community system of interconnected warehouses.

Proposals by Lord Cockfield were to harmonize excise duties at common rates and these would have major repercussions; for example, Danish prices would fall across the board, hitting government revenue heavily. Greece, on the other hand, would experience massive price rises for some products, such as cigarettes and spirits. These price changes would be so disruptive for some countries' products that the Commission has recognized subsequently that some flexibility will have to be retained. However, it cannot allow such wide differences to continue in rates of excise duties on mineral oils because of the adverse effects on competition, and it will need greater uniformity in this area. However, it was decided that in the case of products such as alcohol and tobacco there was scope for more flexibility, laying down some minimum rates, leading towards greater target convergence over time. The last has become more urgent to avoid the normal incentive to smugglers to exploit the different excise duties.

*Corporation tax*   One missing element of the internal market as it progressed in the 1990s was that relating to a common taxation policy for companies. The absence of tax neutrality has distorted the location of business investment, with some countries such as Ireland treating inward investment more favourably than others. Despite a draft directive in 1975 which was to create a range for corporation tax of 45–55 per cent, this was not adopted. In 1977 there was a directive to encourage collaboration between tax authorities, though its implementation was incomplete. In 1988 another draft directive addressed the different asset bases on which taxes are charged. The rationale for harmonizing corporation tax is that capital is highly mobile, seeking to avoid multiple taxation and preferring to exploit different tax jurisdictions; for example, countries with lower rates of corporation tax will attract capital and MNCs are able to benefit by minimizing their tax bills. There are losses to governments with higher rates of corporation tax which are forced to increase the level of other taxes to obtain revenue (and if taxes were raised further on labour, this would push up unemployment even more). If the different corporation tax rates were reflected in lower prices, then it would affect not only the capital market but competition in the goods market as well. While corporate tax rates have fallen, they ranged from 28 per cent in Finland and Sweden, 30 per cent in the UK to around 50 per cent in Germany (January 1999). (See Table 9.2.) Furthermore, statutory tax rates may differ from effective tax rates paid by companies. Depreciation allowances often differ, with some countries using accelerated depreciation allowances to subsidize capital investment.

Three different tax systems have been used in EU countries. First, there is the classical system used in countries such as the Netherlands and Luxembourg, under which dividends paid to shareholders are subject to tax without any credit against corporate tax; that is, they are taxed twice. The Van den Tempel Report in 1970 favoured this system.

*Table 9.2    Corporate tax rates in the EU 1999 (%)*

|  | Tax rate (%) |
| --- | --- |
| Germany | 43.6–56.7 |
| France | 41.7 |
| Italy | 41.3 |
| Belgium | 40.2 |
| Greece | 35.0–40.0 |
| Portugal | 39.6 |
| Luxembourg | 37.5 |
| Netherlands | 35.0 |
| Spain | 35.0 |
| Austria | 34.0 |
| Denmark | 34.0 |
| Ireland | 32.0 |
| UK | 30.0 (after 1999 budget) |
| Sweden | 28.0 |
| Finland | 28.0 |

*Note*:    Japan 51.6% and USA 40.0%.

*Source*:    KPMG corporate tax rate, *Financial Times*, 3 March 1999, p. 2.

The second type is an imputation system: in the UK corporate tax has been charged at one rate, and if profits are distributed, shareholders are given a tax credit which reduces their personal tax liability; in other words, part of personal tax has been included in the corporation tax payment. Third, there is the split-rate or two-rate system in which distributed profits are charged a lower rate of corporation tax than undistributed ones. The Neumark Committee in 1963 favoured the split-rate system used in Germany.

Withholding taxes imposed by countries on the payment of dividends from a subsidiary to its parent company in another country have also differed; for example, French subsidiaries operating in Italy have had to face higher withholding taxes than Dutch subsidiaries operating in Italy when seeking to return money to their own countries. In 1990 a directive laid down that subsidiaries do not have to deduct withholding taxes when payments were made to a parent company. The EU has made little and slow progress in implementing company-tax harmonization, though unfair favourable treatment in corporation taxation (or capital income tax as in Luxembourg) has necessitated closer co-operation and new initiatives. In 1997, the Council of Economics and Finance Ministers (ECOFIN), conscious of the loss of governmental revenue in high-tax regimes, agreed on a code of conduct against harmful tax competition. This included the necessity to introduce a minimum taxation of savings; also, to deal with double taxation of company activities, especially interest and royalty payments within MNCs. Finally, it was necessary to examine state aids which encompass tax elements. However, governments are reluctant to harmonize when it involves sacrificing their own system and the flexibility which they believe it provides, with the need for unanimity impeding rapid progress.

## The Community Budget

*Relationship to national budgets*   The Community Budget differs from national budgets in two respects. The first is that the Community Budget is relatively small in size and Community expenditure is just over 1 per cent of EU GDP – 1.20 per cent of EU GDP in 1993 and rising to 1.27 per cent in 1999. This underdevelopment of the Community Budget is in marked contrast to the high and much increased levels of national expenditure as a percentage of GDP – up to some 45 per cent of member countries' GDP. The key functions which one normally expects to be conducted in a federation, such as defence, were excluded from the Community. Defence expenditure has remained in the province of national governments and organizations such as NATO.

The second important difference is that national budgets are functional budgets, whereas that of the EU is an accounting type of budget which is expected to balance – despite difficulties in achieving this aim. Some borrowing facilities exist and these are extensive for the ECSC and Euratom, and for the EU they included the EIB, the Community loan instrument after 1975 and the Community instrument after 1978, and so on. The Budget itself is concerned mainly to raise revenue to balance its financial expenditure; it is not engaged in macroeconomic Keynesian stabilization policies of running budgetary deficits to stimulate demand in order to reduce persistently high levels of unemployment. While a case could be made for the EU to run deliberate budget deficits, given the mounting level of EU unemployment, particularly during the 1990s, some governments consider higher expenditure to be undesirable because of its inflationary consequences. The Community Budget finances specific sectoral activities and exogenously determined factors have influenced the large agricultural expenditure. Indeed, the EU's major preoccupation in recent years has been to contain pressures towards budgetary imbalance.

*Budgetary receipts*    The separate budgetary arrangements for the ECSC, Euratom and the EEC were brought together into a General Budget after their merger in 1968. Both Euratom and the EEC were initially dependent for their receipts on national contributions and a key was constructed to determine these, based on national income and the degree of involvement in different activities. This was a reasonably fair system, but the Community decided in the mid-1960s to introduce its own direct sources of revenue. It started to use both customs duties and agricultural levies on imports from outside the Community. Customs duties and agricultural levies for the EU are collected at important entry points: ports such as Antwerp and Rotterdam. Since the goods' final destination is often elsewhere, such as Germany, it was decided that logically the revenue raised should accrue not to national governments but to the Community. The most open economies with high imports from extra-EU sources therefore contribute disproportionately to these revenue sources.

The EEC was influenced in its desire to have its own direct source of revenue by the ECSC, which imposed levies on coal and steel production, and these are now incorporated in the full EU budgetary receipts. It was decided to introduce the crucial new element of a percentage of VAT to raise the Community's revenue receipts and provide sufficient own resources. These have developed at an earlier stage in the evolution of the EU than in other unions, such as the USA or the German Zollverein. Own resources provide the EU with some independence, although it still depends on member states to collect the revenue for which they have received 10 per cent of the revenue collected – the Commission in 1987 proposed the elimination of this refund.

VAT tends to be a regressive tax, certainly when compared with the progressive nature of income tax. Although with VAT higher-income countries which consume more tend to pay more than others, one has to bear in mind that VAT is excluded on investment and exports, both of which are usually higher in more successful economies. This led to some criticism about the wisdom of relying so much upon VAT as the Community's main source of revenue (El-Agraa 1994). Furthermore, reliance on VAT grew and it became necessary to raise the VAT ceiling from 1 per cent to a maximum of 1.4 per cent from January 1986; there was some pressure to have this raised again to 1.6 per cent in 1988 to finance the Community's growing commitments. After 1994 the ceiling on VAT contributions was reduced downwards again to 1 per cent.

VAT became the major revenue source, outpacing customs duties and levies on agricultural imports which are insufficiently dynamic sources of revenue, because the EU has concluded a wide range of agreements with outside countries and negotiated tariff reductions in GATT. Furthermore, in agriculture levies have been more than used up by export subsidies. The sources of budgetary receipts are shown in Table 9.3.

A search got under way for additional revenue sources for the EU, such as those from excise duties. But progress in the field of taxation has been slow in an area where unanimous voting is required. The most significant proposal by the Commission was to introduce a fourth revenue source linked to GNP. This would be provided from the difference between each country's GNP and its actual VAT base. The proposed ceiling was set at 1.4 per cent of GNP. It represented a significant increase in EU resources, and in 1988 comprised 16.5 per cent of budgetary resources, but is clearly less of an own resource than the other sources. GNP-related income is more equitable since GNP tends to possess greater progressiveness than VAT; also, it was intended to include Italy's 'black' economy. Since the EU has continued with VAT, the compromise of using both this and the new fourth resource of GNP represents the usual Community fudge. However, the fourth resource is a significant improvement, based upon the ability to pay and by 1997 accounted for as much as 40 per cent of EU budgetary finance. That compared favourably with revenue from agricultural duties which had fallen to under 3 per cent, customs duties at 15 per cent and VAT at 42 per cent. Furthermore, by 1999 VAT receipts had dropped below those linked to GNP and it seems best to rely mainly on this fairer source of budgetary finance. It was agreed at the Berlin Summit in March 1999 that this trend would be reinforced with a progressive reduction in the dependence on the value added tax base from a notional 1 per cent to 0.75 per cent in 2002 and 0.5 per cent in 2004. In the long term there may be a further search for additional revenue sources, perhaps related to an environmental tax or new sources, depending on the budgetary needs of an enlarged Community.

*Budgetary expenditure*   A small amount of expenditure goes on financing staff and administration, but the bulk of it finances common

*Table 9.3  Budgetary receipts of the European Communities (millions UA/EUA/ECU)[1]*

| | ECSC levies and others | European Development Fund contributions | Euratom contributions (research only) | Miscellaneous and contributions under special keys | EC budget | | | | | Total EC | Total |
|---|---|---|---|---|---|---|---|---|---|---|---|
| | | | | | Own resources | | | | | | |
| | | | | | Miscellaneous | Agricultural levies | Import duties | GNP contributions or VAT[2,3] | | | |
| 1958 | 44.0 | 116.0 | 7.9 | 0.02 | – | – | – | 5.9 | | 5.9 | 173.8 |
| 1959 | 49.6 | 116.0 | 39.1 | 0.1 | – | – | – | 25.1 | | 25.2 | 229.9 |
| 1960 | 53.3 | 116.0 | 20.0 | 0.2 | – | – | – | 28.1 | | 28.3 | 217.6 |
| 1961 | 53.1 | 116.0 | 72.5 | 2.8 | – | – | – | 31.2 | | 34.0 | 275.6 |
| 1962 | 45.3 | 116.0 | 88.6 | 2.1 | – | – | – | 90.2 | | 92.3 | 342.2 |
| 1963 | 47.1 | – | 106.4 | 6.7 | – | – | – | 77.4 | | 84.1 | 237.5 |
| 1964 | 61.3 | – | 124.4 | 2.9 | – | – | – | 90.1 | | 93.1 | 278.7 |
| 1965 | 66.1 | – | 98.8 | 3.5 | – | – | – | 197.6 | | 201.1 | 366.0 |
| 1966 | 71.2 | – | 116.5 | 3.9 | – | – | – | 398.3 | | 402.2 | 590.0 |
| 1967 | 40.3 | 40.0 | 158.5 | 4.2 | – | – | – | 670.9 | | 675.1 | 913.9 |
| 1968 | 85.4 | 90.0 | 82.0 | – | – | – | – | – | | 2 408.6 | 2 666.0 |
| 1969 | 106.8 | 110.0 | 62.7 | 78.6 | – | – | – | 3 972.6 | | 4 051.2 | 4 330.7 |
| 1970 | 100.0 | 130.0 | 67.7 | 121.1 | – | – | – | 5 327.3 | | 5 448.4 | 5 746.1 |
| 1971 | 57.9 | 170.0 | – | – | 69.5 | 713.8 | 582.2 | 923.8 | | 2 289.3 | 2 517.2 |
| 1972 | 61.1 | 170.0 | – | – | 80.9 | 799.6 | 957.4 | 1 236.6 | | 3 074.5 | 3 305.6 |
| 1973 | 120.3 | 150.0 | – | – | 511.0 | 478.0 | 1 564.7 | 2 087.3 | | 4 641.0 | 4 911.3 |
| 1974 | 124.6 | 150.0 | – | – | 65.3 | 323.6 | 2 684.4 | 1 964.8 | | 5 038.2 | 5 312.8 |
| 1975 | 189.5 | 220.1 | – | – | 320.5 | 590.0 | 3 151.0 | 2 152.0 | | 6 213.6 | 6 623.1 |
| 1976 | 129.6 | 311.0 | – | – | 282.8 | 1 163.7 | 4 064.6 | 2 482.1 | | 7 993.1[4] | 8 433.7 |
| 1977 | 123.0 | 410.0 | – | – | 504.7 | 1 778.5 | 3 927.2 | 2 494.5 | | 8 704.9 | 9 237.9 |
| 1978 | 164.9 | 147.5 | – | – | 344.4 | 2 283.3 | 4 390.9 | 5 329.7 | | 12 348.2 | 12 660.6 |
| 1979 | 168.4 | 480.0 | – | – | 230.3 | 2 143.4 | 5 189.1 | 7 039.8 | | 14 602.5 | 15 251.0 |
| 1980 | 226.2 | 555.0 | – | – | 1 055.9[5] | 2 002.3 | 5 905.8 | 7 093.5 | | 16 057.5[6] | 16 838.7 |
| 1981 | 264.0 | 658.0 | – | – | 1 219.0 | 1 747.0 | 6 392.0 | 9 188.0 | | 18 546.0[7] | 19 468.0 |
| 1982 | 243.0 | 750.0 | – | – | 187.0 | 2 228.0 | 6 815.0 | 12 197.0 | | 21 427.0 | 22 420.0 |
| 1983 | 300.0 | 700.0 | – | – | 1 565.0 | 2 295.0 | 6 988.7 | 13 916.8 | | 24 765.5[8] | 25 765.5 |

| Year | | | | | | | | | | | |
|---|---|---|---|---|---|---|---|---|---|---|---|
| 1984 | 408.0 | 703.0 | — | — | — | — | 1 060.7[9] | 2 436.3 | 7 960.8 | 14 594.6 | 26 052.4[10] | 27 163.4 |
| 1985 | 453.0 | 698.0 | — | — | — | — | 2 491.0[11] | 2 179.0 | 8 310.0 | 15 218.0 | 28 198.0 | 29 349.0 |
| 1986 | 439.0 | 846.7 | — | — | — | — | 396.5 | 2 287.0 | 8 172.9 | 22 810.8 | 33 667.2 | 34 952.9 |
| 1987 | 399.3 | 837.9 | — | — | — | — | 74.8 | 3 097.9 | 8 936.5 | 23 674.1 | 35 783.3 | 37 020.5 |
| 1988 | 567.0 | 1 196.3 | — | — | — | — | 1 377.0 | 2 606.0 | 9 310.0 | 28 968.0 | 42 261.0 | 44 024.3 |
| 1989 | 404.0 | 1 297.0 | — | — | — | — | 4 018.4 | 2 397.9 | 10 312.9 | 29 170.6 | 45 899.8 | 47 600.8 |
| 1990 | 488.0 | 1 256.5 | — | — | — | — | 5 191.5 | 1 875.7 | 10 285.1 | 29 252.4 | 46 604.7 | 48 349.2 |
| 1991 | 495.0 | 1 191.0 | — | — | — | — | 3 749.2 | 2 486.8 | 11 476.0 | 38 874.5 | 56 586.5 | 58 272.5 |
| 1992 | 535.3 | 1 942.1 | — | — | — | — | 385.9 | 2 328.6 | 11 599.9 | 48 513.2 | 62 827.6 | 65 605.0 |
| 1993 | 551.8 | 1 353.6 | — | — | — | — | 1 266.2 | 2 930.0 | 11 055.6 | 50 987.9 | 66 239.7 | 68 145.1 |
| 1994 | 393.0 | 1 781.0 | — | — | — | — | 516.1 | 2 038.9 | 12 619.3 | 54 839.2 | 70 013.5 | 72 187.5 |
| 1995 | 268.0 | 1 650.0 | — | — | — | — | 515.9 | 1 901.5 | 12 340.9 | 57 196.9 | 71 955.2 | 73 873.2 |
| 1996 | — | 950.0 | — | — | — | — | 568.2 | 1 963.3 | 12 852.9 | 66 504.0 | 81 888.4 | — |
| 1997 | — | 1 560.0 | — | — | — | — | 612.0 | 2 015.4 | 12 203.2 | 67 534.9 | 82 365.5 | — |
| 1998 | — | 1 830.0 | — | — | — | — | 668.1 | 2 718.1 | 11 144.3 | 70 046.7 | 84 577.2 | — |

*Notes:*
1  UA until 1977; EUA/ECU from 1978 onwards.
2  GNP until 1978; VAT from 1979 until 1987; GNP from 1988 onwards.
3  This column includes, for the years to 1970, surplus revenue from previous years carried forward to following years.
4  As a result of the calculations to establish the relative shares of the member states in the 1976 budget, an excess of revenue over expenditure occurred amounting to 40.5 million UA. This was carried forward to 1977.
5  Including surplus brought forward from 1979 and balance of 1979 VAT and financial contributions.
6  Including surplus of ECU 82.4 million carried forward to 1981.
7  Including surplus of ECU 661 million.
8  Includes surplus of ECU 307 million.
9  Includes ECU 593 million of repayable advances by member states.
10  There was a small deficit in 1984 in respect of the EC budget, due largely to late payment of advances by some member states.
11  Includes non-repayable advances by member states of 1981. ECU 6 million.

From 1988 onwards, agricultural levies, sugar levies and customs duties are net of 10 % collection costs previously included as an expenditure item.

*Sources:*  1958–89: management accounts; 1990–93: Court of Auditors' Report; 1994: general Budget of the European Community; 1995–97: general Budget of the European Union. DG for Economic and Financial Affairs, *European Economy*, no. 66, 1998.

Table 9.4  Budgetary expenditure of the European Communities (millions UA/EUA/ECU)[1]

| | ECSC operational budget | European Development Fund | Euratom[2] | EC general Budget | | | | | | | Total |
|---|---|---|---|---|---|---|---|---|---|---|---|
| | | | | EAGGF[3] | Social Fund | Regional Fund | Industry energy research | Administration[4] | Other | Total EC | |
| 1958 | 21.7 | – | 7.9 | – | – | – | – | 8.6 | 0.0 | 8.6 | 35.5 |
| 1959 | 30.7 | 51.2 | 39.1 | – | – | – | – | 20.3 | 4.9 | 25.2 | 146.2 |
| 1960 | 23.5 | 63.2 | 20.0 | – | – | – | – | 23.4 | 4.9 | 28.3 | 135.0 |
| 1961 | 26.5 | 172.0 | 72.5 | – | 8.6 | – | – | 27.9 | 2.9 | 39.4 | 305.0 |
| 1962 | 13.6 | 162.3 | 88.6 | – | 11.3 | – | – | 34.2 | 46.8 | 92.3 | 356.8 |
| 1963 | 21.9 | 55.5 | 106.4 | – | 4.6 | – | – | 37.2 | 42.3 | 84.1 | 267.9 |
| 1964 | 18.7 | 35.0 | 124.4 | – | 7.2 | – | – | 43.0 | 42.9 | 93.1 | 271.1 |
| 1965 | 37.3 | 248.8 | 120.0 | 102.7 | 42.9 | – | – | 48.1 | 7.4 | 201.1 | 607.2 |
| 1966 | 28.1 | 157.8 | 129.2 | 310.3 | 26.2 | – | – | 55.4 | 10.4 | 402.3 | 717.3 |
| 1967 | 10.4 | 105.8 | 158.5 | 562.0 | 35.6 | – | – | 60.4 | 17.1 | 675.1 | 949.8 |
| 1968 | 21.2 | 121.0 | 73.4 | 2 250.4 | 43.0 | – | – | 91.8 | 23.5 | 2 408.7 | 2 624.2 |
| 1969 | 40.7 | 104.8 | 59.2 | 3 818.0 | 50.5 | – | – | 105.6 | 77.1 | 4 051.2 | 4 255.9 |
| 1970 | 56.2 | 10.5 | 63.4 | 5 228.3 | 64.0 | – | – | 114.7 | 41.4 | 5 448.4 | 5 578.5 |
| 1971 | 37.4 | 236.1 | – | 1883.6 | 56.5 | – | 65.0 | 132.1 | 152.2 | 2 289.3 | 2 562.8 |
| 1972 | 43.7 | 212.7 | – | 2 477.6 | 97.5 | – | 75.1 | 177.2 | 247.1 | 3 074.5 | 3 330.9 |
| 1973 | 86.9 | 210.0 | – | 3 768.8 | 269.2 | – | 69.1 | 239.4 | 294.4 | 4 641.0 | 4 937.9 |
| 1974 | 92.0 | 157.0 | – | 3 651.3 | 292.1 | – | 82.8 | 335.7 | 675.2 | 5 038.2 | 5 287.2 |
| 1975 | 127.4 | 71.0 | – | 4 586.6 | 360.2 | 150.0 | 99.0 | 375.0 | 642.8 | 6 213.6 | 6 412.0 |
| 1976 | 94.0 | 320.0 | – | 6 033.3 | 176.7 | 300.0 | 113.3 | 419.7 | 909.5 | 7 952.6 | 8 366.6 |
| 1977 | 93.0 | 244.7 | – | 6 463.5 | 325.2 | 372.5 | 163.3 | 497.0 | 883.4 | 8 704.9 | 9 042.6 |
| 1978 | 159.1 | 394.5 | – | 9 602.2 | 284.8 | 254.9 | 227.2 | 676.7 | 1 302.4 | 12 348.2 | 12 901.8 |
| 1979 | 173.9 | 480.0 | – | 10 735.5 | 595.7 | 671.5 | 288.0 | 863.9 | 1 447.9 | 14 602.5 | 15 256.4 |
| 1980 | 175.7 | 508.5 | – | 11 596.1 | 502.0 | 751.8 | 212.8 | 938.8 | 2 056.1 | 16 057.5[5] | 16 741.7 |
| 1981 | 261.0 | 658.0 | – | 11 446.0 | 547.0 | 2 264.0 | 217.6 | 1035.4 | 3 024.6 | 18 546.0[6] | 19 465.0 |
| 1982 | 243.0 | 750.0 | – | 12 792.0 | 910.0 | 2 766.0[7] | 346.0 | 1 103.3 | 3 509.7 | 21 427.0[8] | 22 420.0 |
| 1983 | 300.0 | 752.0 | – | 16 331.3 | 801.0 | 2 265.5 | 1 216.2 | 1 161.6 | 2 989.9 | 24 765.5[9] | 25 817.5 |
| 1984 | 408.0 | 703.0 | – | 18 985.8 | 1 116.4 | 1 283.3 | 1 346.4 | 1 236.6 | 2 150.8 | 26 118.3[10] | 27 239.3 |
| 1985 | 453.0 | 698.0 | – | 20 546.4 | 1 413.0 | 1 624.3 | 706.9 | 1 332.6 | 2 599.8 | 28 223.0[11] | 29 374.0 |
| 1986 | 439.0 | 846.7 | – | 23 067.7 | 2 533.0 | 2 373.0 | 760.1 | 1 603.2 | 4 526.2 | 34 853.2 | 36 148.9 |

| Year | EAGGF – Guarantee | Structural Funds | Community initiatives | Cohesion Fund | Other structural | Total structural | Internal policies | External policies | Administration | Other | Total budget |
|---|---|---|---|---|---|---|---|---|---|---|---|
| 1987 | 399.3 | 837.9 | – | 23 939.4 | 2 542.2 | 2 562.3 | 964.8 | 1 740.0 | 3 720.5 | 35 469.2 | 36 706.4 |
| 1988 | 567.0 | 1 196.3 | – | 27 531.9 | 2 298.8 | 3 092.8 | 1 203.7 | 1 947.0 | 6 186.8 | 42 261.0 | 44 024.3 |
| 1989 | 404.0 | 1 297.0 | – | 25 858.8 | 2 676.1 | 3 920.0 | 1 353.0 | 2 063.0 | 9 978.9[12] | 45 859.8 | 47 560.8 |
| 1990 | 488.0 | 1 256.5 | – | 27 233.8 | 3 212.0 | 4 554.1 | 1 738.0 | 2 298.1 | 7 567.9 | 46 604.6 | 48 349.1 |
| 1991 | 495.0 | 1 191.0 | – | 33 443.2 | 3 869.3 | 5 179.9 | 1 918.8 | 2 519.2 | 9 655.6 | 56 586.0 | 58 272.0 |
| 1992 | 535.3 | 1 942.0 | – | 38 461.6 | 4 817.2 | 7 578.7 | 2 423.7 | 2 927.4 | 6 619.0 | 62 827.6 | 65 304.9 |
| 1993 | 551.8 | 1 353.6 | – | 37 135.3 | 5 097.2 | 8 172.4 | 2 833.8 | 3 296.4 | 9 704.6 | 66 239.7 | 68 145.1 |
| 1994 | 37 465.0 | 17 555.7 | 1 860.2 | 1 679.0 | 433.9 | 21 528.8 | 3 733.8 | 3 348.3 | 3 617.6 | 320.0 | 70 013.5 |
| 1995 | 38 422.5 | 18 688.3 | 2 068.0 | 1 749.7 | 1 221.6 | 23 727.6 | 4 256.0 | 4 162.8 | 4 008.3 | 1 950.0 | 76 527.2 |
| 1996 | 41 328.0 | 21 099.2 | 2 204.6 | 1 919.3 | 782.5 | 26 005.6 | 4 780.3 | 4 718.2 | 4 128.6 | 927.7 | 81 888.4 |
| 1997 | 41 305.0 | 21 544.0 | 2 349.3 | 2 326.0 | 413.6 | 26 632.9 | 4 870.6 | 4 796.5 | 4 283.5 | 477.1 | 82 365.6 |
| 1998 | 40 937.0 | 23 084.4 | 2 558.8 | 2 648.8 | 302.7 | 28 594.7 | 4 678.5 | 4 528.5 | 4 353.4 | 437.0 | 83 529.2 |

*Notes:*

1. UA until 1977; EUA/ECU from 1978 onwards.
2. Incorporated in the EC budget from 1971.
3. This column includes, for the years to 1970, substantial amounts carried forward to following years.
4. Commission, Council, Parliament, Court of Justice and Court of Auditors.
5. Including surplus of ECU 82.4 million carried forward to 1981.
6. Including ECU 1173 million carried forward to 1982.
7. Including ECU 1819 million UK special measures.
8. Including ECU 2211 million carried forward to 1983.
9. Including ECU 1707 million carried forward to 1984.
10. There was a small deficit in 1984 in respect of the EC budget due largely to late payment of advances by some member states.
11. There was a cash deficit in 1985 of ECU 25 million due to late payment of advances by some member states.
12. Includes a surplus of ECU 5080 million carried forward to 1990.

*Sources:* 1958–89: management accounts; 1990–93: Court of Auditors' Report; 1994: general Budget of the European Community; 1995–97: general Budget of the European Union. DG for Economic and Financial Affairs, *European Economy*, no. 66, 1998.

sectoral policies. The most significant area of expenditure has been agriculture, as shown in Table 9.4. Its share of the Budget, for example, was about three-quarters in 1973 and around three-fifths in 1988, falling to around a half by the late 1990s. While the percentage of budgetary expenditure devoted to agriculture has fallen, in absolute amounts it has continued to increase. Claims on the Budget were high when the Community was disposing of its agricultural surpluses on the world market with heavy export subsidies. The search for agricultural solutions has continued somewhat elusively, though with some success, such as that in the last GATT round to reduce export subsidies. Another significant earlier commitment was that in the Brussels Council Agreement in 1988, which laid down that the annual growth of EAGGF Guarantee expenditure should not exceed 74 per cent of the annual growth of the Community GNP. Agricultural policy has continued to squeeze agricultural prices, helping to erode the large and costly surpluses, but much hinges in terms of expenditure on the degree of income compensation that is made available to cushion farmers.

Despite encroaching bankruptcy, caused mainly by the overdominance of agricultural expenditure, there have been pressures to increase spending in other desirable policy areas, to raise the profile of the Community and to offset uneven distributional effects of the Budget. Although expenditure on the Social Fund pre-dated agricultural spending, the introduction of agricultural spending by the Community in 1965 swamped that of the Social Fund. It was only with the recognition of the case for enhanced Structural Fund expenditure to help weaker regions and the role of the ESF on the supply side, especially in training, and of the ERDF in raising demand-side expenditure, that by the 1990s the EU had marginally improved towards a redistributive Budget. Furthermore, the setting up of the Cohesion Fund to countries with less than 90 per cent of EU average per capita GNP established a small built-in mechanism of redistribution to member states; for example, in 1999 Spain received about £6 billion from Structural Funds and over £1 billion from the Cohesion Fund.

There are particular obstacles impeding the redirection of budgetary expenditure. Those countries, especially agricultural ones benefiting from the existing pattern of expenditure, have been reluctant to see these eroded. Agricultural countries benefit substantially in terms of total receipts, and the smaller countries, such as Ireland and Denmark, have fared particularly well in terms of per capita receipts. Such a redistribution of income on welfare grounds may be justified for Ireland, but not for Denmark. Other small countries, such as Belgium and Luxembourg, have also gained significantly from playing the host to Community institutions, though part of their income does not accrue to their own citizens but is repatriated by EU employees. The EU has been worried that focus on net budgetary transfers *per se* is conflictual and encourages 'juste retour'. However, estimates are shown by the Court of Auditors' Report, exemplified in 1997 by Germany paying 28.2 per cent of the EU Budget (and down from 33.3 per cent in 1994), while budget expenditure in Germany was only 13.1 per cent. The Netherlands was a net contributor and paid in 6.4 per cent and received back 3.3 per cent of EU budgetary expenditure. Other net contributors, apart from the UK, included Austria, which paid in 2.8 per cent and received 1.7 per cent, and Sweden, which paid in 3.1 per cent and received 1.4 per cent. France also paid in 17.5 per cent and received 16 per cent. Italy was in balance with 11 per cent paid in contributions and 11 per cent in receipts in 1997.

The Community is divided in its approach between the Commission, Parliament and the Southern European members which generally favour more expenditure. On the other hand, the UK, Germany and more recently France, which pay most towards financing the Community, want to limit their excessive expenditure. However, increasing the level of expenditure would enhance the Community's role, making agreement easier, though there are strong constraints on expansion. Governments are concerned about a rising proportion of budgetary expenditure as a percentage of Community GDP, even though this is far below the minimum proposed by the MacDougall Report. National governments involved in making cutbacks in domestic expenditure to create room for the private sector – which they perceive to be the basis of success of their major competitors in the USA and Japan – find it hard to acquiesce to more expenditure at Community level. By the late 1990s Germany under the new Schröder government appeared to have become more like the British in seeking to reduce its large underwriting of Community expenditure, some of which is wasteful and targets inappropriate objectives.

The EU wished to plan its future development on the basis of adequate, stable and guaranteed resources. The financial perspective during the 1990s was set at the Edinburgh Summit in 1992 which linked the percentage of EU GNP to the performance of the EU economy, reaching an own-resources ceiling up to 1.27 per cent of GNP by the end of the century. For example, in 1997 the share of the Budget was 46.3 per

*Table 9.5   EU Budget for the millennium (in million euros)*

| | Year | | | | | | |
|---|---|---|---|---|---|---|---|
| | 2000 | 2001 | 2002 | 2003 | 2004 | 2005 | 2006 |
| Agriculture (including rural development) | 40 920 | 42 800 | 43 900 | 43 770 | 42 760 | 41 930 | 41 660 |
| Structural operations | 32 045 | 31 455 | 30 865 | 30 285 | 29 595 | 29 595 | 29 170 |
| Pre-accession aid | 3 120 | 3 120 | 3 120 | 3 120 | 3 120 | 3 120 | 3 120 |
| Total appropriations for payments | 89 590 | 91 070 | 94 130 | 94 740 | 91 720 | 89 910 | 89 310 |
| Appropriations for payments as a % of GNP | 1.13 | 1.12 | 1.13 | 1.11 | 1.05 | 1.00 | 0.97 |
| Available for new members | – | – | 4 140 | 6 710 | 8 890 | 11 440 | 14 220 |
| Own-resources ceiling (%) | 1.27 | 1.27 | 1.27 | 1.27 | 1.27 | 1.27 | 1.27 |

*Source:*   EU Presidency, *Financial Times*, 27/28 March 1999, p. 2.

cent for the CAP; with structural operations having risen to 35.7 per cent; internal policies 6.7 per cent; external policies 6.6 per cent; administrative expenditure 4.8 per cent; and reserves 0.5 per cent.

The Budget agreement at the Berlin Summit in March 1999 agreed on a total EU expenditure over seven years of 640 billion euros. This is shown in Table 9.5.

It was important to establish another firm Budget to accommodate East European enlargement, but to ensure that it would not be overwhelmed by massive new agricultural expenditure there. It was also important to ensure that agriculture's share of the Budget was constrained. French opposition resisted really radical CAP reform, which exacerbates the agricultural costs of East European enlargement. Pre-accession aid of 3.1 billion euros per annum, and from 2002 the sum of 4.1 billion euros, rising to 14.2 billion euros in 2006, is available for new members only (and not for use by existing member states).

*The role of the institutions in the budgetary process*   The Commission has continued in its role of providing new initiatives for further integration, with an accompanying need to finance such development. The Commission prepares preliminary draft budgets which set out the spending priorities for the coming year and are examined by the Council of Ministers. The final draft is then sent to the EP for the first reading. Normally the EP makes amendments and modifications and sends it back to the Council for the second reading. The Council can accept it or make recommendations and refer it back to the EP for its second reading. The Budget Council, comprising ministers from national finance ministries, reaches its decisions by qualified majority voting and usually trims back budgetary expenditure. If the EP does not accept the outcome, the Commission, Council and EP Budget Committee try to resolve the problem in a conciliation meeting. If there is no agreement, then the institutions are forced to operate under the old Budget until a new preliminary Budget has been renegotiated as soon as possible.

The EP has tried to increase its powers, particularly in the budgetary field. It has been given the last word on so-called 'non-compulsory expenditure' (NCE) – this differs from the 'compulsory expenditure' that is necessary to carry out the provisions of the Treaty. Thus non-compulsory expenditure related largely to EU spending on regions, social policy, energy, industry, transport, and so on. The Brussels Agreement in 1988 raised spending on Structural Funds into privileged NCE, or what has been called 'compulsory non-compulsory expenditure'

(Shackleton 1990, p. 20). Compulsory expenditure is mainly on agriculture, especially on Guarantee spending and some Guidance spending. The Council therefore still controls the bulk of expenditure, and even on the NCE there is a limit to which this may be raised by the Parliament. The three objective criteria used to determine the maximum NCE are: the trend in GNP (in volume terms); the average variations in the budgets of member states; and the trend in the cost of living during the preceding financial year.

Since 1979 the elected EP and the Council have been locked in a struggle almost every year over the size and shape of the Budget and their respective powers. Parliament has succeeded in raising annual expenditure marginally, even though its room for manoeuvre is mainly confined to NCE. Parliament and Council clashed quickly in 1979 when the latter failed to obtain the qualified majority necessary to reject the EP's increase in the Regional Fund. The conflict between the two institutions became even more intense in 1980 when the EP rejected the Budget for the first time. Clashes continued in the early 1980s over contentious issues such as the CAP and British budgetary rebate. The Fontainebleau Summit in 1984, in tackling the latter, appeared to have settled the budgetary problem, paving the way to greater progress. In practice it failed to do this completely, and there has been continuing turbulence over the Budget.

Expenditure claims have tended to overstretch resources and disagreements have been resolved by the use of creative accounting and by asking the Court of Justice to resolve the respective roles of the Council and Parliament in budgetary matters. The EP has generally favoured a more expansive budget and continued to challenge the interpretation of what is compulsory and what is non-compulsory expenditure, trying to switch more elements into non-compulsory spending. A clearer financial perspective has been agreed between the institutions to lessen conflict, with the Council of Ministers adopting a plan of financial perspectives for a six-year programme (1994–99), and also an interinstitutional agreement on how the three institutions are to co-operate.

To monitor budgetary procedures, the Court of Auditors was established in 1977 and its powers were increased under both the Maastricht and Amsterdam Treaties to include investigation of irregularities. It comprises independent members who audit the Budget; and operates along with the Parliament's Committee of Budgetary Control. They are concerned to ensure that money is spent effectively to avoid waste. There is a big problem of fraud with lost revenue through smuggling of cigarettes and alcohol. Meanwhile, on the expenditure side, agriculture, Structural Funds and overseas aid have led to many cases of fraud and irregularity. In 1998 the Commission established a special anti-fraud unit UCLAF (Unité de Co-ordination de la Lutte Anti-Fraude).

## Taxation in the UK and the problem of the Community Budget

*Taxation*
Before the UK joined the Community, its tax system was distinctive in showing a greater reliance on direct taxation than in other countries (particularly France and Italy), whilst its indirect taxation was based mainly on purchase tax across a wide range of consumer goods. This was levied at the wholesale stage and charged as a percentage of the wholesale price, originally at two rates, though both the rates and their number increased. Purchase tax came under criticism for its adverse effects on the performance of particular sectors, such as the motor industry. The problems of manufacturing industry and its excessive taxation in relation to services led to the introduction of the Selective Employment Tax (SET) in 1966 – this was a tax on the employment of workers in the service sector.

VAT offered the advantage of replacing these taxes by a single sales tax levied at the retail stage. But a disadvantage was that it proved more costly to collect since purchase tax had been collected from fewer than 100 000 taxpayers; a seven-fold increase in tax officers was needed to collect VAT from more taxpayers. When the Richardson Committee first examined the replacement of purchase tax by VAT in 1964, they concluded that purchase tax was preferable to VAT. In 1973 the UK altered its system (as it did in other areas, such as its agricultural deficiency payments), not so much because of major defects but as measures to harmonize within the Community. After 1979 the Thatcher government increased the rate of VAT from 8 per cent to 15 per cent (and to 17.5 per cent in 1991), with offsetting reductions in direct taxation as part of its supply-side policy. Nevertheless, UK governments showed some sensitivity to Community proposals to have two rates of VAT as part of the creation of a full internal market, since this would affect British zero-rating on a wide range of goods and services such as food and housing. While phasing out zero-rating would raise VAT revenue significantly, it would also raise the retail price index and be even more regressive. Similarly a reduction in excise duties and harmonization at Community level would result in a further fall in government revenue, but would dampen the retail price index. The disparity in excise duties, with higher duties in the UK on tobacco and alcohol in particular, have led to widespread smuggling. This is sometimes highly sophisticated, especially in non-bulky cigarettes, with UK-made cigarettes being exported and exempt from duty to various destinations, such as Andorra, and then mainly re-exported back to the UK illegally, avoiding duty. There are also significant disparities now in petrol and diesel prices as a consequence of higher 'green' taxes in the UK, with marked consequences, for example, between the Irish Republic and Northern Ireland.

### Budgetary problems for the UK

Budgetary problems have been a source of continual friction and strain in the UK's membership of the Community. Although in other EU countries few citizens consider that their own country benefits most from the EU, in the UK a large majority perceived not only that the UK benefits least but also contributed most (Hewstone 1986). Problems have arisen with regard to both revenue and expenditure.

On the revenue side, since the UK has a highly open economy (particularly in its trade with the rest of the world) it has contributed disproportionately to the EU's revenue in the form of customs duties and levies on agricultural imports. For example, during 1984–9 the UK was the second largest source of customs duties (behind Germany) and was the second largest source of agricultural levies (behind Italy). While the pattern of UK trade has changed, with greater imports from the Community, this has not really solved the problem. If the UK imports more foodstuffs from the EU, obviously no import levies are payable but the UK simply substitutes higher trade costs for higher budgetary costs. In other words, instead of importing low-cost foodstuffs from the rest of the world and paying an import levy to raise the price to the level prevailing in the Community, the UK pays the high price directly to import from a Community supplier.

The choice of VAT as the major source of Community revenue is also unfavourable to countries with high consumption and low investment and which have imports in excess of exports. From a UK perspective, some additional source of revenue may have been preferable, such as a tax on imports of oil. But this would have resulted in the Community having an energy policy similar to its agricultural policy and, given the criticisms of the latter, it would not be desirable to advocate yet another high-price policy. Furthermore, if the tax were imposed not on oil

imports but on oil production, the UK would actually suffer disproportionately. If a tax on oil (and other energy sources) were introduced,
then from the viewpoint of conserving energy it would be better to tax
consumption. While this would be a useful Community tax measure,
unfortunately it would not solve the UK's budgetary problems. In practice it is difficult to find additional revenue sources which are good
taxes and which also result in a lower budgetary contribution by the
UK.

As a small agricultural producer, the UK has not been able to secure
a net budgetary inflow from the overdeveloped level of CAP expenditure; for example, Guarantee payments to the Netherlands have in some
years been around twice those of the UK. Although a system of 'juste
retour', in which every country receives exactly the same as it contributes, cannot be recommended, a system in which low-income countries
are net contributors to the Budget is a very perverse outcome. It has
proved extremely difficult to develop other common policies that are as
favourable to the UK as the CAP is to the more agricultural countries.
Although new areas of expenditure could be opened up, it is necessary
to ensure that the Community level is appropriate to conduct these
policies instead of the national level.

Expenditure by the EU on defence, social expenditure, and so on,
would particularly suit the UK. Changes like this would be fundamental and to date have been mainly piecemeal, since politically the EU has
found it necessary to retain the expensive CAP, which has constituted
an unfortunate restraint on expanding expenditure in other areas. While
Structural Funds have provided significant benefits to the UK, its share
of these has now diminished significantly with southern enlargement,
German reunification and impending Eastern European enlargement.

### Budgetary dialogue with the UK

When it joined the Community, the UK accepted that it would contribute to the Budget in accordance with a fixed percentage key, beginning
at 8.78 per cent in 1973 and increasing to 19.24 per cent in 1977. The
Labour government became concerned that this would represent an
undue burden on the UK, since its relatively slow rate of economic
growth meant that its share of Community GNP was likely to decline.
This happened, particularly when measured using current exchange
rates rather than rates designed to reflect the purchasing-power parity
of currencies. The government focused on reducing UK contributions,
because it was dubious about being able to change Community ex-

penditure in a way more favourable to the UK. It pressed forward with renegotiation, and agreement was reached at the Dublin Summit in 1975 for a payback system for countries which oversubscribed to the Budget. It applied to gross contributions, and a complex formula was established for a sliding-scale reimbursement. Despite a favourable referendum vote in 1975, the UK's budgetary terms worked out badly.

Budgetary problems soon resurfaced and were brought to a head in 1979 by the new Conservative government, again at a Summit in Dublin. The UK pressed for a cut of £1 billion in its contribution, but the maximum reduction offered was £350 million. The government tried, relatively unsuccessfully, to increase Community expenditure in the UK by, for example, proposals for greater Community aid for investment in the coal industry. Budgetary confrontation resulted in stresses and acrimony, deflecting the Community's attention from much-needed developments in other areas. Although the UK appeared to have a strong case in pointing to the inequities in the Budget, its pleas were frustrated; France constantly argued that the only concessions could be lump-sum, degressive and temporary (Butler 1986).

Early in 1980 the UK was offered a better deal after linking the Budget discussion to the setting of agricultural prices. On average between 1980 and 1982 the UK received a refund of about 70 per cent of its net budgetary contribution. The British government agreed at the Brussels Summit in March 1984 that its contributions would be redefined to exclude the counting of levies and customs duties in its search for some permanent solution. It appeared that this had been achieved at the Fontainebleau Summit in 1984, and in return for agreement to raise the Community VAT contribution the UK obtained a guaranteed percentage rebate every year – whereas the earlier rebates received under the 1980 agreements had been for absolute financial amounts (Denton 1984). At Fontainebleau the UK accepted the Budget rebate of ECU 1 billion for 1984; it agreed a compensation mechanism for 66 per cent of the difference between its share of VAT payments and its receipts from the Budget. The Fontainebleau Agreement in its technically complex calculation of rebates to the UK created a special position which was resented by other countries. While German contributions to the British rebate have been reduced, Germany is still concerned about the British abatement, plus the fact that rich countries such as Denmark continue to be net beneficiaries from the Budget.

Some improved settlement had to be reached eventually in order to avoid an impasse which would distract the Community from new progress towards southern enlargement. It was recognized that the UK had a genuine grievance, but member states were upset by its tactics in demanding the return of its own money and threatening the established pillars of the Community, such as the CAP. British policy continues to be based on keeping tight budgetary finance to encourage agricultural reform; it has been adamant about better husbandry before sanctioning further expansion in expenditure.

The resolution of the basic budgetary problem still falls short of UK aspirations, being inequitable to the extent that a country with a relatively low income per head remains a net contributor. Between 1973 and 1986 the UK's total budgetary imbalance with the Community was –£7785 million. The UK's percentage share of annual contributions to the Budget compared with payments from it show that the UK had has the largest net gap, apart from Germany. The net gap in 1987 was 6.1 per cent and an unyielding UK position resulted in deadlock at the European Summit in Copenhagen in December 1987. There the UK's compensatory offer was less than that reached at Fontainebleau, though use of the additional GDP base was welcomed. Fortunately greater progress was possible, with a new agreement at the emergency European Summit in Brussels in February 1988. This resolved budgetary disagreements up to 1992, after which a new agreement was reached at the Edinburgh Summit in December 1992 on the financial perspective to 1999.

For the UK it has been necessary to defend stubbornly its abatement mechanism and much depended on whether its relative income position was still below the EU average; also, it was complicated not just by growth rates (and numbers of new members), but by fluctuations in the sterling exchange rate outside the EMU. Political pressure from the largest net contributing countries, especially Germany, continued for the end of the UK rebate (of about £2 billion per annum) or new rebates for themselves. This has been brought to a head by enlarged budgetary costs of Eastern European enlargement and a reluctance by France to move to joint member-state financing of CAP and a determination by Southern European countries to hold on to their large gains from the Structural Funds. The defusion of budgetary conflict depended upon concessions by all sides, especially by Germany's willingness to continue financing budgetary costs as a *quid pro quo* for its large trade gains in a constantly enlarging union. The Berlin Summit in March 1999 conceded the continuance of the UK Budget rebate, but made certain modifications to it. For example, the costs of financing it were altered, reducing the contributions of Germany, Austria, the Netherlands and Sweden to 25 per cent, with the balance paid by the other ten member states. The UK also agreed to forgo windfall gains which would have accrued to it through reducing EU budgetary dependence on VAT (through which the UK contributed more than under the increased dependence on GNP). In addition, the UK agreed to forgo the 25 per cent of customs duties and agricultural levies for collection costs. Finally, the UK will not receive any rebate for the pre-accession aid to Eastern Europe, to which the UK would have been entitled after enlargement.

# 10 World-wide trading links

## External background

Although the EU has been concerned very much with the process of internal integration and with fostering intra-trade, it has had to institute a common external policy towards the rest of the world. The EU is a giant in world trade and has created a distinctive preferential system in its extra-trade arrangements. It has focused its closest links in key areas with which the major ex-colonial powers, such as France and the UK, have had historic links. It was natural that the EU should seek to consolidate these links in using trade and aid to exercise its political influence in strategic areas such as the Mediterranean and Africa. They are important sources of supplies of energy and raw materials which need assistance, such as foreign investment from the Community, to develop more rapidly.

The Community's external policy has become intertwined with its policies in other sectors. For example, the consequences of the CAP have resulted in outside countries seeking to preserve their exports to some extent by reaching special trade arrangements with the EU, though the EU has been least liberal towards competitive agricultural imports. Outsiders have also sought to reduce the diversion of their manufactured exports caused by the Common External Tariff (CET). Modifications to this tariff represent the Community's most potent weapon in dealing with outsiders. EU preferential agreements have multiplied to such an extent that very few countries are subjected to the full CET. However, an open trading policy has accelerated the decline of the Community's traditional industries, with related regional problems in those areas affected by imports. The EU has recognized the need to expand the new high-tech industries, but some countries such as France made progress towards this conditional upon using the EU's Common Commercial Policy in a more protectionist way to outsiders (Pearce and Sutton 1986).

There was also concern by outside countries that the EU internal market programme might strengthen Community industry at external expense. However, to the extent that EU GDP rises and sucks in imports, there is little evidence of outside countries being affected very adversely. Also, multilateralism triumphed in the Uruguay Round, though preferential arrangements still conflict with this. The benefits of multilateral free trade over protectionism have been recognized increasingly not just by developed but also by developing economies which have become more outward-looking. The less-developed economies still possess some advantages in being able to subsidize their industries and in not applying the same social measures as the EU. They have also learnt from the EU example of bloc trade, seeing advantages from participating in customs unions or more especially in Free Trade Areas (FTAs) within their own region. These are important in enabling them to exploit dynamic infant industry economies of scale. Outside countries have had to review their trading strategies with the EU and less-developed economies have sought a more balanced and less exploitative neo-colonial type of relationship.

This chapter examines some of the EU's world-wide trading connections. How beneficial are these special trading arrangements to the Community, and what have been some of the effects on other countries? It pinpoints those areas that have special arrangements with the Community. The EFTA countries were most favoured, at the top of the hierarchy, with the majority moving from free trade to full membership of the EU (and hence are mainly covered in the following chapter on enlargement). Next in importance were those in the Mediterranean area and the Mediterranean agreements were condemned for being against both the letter and the spirit of GATT (Pomfret 1986). A hierarchical ranking of links with outside countries has resulted in a clear 'pecking order', but there have been movements within this, with the CEECs moving upwards from the bottom and most discriminated level. In this chapter considerable emphasis is given to the ongoing links which the EU has established with the Mediterranean and especially with those countries of the Lomé Convention in Africa, the Caribbean and the Pacific (ACP).

The geographical distribution of EU trade is shown in Table 10.1. More than half was intra-trade by 1973 and this rose further with subsequent enlargements. Its major external trading partners are the USA, Japan and the developing countries.

Table 10.1   EU(12): exports and imports by main country groups (in per cent[1])

| | Exports | | | | | Imports | | | | |
|---|---|---|---|---|---|---|---|---|---|---|
| | 1963 | 1973 | 1980 | 1985 | 1994 | 1963 | 1973 | 1980 | 1985 | 1994 |
| EU | 48.4 | 56.1 | 55.8 | 54.7 | 58.4 | 43.1 | 53.2 | 49.4 | 52.9 | 57.0 |
| EFTA(6) | 13.4 | 11.3 | 11.0 | 10.0 | 10.7[2] | 9.0 | 8.3 | 8.6 | 9.3 | 11.1[2] |
| Eastern Europe | 3.0 | 3.8 | 3.5 | 2.8 | – | 3.4 | 3.1 | 3.7 | 3.9 | – |
| United States | 7.3 | 7.6 | 5.6 | 10.1 | 7.3 | 11.8 | 8.7 | 8.6 | 8.0 | 7.4 |
| Japan | 1.0 | 1.4 | 1.0 | 1.2 | 2.1 | 0.9 | 2.1 | 2.6 | 3.4 | 3.9 |
| Developing countries | 22.3 | 17.0 | 21.3 | 18.4 | 14.2 | 25.8 | 21.3 | 25.1 | 20.4 | 12.8 |
| of which:   OPEC | 4.1 | 3.9 | 8.1 | 6.0 | 2.9 | 8.6 | 8.9 | 13.8 | 8.4 | 3.2 |
| NICs | 5.6 | 5.1 | 4.5 | 3.9 | 11.3 | 5.4 | 4.9 | 4.4 | 4.8 | 9.6 |
| Rest of world | 4.6 | 2.8 | 1.9 | 2.8 | 7.3 | 5.9 | 3.2 | 2.0 | 2.1 | 7.8 |

*Notes:*
[1]   Because of different data sources, some figures may deviate slightly from some of those in other tables.
[2]   Other European OECD countries.

*Sources:*   UN COMTRADE Data Base in A. Utne, *EFTA Bulletin*, no. 4, vol. XXVII, October–December 1986. For 1994, adjusted from *European Economy*, no. 66, 1998, pp. 152–3.

## The EU's non-preferential and preferential links

*The EU's non-preferential links with developed countries*

*The United States*  The EU and USA have enjoyed very close links because the USA has generally supported EU integration, though their harmonious relationship has deteriorated in recent years. Friction has arisen in specific economic sectors such as agriculture, with the USA pressing for the removal of farm subsidies. The EU's obstinate approach to agricultural protection has persisted, despite the agricultural concessions to freer trade which were made in the last Uruguay Round. However, bans on beef treated with hormones and restrictions on genetically modified seed imports exemplify continuing trade friction. In other industries such as steel, the Americans opted for import controls, arguing that European imports were highly subsidized (Hine 1985, p. 234; Tsoukalis 1986, p. 23). The EU has also resorted to other non-tariff barriers (NTBs) to concoct protectionist rules, such as noise regulations to limit US planes, and justifying quotas on US TV programmes and films as defence of culture.

In relation to Eastern Europe, the EU has always adopted a less hostile view than the more distant Americans. The USA was prepared to use trade sanctions as a way of putting pressure on the Soviet Union. Security-related exports have been controlled through the Co-ordinating Committee on Multilateral Export Controls (COCOM). The attempt by the USA to control exports of high-technology products to Eastern Europe by its many business subsidiaries and by European companies operating under licence in the EU resulted in disagreements between the EU and the USA. The USA likewise objected to Community countries subsidizing export credits and loans to Eastern Europe, though such opposition lessened with better relations from the 1990s.

Political–military differences between the USA and some EU countries have existed, particularly France, though the EU supported UN action in the Gulf conflict. While the two blocs remain allies with common interests, the traditional close coupling between them is now questioned much more widely than in the past. Economically, the USA has faced massive budgetary and particularly trade deficits, and the latter are likely to be cut only by reduced expenditure abroad, continued depreciation of the dollar and by further protectionist sentiments; these are likely to work against EU interests. Conflict in the WTO over EU preferential imports of bananas and US retaliatory action in 1999 was yet another indication of some diverging and conflicting interests.

*Japan*  Japan began its trade dialogue with the Community in the early 1960s, although only bilateral deals were reached. The imbalance in trade has arisen since imports from Japan have risen much more rapidly than exports to Japan. The Japanese have conducted a very effective strategy via their Ministry of International Trade and Industry (MITI), based upon finance underpinning mass investment and economies of scale creating the competitiveness from which to promote a laser-beam focus on specific European product markets (Nester 1990). Although the virtue of a multilateral trading system is that it is unnecessary to achieve bilateral balance with each country, the EU and Japan agreed in 1983 to a voluntary export restraint (VER) on various sensitive products. By the mid-1980s VERs were applied to just over a third of Japanese exports to the Community. Despite these, Japan's trade surplus with the EU has continued to widen.

The trading problems can be attributed largely to Japanese NTBs. Although Japan has the lowest tariff rates of any country, NTBs abound as part of Japanese culture. Different technical standards, bureaucratic delays and a fragmented distribution system, plus its high savings ratio, have combined to reduce imports. Japanese firms, their suppliers and distributors, are organized in Keiretsus (links/networks) which are the survivors of prewar Zaibatsus, and which Europeans have found difficult to penetrate. European businesses have manifested many deficiencies of their own, including low capital investment in high-tech sectors, and weak marketing, with far fewer European business executives in Japan than Japanese business executives in Europe.

## The EU's preferential trade relations

*The Mediterranean*  The importance of the Mediterranean to the Community has grown from the initial preferential trade links which France conducted with its former north African colonies in Morocco, Tunisia and Algeria. Algeria has the largest population and income per head of the three countries, drawing much of its revenue from oil exports. The whole region is of crucial importance to the EU to secure economic development and stability, and to lessen migratory labour pressure. The agreement with these three Maghreb countries is separate from the Community's agreements with other countries in Africa under the ACP.

Economically, countries like Tunisia have responded more positively to Community preference than others such as Morocco, though both countries have achieved good rates of economic growth. Morocco showed concern at Iberian enlargement of the Community, with estimates that this might cost Morocco some 2 per cent of its GDP. In July 1987 Morocco surprised the Community by applying for membership, though this is impossible since membership is open to European countries only. However, Morocco's persistence led to the improved Euro-Mediterranean free trade agreement and in 1995 new and more comprehensive preferential agreements were negotiated with Tunisia and Morocco. The projected static and dynamic effects have been estimated, with agricultural restrictions limiting the benefits (Galal and Hoekman 1997). Unfortunately the Community appears to have got itself into a zero-sum game in which trade concessions to certain countries are at the expense of others.

The signing of an Association Agreement with Greece in 1961 established a precedent which has carried its association to full membership (and which is discussed in Chapter 11). It became difficult to reject other preferential applications and one was reached with Turkey when it became an Associate Member of the Community by the Treaty of Ankara 1964. However, problems in applying the trade agreements successfully contributed to the Community's rejection of Turkey's application to join the EU in 1989.

The proliferation of Mediterranean agreements in the early 1970s included an association with Cyprus after 1972 which established a customs union for free industrial trade. This has ensured that the application for full membership of the EU is likely to ensue in the early years of the new century. Economically Cyprus is a highly suitable island for EU membership but politically the divisions between the majority Greek part of the island and the minority Turkish Republic of Northern Cyprus pose problems. The EU will accept access of Cyprus either, it is hoped, as one island, or if not, then just Greek Cyprus. It is quite a risky strategy by the EU since although the majority in Cyprus want accession (Greeks as well as some Turks), the Turkish leadership in Cyprus does not want its accession to the EU without recognition of its separate position and also before the entry of Turkey itself into the EU. Whilst a customs union for industrial products was finally achieved by 1996, Turkey seems to have fallen back from the accession envisaged in the Ankara agreement. The EU considers that it would be difficult to digest such a large Islamic country with low GDP, very high dependence on agriculture, and poor record on human rights. Also, Germany does not want further free-labour mobility from Turkey as a full EU member. The EU has downgraded the strategic role of Turkey post-cold war and *vis-à-vis* Russia. Hence if Turkey is frozen out of EU membership it makes it less likely that there can be a successful entry of a united Cyprus into the EU.

The Community established a preferential agreement with Israel in 1970 which led to a free trade agreement. In order not to upset its close relations with the USA, Israel subsequently also signed a separate FTA agreement with the USA. It was important for the EU to maintain a balance with Arab countries and therefore co-operation agreements were signed with the important Mashreq (Egypt, Lebanon, Syria and Jordan). There was also an association with Malta after 1970 which enabled it to raise its exports to the EU significantly and to attract inward investment, especially in industries such as clothing (Pomfret 1986, pp. 68–75). Malta is likely to join the EU fully within a few years (Redmond 1993).

Yugoslavia also signed a non-preferential agreement, so that by the 1970s the only Mediterranean countries lacking special relations with the Community were Albania and Libya. The complicated pattern of individual agreements required some rationalization, and after Commission proposals in 1972 the Community sought to replace individual agreements by a more global approach to the Mediterranean. The Community has identified this area as one of strategic importance and has used its commercial policy to exercise political influence – whereas the USA has used its naval presence. The EU draws its oil and other raw materials from the area. The Mediterranean countries themselves have perceived economic advantages in securing access to the EU market to stimulate their own industrial development and agriculturally to offset some of the protectionist nature of the CAP. The EU has brought the Mediterranean into its orbit, though the extension of its influence in the area infringes GATT and provides a poor example to other countries.

During the 1990s EU interest in the CEECs, especially by the northern member states, exceeded and overtook that of the Mediterranean, with more aid per capita plus quicker and more favourable trade treatment for the CEECs to prepare them for eventual membership. It became necessary to placate Mediterranean aspirations and therefore, partly with Spanish support in order to maintain some kind of balance, the EU(15) in 1995 set about creating an FTA for the EU and Mediterranean(12) to be achieved more slowly by about 2010. The key features are not just FTAs between each of the Mediterranean countries and the EU, but also the opening up of intra-Mediterranean free trade. The EU made provisions for increased aid to the region and the increased aid and technical assistance were in return for a further reduction in most barriers to the movement of goods and investment over a period of 12 years. The EU has largely dictated the terms of the agreement, seeking to maximize its own advantage in industrial free trade. It has imposed its own standards and constrained trade in key sectors such as petro-chemicals, services and agriculture (Tovias 1997).

The effects of preferential agreements are contested and may have become more marginal as a consequence of tariffs having been lowered successively in GATT. Preferences have had a more substantial impact on particular products in which EU protection has been high, such as textiles and agriculture. However, the EU is still highly resistant to opening up agricultural trade, being mainly concerned with industrial trade. The more outward-looking Mediterranean countries have been the ones to benefit most, and they have provided an attractive source for multinational inward investment, which traditionally was very low in the region because of political instability. Preferential agreements are helpful in underpinning liberalization and hence in attracting FDI. However, limited intraregional Mediterranean trade in the past constituted a restriction on further FDI. Hence it is a logical development for Mediterranean countries to develop free trade not just with the EU but between themselves, and the reduction of trade barriers should stimulate more inward FDI.

The southern enlargement of the Community aggravated its relations with outsiders such as the USA and partly with other Mediterranean countries. The countries with products similar to those of the new entrants are the ones most vulnerable to displacement. New entrants to the EU not only added to its immediate problems, but dynamically the effects of higher agricultural prices tended to increase supply, further threatening outside Mediterranean countries. For example, there are some highly competitive agricultural products such as citrus fruits between the full northern Mediterranean members of the EU competing with those of the southern Mediterranean countries. The EU since enlargement has increased its self-sufficiency in many products, making it less receptive to imports and those from the rest of the world seem likely to bear the brunt of any future protectionism. Even within the Mediterranean it has hampered negotiations with countries highly dependent on agriculture, such as Egypt.

*ACP countries: problems of trade and aid*   ACP countries, as LDCs, are characterized by low income per head and overdependence on agriculture. Most endure a precarious agricultural existence and some have suffered badly from drought in recent years. Many of the younger skilled and more mobile people have been forced to emigrate from arid African countries to take advantage of opportunities elsewhere in countries like Senegal or the Ivory Coast.

The oil-exporting countries have naturally benefited from the rise in oil prices (including ACP countries such as Nigeria, Congo, Gabon, Trinidad and Tobago). Other ACP countries which are oil importers have suffered, and also their exports to OPEC have not consisted of sufficient industrial products to increase sales there significantly. Apart from exogenous shocks, many LDCs have been moulded by their colonial inheritance, with Africa carved up into particular spheres of separate French and British interests. Their dominance led in some instances to a legacy of minimum-wage legislation and high wages in the public sector which distorted resource allocation. The influx of overseas multinationals has further reinforced the bias against investment in the indigenous private industrial sector. High wages militate against labour-intensive employment (yet labour is the abundant factor), and also generate inflationary pressure. ACP countries have tended to experience higher wage costs and inflation than many of the NICs in Asia.

LDCs require financial aid to fill both their savings/investment gap and their gap in foreign exchange. They can see the benefits from aid, even though they prefer to earn their living in the world to a greater extent by engaging in trade. Indeed, the latter is of far greater significance, since aid under Lomé was only equivalent to about 3 per cent of ACP exports to the EU (Stevens 1984).

Aid has created some problems with regard to debt servicing and passive overdependence on donor countries. However, many development economists still maintain that the benefits exceed the costs and that the quality and quantity of aid should be improved. A growing amount of national aid has been channelled through the Community. Member states' contributions to the EU as a share of EU member states' total overseas development assistance 1991–94 on average was 15.7 per cent in the EU, with the UK being particularly high at 23.4 per cent (House of Commons 1998, vol. II, p. 117). The amount of aid given has had to keep up with inflation and the growing membership of the ACP. Many criticisms have been levelled at EU aid administration. Whilst in principle the ACP is responsible for selecting aid projects, the

EU has used its financial powers to influence the choice and implementation of projects. Aid policy is overcentralized, with tight bureaucratic control from Brussels, requiring considerable documentation and slow disbursement. The European Development Fund remains outside the EU Budget, which means that the EP cannot examine in detail the Convention's work. However, if it were to be incorporated in the EU Budget, it could result in the ACP receiving less, despite acute poverty, in relation to the EU's new priorities in the Mediterranean and Eastern Europe. Some Lomé aid has been used to repay growing debts to the IMF and the World Bank which have imposed unpopular programmes of structural adjustment.

*EU association with the ACP*    Links with LDCs were not provided for in the Spaak Report in 1956 but were proposed subsequently by France and included in the EC, since France regarded its colonial territories as a natural extension of France itself. It was also a means of ensuring that some of the financial costs of aiding overseas territories would be shared between Community countries. A European Development Fund (EDF) was established to channel aid to the associates, and over the first five years it was agreed that France and Germany should subscribe the lion's share equally.

France has been very successful in charging high prices for its exports to the associated countries. Where French production costs have been above the world price, this has had the adverse effect of diverting trade towards less efficient French producers. Close francophone co-operation has been maintained in Africa, helped by monetary union between France and the West and Central African states. The large-scale presence of French advisers and a tendency to tie aid to French exports enabled France to supply on average 40 per cent of francophone imports between 1975 and 1982 and to enjoy a massive trade surplus with francophone Africa. Trade with associates has tended to provide a significant balance-of-trade surplus for the Community which has helped it to offset trade deficits with countries at a higher level of economic development, such as the USA and Japan.

*From Yaoundé to Lomé*    By the early 1960s many of the overseas territories had been given independence, and a new basis of association signed at Yaoundé (Cameroon) in 1963 came into effect in 1964. It covered 18 associated African states and Malagasy (AASM), and was later joined by Mauritius in 1971. Under Yaoundé I, expenditure was

730 million units of account and under Yaoundé II from 1969 to 1975, 918 million units of account were spent. The aid was generous since most of it was given in grants and much of it went to heavily populated countries such as Zaire (the ex-Belgian Congo, now called the Democratic Republic of Congo). Some of the interior states, such as Chad, are very backward and much in need of aid, whereas many of the coastal states in Africa enjoy greater scope for trade.

Yaoundé was essentially neo-colonial, with no pretence of economic equality between the EC and the African associates. Trade relations were based on the reciprocity of trade advantages. However, under Lomé, countries succeeded in ending the process of having to grant reverse preferences. The first agreement at Lomé (the capital of Togo) in 1975 was between the EC and 46 ACP countries; it was considered an inspiring and exemplary step forward towards a more balanced relationship with LDCs. Yet this is something of a façade since the ACP countries are so dependent upon the Community for trade and aid, whereas for the Community the ACP constitutes a much less significant trading partner. Nevertheless, the fact that the Caribbean and Pacific countries could form a joint group with the Africans was remarkable and their co-operation has created a group with some bargaining power and an ability to speak with one voice.

Nigeria, the Ivory Coast and the Democratic Republic of Congo (formerly Zaire) account for nearly half of total ACP exports to the Community. The EU is much less important for the Caribbean countries, for whom the USA is a greater trading partner. Poverty is endemic: about 40 per cent of ACP countries recorded no growth in income per head during the 1970s and by 1984 only 16 Lomé countries had an income per head of over $1000. Their dilemma is which path to take in development, since the formation of horizontal regional trading blocs separate from vertical links with the Community is very appealing, and there is some very modest funding for regional economic integration in Lomé IV. Unfortunately, intra-trade in LDCs is low and disagreements have arisen over the location of industries. This has not been an insuperable problem in all horizontal trading blocs, but continuing difficulties have forced LDCs into traditional trade links with the Community.

Second, third and fourth Conventions were signed at Lomé, based upon the same principles of legality as the first agreement, though the duration of Lomé IV was increased from five to ten years. Although these agreements manifested improvements in some areas, the Community in recession could never match the aspirations and needs of the

ACP. In Lomé II, on which agreement was finally reached on 31 October 1979, the EC exploited the divisions and lack of leadership in the ACP (Long 1980, ch. 2). Negotiations were further protracted during Lomé III, since the ACP was tied up with negotiations relating to the reduced funding from other international agencies at that time. Negotiations for Lomé IV began in October 1988, with the EC again being better briefed and organized than the ACP.

*Table 10.2    Volume of aid for the first five years of Lomé IV in comparison with Lomé III*

|  | Lomé III | | Lomé IV | |
|---|---|---|---|---|
|  | Value (million ECU) | % | Value (million ECU) | % |
| Aid | 4 790 | 64.54 | 6 845[1] | 63.38 |
| Risk capital | 635 | 8.58 | 825 | 7.64 |
| STABEX | 925 | 12.50 | 1 500 | 13.89 |
| SYSMIN | 415 | 5.61 | 480 | 4.44 |
| Structural adjustment support | – | – | 1 150 | 10.65 |
| Soft loans | 635 | 8.58 | – | – |
| Total EDF | 7 400 | 100 | 10 800 | 100 |
| EIB | 1 100 | | 1 200 | |
| Total resources | 8 500 | | 12 000 | |

*Notes*:
[1]  Part of it can be used for Structural Adjustment Support.
ACP states: Angola, Antigua and Barbuda, Bahamas, Barbados, Belize, Benin, Botswana, Burkina Faso, Burundi, Cameroon, Cape Verde, Central African Republic, Chad, Comoros, Congo, Djibouti, Dominica, Equatorial Guinea, Ethiopia, Fiji, Gabon, The Gambia, Ghana, Grenada, Guinea, Guinea Bissau, Guyana, Ivory Coast, Jamaica, Kenya, Kiribati, Lesotho, Liberia, Madagascar, Malawi, Mali, Mauritania, Mauritius, People's Republic of Mozambique, Niger, Nigeria, Papua New Guinea, Rwanda, St Christopher and Nevis, St Lucia, St Vincent, São Tomé and Principe, Senegal, Seychelles, Sierra Leone, Solomon Islands, Somalia, Sudan, Suriname, Swaziland, Tanzania, Togo, Tonga, Trinidad and Tobago, Tuvalu, Uganda, Vanuatu, Western Samoa, Zaire, Zambia, Zimbabwe; plus Haiti, Dominican Republic in Lomé IV.

*Source*:    *Lomé Briefing*, no. 14, January–February 1990.

The financial endowment of the various Lomé agreements increased from ECU 3.5 billion under Lomé I to ECU 5.5 billion under Lomé II, ECU 8.5 billion under Lomé III and ECU 12 billion in the first five years under Lomé IV, as shown in Table 10.2. This was reviewed and raised again in 1995 by the EU(15) to ECU 14.6 billion. However, this has had to cover a growing ACP membership from 46 states under Lomé I to 68 states under Lomé IV and subsequently to 71 states. Details of the Financial Protocol 1995–2000 are shown in Figure 10.1.

ACP aid has to be measured against growing difficulties: falling commodity prices; a rising ACP debt burden (estimated at about $130

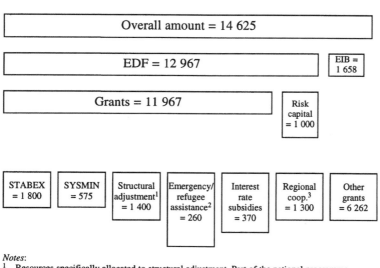

*Notes*:
1  Resources specifically allocated to structural adjustment. Part of the national programme monies may also be allocated for this purpose.
2  Consisting of: Emergency aid = 140 (also ECU 160 mn from the Community Budget)
   Refugees = 120.
3  Including:   – CDI = 73
   – Regional trade promotion = 85
   – Joint Assembly = 4
   – Institutional support = 80

In addition to the ECU 14 625 allocated to ACP states the sum of ECU 200 mn has been earmarked for overseas countries and territories (EDF = 165, EIB = 35).

*Source*:  *The Courier*, no. 155, January–February 1996, p. 12.

*Figure 10.1  Lomé IV Convention – Financial Protocol 1995–2000 (in millions of ECU)*

billion); and stagnation in many sub-Saharan African countries (necessitating since 1988 a special Community programme to aid some very highly indebted, low-income countries there). Many countries have also had to adopt painful macroeconomic restructuring programmes at the behest of international aid agencies.

Most of the Community financial aid (around two-thirds) has been programmed, consisting mainly of outright grants or loans on soft terms. The remaining aid has been non-programmed, with the various categories under Lomé III and Lomé IV shown in the tables.

A new feature of Lomé IV was the provision of 10.65 per cent of lending via the seventh EDF for structural adjustment support, rather than long-term development. There was a move onwards from microeconomic projects to structural adjustment at the macro-level which was conditional on economic performance. Both Lomé III and IV have recognized the potential of a wide range of developments, including tourism and fisheries, but have focused mainly upon agriculture. The priority of rural development is shown in over three-quarters of the National Indicative Programmes drawn up for each state. These mainly reflect a centralized approach despite efforts to encourage more local participation. There was also a new emphasis on environmental protection in Lomé IV, though it seems doubtful whether environmentally damaging developments will be cancelled. Whilst each new agreement has tried to be innovatory to break new ground, constraints are imposed by the different perspectives of member states. For example, some Community members such as France and Italy favour the donation of more aid, whilst others such as Germany and the Netherlands would prefer to focus on the provision of better trade access into the Community market. Further liberalization of agricultural imports tends to be marginal because of the CAP. However, four special protocols give preferential access for beef and veal, sugar, rum and bananas. These have helped particular countries, including Botswana and Zimbabwe for beef and veal, Fiji for sugar, the West Indies for rum, and the Windward Isles for bananas. Unfortunately it has been difficult for smaller countries to diversify, but any further reduction in EU agricultural prices for beef and sugar will erode benefits for the ACP, unless quotas are raised. In addition, the preferential access for bananas has come under most threat from American pressure in the WTO.

*STABEX*   While the Community's Export Revenue Stabilization Scheme (STABEX) was pre-dated by the IMF's own compensatory finance scheme, the conditions of STABEX have been less strict and it has given preferential treatment to very disadvantaged countries. The numbers of primary products covered under the scheme increased in each Convention, and 48 products were listed in the appropriate Article of the third ACP–EC Convention. In addition, the restrictive threshold qualifications were reduced. To obtain assistance the commodity must exceed a dependence threshold of export earnings in the previous year, and export earnings had to fall by a minimum amount below a reference level averaged from the years preceding the claim. The dependence threshold and reference level were cut from 7.5 per cent in Lomé I to 6.5 per cent in Lomé II, 6 per cent in Lomé III and 5 per cent in Lomé IV. For the least-developed, island and land-locked states, the dependence and reference levels were reduced from 2.5 per cent in Lomé I to 2 per cent in Lomé II, 1.5 per cent in Lomé III and 1 per cent in Lomé IV.

A defect of STABEX is its limited funding and, with some falling commodity prices for products such as groundnuts and coffee, transfers have had to be scaled down significantly. For example, total STABEX spending allocated by the end of 1988 was already ECU 919 million. Particular products have dominated total STABEX expenditure, such as groundnut products, coffee and cocoa. These primary products have influenced the distribution of STABEX expenditure between ACP states, with Senegal topping the list of beneficiaries. This is shown in Table 10.3 for the period 1975–85.

*Table 10.3  The top ten beneficiaries from STABEX, 1975–85*

|  | Receipts (in ECU) |
| --- | --- |
| Senegal | 183 257 156 |
| Sudan | 125 042 319 |
| Ivory Coast | 113 324 801 |
| Ghana | 90 647 339 |
| Ethiopia | 53 807 619 |
| Papua New Guinea | 50 690 742 |
| Tanzania | 50 473 947 |
| Kenya | 44 865 565 |
| Togo | 41 775 242 |
| Mauritania | 37 000 450 |

*Source*:   Eurostat, *ACP Statistics 1987*

In some respects the distribution is arbitrary, since some poor countries which fail to meet the qualifications have suffered *vis-à-vis* a few relatively prosperous countries which have had their export earnings included. Many other criticisms have been levelled at STABEX, such as its bias against countries that have efficient domestic commodity policies and balance-of-payments management (McQueen 1977; Hewitt 1984; Hine 1985). In Lomé IV STABEX transfers no longer had to be repaid; there was an increased allocation to ECU 1.5 billion; and a few new commodities were added; but all this could hardly cushion countries from the collapse of international commodity agreements for products such as cocoa and coffee. Overall, commodity compensation schemes have been strongly criticized (except by the ACP themselves), since they were too automatic, with slow disbursement, and kept some countries in commodities for too long. Instead, they should probably have moved out from such narrow specialization and diversified earlier.

*SYSMIN*   The Système Minérais (SYSMIN) was an innovation in Lomé II and is a scheme for mineral products similar to that for primary products in STABEX. Minerals, with the exception of iron ore, had been excluded from STABEX. Iron ore has been switched into SYSMIN, along with various other mineral products, though the cost of financing these is less than if they had been included within STABEX (Long 1980, pp. 104–6). The rationale of SYSMIN is to tackle the depletion of mineral resources, although the high demand in the 1960s and the 1970s was in fact dampened by slower economic growth during the 1980s. Africa is very well endowed with minerals and metals, far better than the Caribbean or the Pacific. The scheme helps mineral producers where earnings fall below production costs and where production is threatened. A trigger threshold was set at 10 per cent with a dependence threshold of 15 per cent (and 10 per cent in the case of the least-developed, island and land-locked states). The range of products included iron ore, copper, phosphates, manganese, bauxite, alumina and tin.

Criticisms have been levelled at the restrictive coverage of products and countries covered by the scheme. One modification made under Lomé III was the opening of a second 'window' for ACP countries that derived 20 per cent of their export earnings (12 per cent for the least-developed, island and land-locked countries) from a combination of mining products – other than precious minerals, oil and gas, but not necessarily those mentioned specifically in the Convention. This was expected to broaden the number of beneficiaries, since in the first four years of SYSMIN only four countries benefited: Zambia, Zaire, Guyana and Rwanda. The modified scheme was considered likely to benefit ACP states such as Botswana, Niger and Zimbabwe. It was also agreed that SYSMIN funds could be used to tackle problems emanating from adverse developments such as new technology. In addition, SYSMIN ceased to be concerned solely with maintaining productive capacity, and where it was in the interests of the ACP, orderly reductions in capacity could be financed. Few of the ACP countries received help and SYSMIN was underspent because of insufficient projects. It has little support for renewal in Lomé renegotiations.

*The consequences of association with the ACP*    ACP countries in association with the Community have naturally derived some economic benefits, although the trading benefits have been less than anticipated. Under both the Yaoundé and the Lomé agreements the associates' share of total EC imports has fallen, and surprisingly they have had a slower rate of export growth to the Community than those from some other developing countries. ACP performance has been disappointing in several respects. Its share in all extra-EC imports fell from 8.1 per cent in 1974 to 5.5 per cent in 1982 and 3.7 per cent in 1992 (Hewitt 1984; *The Courier* 1986; Davenport, Hewitt and Koning 1995). The ACP share of world trade also fell from its quite low level, being outpaced by Asia's share of extra-EU imports which rose from 5.9 per cent in 1980 to 13.6 per cent by 1992 (Eurostat). Furthermore, the degree of intra-ACP trade has remained low – only about 4 per cent – with a high proportion of this being conducted in regionally integrated blocs such as the Economic Community of West African States (ECOWAS).

The apparent liberalism of the Lomé agreements, with their lack of formal quantitative restrictions, conceals certain weaknesses. For example, most ACP exports – tropical foodstuffs and raw materials – enter the EU duty-free in any case. Exports of energy and mineral products come in zero-rated, meaning that many countries, such as Zambia, have benefited very little. For those products where the ACP does enjoy an advantageous margin of preference over other LDCs, this has been reduced by multilateral tariff reductions under GATT, plus other special arrangements such as the Generalized System of Preferences (GSP). The CAP has been mentioned as one obstacle to agricultural exports, while industrially many ACP countries have been unable to benefit significantly because of their low level of industrial development. Furthermore, restrictive rules of origin were imposed under Lomé I, whereby 50 per cent of value-added had to take place within ACP states. This was a high level of added value to set for countries with limited manufacturing industry and which needed to co-operate with other non-Lomé states. The EU has responded by making the rules more flexible where they were found to be inhibiting industrial development. Under Lomé IV, requests could be made for a derogation reducing the ACP added value to 45 per cent and the EC had to respond within 60 working days, otherwise the request would be deemed to have been accepted.

In industries favoured by LDCs, such as textiles, the ACP share of exports by LDCs to the Community has been very low. Furthermore, a few countries, such as entrepreneurial Mauritius, have accounted for a high proportion of these exports, having attracted considerable inward investment into the textile industry. The benefits derived by Mauritius eventually led to national safeguards being imposed in the form of VERs by the UK and France. Another country that has been quite successful in developing and diversifying its trade has been the Ivory Coast. Hence the consequences of Lomé depend upon which countries are examined, and to focus on overall ACP performance, dominated by some countries with poor performances such as Ghana, Zaire and Zambia, may result in a misleading conclusion (Stevens 1984, ch. 2).

While ACP trade gains may have been relatively limited, this has not placated other countries which have expressed continuing concern that in the long run their own exports will tend to be displaced from the Community market. Furthermore, some trade diversion has been observed in particular products (Balassa 1975). However, in many products the ACP preference is ineffective either because the ACP is quite competitive without the preferences or, at the opposite extreme, because even with the benefit of the preferences it still remains insufficiently competitive, for example, because of excessive costs or non-price failings. The ACP preference has been decisive for about a third of exports, especially products such as palm oil, coffee, cocoa and bananas, in which countries such as Senegal, the Ivory Coast, Kenya and Zimbabwe have raised their competitiveness.

The ACP importance as a supplier to the Community is particularly high for specific products. For example, in 1985 it supplied 83 per cent of EC sugar imports (though only to top up heavily protected EC beet output), but it has been of benefit to countries such as Mauritius, Swaziland, Belize and Fiji. The ACP also supplied 79 per cent of EC cocoa imports, 64 per cent of its aluminium imports, 41 per cent of its coffee imports and 24 per cent of its copper imports.

Outside (non-ACP) countries have considered it vital to try to reach some agreement with the Community to minimize perceived disadvantages and to safeguard their interests. To outsiders the attraction of the large Community market is very clear and there has been a scramble to reach some kind of trading agreement with it. Lomé-type preferences have been extended to least-developed countries outside the ACP group, which now conforms to the WTO in this respect.

*A grim future for Lomé preferences*   Renegotiations began on Lomé V for the new millennium amidst disappointment with the ACP and recognition of the need to encourage greater liberalization of markets and trade. Lomé preferences require a continued waiver from the WTO, yet the ACP, despite massive trade preferences, has performed weakly, with insufficient diversification into new product areas. Some critics have blamed the preferences themselves in guaranteeing high market prices; also, non-reciprocal preferences meant that they did not open up their own markets sufficiently to competition. However, others argued that the margin of preference was not high enough; but whatever the explanation for ACP failings, their future may be even bleaker in the new millennium as preferences are gradually withdrawn. The World Trade Organization (WTO) has underpinned globalizing and liberalizing aspirations; for example, it has ruled against the discriminatory preferential EU banana policy which has adversely affected non-Lomé suppliers. The USA has sprung to the defence of equally poor countries in Latin America, partly to assist its own large multinational corporations which are involved there. The future is likely to see continued pressure to withdraw non-reciprocal preferences, especially for the more advanced ACP countries. The Lomé Convention expires in the year 2000 and although there is likely to be some transitory continuity of the present arrangement for a few years beyond that, Lomé is likely to be replaced by free trade areas (FTAs). There would be an FTA for each region: Africa; Caribbean; and Pacific. An FTA would cover duty-free access for substantially all their exports, but it would also involve opening up their market to EU imports. The ACP is worried about being split into groups and is loath to provide full reciprocity. The proposed regional FTAs have insufficient regional integration. Reciprocal liberalization to EU imports, though reducing inflation in the ACP, would kill off many nascent industries and adversely affect governmental revenue from tariffs (House of Commons 1998, p. xxvii).

*The Generalized System of Preferences (GSP)*
Those LDCs not in association with the Community have been eligible
under the GSP. Both the EC and the UK introduced a GSP scheme in
1971, though the former scheme was less extensive in coverage. The
enlarged Community operates one GSP which gives tariff concessions
on industrial and agricultural imports – though the agricultural imports
are highly restricted by the CAP. The GSP has offered much less than
either Yaoundé or Lomé: it is more restrictive and excludes many of the
products that are important to the associates. It has quotas and covers
fewer products, with restrictions on products such as textiles. The GSP
lacks the binding and permanent nature of Lomé. Although the GSP
covers a given time period, the Community can make withdrawals from
it at any time without breaching its legal obligations. Where there has
been a surge in imports from the successful NICs, the Community has
introduced safeguards. It also applies rules of origin which do not allow
cumulation apart from the imports of regional groupings.

The effects of the GSP have generally been positive but very limited
(Balassa 1975; Hine 1985; Pomfret 1997). Most LDCs naturally have
only a limited base for the production of industrial exports and it is the
NICs that have been most successful; these, while being relatively
efficient, are often not the neediest countries. Seven countries – Yugoslavia, Malaysia, Hong Kong, India, South Korea, Brazil and Romania
– have been responsible for over half the Community's GSP imports
(Hine 1985, p. 210).

China is now covered by the GSP. It has been seeking closer links
with the Community to offset the dominance of the superpowers. In
1978 a non-preferential trade agreement was signed with China, followed in 1985 by a trade and co-operation agreement.

Disenchantment with the GSP and withdrawals of access led LDCs to
take a more favourable view of general tariff cuts in the Uruguay Round.
These are obviously better for global welfare in removing trade diversion
in the future. In any reformed Lomé replaced by FTAs, those countries
that did not agree to partnership agreements would be downgraded to the
GSP. In such circumstances the UK favoured further improving the GSP
towards the levels and stability enjoyed under Lomé. Meanwhile, the
more developed countries could be gradually removed from the GSP.

**The British Commonwealth**
When the UK joined the EC in 1973 it was natural that some arrangements would be made to fit the British Commonwealth into a modified

association with the Community. What was at issue was whether this was to embrace both the less-developed and the developed countries in the Commonwealth which had enjoyed Imperial Preference. Provisions had been made by the EC largely to suit French overseas interests, and the overall outcome tended to reflect a French view of the outside world. The UK successfully negotiated agreements to replace its special links with most less-developed countries, and in addition special treatment was provided for New Zealand despite the dissatisfaction of French farmers about imports of New Zealand dairy products. The old dominions, Canada and Australia, though important suppliers of products such as minerals to the Community, have refocused their links in their own region, establishing closer relationships with countries such as the USA and Japan.

Even before the UK entered the Community, some less-developed Commonwealth countries had already reached their own agreements with the EC. They had been encouraged to do so in the expectation that the UK would enter the Community. It was paradoxical that in the 1960s some of these LDCs were successful in joining the EC and began to discriminate in favour of the EC and against the UK. Nigeria was the first Commonwealth country to appreciate the benefits of an agreement with the expanding Community market which was importing more than twice as much of its important cocoa exports than the UK. There was recognition of the need to become associated to prevent a displacement of sales by competitors already enjoying association under the Yaoundé Convention.

By 1969 the three East African countries – Tanzania, Uganda and Kenya – had reached agreement with the EC, but their terms were less favourable than those accorded to the Yaoundé associates. They were only able to reach an agreement on trade (not on aid), and in trade they not only had to accept quotas on some of their exports which were in strong competition with the Yaoundé producers, but also had to grant even more beneficial reverse preferences to the EC.

The incorporation of 21 Commonwealth countries into the first Lomé Convention helped to bridge Anglo-French divisions which had resulted in a carving up of the African continent. The Commonwealth associates were in many cases more developed than their counterparts and less prepared to accept a subservient position. The UK has helped to turn the Community into a more outward-looking bloc. Prior to UK entry into the Community, imports from LDCs were about a quarter of the UK's total imports, whereas about a fifth of total EC imports came from LDCs. The liberal trading policy of the UK, and support from the USA, moved the Community towards the approach of those two countries of requiring no reverse preferences from associated countries. Although the UK is still a major importer from LDCs, the growth of its imports from ACP countries has been relatively slow. France has overtaken the UK as the major market for the ACP, while Germany imports more manufactured goods from the ACP than does the UK.

Whereas there was no sugar agreement in the Yaoundé Convention – the Congo being the only significant producer until Mauritius joined in 1972 – the Commonwealth sugar agreement with the UK was used as the basis of a new ACP agreement. The Community agreed to buy 1.2 million tonnes from the ACP; this was about 60 per cent of total exports. While the price had to be negotiated between ACP exporters and EU consuming countries, it could not be lower than the price agreed by the Community for its own producers. The guarantees have been helpful, though unfortunately offset by the Community's overproduction of beet sugar and its dumping on the world market which has tended to depress world prices.

One area of the Commonwealth that has suffered is the part in Asia which was deemed ineligible for inclusion in Lomé. It was argued that Bangladesh, India, Malaya, Pakistan, Sri Lanka, Singapore and Hong Kong differed in economic structure and their inclusion in Lomé would dilute the benefits enjoyed by other ACP associates. They have been covered instead by the Community's GSP scheme, though this was tighter than the UK's own GSP. Over time, the UK has fallen into line with a less liberal policy towards those countries not covered by the Community's preferential arrangements. Those groups (ACP) for which the UK was able to negotiate special terms have been able to increase their share of trade with the Community; but other LDCs have been squeezed by such preferential agreements and by the primacy accorded to trade with other groups such as the Mediterranean and the ACP.

The UK and France have started to co-operate more closely in some parts of Africa, partly to ensure their continuing dominance in the area, as shown by the British making some inroads into the Ivory Coast and France into Kenya. However, apart from this bilateral co-operation, much of the trade and aid policy has been channelled through Lomé. For example, Lomé aid has risen to about 30 per cent of the budget of the UK Department for International Development, and in 1998–99 the UK's contribution to the EDF was £216 million (House of Commons 1998). In the renegotiation of the Lomé Convention after the expiry of

Lomé IV, the UK would like to see greater differentiation on the basis of eradicating poverty. The UK is keen on tranches of finance with additional finance being not automatic but related to performance. In addition, other conditions for aid would consist of having the right macroeconomic framework, concentrated anti-poverty policies and meeting conditions of human rights. With regard to altering the Lomé preferential trade system towards one of FTAs, there is concern that reciprocal liberalization would be asymmetric and any adverse effects on the ACP need to be taken into account and monitored closely.

# 11 Enlargement and integration

## The new European Union

The original Six (West Germany, France, Italy, Belgium, the Netherlands and Luxembourg) reflected many differences; for example, Italy with its particular problems in the Mezzogiorno for which special provisions were necessary. Nevertheless, the Six constituted a much more homogeneous and optimal grouping than the EU(15). The first enlargement of the Community in 1973 enhanced its northern bias, bringing in the United Kingdom, Ireland and Denmark. Ireland and Denmark benefited significantly agriculturally. The second enlargement in the 1980s shifted the balance of influence towards Southern Europe after the entry of Greece in 1981. The third enlargement involved the accession of Spain and Portugal in 1986. The reunification of Germany in 1990 was simply one of absorption of Eastern Germany and has reinforced the centrality and dominance of Germany. The fourth enlargement, the entry of Austria, Finland and Sweden in 1995, was less problematic in bringing in richer countries with fewer problems. The critical test for the EU is in absorbing the former Communist countries of Eastern Europe in the coming years.

Why has the EU grown so much in terms of membership, and are there no limits to this, provided countries can meet the entry criteria? These are based upon members being European, democratic, upholding human rights, having a competitive market economy and accepting the basic Treaties. Countries outside the EU regard it with awe, often seeing it as a much stronger, united and more attractive organization than it appears once they have gained membership. The EU has generally looked upon applications favourably since its image is strengthened by its new-found popularity, and it has been flattered by applications to join. It has become a more powerful actor with an enhanced capacity to exercise its economic and political influence in international affairs. The EU has been greatly strengthened in size and potential power; for example, the EU(12) population was 339 million, and its share of world trade 21 per cent of exports and 22 per cent of imports. Austria, Finland and Sweden together added 21.3 million to its population size.

Unfortunately, enlargement of the EU has also multiplied its problems, making it a less optimal grouping. The addition of more members has aggravated procedural difficulties. A system of majority voting on more issues becomes imperative if effective progress is to be made in such a large union, though this has to be balanced to avoid ill-will if countries are outvoted on issues which they perceive to be important. The incorporation of extra members has resulted in new official languages, with a multiplication of interpretation and translation services. The EU(15) has 11 official languages: Danish, Dutch, English, French, German, Greek, Italian, Portuguese, Spanish, Finnish and Swedish. These 11 languages generate 110 different language combinations (and five new East European members would raise this to 240 combinations). Economic disparities have similarly been increased, with wider national and regional variations in income per head within an even more diverse agricultural Community.

The countries in Southern Europe have been highly dependent on the EU, relying upon tourist receipts and migrant remittances to support their low income levels. As full members of an enlarged single market, there have been significant readjustment costs, with trade leading to the decline of less efficient nascent technological sectors in Southern Europe. Whereas in Chapter 3 attention was drawn to the predominance of intra-industry trade, the more significant differences in factor endowments between Northern and Southern Europe are likely to reinforce Southern European specialization in more labour-intensive industries. There are also dangers from this inter-industry specialization that the less competitive countries that have joined the EU will push it towards greater protectionism against non-members. To avoid the growth of such protectionist pressures, enhanced structural funding continues to cushion the costs of readjustment.

The focus on Southern Europe in the 1980s was diluted in the 1990s by the switch in emphasis towards Northern and Eastern Europe. A reunified Germany is the hub of the Community, inevitably providing a new eastern focus as investment is redirected to areas with lower wage costs and skilled labour, which are centrally located for European sales. Despite the special trading relationship which existed between East and West Germany, reunification posed new implications for EU policies in terms of wider regional disparities, adverse environmental problems, the need to cut industrial state subsidies, and the dangers of adding to agricultural overproduction.

## Enlargement and integration

### Southern enlargement

*Greece*   The entry of Greece as the tenth member of the EC in 1981 completed its links with the Community. These had been established 20 years earlier with the signing of the Athens Agreement in 1961 which commenced its association. Greece has encountered both political and economic problems. Politically it moved from a military *coup* in 1967 back to a democratic civil regime in 1974. Economically, Greece has a larger percentage of its labour force in agriculture than either Portugal or Spain; furthermore, the contribution of agriculture to Greek GNP is much lower than its contribution to total employment. Nevertheless, Greece enjoyed both a food surplus in its trade with the Community and also with the rest of the world (Tsoukalis 1986). Greece submitted a memorandum to the EC in 1982 outlining the problems of the Greek economy and the inadequacy of Community policies; this included the CAP market organization which at that time covered only 75 per cent of Greek agricultural production compared with 95 per cent of agricultural production in other member countries (Nicholson and East 1987, p. 198). While Greek agriculture has benefited from high CAP expenditure, its export surplus in agricultural products turned into a deficit, partly because of the high income elasticity for imports such as meat and milk (Baltas 1998, p. 113). In addition to overdependence on agriculture, Greece also has an overdeveloped service sector, whilst its industry manifests serious deficiencies, with some economists referring to its de-industrialization before it has even reached the stage of industrial maturity.

The dissatisfaction of Greece with some aspects of the Community has been alleviated by a positive response to dealing with its problems. Currently there seems little likelihood of any withdrawal by Greece from the Community since its net impact on the Greek economy has generally been positive and Greece is a net beneficiary from the CAP (Yannopoulos 1986). Greece used its bargaining power to obtain favourable treatment in the Integrated Mediterranean Programmes (IMPs) before agreeing to Iberian enlargement of the Community. Greece has also enjoyed leverage in the Community over its rival Turkey, and it has taken a hard line against Turkish membership of the EU because of the occupation by Turkish forces in the northern part of Cyprus.

The Greek economy has shown the lowest rate of economic growth of any member state. Although this has not been manifested in very high unemployment, it is due mainly to its lax economic policies. There has been pressure from the EU to improve its macroeconomic policies, to reduce government debt and to bring down inflation, in return for greater EU financial help. Greece was the only country which was unable to meet the tough Maastricht conditions for the drachma to be abandoned and replaced by the euro.

*Portugal*   Unlike Greece, which enjoyed close links with the Community over many years, Portugal enjoyed a more outward-looking role towards its empire in Africa. Like Britain, it had its back to the continent, facing the open sea. Within Western Europe it retained its close links with the UK by joining EFTA. At that time Portugal lacked a democratic political system. It fared well in EFTA since it had a long timetable for cutting its tariffs on imports, whereas those tariffs against its exports were eliminated more quickly.

Portugal's decision to become a full member of the Community coincided with its more European outlook and the shedding of its colonial empire, even though immense trading opportunities still remain in mineral-rich Angola and Mozambique. The trade agreement between Portugal and the Community in 1973 offered less generous terms than those that had been granted to Greece. With the return to full democracy in Portugal after the departure of Caetano in 1974, public opinion gave wide support to pursuing full membership of the Community – even to a greater extent than in Greece.

Unlike Greece, Portugal is weak in agriculture but stronger industrially. Portugal had by far the lowest income per head in the Community but has had a good rate of economic growth since joining. It has benefited from its low labour costs, helping industries such as textiles and ship repair, and proving attractive to foreign investment, though some of this may now be diverted towards Eastern Europe. In 1986, on its entry to the EC, Portugal lost its narrow trade surplus with the Community, and in key sectors such as textiles (which accounts for about a third of Portugal's export earnings) there is strong competition; for example, the granting of a large Community textile quota to Turkey was unpopular.

Investment priority to industry led to low agricultural investment, and for many years Portugal has been a net importer of food. After 1974 its food imports rose again to help feed the people displaced from the colonies (*retornados*). Agricultural productivity is low and production of wheat per hectare, for example, is only about one-quarter of that in countries such as the Netherlands. The dairy industry is particularly inefficient, with on average only three or four cows per farm. Portugal has benefited significantly from Community Guidance expenditure, though with relatively small amounts from guaranteed prices, partly because of its agricultural structure; it has been adapting over a ten-year transition period to lower Community prices such as for cereals, which were 50 per cent lower than in Portugal. To ease the burden the EU has agreed to extend the transition period to 2001, provided that the extra support is given through direct income aids and not through guaranteed prices. Portugal needed continuing massive structural assistance for both agriculture and industry, for example, after the PEDIP (Portuguese Economic Development and Industrial Programme) expired in the early 1990s. Portugal has drawn strongly on the Structural Funds to improve its economic performance and with financial help has been able to bring down its high inflation rate, place the escudo in the ERM and join the euro.

Portugal was worried about suffering in some respects from the opening up of trade in Iberia with Spain. Historically their joint trade was low, and in 1984 only 4.4 per cent of Portugal's exports and 7.2 per cent of its imports were conducted with Spain. For Spain, 2.4 per cent of its exports and 0.7 per cent of its imports were with its Portuguese neighbour. Although Portugal has the advantage of lower wages, too few of its companies do much marketing outside Spain or have set up abroad. Meanwhile, Spain benefits from its larger home market and stronger companies, reinforced by an influx of much multinational investment in recent years. Iberian links have been transformed in the EU, with Spain becoming Portugal's second biggest customer, while Spain has moved up to first place and supplied 16.6 per cent of Portugal's imports in 1992 (Lopes 1993).

*Spain*    Spanish membership of the Community was a justified reward for its return to democracy, but Spain probably posed the greatest economic challenge for the EU – certainly after digesting the UK in 1973. Spain under Franco was very much a closed economy, and until 1970 it had not established trading links with either EFTA or the EC. In 1970 it began a trade agreement with the EC which reduced tariffs, but with some exceptions in sensitive products and with a slower pace for dismantling tariffs on the Spanish side.

Full membership of the Community provided new export opportunities for Spain, but also much stiffer import competition, previously contained by higher tariffs. This tariff protection was particularly high in sectors such as the car industry, and in 1986 the tariff was cut from 36.5 per cent to 22.5 per cent as a first stage towards its eventual removal. The introduction of Community policies such as VAT and abolition of the former tax rebate, plus weak expertise in marketing, handicapped Spain's export potential, resulting in a long-term trade deficit. The substantial trade deficit on current account has been partly offset by large inflows on the capital account. Community exporters such as Germany have taken full advantage of the opening up of the Spanish market, with Germany replacing the USA as its major supplier. In its first two years of Community membership the Spanish economy grew rapidly with high investment, though the surge of imports resulted in a huge trade deficit. Spain has proved a very attractive location for multinational corporations (MNCs), though this may have aggravated regional imbalance, favouring Madrid and Catalonia. With a transition period of seven years for most goods, full completion of the customs union coincided with that of the single market, exposing Spain's generally low level of industrial competitiveness in up-market sectors. Spain had about a 30 per cent gap in productivity compared with the Community average, and also low quality standards. The issue of renegotiation with the Community was raised, since its budgetary gains were being outweighed by its massive trade imbalance. Also, austerity policies have led to high unemployment because of a growing young labour force and tight demand policies have been imposed to dampen inflation to enable Spain to participate in the ERM and the euro.

The size of Spanish output in agriculture and fishing and in industry posed problems for the Community. Although agricultural production in Southern Europe is to some extent complementary to that in Northern Europe, there were some adverse effects, especially in southern France and Italy. An even greater problem was the prospect of generating additional farm surpluses; for example, Spanish olive oil production was almost as large as that in the rest of the Community. The dilemma for the Community was the extent to which it should extend price support to Southern European products (Leigh and van Praag 1978). Spanish producers possess a worrying capacity to add to overproduction, and its fishing fleet tends to complicate agreements to control overfishing. Industrially, Spain is a major world producer in some staple industries such as steel and shipbuilding, in which the EU has already had to introduce policies for restructuring because of overcapacity. Spain is also a major competitor in other traditional industries such as footwear and textiles.

*The fourth enlargement: Austria, Finland and Sweden*   The entry of Austria, Sweden and Finland into the EU in 1995 was in many ways a natural step, building upon their existing free trade in EFTA. All three countries decided that the European Economic Area would be inferior to full membership of the EU since they would be frozen out of crucial decision-making. Instead of continuing to get the 'best of both worlds', they worried that they would have the worst. The newly admitted countries were welcome since they lacked major economic problems, being quite rich and net contributors to the Budget. As in most countries, the business interest has favoured belonging fully to the EU to avoid companies suffering adverse effects on trade with the EU. Sweden had already started to falter in its economic growth and company performance, compounded by its high tax policies to finance welfare spending.

The main reservations about the EU were held by agricultural and environmental groups. Agriculture traditionally was subsidized even more heavily than the EU. The new members had agricultural sectors which were highly protected and in the negotiations there were requests for special interests, such as Alpine farmers in Austria, and the Arctic regions of Sweden and Finland. The EU created a new Objective 6 in order to support the lowly populated regions. However, expenditure for these was minor compared with that for the Objective 1 regions in Southern Europe (though Burgenland in the east of Austria was also declared an Objective 1 area). Objections on environmental grounds surfaced, for example, in Austria, where a significant issue was pollution from commercial vehicles involved in EU transit.

The greatest problem faced in the past by Austria, Finland and Sweden which related to neutrality was removed by the collapse of the menacing USSR and the end of the cold war. This means that the EU Maastricht and Amsterdam proposals for deeper political integration are not such a major problem for these countries as it would have been in the past. All countries have recognized the growing importance of the EU market, especially Finland, which suffered most from the marked contraction in East European trade. There was also a kind of domino effect in Scandinavia between Swedish and Finnish entry, though unfortunately this was not maintained for Norway.

*Eastern European enlargement*

*A united Germany*   The German Democratic Republic (GDR) enjoyed a special trading relationship with West Germany, but these intra-German links took on a new significance when the GDR was absorbed with reunification in 1990. They accelerated pressure for faster EU integration to lock Germany rigidly into the Community. Reunification has elevated Germany to an even stronger position as the Community's dominant economic power. West Germany's total exports were already in excess of those of Britain and France combined, but now Germany is by far the biggest in terms of population size and labour force. Its total share of EU GDP was around 30 per cent, even though the East German GDP was only about 7 per cent of that in West Germany. Berlin, which was a pawn in the struggle between East and West, has now regained its central influence as the capital again, with the parliament moving from Bonn, and further power moving eastwards from Western capitals such as London, Paris and Brussels.

Reunification took place swiftly, because the exodus of people which began in August 1989 was weakening the GDR and aggravating problems in the receiving West Germany. Hence reunification after the Berlin Wall was breached in November 1989 occurred more quickly than was really justified by economic conditions. In March 1990 there were free elections in East Germany; monetary union in July; and in September a Treaty was signed between the two Germanys and the four wartime allies. By the end of the year in the first all-German postwar elections Helmut Kohl was elected Chancellor.

EU integration is not unfamiliar with the problems which arise for a weaker economy when it is linked to a highly developed economy. However, in the case of German economic, monetary and social union (GEMSU) from 1 July 1990, this has involved not only the joining together of a weak Eastern economy to a strong Western economy, but also a switch from a centrally planned system; that is, it was a capitalist takeover by the West. Furthermore, monetary union preceded economic convergence, with a common monetary system based on the D-mark (which replaced the Ost-mark in the east of the country). The Bundesbank was overruled and accepted somewhat reluctantly a generous exchange-rate conversion between Ost-marks and D-marks. For adults, this was a one-to-one conversion rate up to 4000 Ost-marks with the rest at two-to-one. For children the one-to-one limit was 2000 Ost-marks, and for pensioners, 6000 Ost-marks.

In terms of demand and supply analysis, immediate problems arose from excess monetary demand and inadequate supply of goods in the East because of the lack of competitiveness and the collapse of many firms. Other sources of inflation arose from the removal of subsidies on

292 Political economy of integration in the European Union

basic goods in the East and pressure for higher wages, partly to compensate for higher food prices, but also in comparability claims with workers in West Germany. East Germany found that having the D-mark was illusory wealth, since an already feeble economy had become even more uncompetitive through higher costs. It was proposed that wages in the two Germanys should be fully equalized, even though productivity gaps will remain into the twenty-first century. Hence unemployment soared and by the second half of 1991 about 45 per cent of the labour force in the East had lost their jobs (Lange and Pugh 1998, p. 19).

There have been some potential advantages for firms from locations in East Germany, such as relatively low labour costs. In the motor industry Volkswagen, Opel and Mercedes-Benz all announced plans to produce cars in the East. Unfortunately there was a lag between the opening of new plants, such as the Opel plant in Eisenach, and contraction of existing plants such as Wartburg, creating heavy unemployment. Furthermore, basic infrastructure deficiencies and legal problems over ownership of capital led many businesses, especially the smaller ones in West Germany, to take the less risky option of supplying their highly demanded goods directly from the West. The outdated and polluting chemical and power-generating industries faced decimation because of their conflict with environmental standards. GNP in East Germany fell into decline in the early 1990s along the familiar J-curve before recovering later.

West Germany took over an economy with some useful assets, particularly in the longer term. However, hopes that a fifth of East German industry could be competitive were too optimistic and even some of the stronger sectors have had to be slimmed down radically. Also, East Germany had a similar type of industrial economy to West Germany, with the East being weaker technologically; for example, the machine tool industry is also strong in East Germany but it lacked the modern electronic controls on the machines incorporated by the more advanced Western producers. The Treuhandanstalt (THA) was set up as a transitional institution to dispose of industry in East Germany, privatizing firms often at 'knock-down' prices, mainly to West German companies. The THA, now dissolved, had to come to terms with the overmanning and inefficiency built up during the years of Communism, which was the root cause of the subsequent de-industrialization and high unemployment.

Convergence between East and West Germany is occurring much more slowly than anticipated. The political rhetoric that monetary reform *per se* would create the same miraculous effects as it had in 1948 has proved a myth. Investment has remained too low and goods from East Germany have not been very competitive. There was also general uncertainty, including that over property ownership, which further dampened investment. Fortunately, East Germany has been cushioned by inward transfers of about 5–6 per cent of total German national income (Lange and Pugh 1998, p. 12). Reintegration burdened the German economy with excessive demand, which led to both a trade deficit and excessive inflation. To correct the excessive demand, interest rates were raised, but this led to overvaluation of the D-mark, accentuating German recession even more. This also had the unfortunate effect, as shown in Chapter 8, of destroying the hard-won stability of the ERM in the early 1990s, as some other member states were not prepared to continue raising interest rates indefinitely to maintain the ERM if this condemned them to continued recession.

*The fall of Comecon*   Comecon was the acronym usually used to describe the Council for Mutual Economic Assistance (CMEA) which was founded in 1949. It was a means of ensuring Soviet hegemony in Eastern Europe and its main membership consisted of the USSR, the German Democratic Republic (until reunification in 1990), Bulgaria, Czechoslovakia, Hungary, Poland and Romania. The aim of Comecon, like that of the EC, was to promote integration of trade in order to prevent wasteful duplication in production. Thus the Soviet Union supplied much of the energy, raw materials and aircraft, whilst other countries specialized in different products, such as Hungary in supplying buses. Disagreements arose over specialization and some countries, for instance Romania, pressed ahead despite objections by the Soviet Union with industries such as petrochemicals.

Compared with the EC, Comecon was a more intergovernmental and less supranational organization. The satellite states preferred this, given the weight of the USSR. Factor mobility was also less in Comecon, and although capital flowed from the USSR to countries like the GDR, and labour moved from Poland to the GDR, these movements were less easy than in the EC. Intra-bloc trade was a marked feature of both blocs, and in 1986, for example, 53 per cent of Comecon trade was intra-trade and most of its members conducted more than half of their trade within the bloc. One exception to this was Romania, which significantly reorientated its trading pattern towards the West.

Comecon's original autarkic view of trade eventually gave way to the realization that trade was a means of economizing on resources and of obtaining sophisticated products from the West. The EC offered trade agreements to individual states in 1974, though only Romania responded in 1980. By 1986, 12 per cent of Comecon trade was with the EC, but only 3 per cent of EC trade was conducted with Comecon. The dominant trading country on the EC side was Germany and in Comecon it was the USSR. Trade was stimulated since the EC granted most favoured nation (MFN) status to Eastern European countries, enabling them to benefit from tariff reductions. However, the links between the EC and Comecon were bedevilled by a variety of limiting factors. Both systems were based on competing philosophies and they were loath to recognize each other legally, since Comecon was dominated by the USSR. The links were mainly on a bilateral level between individual countries, or between the EC and Eastern European countries, in specific areas such as fisheries, in which countries like the USSR entered into negotiations with the Community. The EC did not wish to legitimize Soviet hegemony in Eastern Europe by its actions, though under Gorbachev agreement was reached to give belated formal mutual recognition to the two organizations, with a mutual recognition agreement signed in Luxembourg in June 1988.

The trade of Comecon with the Community was inhibited by various elements over the years; for example, Iberian enlargement increased EC protectionism in products such as textiles and clothing. However, East European exports actually suffered less from discriminatory trade agreements than from Comecon's own internal and fundamental deficiencies. For example, East European countries lacked a proper pricing policy for their products, often underpricing them to obtain Western currency, and partly to undermine Western markets – this resulted in numerous anti-dumping cases against Eastern Europe. They also faced problems in exporting agricultural products, though in some respects agricultural exporters have fared better than those selling industrial products because of the generally poor quality of the latter and severe competition from the NICs. The import needs of Comecon for industrialization generally exceeded their export capabilities. Currency inconvertibility led to bilateral deals involving different forms of counter-trade: these involve complex and rather inefficient forms of trading.

The desire of Eastern Europe to catch up with the West led to massive borrowings to finance their industrialization. This resulted in major indebtedness because of rising interest rates and economic recession which reduced the propensity of Community countries to import from Comecon. Poland was the first country to experience problems in servicing its massive external debt. According to the Economic Commission for Europe, Poland's gross debt in 1988 was $38.9 billion, which was more than half Poland's GNP. The root cause of the Polish crisis was lack of incentive and poor morale (Drewnowski 1982). Gross debts elsewhere in Eastern Europe in 1988 in US$ billion were: GDR (19.9); Hungary (17.3); Bulgaria (7.6); Czechoslovakia (5.1); with Romania (2.7) being relatively underborrowed.

After the disintegration in Eastern Europe which began in 1989, the EU became the forum for channelling aid there, including that from the USA. The PHARE (Poland and Hungary Aid for Reconstruction of the Economy) programme was set up by the Group of Seven (G7) Summit in July 1989 on behalf of 24 donor countries. Financial grants from PHARE have not been on the scale of the early postwar Marshall Plan and some of the aid has also been used to service existing debts. The EU invited the other G24 members to participate in the TEMPUS programme of academic exchanges. Grant aid has been helpful in providing much needed expertise and has concentrated increasingly on improving basic infrastructure. It has also been supplemented by EIB loans. Eastern Europe, too, also received substantial financial support from the European Bank for Reconstruction and Development (EBRD), which was created in 1990 with an initial share capital of ECU 10 billion, and based in London. It involved 40 countries plus the EU and the EIB; it has received strong British support because of a lending commitment focused particularly upon a stimulus to the development of the private sector.

The massive needs in Eastern Europe for aid and trade had major implications for the EU and the rest of the world. New trade agreements were granted to Eastern Europe, along with the removal of import quotas and tariff reductions, to give imports from Eastern Europe the same entry conditions as those for developing countries – Romania already enjoyed this privilege under Ceausescu, and other countries such as Poland and Hungary soon had to be treated similarly. During the 1990s the EU replaced Comecon as the principal trading partner for the countries of Eastern Europe. These new trade agreements led on to association agreements (though excluding the USSR), and the effects of these are covered in a separate section on association. The EU also provided economic and technical co-operation, financial assistance and a political dialogue.

It is important not to rush the full integration of Central and East European countries (CEECs) into the EU but to provide a sufficient breathing space for their adaptation, especially in the light of East Germany's difficult adjustment in even more favourable circumstances. Successful economic development depends partly upon attracting sufficient new Western investment to benefits from low wage rates. East European countries have also started to manufacture to West European norms and standards. While there are enormous opportunities for trade benefits to both sides, in which the EU is stronger in more sophisticated industrial products, it will have to brace itself for some structural re-adaptation in particular industries because of increased imports from Eastern Europe such as glass from Czechoslovakia, cement from Poland, and so on.

For the USSR itself a Trade and Economic Co-operation Agreement came into effect in 1990, with both sides granting the other MFN status with the EU removing quotas and financial aid. However, the Partnership and Co-operation Agreements with Russia and the former republics of the USSR are far less liberal than those granted to the CEECs. Economic reform (*perestroika*) introduced after Gorbachev came to power in 1985 faced immense problems and contributed to his demise. His alluring offer of a 'common European home' received a cautious reception by the EU. Whilst an enlarged EU including the former East European satellite states will consolidate the Community as a major world power, it would be folly to go further by incorporating the CIS. While Russia has been seriously weakened, it is still a powerful threat, particularly if the American presence in Europe is to be diminished.

*Economic transition*   Transition to a market-oriented system, ultimately in preparation for application to join the EU, has rested upon several main pillars such as political democracy, and economically in a switch to a market system in which prices have been freed to find their own equilibrium. The result initially was significant inflation, but over time it should result in a more efficient allocation of resources. At a macroeconomic level governments have tried to pursue stabilization policies such as controlling the money supply, tightening budgets partly by cutting finance to state firms, and seeking to control excessive wage pressure. The movement from complete state ownership of industry has been undertaken via a policy of privatization, though this has added to open unemployment, since firms are easiest to sell when they can be made profitable by restructuring and shedding labour.

The transition from a planned socialist system to a free capitalist system based on private markets has naturally proved traumatic. The 'big bang' approach in pursuit of gain has not been achieved without great pain, particularly in the CIS where only slow economic gains have been realized. Nevertheless, sometimes even where slow adjustment policies have been pursued, some countries have performed worse than others; for example, Lithuania has made slower progress than the more liberal market-based policies of Estonia which have brought the latter to the brink of EU membership. Market reforms in Eastern Europe led initially to a marked decline in income per head, with falls similar to those in the Great Depression in the early 1930s.

Electoral discontent resulting from painful economic reforms may lead to some recovery of Communist support amongst a minority of the population. Clearly there are winners and losers, with the main gainers being the successful entrepreneurs and the more adaptable young people, and the losers being many former state employees previously with jobs for life, now experiencing unemployment. The elderly have found it difficult to adapt to new values and also have seen their savings eroded by inflation. There are also fragile and delicate ethnic relationships in Central and Eastern Europe with a need to avoid these minorities being scapegoats for societal problems.

The further east one goes, the greater are the risks generally for business since these countries are furthest from the core EU market. Eastern Europe has seen the collapse of its former trade to the CIS market and this has reinforced its trade links with the EU. Eastern European countries have moved to make currencies freely convertible, though high inflation has placed severe pressure on attempts to fix exchange rates. Apart from Russia, most of the other East European countries have recovered strongly, with more goods being produced and a successful new capitalist class having emerged. East European countries enjoy some comparative advantage, such as low labour costs and relatively highly skilled human capital.

*Association*   The CEECs have moved steadily up the pecking order of trade relations with the EU, initially through the GSP and then the Europe Agreements signed in December 1991 with Poland, Hungary and Czechoslovakia; in spring 1993 with Bulgaria and Romania; and in 1995 with Estonia, Latvia, Lithuania and Slovenia. At first these were not envisaged as a step towards enlargement, though subsequently the EU recognized the desire of the CEECs to go further. The Europe Agreements defined relations between the EU and East European countries. They consist primarily of nine titles: political dialogue; general principles; free movement of goods; movement of workers, establishment of supply and services; payments, capital, competition, and other economic provisions, approximation of laws; economic co-operation; cultural co-operation; financial co-operation; institutional, general and final provisions. An additional title was included in the latest Agreements on co-operation to prevent illegal activities. Institutions were established consisting of an Association Council, Association Committee, Association Parliamentary Committee and a disputes resolution procedure (Mayhew 1998, pp. 151–9).

The Europe Agreements were significant in developing and overcoming the limited and artificial trade under Comecon, though increasing European bloc trade is criticized globally for further discrimination and being inferior to world-wide free trade. The Agreements aimed to establish a free trade area for non-agricultural products over ten years, with slower progress for sensitive products, such as textiles, clothing and steel. On the free movement of goods, protectionism within the EU was to be abolished asymmetrically by the end of the fifth year at the latest, and for the East European countries it was slower, with up to ten years for certain products. The later entrants in the Baltic states had shorter transition periods and free trade with Estonia was established quickly from the beginning of 1995. Although about a fifth of East European exports to the EU are textiles and clothing, the scope for increasing these significantly is limited by global competition and by severe competition from Portugal and Greece which are even more dependent on textiles and clothing than any CEEC. The EU has a large trade deficit on clothing and many EU firms have engaged in outward processing trade, producing the most labour-intensive parts of the product in Eastern Europe which is favoured generally by having no tariffs on re-imports (and this limits technology transfer). The EU in sensitive sectors also has anti-dumping and safeguard clauses, and it has been necessary to impose controls, especially on steel, where some East European countries are very competitive. However, the scope for using these excessively in sectors such as steel is limited since they are allowed to use subsidies for restructuring. Also, there is a lengthy period involved between filing an anti-dumping complaint and the final measure being taken. There is a commitment to helping Eastern European industry to develop, and to help through industrial co-operation in industries such as steel to reduce the overcapacity of older plants and to introduce proper accounting methods, so that East European prices are not artificially too low. In relation to production in steel, this means reducing even further open-hearth furnace production which has low productivity and heavy energy use. Companies have begun to concentrate more on modern oxygen-blown converters; the other main production method is electric.

The association agreements in the 1990s moved Eastern Europe from a position of negative discrimination against it towards positive discrimination in its favour. Given the asymmetry in which the EU brought down its trading barriers more quickly, one might have expected a huge trade surplus in favour of Eastern Europe. Despite a vast growth in their exports, partly switched from CIS markets, this has not materialized; for example, Poland in the mid-1990s had a trade deficit with nearly all the 15 EU countries, and these were particularly large with its main trading partners Germany and Italy. In trade with Italy, Poland was in deficit on imported components for Fiat vehicles (which was partly offset by sale of final vehicles), and also had a big deficit on white goods, and so on, due to Poland's high propensity to import consumer products. To deal with balance-of-payments problems some countries such as Poland and Hungary were forced to introduce small import charges. The CEECs can impose exceptional measures of protection, such as those for infant industries and restructuring, though the EU has used its powerful position to inhibit their widespread application. Fuller application of the agreed EU policies on competition and restriction of state aids will over time enable the dismantling of EU trade controls.

The trade imbalance can be attributed to various elements including some continuing restrictive impediments to trade. Imports in sensitive sectors, such as iron and steel, textiles and agriculture, have been highly restricted and yet these are key sectors, accounting for a significant percentage of East European production and exports. The EU has also invoked its various safeguard clauses and anti-dumping measures, not just because of low prices but also in response to protectionist lobbies. For example, agricultural imports have been restricted even further by using health scares to ban unsanitary imports of meat and other products. Trade flows are a function of both demand and supply pressures. Growing recession in the EU has reduced the growth of imports, whilst improved economic expansion in Eastern Europe has sucked in more imports. Also on the supply side, Eastern Europe has still continued to have some problems in the quantity of goods produced, such as in agriculture because of changes in land ownership, underinvestment and poor organization; and especially low quality because of problems of processing and marketing goods to Western standards. In relation to the benefits from tariff cuts, rules of origin restrictively laid down that a high percentage of goods (generally 60 per cent of value added) had to originate within the area, while tariff cuts with the rest of the world via the Uruguay Round further eroded the benefits of preferences to Eastern Europe. Bilateral, diagonal and full cumulation of rules of origin also apply (Mayhew 1998, pp. 68–9).

The EU and the CEECs especially could benefit enormously from the growth of free trade, and estimated benefits have been shown from modelling this (Black 1997). However, the EU is torn between an ambitious, quick and risky full enlargement and a more cautious, selective and prudent approach. Initially the EU appears to have a vested interest in supporting even closer intra-trade in the CEECs, via CEFTA (Central European Free Trade Area) and prolonging the association agreements in which on balance the EU is probably the major beneficiary. Delaying the enlargement process as long as possible economically postpones costly budgetary transfer payments to the CEECs via the reformed CAP and the Structural Funds. However, much hinges on the pressures from the CEECs since there is generally popular support for EU membership and delays could reinforce anti-EU concerns of the minorities over issues such as capitalist market domination, especially to Germany, for which the CEECs would be the main supplier of cheap labour and raw materials. Also, migratory labour pressures could increase if reforms in Eastern Europe fail. EU borders are quite porous and it is surprising, given the big differences in income per head between the EU and Eastern Europe, that there has not been even more immigration from Eastern Europe (Siebert 1994). Much depends on people's expectations that their situation will improve significantly and if this cannot be achieved successfully through reforms and association agreements, the enlargement issue will have to be dealt with sooner rather than later. For example, the EU has made progress internally through a process of setting target dates to achieve economic integration such as EMU, yet has shied away from setting firm dates for eastern enlargement.

*Favoured applicant countries for accession*   Eastern enlargement is the biggest challenge of all, but it offers immense economic and political benefits to both the EU and even more so to the CEECs. There will be huge benefits from increased competition, growth of trade and higher investment. Failure by the EU to deliver full membership eventually would stall the pace of economic and political reform with a fallback encouraging Russia to reassert its ambitions for control again. The CEECs, unlike previous enlargements, have already been pressured into taking on much of the *acquis communautaire*. Market measures contribute to free trade and a much higher rate of economic growth which will more than cover the increased Budget costs of enlargement.

Accession will add significantly more to the EU land area and population than to its GDP since essentially the CEECs consists of poor member states with low per capita GDP. There are problems and deficiencies in the measured data, with a thriving 'black' economy, but after an initial contraction in GDP, evidence shows rapid recovery with a GDP growth 1995–99 of just under 4 per cent per annum on average for the 10 CEECs. This is shown in Table 11.1, in which only the Czech Republic has a per capita GDP of more than 50 per cent of the EU average. Furthermore, there is great heterogeneity among the CEECs, with per capita GNP in the Czech Republic being three times as high as that in Latvia. In fact, the Czech Republic is probably best placed, having maintained a good rate of economic growth and a better trade-off between unemployment and inflation than most other countries (see Table 11.2). The Czech Republic was highly industrialized as part of the Austro-Hungarian Empire and had a similar standard of living. It possesses considerable industrial potential and may have benefited from the split with the poorer Slovakia which is far more agricultural and has had also to restructure its heavy dependence on arms. Slovakia may well regret the split since it has been rejected by the EU for the time being.

Hungary, with a population size similar to the Czech Republic, has a per capita GNP of just over a third of the EU average. It has a slightly higher percentage of its labour force employed in agriculture. Its macroeconomic trade-off has been worse than that of the Czech Republic. Like the Czech Republic it has striven to raise its share of GDP generated by the private sector (55 per cent of GDP in 1994) and to attract FDI. It has been most successful with a cumulative FDI inflow 1989–95 of $11 466 million, compared with the Czech Republic in second place with $5481 million (EBRD 1995). Invariably FDI in some sectors, such as the motor industry, has been accompanied by higher tariffs to outsiders, partly at the behest of Western companies.

Poland is the largest of the new applicant countries with a population of just over 38 million. Its per capita GNP was just under 30 per cent of the EU average. It poses special problems for the EU especially in

Table 11.1    *CEECs' economic statistics*

| | Population 1994 (millions) | Area (1000 sq. km) | GDP (1996) in million ECU | Per capita GNP (World Bank) in PPP EU=100 (1995) | Labour force % in agriculture | Cumulative FDI inflow, 1989–95 million US$ |
|---|---|---|---|---|---|---|
| Czech Republic | 10.3 | 78.9 | 43 920 | 53.1 | 11.2 | 5 481 |
| Hungary | 10.3 | 93.0 | 32 925 | 34.9 | 15.2 | 11 466 |
| Poland | 38.6 | 312.7 | 105 908 | 29.4 | 27.5 | 2 423 |
| Slovakia | 5.3 | 49.0 | 14 497 | 19.6 | 12.1 | 623 |
| Slovenia | 2.0 | 20.3 | 14 244 | 28.4 | 6.0 | 505 |
| Bulgaria | 8.4 | 110.9 | 7 437 | 24.4 | 13.4 | 302 |
| Romania | 22.7 | 237.5 | 23 102 | 23.7 | 24.0 | 879 |
| Estonia | 1.5 | 45.1 | 3 324 | 22.9 | 14.4 | 637 |
| Latvia | 2.7 | 64.5 | 3 921 | 18.3 | 15.8 | 409 |
| Lithuania | 3.7 | 63.5 | 4 942 | 22.4 | 18.5 | 228 |
| Total (CEEC10) | 105.5 | 1 075.4 | 254 220 | 29.0 | 20.9 | 22 953 |
| EU(15) | 372.7 | 3 234.1 | 6 764 100 | 100.0 | 5.3 | – |

*Sources:*   EP/Statistical Service 1998; for FDI, *EBRD Transition Report 1995.*

*Table 11.2*    *Macroeconomic performance, selected CEECs*

| | Real GDP growth rate | | | Inflation rate (1996 December on December) | Unemployment rate (1996, in per cent with ILO definition) |
|---|---|---|---|---|---|
| | 1994 | 1995 | 1996 | | |
| Hungary | 2.9 | 1.5 | 1.0 | 19.8 | 9.2 |
| Poland | 5.2 | 7.0 | 6.0 | 18.7 | 12.4 |
| Estonia | −1.8 | 4.3 | 4.0 | 14.8 | 10.2 |
| Czech Republic | 2.6 | 4.8 | 4.0 | 8.6 | 3.4 |
| Slovenia | 5.3 | 3.9 | 3.1 | 9.1 | 7.3 |

*Source*:    *Commission opinion 1997* (National Sources, EBRD, Commission service).

relation to its large agricultural sector which is the largest of the applicant countries. Furthermore, its agriculture is extremely inefficient since it accounts for only around 7 per cent of its GDP . Agricultural productivity is very low, with small farms (on average 15 hectares), low technology and agricultural prices below the EU average. Polish industry is becoming more efficient through privatization and modernization, with its steel output being used increasingly in the rapidly expanding motor industry. The latter constitutes by far the largest car market in Eastern Europe, offering benefits from economies of scale. The Polish labour force is highly skilled, young and quite entrepreneurial. Poland is impatient for early membership, being prepared to accept the full *acquis communautaire*.

Slovenia had a per capita income of over 28 per cent of the EU average, with some estimates much higher (Commission 1999), and was by far the wealthiest of the Yugoslav Republics from which it declared its independence. It has only a small percentage of its labour force in agriculture, close to the EU average, and an average level of agricultural efficiency. Slovenia has some strengths in never really being under a central planning system; also, it is highly ranked by international credit-rating agencies. However, its weaknesses included quite an inflexible and relatively high-waged labour market. This, plus an incomplete legal framework and some fears by foreign investors, led to a relatively small amount of foreign investment. The cumulative FDI inflow was estimated at US$505 million during 1989–95 (EBRD 1995).

Estonia is the small Baltic state most favoured by the EU, partly because it has become a very free economy, with liberal economic reforms and extremely low tariffs. It receives strong support for entry from its Scandinavian neighbours, especially Finland. It is the smallest of the applicant states in terms of population and GDP. It has a slightly higher per capita income than its Baltic neighbours, Latvia and Lithuania. It has privatized significantly and also attracted more cumulative FDI than either Latvia or Lithuania. Estonia went through successful monetary reform starting with a parallel currency, dollarization, followed by an interim currency, the cheap rouble, leading to the permanent currency of the kroon since June 1992. Pegging the exchange rate to the D-mark helped to dampen its high inflation rate. However, a high exchange rate made exporting harder, especially where Estonian exporters failed to modify their exports sufficiently for the EU market.

*Enlargement*  There will have to be another IGC before enlargement takes place, since many important matters still need to be settled, including institutional arrangements. However, the Commission in its Agenda 2000 Report in 1997 assessed the applicants on the criteria agreed at the Council meeting held at Copenhagen in June 1993. The meeting laid down the three criteria which candidate countries should fulfil: the political, economic and *acquis communautaire*. With regard to the stability of institutions, guaranteeing democracy, the rule of law, human rights, and respect for and protection of minorities, progress has still to be made in a few countries. However, only one applicant, Slovakia, was deemed not to satisfy the political criteria.

The economic criteria require the existence of a functioning market economy as well as the capacity to cope with competitive pressure and market forces within the EU. The Commission has divided the applicants into two groups, with the favoured group consisting of the Czech Republic, Hungary, Poland, Slovenia and Estonia (plus Cyprus). These have a functioning market economy, while the capacity to withstand competitive pressures and market forces is also met by most of these countries, though Estonia is failing on the latter (whereas paradoxically it is considered more successful on the former).

The obligations of membership have risen with a bigger *acquis*, for example, now including the SEM, CFSP, EMU, justice and home affairs. The Commission's indicators for progress are: (a) meeting the obligations in the Europe Agreements; (b) progress in transposition and effective implementation of measures set out in the White Paper, especially single-market measures; (c) transposition and implementation of other measures, for example, relating to the environment, energy, agriculture, industry, telecommunications, transport, social affairs, customs administration, and justice and home affairs.

On the third criterion, the obligations of membership, the Commission's opinion is that Hungary has made the best progress on (a), (b), and (c). Poland has problems with (a), is reasonable on (b), and needs slightly more effort on (c). The Czech Republic has problems on (a), is reasonable on (b), and needs continuing efforts on (c). Slovenia is behind on (a) and unsatisfactory on (b) and (c). Also, Estonia has significant problems on (b) and (c) (Commission 1997). The administrative and judicial capacity to apply the *acquis* is important and efforts undertaken are bringing results in the Czech Republic, Hungary, Poland and Estonia. In reality only the first three countries are able to adopt the *acquis* in the medium term, while others such as Slovenia and Estonia need a more sustained effort and to establish a better administrative structure.

The EU's pre-accession strategy has been one of helping to accelerate economic convergence through PHARE funds and help with legal harmonization and reshaping of institutions; for example, to strengthen competition policy and to reduce state aids. The EU has seconded officials to help with specific projects, and annual progress reports record the degree of success in preparing the applicants for membership.

The EU made a political choice of vision in accepting half of the applicants, showing a gesture of goodwill towards Slovenia and Estonia. One hopes the rejection of the other five weaker applicants for the moment – Bulgaria, Romania, Slovakia, Latvia and Lithuania – does not dash their hopes. The other alternative was to open negotiations with all applicants (with the exception of Slovakia, ruled out on political grounds, especially in relation to human rights). Instead, the Commission has drawn the line, though it is emphasized that it is merely a difference of degree, with those favoured being the 'pre-ins'.

The decision to split off Estonia favourably from the other Baltic states of Latvia and Lithuania was partly justified by its stronger economic performance, but has been a much-criticized decision since it has been argued that it could send the wrong signal that Russia can pick off the Baltic states (Lofgren 1997). Some of the evidence on which the Commission reached its judgement has been challenged; for example, Latvia has cited a few facts and statistics used by the Commission which are out of date and mistaken (*Latvian News Bulletin*, July 1997). Similarly, there have been responses in defence of Lithuania, suggesting that it appears no worse than some other applicants such as Poland in particular respects, such as restructuring after privatization (Samonis 1997, p. 5). He argues that Lithuania's main problem can be attributed to its poor image in failing to sell its success in economic transformation.

The EU has drawn up a new financial framework for the years 2000– 2006, in which its expenditure is set to increase (at 1997 prices) from ECU 35.2 billion in the year 2000 to ECU 42.8 billion in 2006. Of this, the new member states are to receive ECU 11.6 billion in 2006, plus ECU 1 billion in pre-accession aid each year. Clearly the EU also has to make adjustments and the financial implications are that the existing member states face a reduction in their share of the Structural Funds and further reform of the CAP through continued reduction of EU prices towards world levels. Whilst EU farmers are compensated for price cuts by direct income aids, these will not apply to farmers in the CEECs.

There is a lack of general administrative expertise in the CEECs, and weaknesses, especially in regional or local administrative institutions that are able to manage the EU-funded projects. The EU recognizes the need to strengthen institutions at the local and regional level, but for the moment accepts that the low general level of economic development and small size of most of the potential new members does not make the creation of new administrative structures an immediate priority. However, Poland, the largest new applicant, has switched from its 49 centrally administered provinces to 16 self-governing regional authorities (voivodships) to promote regional economic development. This will improve its relations with the EU, which prefers to work with a few large regions. While most in Poland favour regional self-government, there is some opposition to autonomous regions (Winiarski 1995). For example, Poland post-1945 was concerned with cementing nationhood, rather than splitting up the country. Membership of the EU would mean that areas west of the Vistula are best able to cope with EU competition, with regional problems likely to increase in the east.

The EU tends to strike a hard bargain with enlargement, if past experience is any guide (Redmond 1993). Its approach so far to Eastern Europe has been cautious and particularly ungenerous in relation to agricultural imports, reflected by an unexpected shift in the EU's favour in relation to agricultural trade. However, at the end of the day, despite protestations by new applicants over particular issues, be they agriculture or concerns over restricted transition arrangements for labour mobility, and so on, they would appear to have few alternatives other than to accept EU entry terms. For example, Poland's worry about Germans buying up land cheaply in western Poland, and its attempt to prevent this, seems unlikely to prevail.

Finally, the process of enlargement involves quite a long time-scale through the different stages from the initial application to the Commission opinion, the start of negotiations, Treaty of Accession and accession itself. On average a period of six years is involved (Nicolaides and Boean 1996, p. 7), being shorter where negotiations are easier (for example, the last EFTA enlargement), but it will be more protracted for Eastern Europe. For example, eastern enlargement of NATO was quicker and less costly than EU enlargement.

*Differentiated and flexible integration*
Enlargement is likely to accelerate the more pragmatic and flexible approach to integration. However, a range of basic common policies have formed the building blocks of the Community. Countries have to conform to the Treaties and to the ongoing legislation from Community institutions. The basic foundations of the EU, such as the principle of non-discrimination against its members, have to be respected and countries cannot reimpose trading barriers against other members of the Community. Unless these principles are applied, the EU cannot operate effectively and will be undermined. Nevertheless, a pursuit of excessive common standardization and an attempt to impose uniformity for its own sake are undesirable and certainly less practicable for a Community of 15 or more different countries. The Community has acknowledged this, using various instruments such as gradual and phased directives, plus some derogations, and some national discretion in how measures are to be applied (Wallace 1985).

Some differentiation in approach has also existed in other organizations, such as French and Spanish arrangements in NATO. The crucial issue, however, is how much flexibility is possible and whether it can be provided without creating so many exceptions and special cases that ultimately it distorts and discredits the whole organization. In the new Community the less standard and more diverse pattern of integration which has had to emerge is likely to be reinforced in the future. The first enlargement of the EC in 1973 created a situation of differential treatment by the transition phases of adjustment. It is no coincidence that this first enlargement resulted in greater discussion about a two-speed Europe which was suggested by W. Brandt in West Germany in

1974; this was followed by the Tindemans Report in 1976 in which there were further proposals for differentiated development. In a two-speed Europe at least there is an obligation on those countries that are forging ahead faster to help the weaker countries, for example by greater regional assistance.

There is little doubt that since enlargement the EU has shown a tendency to split into at least two tiers. There is not only a reluctance to support weaker countries sufficiently, but also doubts about whether such fiscal transfers would actually produce long-run convergence. The pattern that is inevitably emerging is one in which some countries, usually the original Six, are better able to push forward with policies in new areas. The two countries, France and Germany, that have taken most initiatives have provided the momentum in fields such as the EMS and EMU, which finally started in 1999 with 11 members. Countries not participating in new initiatives are free to join and encouraged to take up the option when conditions become more propitious for them. The Schengen Treaty, which was signed in 1985 by France, West Germany and Benelux, was another example of the more progressive countries pressing ahead to abolish frontier controls from 1 January 1990. The two-tier approach may even prove to be the most practical way of progressing in other fields, such as that of removing tax barriers; for example, tax rates and yields on VAT and excise duties have been much wider in the UK, Denmark and Ireland than in the original Six. The diversity of member states in the EU has increased the differentiated application of the *acquis communautaire*, and also in relation to environmental and social policies (especially during the UK opt-out).

The Community is likely to be confined to core policies, though there is no consensus over what they should be; for example, R. Dahrendorf's list in a Europe *à la carte* included foreign policy, trade, monetary policy and overseas development. However, one has to be careful to prevent the loosest *à la carte* approach, since if countries are completely free to choose which policies they want to participate in, this will ultimately create only a minimum level of integration which will fail to sustain a durable level of union. France approved a variable-geometry Community in the 1970s, particularly in industrial and technological policy. The *acquis communautaire* applies to core policies, but in other areas countries may choose whether to participate or not. Even some non-members of the EU have participated in the EUREKA project and projects of nuclear fusion, such as the Joint European Torus (JET).

Hence the better approaches consist of a provision for multi-speed progress by member states to the same policies and/or a variable-geometry approach in which the most dynamic and integration-minded core countries steam ahead with the more peripheral countries invariably lagging behind. There is a danger of geographical divisions with variable geometry and hence a preference for flexible integration based on policy areas through a common base for all, plus open partnerships (CEPR 1995, p. 58). This provides a compromise between accelerated supranationalism on the common base and more intergovernmentalism for open partnerships. It is the most realistic way of coping with the much-enlarged EU.

For efficient operation of the EU qualified majority voting (QMV) is better since opponents would be excluded from the blocking process. A more variegated pattern of integration enables the more dynamic countries to press on ahead, acting as catalysts to new policy areas and providing a way of breaking the soul-destroying deadlock and paralysis of the Community; this would help to overcome a damaging split of the Community into two groups. It also gives the 'outs' the right to join when convergence enables them to participate. In the run-up to Amsterdam, France and Germany were keen to press ahead without any veto by other member states, but the UK under the new Blair government was averse to enhance co-operation in pillar 1, since the UK had decided to end its opt-out of social policy. The Amsterdam Treaty was more of a compromise, and in pillars 1 and 3 authorized flexible co-operation by member states. This is done by QMV (but with the safeguard that any member state may prevent a vote being taken by invoking important reasons of national policy). Also, the 'outs' must be permitted to join at any time. Under the flexible co-operation the policy decisions also still have to be taken under the normal Treaty provisions; for example, since unanimity is required on taxation, whatever the number of member states involved in enhanced co-operation in this field, unanimity would still be required.

The new Community of 15 cannot be optimal for all activities. It has striven hard to obtain basic agreement in key areas and indeed it is surprising in some respects that the Community has been able to make as much progress as it has, given the differences and at times the unco-operative nature of new members. A much looser pattern of integration seems inevitable in the future and the UK may look back wistfully on why it could not attain flexibility to a greater extent in the first place in sectors such as agriculture.

**Enlargement and the UK**

The UK has favoured enlargement, particularly of countries with which it has had close relationships historically, such as Portugal and the Scandinavian countries. These were a natural development from existing EFTA links. The policy of encouraging enlargement has continued in relation to Central and Eastern Europe. The main reservation existed in relation to German reunification *per se*, with concerns about this voiced by Prime Minister Thatcher and by Nicholas Ridley, with the latter being removed specifically over the issue.

The UK has supported EU enlargement and favoured admitting the CEECs for two main reasons: first, it helps to underpin political and economic democracy within a peaceful Europe; second, an enlarged EU containing the CEECs will create greater diversity and slow down the deepening process of internal integration. In other words, there is a trade-off between enlargement and deepening, and the UK has always held major reservations about the extent and pace of policy deepening. The UK Conservative government pressed for subsidiarity to provide a brake on what seemed like inexorable deepening. Continued EU enlargement will provide an even greater constraint, with slower progress and more opt-outs across an increasing range of flanking policies.

It is unfortunate that the UK approach has been based so much on a negative view of EU internal integration. Furthermore, UK policy economically is weak to the extent that the UK economy is not naturally well placed to be the main beneficiary either from Southern European or CEE enlargement. While the UK has little alternative but to see Germany anchored firmly in the EU, the main effects of East European enlargement seem likely to consolidate German hegemony. Germany is dominant in terms of population size and economic strength. Although it inherited heavier burdens than anticipated, with slow progress in transforming East Germany, in the long run it will be strengthened. In recent years the German economic miracle has disappeared, giving way to a more stagnant, high unemployment and over-regulated economy. However, the opportunities exist for Germany to recover economically by reclaiming its economic hegemony in the CEECs. In contrast, the more peripheral and geographically distant UK seems likely to benefit less from market gains compared with Germany, but still pays a significant part of the heavy budgetary costs of enlargement. Clearly the political objectives of the Foreign Office seem to have dominated the economic objectives of the UK, unless there is a surprising British entrepreneurial boost of activity in the CEECs.

On the basis of past trends in trade and FDI in the CEECs, the UK shares are relatively small compared with those of Germany. Germany in the early 1990s was responsible for over half of EU exports to the CEECs (and geographically this was to be expected from the gravity model of trade flows). The German share has risen further, with Germany enjoying a huge trade surplus, while that of the UK fell. The UK was not among the five major trading nations for the Czech Republic or Hungary, though it was in fifth place in Poland. Similarly in FDI Germany accounted for over a fifth of FDI, compared with less than 5 per cent for the UK (Hughes 1996, p. 106). FDI is partly a substitute for trade but also complementary to it. German business has seized the opportunity to purchase assets cheaply and to link them into its production chain. It has been able to exploit the cheap but fairly skilled labour in the CEECs, and this should help to create greater flexibility and profitability for German companies. Unlike American companies, which have been more concerned with markets, German companies have mainly sought out new locations in the CEECs to lower production costs. It is not just large companies, but many SMEs that have been active in building up close cross-border links enabling them to exploit 'just-in-time' production methods. It is this level and aspect of German FDI which tends to mark it out from that of British FDI in the CEECs. For example, there has been a growing concentration of German FDI in the former German part of Poland. At a microeconomic level a sample of companies has shown that most have been successful, including those such as British Vita, which moved following its suppliers and customers from Germany to Poland; Glaxo, which produces pharmaceutical products in the Czech Republic (but maintains its R&D in the UK); and United Biscuits in Hungary. However, one failure was Lycett, a UK engineering firm in Hungary (Estrin, Hughes and Todd 1997).

# 12 Prospect and retrospect

## Integration in the EU

Integration in the EU has been a major contributor in restoring postwar prosperity after two disastrous world wars. US support was vital in underpinning initial European economic recovery via the OEEC, the forerunner of the EEC. European defence arrangements owed more to NATO than the EU, though the EU is making progress in developing its own CFSP (Common Foreign and Security Policy) and ultimately a stronger defence role. Nations were prepared to surrender some degree of power to supranational institutions such as the EU.

Hopes for a federal Europe were dashed by the loss of momentum, especially after the early idealism and the dynamism of super-economic growth in the 1960s. Recession after the oil crisis in 1973 and rising unemployment created a setback, and it was only in the late 1980s that attempts were made to restore a new sense of direction to the Community: this was provided by the Single European Act which came into force in 1987. It was much less ambitious than many supporters of European union had hoped for, and in some respects was the lowest common denominator which could be agreed by the EU(12). It represented a recommitment to completion of the internal market for which majority voting was introduced. The fact that a vote can be taken encourages compromise, though there are still many areas where unanimity is necessary. A greater use of majority voting became a prime requirement to ensure that an enlarged Community works effectively and is not paralysed in its decision-making. The SEA also brought about more commitment to policies in other fields, such as economic and social cohesion, research and technological development, the environment, and greater political co-operation, enhancing the role of the EP and leading towards a common foreign policy.

Whilst any annual appraisal of progress might indicate that this has occurred at a snail's pace and at times the EU has had to back-pedal, when one cumulates the developments retrospectively, it indicates a massive step forward. Despite continued dominance of the Council of Ministers in the Community's decision-making process, slow progress towards rendering the EU's decision-making more democratic has been made; for example, direct elections to the EP finally materialized in 1979. Since then the EP has gradually seen an accretion of its powers which were consolidated in the Single European Act, the Maastricht Treaty and the Amsterdam Treaty. The Maastricht Treaty constructed a new European architecture of three pillars. The central pillar 1 of the EC was strengthened in many respects and mobilized support around the grand EMU project. The EC was also flanked by two more inter-governmental pillars: pillar 2, the CFSP, and pillar 3, JHA (Justice and Home Affairs), in which the role of the EU institutions was much more constrained. The Maastricht Treaty enshrined the principle of subsidiarity, whereby the EU would take action only where it could demonstrate clear superiority of competence and performance by reasons of scale or effects over those of member states. The Amsterdam Treaty built on the proportionality of EU action having to be fully justified. In addition the Amsterdam Treaty in 1997 reflected further complexity, with some continuing intergovernmental tendencies and it fell short of the federalist progress achieved at Maastricht.

The economic benefits from the customs union and the growing intra-trade were enhanced further with the internal market in 1992, which focused particularly upon removing NTBs. This provided the prime focus of economic interest and activity, giving the EU a new lease of life. Glittering economic prospects *ex ante* were painted from the realization of a single market. A virtuous circle of benefits was expected, especially in the long term, from more competition, industrial reorganization, the reaping of economies of scale and through greater innovation. The methodology has been criticized on various grounds, including that of exaggerating the significance of economies of scale. At a macroeconomic level the benefits accruing from the successful completion of the single market were intended to provide the EU with a better trade-off between conflicting policy objectives. Certainly its impact in lowering the rate of inflation has been significant, especially when accompanied by tight monetary policy in preparation for EMU. Whilst in the short run some job change and displacement was inevitable, unfortunately a high level of unemployment has persisted, particularly in the traditional motor of the EU, Germany. *Ex post* the expected benefits have materialized more gradually, and progress has been slowest in opening up public procurement fully. It will always be necessary to maintain a vigilant watch on state subsidies, since countries are always on the look-out for some way in which they can bend the rules to increase their own national competitiveness.

Unfortunately the CAP, which has been the cornerstone of the Community and its most fully developed policy, has faced continuing problems. Economic events have changed greatly since its inception as worries over food shortages have been replaced by massive surpluses. These have arisen as a result of inexorable technical progress and overgenerous price support policies. They have had increasingly adverse effects on the pattern of agricultural trade with the rest of the world. Agricultural reforms have tended to be piecemeal and belated, always falling short of sufficiently fundamental changes in policy to deal with the problems. Prospects for successful reform are limited, with some countries holding the Presidency of the Council being expected to solve many of the agricultural problems for which they were partly responsible. It is only external pressures from outside the EU and the need to make changes before enlargement to the CEECs that have provided a greater impetus to reform. Yet at the Berlin Summit early in 1999 some of the agricultural proposals by the Commission were diluted, mainly because France could not stomach the strong proposals for joint national financing of agriculture, nor the significant loss in agricultural benefits which it has enjoyed since the formation of the EEC.

The CAP has swallowed up much of the finance which could have been used far more effectively in other ways, such as much-needed support to expand high-technology industry to keep pace with the USA and Japan. The main thrust of policy has been through completing the negative integration of the single market, and where positive industrial policy has been pursued this has covered both old and new industries. Ideally, apart from short-run cushioning of declining traditional industries, a more effective policy has to be based on assisting the development of new high-tech sectors for the millennium. While there has been significant progress in the aerospace industry in the EU, it is important to improve even further on the performance of the electronics industry. This will involve increasing the EU's R&D programmes to account for a larger part of the Budget. Also, it will be necessary to increase further the role of SMEs, some of which will constitute the large employers of the future.

The EU's origins were connected very much with the problems of the energy sector, but despite significant progress there was a failure to include a section on energy in the Maastricht Treaty. Also, EU import-dependence seems likely to increase despite the common measures that have been introduced. Likewise, there was an explicit commitment to develop a common transport policy from the start, but progress was very slow for many years until it was decided that SEM measures, including those for transport, would be implemented by a majority vote. During the 1990s there was great emphasis given to the construction of TENs to link up the EU's infrastructure to facilitate trade and speedy access across borders to the periphery. Emphasis was also given to creating a more competitive market for the most rapidly growing new mode of air transport. Unlike energy and transport, environmental policy only came on to the agenda from the early 1970s but has received strong support from the EP and ECJ, and it has become increasingly connected to many sectors of economic integration. These include not only energy and transport, but also industrial and agricultural policy. Environmental policy was reinforced later by the SEA and the Maastricht Treaty, which provided a firm legal base for environmental policy. The Maastricht Treaty ushered in majority voting on environmental matters connected to the single market, but in addition it brought in the issue of subsidiarity. The Amsterdam Treaty extended majority voting on environmental policy, though unanimity is still required on some aspects, such as environmental taxation. The EU also has external competence, manifested by signing many international environmental agreements.

One of the main changes in the EU over recent years has been the growth of regional and social policy and its concentration on the areas and groups most in need. This can be explained partly in terms of the need to help peripheral less-developed regions to 'take off', and also to supplement industrial policy support for industrial areas experiencing de-industrialization. However, there have been other influential elements provided by an enlarging union with wider regional differentials, and also the recognition that in the new Europe there needs to be a stronger role for the regions. This is exemplified not just in the creation of the Committee of the Regions to provide an input into the decision-making process, but also in the growing emphasis on partnership in the use of the Structural Funds. For Southern Europe in particular the Structural Funds have been seen as part of the complementary bargain and linked to the single market. To the extent that stronger countries have benefited most from the single market, there has been growing recognition of the need to provide a redistributive element.

Progress in the EU has been gradual and largely incremental, running into periodic crises. Proposals for a great leap forward towards the major transformation of EMU in the 1970s suffered a setback, partly as a result of the oil crisis and the move to floating exchange rates.

Nevertheless, the case for EMU remains strong to facilitate trade and to maintain the common system of agricultural prices. Hence, in 1979 a new Franco-German initiative led to the EMS, which operated more flexibly during the 1980s. The success of the ERM reactivated the elusive goal of full EMU. This was the big project of the Maastricht Treaty and during the 1990s the EU economies showed an increasing degree of convergence, particularly towards a lower and more uniform level of inflation. Despite the turbulence in foreign-exchange markets, caused by the removal of controls on capital mobility, and the widening of exchange-rate margins, most countries tried to limit these to the narrower ERM band. Undeterred by speculative activity, the EU decided politically that if it did not press on towards full EMU, it would again fall back from this important goal. Hence from the beginning of 1999 the decisive development occurred with the establishment of the euro which confirms the global role of the EU, with its own currency rivalling the postwar dominance of the US dollar. Whilst the euro depreciated initially against the dollar in 1999, this should help export-led growth to reduce the high level of unemployment. Unfortunately there are continuing doubts about economic convergence, with higher inflation in Southern Europe and high budgetary deficits and debt in countries such as Italy. However, unless there are further delays to the programme, eventually the euro will replace national currencies from 1 January 2002, when there will be a six-month transition period for dual currencies.

EU fiscal integration has taken place, originally to harmonize sales taxes through the introduction of VAT to avoid distortions in trade. Despite a minimum level of VAT of 15 per cent, rates of VAT still differ, as do those of excise duties. The latter have led in some instances to profitable cross-border shopping and smuggling within the EU. There is also pressure to go further in relation to corporate taxation to avoid distortions in capital mobility. However, the main focus has been on VAT, partly since this was used to underpin the EU's own budgetary sources of finance. In some respects VAT was not a judicious choice of EU finance and the switch towards the more equitable resource of GNP represents a vast improvement in terms of being based upon a country's ability to pay. That leaves the main problem with the EU Budget still centred on the continuing overexpenditure on agriculture, given the declining importance of agriculture in employment and as a percentage of GNP. The EU Budget for the millennium has tried to stabilize agricultural expenditure at just over 40 000 million euros per annum.

Also, a policy of income support for farmers avoids the microeconomic problem of surpluses and enables prices to fall closer to world levels, lessening conflict with the rest of the world. However, compensation to farmers still seems excessive, but at least a rural development policy offers more scope for success than reliance upon the CAP *per se*. In addition, the increasing expenditure on Structural Funds in recent years is to be welcomed both as a means of reducing inequalities and improving solidarity. Ideally one would like to see a more positive role by the EU through the use of its federal Budget, but contrary to the MacDougall Report, budgetary expenditure remains modest, and the own-resources ceiling remains fixed at 1.27 per cent of EU GDP. Whilst one recognizes that there may be concerns about inefficient EU expenditure, especially when national expenditure is being severely constrained, it would be unfortunate if the stability pact as part of EMU further reduced national fiscal flexibility without enhancing this further at the federal level.

Apart from the increasing level of internal integration in the EU, both micro and macro, the EU has not neglected the establishment of appropriate external trading relations with particular groups of countries. These have reflected historical, strategic and foreign-policy goals. A clear pecking order of relations has been established including the EFTA countries, the Mediterranean and the ACP. While trade preferences have not been as helpful as expected in promoting the development of the ACP, preferences only offer opportunities for more competitive trade and are no guarantee of this if countries are not sufficiently entrepreneurial and have supply-side deficiencies. The existence of preferences as a result of the EU's common external trading policy has still provided an attractive incentive for a host of other countries to enter into trade agreements with the EU. These preferential arrangements have been a continued threat to multilateralism, but fortunately global pressures predominated in the last Uruguay Round. It is important that EU trade preferences are made consistent with the WTO, otherwise they are likely to be a source of continued trade friction with the rest of the world, especially the USA. For example, conflict over bananas led the WTO to rule against EU preferential ACP treatment. It has raised prices for EU consumers far in excess of the benefits for the ACP which need more aid to diversify. In the future the Lomé preferential system is likely to be transformed into regional FTAs.

For European countries the lure of moving to full membership of the EU has proved immensely powerful, especially for the CEECs, which were previously the most discriminated bloc because of the Communist system and central planning, lacking market prices. It is in terms of the ever-enlarging membership that the EU now faces major problems. Having successfully grown from the EU(6) to the EU(9), EU(10), EU(12) and in 1995 to the EU(15), the future opens up an unknown final level of membership, dependent upon successful transition in the CEECs. The enlargement problems of Southern Europe pale into insignificance compared with those of moving on from the association agreements to full membership of the EU. While this has occurred already in NATO for the Czech Republic, Hungary and Poland, the economic costs are much greater and more intractable for the CEECs in the EU. The EU at Amsterdam failed to agree on all of the institutional reforms which will be necessary before enlargement can occur. It is necessary to maintain a balanced decision-making process by re-weighting votes in the Council of Ministers to ensure that an influx of smaller member states are not over-represented.

One month after the Amsterdam European Council, the European Commission presented its 'Agenda 2000' which has taken account of the prospects for an enlarged union. The Commission also published its opinions on each of the CEECs, along with Cyprus. The future is likely to see a looser and more flexible pattern of integration which is compatible and suitable for the new enlarged Community. Enlargement is likely to take place more slowly than the CEECs would like, with eventual participation in all three pillars of the EU. While there will be opposition, particularly from sectional interests in the EU, especially in agriculture and declining industries such as textiles in countries like Portugal, the majority will benefit. The CEECs need to be rewarded for the rapid progress that they have made in liberalization and recovering from depression in the early 1990s. Although large gaps exist which will necessitate massive structural transfers, some countries, such as the Czech Republic, are likely to approach the GDP level of Greece in a few years. It is important to prevent nationalist groups, along with Russia, from seizing the initiative to oppose closer integration. The EU has little choice but to press on with enlargement to underpin the process of liberalization and provide the certainty to encourage continued inflows of FDI. As with the single market, there are risks and opportunities, but on balance the potential gains are immense. The trading opportunities are enormous for both sides and could help to spark off economic recovery in both Western and Eastern Europe, recreating a powerful and united single Europe.

**Integration and the UK**

Each chapter of this book has tried to present the story of the unfolding links between the EU and the UK, and the latter in joining the Community in 1973 had to adjust to an organization which it had not initiated itself and which was not the one most suited to displaying its strengths. Meanwhile, politically the UK has preferred intergovernmental co-operation and has been reluctant to embrace further rapid progress towards a supranational Community. By the time the UK joined, its industrial competitiveness had diminished and the pace of EU economic growth had started to slacken.

The UK has been keenest on the EU as a liberal free-trading bloc – despite its tendency to suffer balance-of-payments deficits with the EU. The internal market received considerable support in removing NTBs, and the UK took advantage of its presidency of the Council of Ministers in 1986 to provide a new direction for the internal market. This enabled the UK to exploit its comparative advantage in high-tech sectors and especially in the tertiary sector such as financial and transport services. The UK was a major proponent of opening up the internal market, which offered huge potential opportunities for successful businesses. The reforms introduced during the long period of Conservative government from 1979 to 1997, particularly in the labour market, reduced excessive trade union power; this dampened wage-push inflationary pressure and improved the UK's relative economic performance. British business is strong in particular sectors, such as pharmaceuticals, telecommunications, the oil industry, food and drink, and the defence-related sector. The UK economy has a slightly different sectoral composition from that of continental economies in being heavily dependent on indigenous energy and on services, being less dependent on agriculture and is significantly de-industrialized. Also, after years of underinvestment in capital and the skills of employees, the UK has become increasingly dependent upon inward investment, particularly in key sectors such as the motor industry where indigenous ownership has been extinguished.

Over the years the UK has become more *communautaire*, though to a lesser degree than most other member states. It is attuned particularly to liberal market principles, though in the long term the completion of the internal market psychologically may prove of less significance than the linking of the UK to continental Europe with the Channel Tunnel. This has helped to make a marginal improvement to the competitiveness of UK exports to the continental single market, but its most important effect is that it has become joined to continental Europe. However, the financing of this project, with a preference for private-sector finance and the policy of privatization, has led to a marked underinvestment in British railways, lacking the TGVs pioneered by France for continental railways.

Overall, on most issues the UK has mainly been in the position of responding defensively and in a minimalist way to most new EU developments. In the early years especially it failed to recognize that progress could best be made through the traditional interlinking of issues, making it an 'awkward partner' (George 1990). This led to the UK being reactive rather than proactive on most issues, apart from the SEM. This enabled the EU to be driven mainly on the Franco-German axis, pressing on ahead, with the UK losing influence on events. The main difficulty was the CAP, since not only did it raise food prices, but it was singularly inappropriate for the UK with the smallest percentage of its population on the land and an efficient agricultural sector. In addition, the introduction of the CFP was a further irritant to the UK fishing industry. However, the main problem for the UK was that the CAP dominated EU budgetary expenditure. This led the UK to become enmeshed in a national focus on distributional issues, struggling constantly to offset the budgetary costs of EU membership. After much effort it proved possible to retrieve a refund after the Fontainebleau Summit in 1984 and since then this has been maintained, though only after making minor concessions again at the Berlin Summit early in 1999, which had to set out a new Budget for the millennium to encompass Eastern Europe.

A basic stumbling block between the EU and the UK has been the failure to recognize the momentum of integration and that the SEM could be conceived to involve other aspects including integration of social policies, environmental policies and EMU. The UK Conservative governments had particular problems with the costs of all these developments; for example, they objected to the use of majority voting on social policy issues and also the extending range of social policy which increasingly conflicted with the domestic approach of a flexible and deregulated labour market. Likewise there was a preference for exchange rates to be left to market forces, with constant delays from 1979 until 1990 before finally joining the ERM of the EMS. The time had been ripe to join earlier, and the belated decision to enter resulted in entry at an overvalued exchange rate. The failure to remain in the ERM after 'Black Wednesday' in September 1992 was partly because of the unwillingness to continue raising interest rates towards the higher inter-est-rate level demanded by German reunification, which would aggravate the recession in the UK. The whole vision of Mrs Thatcher, as reflected by her speech at Bruges in 1988, was based upon the limited co-operation of independent states, being opposed to any federal and bureaucratic European superstate with a single currency.

The removal of Mrs Thatcher and the end of the long period of Conservative governments, culminating with that of John Major, have altered the conflictual reactive policy style, leading to significant modi-fications in key areas such as the ending of the UK opt-out on social policy. Tony Blair's new Labour government has struck a new policy seeking to be more proactive and at the heart of the EU. This was reflected in its approach to the Amsterdam Treaty and in the UK Presi-dency of the EU in the first half of 1998, though the government's continued belief in its scope for independent action constrained progress. Its lofty ambitions were much diminished by its absence from the most important development of the euro. The UK is left with the same continuing monetary uncertainty as in the past, this time being depend-ent upon a referendum. Exhortations to British business to prepare for entry seem unlikely to materialize, given the lack of decisiveness in holding a referendum immediately, and with the future outcome con-tinuing uncertain.

At least in relation to enlargement, the UK has taken a more favour-able view, though this may still be partly for the wrong reasons in seeking to minimize the deepening of internal integration and ensuring the continuance of a flexible multi-tier and multi-speed EU. Whilst enlargement offers immense trading potential, UK business was not best placed to benefit from Southern European enlargement, and like-wise it is certainly not well positioned to gain significant trading benefits in the CEECs compared with those of Germany. Instead, the effect of Eastern European enlargement seems likely to consolidate German economic and monetary dominance of the EU. Despite the recent con-cern over slow German economic growth (outpaced over the last few years by France) and heavy unemployment, it will be able to exploit the spatial division of labour in Eastern Europe to offset its high labour costs. Germany is naturally the major EU exporting country to the CEECs, and this seems likely to grow even further with enlargement. There has also been a vast outflow of German investment into the CEECs, with a much lower percentage of outward investment by the UK to the CEECs. Furthermore, the UK economy itself is also heavily dependent on inward investment and faces immense competition from low-wage-cost countries in Southern Europe and the CEECs.

The UK's relative GDP deteriorated in the EU(9), though economically there was a relative improvement in the UK's performance during the 1980s in the EU(12). This was partly a reflection of a long-overdue improvement in UK economic performance, but was mainly a consequence of the lower GDP per head of the three new Southern European entrants. Similarly, the CEECs' enlargement will again move the UK up the EU league table, tending to squeeze the benefits for the UK from the Structural Funds. Although the UK was instrumental in developing a common regional policy, it was motivated mainly by the funding *per se*, rather than a strong belief in the devolution of political and economic power. Under the new Labour government the UK has now moved significantly towards decentralization favoured by the EU to enhance regional autonomy. However, EU structural funding has been concentrated most on less-developed regions (with far more spent on Objective 1 than Objective 2 industrial regions). All the Southern European countries and Ireland have also benefited from the Cohesion Fund and with enlargement of the CEECs will absorb more and more of the funding. While the number of Objective 1 regions eligible in the UK has risen, it will be difficult to maintain these in the face of the CEECs in which whole economies are at such a low level of economic development.

The UK economy faces major problems in the early years of the new millennium, since it will be necessary ultimately to join the euro and this will have to be done at a competitive exchange-rate conversion. Given the unhappy experience of the EMS, this time EMU membership will be irrevocable and strong deflationary pressure will have to be exerted on the UK economy if the UK does not enter at the appropriate rate. Given an inherent bias of the ECB under EMU to low inflation, rather than to low unemployment, the UK could find that its unemployment level rises towards that in France or Germany. However, it seems likely that most of the CEECs will not be strong enough to join EMU, but will the UK want to appear in a lower division of countries lying outside the euro? The euro will consolidate internal market trade, though it would be unfortunate if this were at the expense of externalizing its problems, leading to some disintegration in the Community's trading relationship with the rest of the world and leading to trading friction with its major partner, the USA.

# Bibliography

Albert, M. and Ball, R.J. (1983), *Towards European Economic Recovery in the 1980s*, Report for the European Parliament, Brussels.

Aldcroft, D.H. (1978), *The European Economy 1914–1970*, London: Croom Helm.

Allen, H. (1979), *Norway and Europe in the 1970s*, London: Global Book Resources.

Arbuthnott, H. and Edwards, G. (1979), *A Common Man's Guide to the Common Market*, London: Macmillan.

Armstrong, H. and Taylor, J. (1987), *The Way Forward*, London: Employment Institute.

Armstrong, K. and Bulmer, S. (1998), *The Governance of the Single European Market*, Manchester: Manchester University Press.

Artis, M. and Winkler, B. (1998), 'The Stability Pact: Safeguarding the Credibility of the European Central Bank', *National Institute Economic Review*, no. 163, January.

Balassa, B. (1975), *European Economic Integration*, Amsterdam: North Holland.

Baldwin, R.E. (1989), 'On the Growth Effects of 1992', *Economic Policy*, no. 9.

Baldwin, R.E., Francois, J. and Portes, R. (1997), 'The Costs and Benefits of Eastern Enlargement: The Impact on the EU and Central Europe', *Economic Policy*, no. 24.

Baltas, N.C. (1998), 'Greek Agriculture under the CAP', in C.C. Paraskevopoulos (ed.), *European Union at the Crossroads*, Cheltenham: Edward Elgar.

Barbour, P. (ed.) (1996), *The European Union Handbook*, London: Fitzroy Dearborn.

Barrass, R. and Madhavan, S. (1996), *European Economic Integration and Sustainable Development*, Maidenhead: McGraw-Hill.

Black, S.W. (ed.) (1997), *Europe's Economy Looks East*, Cambridge: Cambridge University Press.

Booz Allen and Hamilton Inc. (1986), *Europe's Fragmented Markets: A Survey of European Chief Executives*, The Wall Street Journal/ Europe.

Buckwell, A., Harvey, D., Thomson, K. and Parton, K. (1982), *The Costs of the Common Agricultural Policy*, London: Croom Helm.

Butler, M. (1986), *Europe: More than a Continent*, London: Heinemann.

Cecchini, P. (1988), *The European Challenge 1992*, Aldershot: Wildwood House Gower.

CEPR (Centre for Economic Policy Research) (1995), *Flexible Integration: Towards a More Effective and Democratic Europe*, no. 26, London: CEPR.

Chisholm, M. (1995), *Britain on the Edge of Europe*, London: Routledge.

Coffey, P. (ed.) (1983), *Main Economic Policy Areas of the EC*, The Hague: Martinus Nijhoff.

Coffey, P. (1995), *The Future of Europe*, Aldershot: Edward Elgar.

Cohen, C.D. (ed.) (1983), *The Common Market – Ten Years After*, Oxford: Philip Allan.

Commission of the EC (1987), *Making a Success of the Single Act*, Brussels, February.

Commission of the EC (1988), *Research on the Costs of Non-Europe*, 16 vols, Brussels.

Commission of the EC (1990), *EC Research Funding* 2nd edn, Brussels.

Commission of the EC (1992), *Second Annual Report on the Implementation on the Reform of the Structural Funds*, Brussels.

Commission of the EC (1993), *Community Structural Funds 1994–99 – Revised Regulations and Comments*, Brussels.

Commission of the EC (1994), *Growth, Competitiveness, Employment*, White Paper, Brussels.

Commission of the EC (1996), *European Energy to 2020*, Special issue, Spring.

Commission of the EC (1997), *Agenda 2000*, Brussels.

Commission of the EC (1997), *Opinions on Applications for Membership in the European Union*, Brussels.

Commission of the EC (1998), 'Aggregate Results of the Single Market Programme, vol. 5', *The Single Market Review*, London: Kogan Page.

Commission of the EC and European Monetary Institute (1998), *Convergence Report Required by Article 109j of the Treaty Establishing the European Community*, Frankfurt, March.

Commission of the EC (1999), *Sixth Periodic Report on the Social and Economic Situation and Development of the Regions of the European Union*, Brussels.

*Courier, The* (1986 and 1996).

Davenport, M., Hewitt, A. and Koning, A. (1995), *Europe's Preferred Partners? The Lomé Countries in World Trade*, London: Overseas Development Institute.

Dearden, S. (1986), 'EEC Membership and the United Kingdom's Trade in Manufactured Goods', *National Westminster Bank Quarterly Review*, February.

De Grauwe, P. (1994), *The Economics of Monetary Integration*, 2nd edn, New York: Oxford University Press.

Denton, G. (1984), 'Restructuring the European Community Budget', *Journal of Common Market Studies*, vol. XXIII, no. 2, December.

Devine, P., Katsoulacos, Y. and Sugden, R. (eds) (1996), *Competitiveness, Subsidiarity and Industrial Policy*, London: Routledge.

Devuyst, Y. (1997), 'The Treaty of Amsterdam: An Introductory Analysis', *European Community Studies Association*, USA, vol. X, no. 3, Fall.

Dinkelspiel, U. (1987), 'Eureka: Co-operation in High Technology', *EFTA Bulletin*, vol. XXVIII, no. 1, January–March.

Dosser, D., Gowland, D. and Hartley, K. (eds) (1982), *The Collaboration of Nations*, Oxford: Martin Robertson.

Drewnowski, J. (ed.) (1982), *Crisis in the East European Economy*, London: Croom Helm.

Duchêne, F., Szczepanik, E. and Legg, W. (1985), *New Limits on Agriculture*, London: Croom Helm.

Dustmann, C. (1996), 'Return Migration, the European Experience', *Economic Policy*, no. 22, April, Centre for Economic Policy.

EBRD (European Bank for Reconstruction and Development), *Annual Reports*.

*Economist, The* (various issues).

El-Agraa, A.M. (ed.) (1994), *The Economics of the European Community*, 4th and earlier edns, Oxford: Philip Allan.

Estrin, S., Hughes, K. and Todd, S. (1997), *Foreign Direct Investment in Central and Eastern Europe*, London: Pinter and Royal Institute of International Affairs.

*European Economy* (various issues), Luxembourg.

*European Investment Bank Annual Reports*, Luxembourg.

Eurostat (1996), *Basic Statistics of the Community*, Commission, Brussels.

Fennell, R. (1988), *The Common Agricultural Policy of the Community*, London: Granada.

*Financial Times* (various issues).

Forder, J. and Menon, A. (eds) (1998), *The European Union and National Macroeconomic Policy*, London: Routledge.

Frankel, J.A. and Rose, A.K. (1998), 'The Endogeneity of the Optimum Currency Area Criteria', *Economic Journal*, vol. 108, no. 449, July.

Fuente de la A. and Vives, X. (1995), 'Infrastructure and Education as Instruments of Regional Policy: Evidence from Spain', *Economic Policy*, No. 20, April

Galal, A. and Hoekman, B. (1997), *Regional Partners in Global Markets: Limits and Possibilities of the Euro-Med Agreements*, London: Centre for Economic Policy Research.

George, K.D. and Joll, C. (1975), *Competition Policy in the United Kingdom and the European Community*, Cambridge: Cambridge University Press.

George, S. (1990), *An Awkward Partner*, Oxford: Oxford University Press.

Greenaway, D. (1987), 'Intra-Industry Trade, Intra-Firm Trade and European Integration', *Journal of Common Market Studies*, vol. XXVI, no. 2, December.

Grennes, T. (1997), 'The Economic Transition in the Baltic Countries', *Journal of Baltic Studies*, vol. XXVIII, no. 1, Spring.

Groeben, H. von der (1985), *The European Community: The Formative Years*, Commission, Brussels/Luxembourg.

Gros, D. and Thygesen (1992), *European Monetary Integration*, Harlow: Longman.

Grubel, H.G. and Lloyd, P.J. (1975), *Intra-Industry Trade: The Theory and Measurement of International Trade in Differentiated Products*, London: Macmillan.

Guggenbühl, A., Vanhoonacker, S. and M. den Boer (1997), 'The New Treaty on European Union: A First Assessment', *Eipascope*, European Institute of Public Administration, Maastricht, no. 1997/2.

Hammar et al. (1997), *International Migration, Immobility and Development*, Oxford and New York: Berg.

Harrop, J. (1978), 'An Evaluation of the European Investment Bank', *23A Société Universitaire Européenne de Researches Financières*, Tilburg, Netherlands.

Harrop, J. (1985), 'Crisis in the Machine Tool Industry: A Policy Dilemma for the European Community', *Journal of Common Market Studies*, vol. XXIV, no. 1, September.

Harrop, J. (1996), *Structural Funding and Employment in the European Union*, Cheltenham: Edward Elgar.

Harrop, J. (1998), 'The EU and National Economic Policy: An Empirical Overview', in J. Forder and A. Menon (eds), *The European Union and National Macroeconomic Policy*, London: Routledge.

Hartley, K. (1982), 'Defence and Advanced Technology', in D. Dosser, D. Gowland and K. Hartley (eds), *The Collaboration of Nations*, Oxford: Martin Robertson.

Heertje, A. (ed.) (1983), *Investing in Europe's Future*, Oxford: Basil Blackwell.

Heller, R. and Willat, N. (1975), *The European Revenge: How the American Challenge was Rebuffed*, London: Barrie and Jenkins.

Henderson, P.D. (1977), 'Two British Errors: Their Probable Size and Some Possible Lessons', *Oxford Economic Papers*, no. 2, July.

Henderson, R. (1993), *European Finance*, Maidenhead: McGraw-Hill.

Heseltine, M. (1989), *The Challenge of Europe – Can Britain Win?*, London: Weidenfeld and Nicolson.

Hewitt, A. (1984), 'The Lomé Conventions: Entering a Second Decade', *Journal of Common Market Studies*, vol. XXIII, no. 2, December.

Hewstone, M. (1986), *Understanding Attitudes to the European Community*, Cambridge: Cambridge University Press.

Hill, B.E. (1984), *The Common Agricultural Policy: Past, Present and Future*, London: Methuen.

Hine, R.C. (1985), *The Political Economy of European Trade*, Brighton: Wheatsheaf.

Hodges, N. (ed.) (1972), *European Integration*, Harmondsworth: Penguin.

Holland, S. (1980), *Uncommon Market: Capital, Class and Power in the European Community*, London: Macmillan.

Holland, S. (1993), *The European Imperative*, Nottingham: Spokesman.

House of Commons (1971), White Paper: *The United Kingdom and the European Communities,* Cmnd 4715, London: HMSO.

House of Commons (1978), Green Paper: *The European Monetary System*, Cmnd 7405, November, London: HMSO.

House of Commons (1998), International Development Committee, Fourth Report, *The Renegotiation of the Lomé Convention*, vols I and II, London: HMSO.

House of Lords (1984), Select Committee on the European Communities, *The Common Fisheries Policy*, December.

Hughes, K. (1996), 'European Enlargement, Competitiveness and Inte-

328 Political economy of integration in the European Union

gration' in P. Devine et al. (eds), *Competitiveness, Subsidiarity and Industrial Policy*, London: Routledge.

Ionescu, G. (ed.) (1979), *The European Alternatives*, The Netherlands: Sijthoff and Noordhoff.

Jacquemin, A. and de Jong, H.W. (1977), *European Industrial Organization*, London: Macmillan.

Jacquemin, A. and Pench, L.R. (eds) (1997), *Europe Competing in the Global Economy: Reports of the Competitiveness Advisory Group*, Cheltenham: Edward Elgar.

Jenkins, R. (ed.) (1983), *Britain and the EEC*, London: Macmillan.

Johnson, C. (1987), 'How Well Are We Doing?' *Lloyd's Bank Economic Bulletin*, no. 41, May.

Johnson, H.G. (1973), 'An Economic Theory of Protectionism, Tariff Bargaining and the Formation of Customs Unions', in M.B. Krauss (ed.), *The Economics of Integration*, London: Allen & Unwin.

Josling, T. (1984), 'US and EC Farm Policies: An Eclectic Comparison' in K.J. Thomson and R.M. Warren (eds), *Price and Market Policies in European Agriculture*, Department of Agricultural Economics, University of Newcastle upon Tyne.

Josling, T. and Harris, J. (1976), 'Europe's Green Money', *Three Banks Review*, March.

Jovanovic, M.N. (1997), *International Economic Integration*, 2nd edn, New York: Routledge.

Kaldor, N. (1971), 'The Truth about the Dynamic Effects', *New Statesman*, 12 March.

*Kangaroo News* (various issues).

Keating, M. and Loughlin, J. (eds) (1997), *The Political Economy of Regionalism*, London: Frank Cass.

Kenen, P.V. (1969), 'The Theory of Optimum Currency Areas: An Eclectic View' in R.A. Mundell and A.K. Swoboda (eds), *Monetary Problems of the International Economy*, Chicago: Chicago University Press.

Klaassen, L.H. and Molle, W.T. (1983), *Industrial Mobility and Migration in the European Community*, Aldershot: Gower.

Knutsen, P. (1997), 'Corporatist Tendencies in the Euro-Polity: The EU Directive of 22 September 1994 on European Works Councils', *Economic and Industrial Democracy*, vol. 18, no. 2, May.

Kohl, W.L. and Basevi, G. (eds) (1980), *West Germany: A European and Global Power*, Boston MA: Heath Lexington.

Krauss, M.B. (ed.) (1972), *The Economics of Integration*, London: Allen & Unwin.

Kreinin, M.E. (1974), *Trade Relations of the EEC*, London: Praeger.

Krugman, P. (1998), 'What's New about the New Economic Geography?', in 'Trade and Location', *Oxford Review of Economic Policy*, vol. 14, no. 2, Summer (special issue).

Kruse, D.C. (1980), *Monetary Integration in Western Europe: EMU, EMS and Beyond*, London: Butterworths.

Lange, T. and Pugh, G. (1998), *The Economics of German Unification*, Cheltenham: Edward Elgar.

*Latvian News Bulletin* (1997), 'Latvia and the European Union', no. 5, July.

Lavdas, K.A. and Mendrinou, M.N. (1999), *Politics, Subsidies and Competition*, Cheltenham: Edward Elgar.

Layton, C. (1969), *European Advanced Technology*, London: Allen & Unwin.

Leigh, M. and van Praag, N. (1978), *The Mediterranean Challenge*, 1, Sussex European Research Paper, no. 2.

Lewenhak, S. (1982), *The Role of the European Investment Bank*, London: Croom Helm.

Lodge, J. (ed.) (1989), *The European Community and the Challenge of the Future*, London: Frances Pinter.

Lofgren, J. (1997), 'The Baltics Join Club Europe', *Transitions*, vol. 4, no. 6, November.

Long, F. (ed.) (1980), *The Political Economy of EEC Relations with African, Caribbean and Pacific States*, Oxford: Pergamon Press.

Lopes, J. da Silva (ed.) (1993), *Portugal and EC Membership Evaluated*, London: Pinter Publishers.

Lossani, M. (1998), 'The European Central Bank and the Objective of Financial Stability', *Economia Internazionale*, Rivista Trimestrale Dell'Instito Di Economia Internazionale, vol. LI, no. 2, Maggio.

Ludlow, P. (1982), *The Making of the European Monetary System*, London: Butterworths.

Mackel, C. (1978), 'Green Money and the Common Agricultural Policy', *National Westminster Bank Quarterly Review*, February.

McKinnon, R.I. (1963), 'Optimum Currency Areas', *American Economic Review*, no. 53.

McQueen, M. (1977), *Britain, The EEC and the Developing World*, London: Heinemann.

Macsween, I. (1987), 'The Common Fisheries Policy', *Royal Bank of Scotland Review*, no. 154, June.

Magnifico, G. (1973), *European Monetary Unification*, London: Macmillan.

Marques Mendes, A.J. (1987), *Economic Integration and Growth in Europe*, London: Croom Helm.

Martin, R. (1998), 'Regional Incentive Spending for European Regions', *Regional Studies*, vol. 32, no. 6, August.

Martin, S. and Hartley, K. (1995) 'European Collaboration in Civil Aerospace: Success or Failure', *The Journal of Common Market Studies*, vol. 33, June.

Mathijsen, P.S.R.F. (1985), *A Guide to European Community Law*, London: Sweet & Maxwell.

Mayes, D.G. (ed.) (1997), *The Evolution of the Single European Market*, Cheltenham: Edward Elgar.

Mayhew, A. (1998), *Recreating Europe: The European Union's policy towards Central and Eastern Europe*, Cambridge: Cambridge University Press.

Midland Bank (1987), 'Setting Priorities for Science and Technology', *Midland Bank Review*, Winter.

Millington, A.I. (1988), *The Penetration of EC Markets by UK Manufacturing Industry*, Aldershot: Gower.

Mizsei, K. and Rudka, A. (eds) (1995), *From Association to Accession*, Institute for East–West Studies and the Windsor Group, Warsaw, Poland.

Molle, W. (1990), *The Economics of European Integration*, Aldershot: Dartmouth.

Mortensen, J. (ed.) (1994), *Improving Economic and Social Cohesion in the European Community*, New York: St Martin's Press.

Moussis, N. (1982), *Les Politiques de la Communauté Economique Européenne*, Paris: Dalloz.

Mundell, R.A. (1961), 'A Theory of Optimum Currency Areas', *American Economic Review, no. 51*.

Myrdal, G. (1957), *Economic Theory and Underdeveloped Regions*, London: Duckworth.

Nedergaard, P. (1995), 'The Political Economy of CAP Reform', in *The Political Economy of European Integration*, Netherlands: Kluwer Law International.

Nester, W.R. (1990), *Japan's Growing Power over East Asia and the World Economy*, Basingstoke: Macmillan.

Neven, D. and Seabright, P. (1995), 'European Industrial Policy: The Airbus Case', *Economic Policy*, no. 21, October, Centre for Economic Policy Research.

Nevin, E. (1990), *The Economics of Europe*, London: Macmillan.

Nicholson, F. and East, R. (1987), *From the Six to the Twelve: The Enlargement of the European Communities*, Harlow: Longman.

Nicolaides, P. and Boean, S.R. (1996), 'The Process of Enlargement of the European Union', *European Institute of Public Administration*, Maastricht, no. 1996/3.

NIESR (National Institute of Economic and Social Research) (1983 and 1989), 'The European Monetary System', *National Institute Economic Review*.

Nugent, N. (1994), *The Government and Politics of the European Union*, London: Macmillan.

Owen, N. (1983), *Economies of Scale, Competitiveness and Trade Patterns within the European Community*, Oxford: Oxford University Press.

Padoa-Schioppa, T. et al. (1987), *Europe in the 1990s: Efficiency, Stability and Equity*, Oxford: Oxford University Press.

Pearce, J. and Sutton, J. (1986), *Protection and Industrial Policy in Europe*, London: Routledge and Kegan Paul.

Pelkmans, J. (1997), *European Integration: Markets and Analysis*, Harlow: Addison Wesley Longman.

Pelkmans, J. and Winters, A.C. (1988), *Europe's Domestic Market*, Chatham House Paper, no. 43, London: Routledge.

Petith, H.C. (1977), 'European Integration and the Terms of Trade', *Economic Journal*, vol. 87.

Pinder, J. (1995), *European Community: The Building of a Union*, 2nd edn, Oxford: Oxford University Press.

Pollard, S. (1974), *European Economic Integration 1815–1970*, London: Thames and Hudson.

Pomfret, R. (1986), *Mediterranean Policy of the European Community*, London: Macmillan.

Pomfret, R. (1997), *The Economics of Regional Trading Arrangements*, Oxford: Clarendon Press.

Presley, J.R. and Dennis, C.E.J. (1976), *Currency Areas: Theory and Practice*, London: Macmillan.

Pryce, R. (ed.) (1987), *The Dynamics of European Union*, London: Croom Helm.

Redmond, J. (1993), 'The Wider Europe: Extending Membership of the

EU', in A.W. Cafruny and G.C. Rosenthal (eds), *The State of the European Community*, vol. 2, Colorado and Harlow: Longman.

Redmond, J. (1993), *The Next Mediterranean Enlargement of the European Community: Turkey, Cyprus and Malta*, Aldershot: Dartmouth.

Robson, P. (1998), *The Economics of International Integration*, London: Allen & Unwin.

Samonis, V. (1997), 'Lithuania's Road to Europe, A Comparative Assessment', *Lithuanian Papers*, no. 11, University of Tasmania.

Servan-Schreiber, J.J. (1968), *The American Challenge*, London: Hamish Hamilton.

Shackleton, M. (1990), *Financing the European Community*, London: Frances Pinter.

Shanks, M. (1977), *European Social Policy Today and Tomorrow*, Oxford: Pergamon Press.

Sharp, M. (ed.) (1985), *Europe and the New Technologies*, London: Frances Pinter.

Siebert, H. (ed.) (1994), *Migration: A Challenge for Europe*, Tübingen: Mohr.

Stevens, C. (ed.) (1984), *EEC and the Third World: A Survey*, no. 4, ODI/IDS, London: Hodder & Stoughton.

Streeck, W. (1997), 'Neither European nor Works Councils: A Reply to Paul Knutsen', *Economic and Industrial Democracy*, vol. 18, no. 2, May.

Svennilson, I. (1954), *Growth and Stagnation in the European Economy*, Geneva: United Nations Economic Commission for Europe.

Swann, D. (1995), *The Economics of the Common Market*, 8th edn, Harmondsworth: Penguin.

Taylor, P. (1983), *The Limits of European Integration*, London: Croom Helm.

Tovias, A. (1997), 'The Economic Impact of the European–Mediterranean Free Trade Area on Mediterranean Non-Member Countries', in R. Gillespie (ed.), *The Euro-Mediterranean Partnership*, London: Frank Cass.

Tsoukalis, L. (ed.) (1986), *Europe, America and the World Economy*, Oxford: Basil Blackwell for the College of Europe.

Tsoukalis, L. (1997), *The New European Economy Revisited*, Oxford: Oxford University Press.

Tugendhat, C. (1986), *Making Sense of Europe*, Harmondsworth: Penguin.

Vanhove, N. and Klaassen, L.H. (1980), *Regional Policy: A Regional Approach*, 3rd edn, Farnborough: Saxon House.

Wallace, H. (1985), *The Challenge of Diversity*, London: Routledge and Kegan Paul.

Wallace, W. (ed.) (1980), *Britain in Europe*, London: Heinemann.

Whitby, M. (ed.) (1979), *The Net Cost and Benefit of EEC Membership*, London: Wye College.

Williams, R.H. (1996), *European Union Spatial Policy and Planning*, London: Paul Chapman.

Winiarski, B. (1995), 'Regional Policy and the Administrative Structure of Poland', *Argumenta Oeconomica*, 1, Wroclaw, Poland, Academy of Economics.

Winters, A. (1987), 'Britain in Europe: A Survey of Quantitative Trade Studies', *Journal of Common Market Studies*, vol. XXV, no. 4, June.

Yannopoulos, G.N. (ed.) (1986), *Greece and the EEC*, London: Macmillan.

Ypersele, J. van and Koeune, J.C. (1985), *The European Monetary System*, Cambridge: Woodhead-Faulker.

Zis, G. (1984), 'The European Monetary System, 1979–1984: An Assessment', *Journal of Common Market Studies*, vol. XXIII, no. 1, September.

# Index

Referendum
  Danish 24
  Irish 24
  Norwegian 24–5
  UK 25–6
Regional and social problems and
  policies 162–93
  funds 170–82
Restrictive agreements 119–121
Romania 305
Rome
  Summit 35, 217
  Treaty 15, 66, 150
Rules of origin 20, 278, 300

SAD 68–9
Santer, Jacques 30, 51
Schengen 48, 308
Schiller Plan 202
Schmidt, Helmut 35, 204, 211
Schuman, Robert 8
  Declaration and Plan 15
SEA 18, 24, 34–5, 46, 51, 66–7, 186,
  312–13, 315
Senegal 275
Service sector 68, 76, 83, 85, 97–8,
  177, 319
Slovakia 55, 301, 305
Slovenia 303, 305
Smithsonian Agreement 202
Snake 202–3, 206–8
Social policy and Charter 183–7
Spaak, Paul-Henri 10, 16, 45, 183,
  270
Spain 99, 101, 115–16, 179–181,
  217, 288–9
Spierenburg Report 45
Spinelli, Altiero 45, 128
SPRINT 133
STABEX 274–6
STAR 168
Steel 15, 21, 127, 298–9
Stockholm Convention 19
STRIDE 168
Sweden 7, 21, 284, 290
Suez 9, 22
Sugar 24, 103–4, 278, 282
SYSMIN 276–7

Target price 92–3
Taxation 233–260
  UK 255–6
Technology 129–34
Thatcher, Margaret 51, 224–6, 310,
  321
Threshold price 92–3
Tindemans, L 203, 205,
  Report 308
Tokyo Round 54
Trade marks 131
Transport 3, 15, 69, 144, 150–54,
  160–61, 315, 319–20
  Trans-European Networks 46,
  153–4, 177–8
Turkey 266–7
Two-speed two-tier Community 308–
  9

UNICE 41, 188
United Kingdom
  Community Budget 256–60
  EU agriculture and fisheries 109–
  16
  EU industry 141–3
  EU institutions 49–51
  EU integration 319–322
  EU membership 21–6
  EU trade 81–6
  EMS 223–232
  Regional and social experience
  190–93
  Trade with Commonwealth 280–
  83
UNRRA 13
Uruguay Round 53–4, 105, 262, 264,
  300, 317
USA 8, 10–11, 14, 23, 103, 106,
  124–5, 135–6, 139–40, 194,
  198, 264–5
USSR 7–13, 296–7

Variable levies 93
VAT 235–40, 244–5, 256, 258, 260
VERs 53–4, 265, 278
Vice-Presidents (Commission) 29
Viner, J 57
Voting 34–5, 50